K

D0498165

BF 431 .M4123 1996
Measured lies : The bell
                220446

MEASURED LIES

OKANAGAN UNIVERSITY COLLEGE
LIBRARY
BRITISH COLUMBIA

MEASURED LIES

THE BELL CURVE EXAMINED

Edited by
Joe L. Kincheloe,
Shirley R. Steinberg, and
Aaron D. Gresson III

St. Martin's Press
New York

MEASURED LIES

Copyright © 1996 by Joe L. Kinchloe, Shirley R. Steinberg, and Aaron D. Gresson III

All rights reserved. Printed in the United States of America. No part of this book may be used or reproduced in any manner whatsoever without written permission except in the case of brief quotations embodied in critical articles or reviews. For information, address St. Martin's Press, Scholarly and Reference Division, 175 Fifth Avenue, New York, N.Y. 10010

ISBN 0-312-12929-7

Library of Congress Cataloging-in-Publication Data

Measured lies : The bell curve examined / edited by Joe L. Kincheloe,
    Shirley R. Steinberg, Aaron D. Gresson III.
        p.   cm.
    Includes bibliographical references and index.
    ISBN 0-312-12929-7
    1. Intellect. 2. Nature and nurture. 3. Intelligence levels—
United States. 4. Intelligence levels—Social aspects—United
States. 5. Herrnstein, Richard J. Bell curve. 6. Racism in
psychology. I. Kincheloe, Joe L. II. Steinberg, Shirley R., 1952-
. III. Gresson, Aaron David.
BF431.M4123 1996
305.9'082—dc20   95-47522
                                                          CIP

First Edition: May 1996
10 9 8 7 6 5 4 3 2 1

CONTENTS

Prelude ix
    Aaron D. Gresson III

PART I
INTRODUCING *THE BELL CURVE*

1. Who Said It Can't Happen Here? 3
    Joe L. Kincheloe and Shirley R. Steinberg

PART II
SITUATING *THE BELL CURVE*

2. Dominance and Dependency: Situating *The Bell Curve*
    within the Conservative Restoration 51
    Michael W. Apple

3. *The Bell Curve* Debate and the Crisis of Public Intellectuals . . . 71
    Henry A. Giroux and Susan Searls

4. The Ape's IQ 91
    Allen Shelton

PART III
RESPONDING TO *THE BELL CURVE:* CHAPTER BY CHAPTER

5. The Set-up: Crocodile Tears for the Poor 109
    Phil Francis Carspecken

6. For Whom *The Bell* Tolls: A Cognitive or Educated Elite? . . . 127
    Yvonna Lincoln

7. IQ as Commodity: The "New" Economics of Intelligence . . . 137
    Richard Cary

8. In the Name of Science and of Genetics and of *The Bell Curve:*
    White Supremacy in American Schools 161
    Ladislaus Semali

9. Bad Luck, Bad Blood, Bad Faith: Ideological Hegemony
   and the Oppressive Language of Hoodoo Social Science . . . 177
   Joyce E. King

10. Speculation Based on Speculation: The Problem of
    The Bell Curve and the Question of Schooling 193
    Jo Anne Pagano

11. Leaps of an Unjust Faith: Missing Links in
    the Causes of Labor Force Participation 203
    Townsand Price-Spratlen

12. Family Matters 211
    Alan A. Block and Don Stephenson

13. Genetic Rationalizations and Public Policy:
    Herrnstein and Murray on Intelligence and
    Welfare Dependency 219
    Maria R. Vidal

14. Parenting in the Promised Land 227
    William F. Pinar

15. Race, Repression, and the Politics of Crime and
    Punishment in *The Bell Curve* 237
    Stephen Nathan Haymes

16. The Last Rational Men: Citizenship, Morality,
    and the Pursuit of Human Perfection 251
    Cameron McCarthy, Ed Buendia, Carol Mills,
    Shuaib Meacham, Heriberto Godina,
    Carrie Wilson-Brown, Maria Seferian,
    and Theresa Souchet

17. *The Bell Curve,* Intelligence, and Virtuous Jews 265
    Sander L. Gilman

18. Chaos and Complexity: A Quantum Analysis
    of *The Bell Curve* 291
    Patrick Slattery

19. Dysgenesis and White Culture 303
    Greg Tanaka

20. A Suburban Tale: Representation and Segregation
     in Special Needs Education 315
     Glenn M. Hudak
21. *The Bell Curve* and Transracial Adoption Studies 331
     William E. Cross, Jr.
22. White Supremacy and the Politics of Fear and Loathing 343
     Peter McLaren
23. *The Bell Curve,* Affirmative Action, and the Quest for Equity . . 351
     Robert M. Hendrickson
24. Attacking Affirmative Action:
     Social Darwinism as Public PRolicy 367
     Catherine A. Lugg
25. Questioning "The Way We Are Headed" 379
     Kyle L. Peck
26. On Refusing One's Place: The Ditchdigger's Dream 391
     Deborah P. Britzman and Alice J. Pitt

PART IV
TALKING ABOUT *THE BELL CURVE*

27. Interviewing and Finding Sound Bites 405
     Ronald E. Chennault and Shirley R. Steinberg
28. Interviews 411
     Interview with Stanley Aronowitz by Shirley R. Steinberg
     Interview with Ellen Willis by Joe L. Kincheloe
29. Scientism as a Form of Racism: A Dialogue 423
     Paulo Freire and Donaldo Macedo
     Coda "Cognitive Elitism" versus Moral Courage 433
     Aaron D. Gresson III

Biographies 441
Index 451

To Jerry Salters and Nathanial Talmadge.
To Miss Tryphena McCaden, Thomas,
Mikell, and Ayana:
People we love and who make truths,
defying the measured lies

PRELUDE

Aaron D. Gresson III

When the Gulf War ended, People Magazine wrote that through the war "a nation learned to feel good about itself again." Prior to the start of the Gulf War, many understood this war to be a deflection from proactively engaging the forthcoming economic recession; they were correct, and George Bush became the first president to lose an election immediately after winning a war. Similar to the Gulf War in its obscurantist mission, *The Bell Curve* attempts to make one segment of America feel good about itself at a high cost: in an interview about *The Bell Curve,* Charles Murray declared that this book would "make them [certain white people] feel better about things they already think but do not know how to say" (cited in Giroux 1995, 342).

For the past three decades American society has become increasingly addicted to blatant or unabashed utterance of the unutterable. It is now fashionable to say what one's parents would not have dared to say: perhaps the poor and aged should be terminated; women ought to be replaced with life-like replicas fashioned by Disneyland engineers; children cost more than they are worth; Blacks really are sub-human and dangerous after all; the Indians better stop bellyaching or they'll get their butts whipped again.

It would be nice if one could merely ignore such utterances; and as Kincheloe and Steinberg argue in their Introduction to *Measured Lies,* it would be nice to be able to ignore Herrnstein and Murray's utterance. But to do so would be much too dangerous, for unutterables have a way of assuming a persuasiveness and realism that often undergird destructiveness of various sorts. So *Measured Lies* had to be written.

Given the complex mission of Murray and Herrnstein's work, we have attempted to provide a multidimensioned response. In part one, several thematic chapters introduce the broad-based social, political, and pedagogical context within which *The Bell Curve* has been constructed. These chapters set the stage for part two, which presents a detailed critical reading of the specific chapters of *The Bell Curve*. Part three is a collection of interviews, letters and dialogues by prominent scholars and social critics on the meaning and significance of *The Bell Curve*.

Elsewhere (Gresson 1995) I have argued that a central crisis within contemporary society pertains to race and its place within the twenty-first century. I also argue that so far the preferred solution to the enlarged cultural crisis that pluralism and multiculturalism have created for the country is "retribalization" (Issacs 1977) The essays, analyses, and reflections contained in this book make clear the importance of rejecting this "retribalization" strategy. It invites the reader to join with the editors and authors in the construction of a critical intellectual and social activist alternative to this "retribalization."

References

Giroux, H. A. (1995). Racism and the aesthetic of hyper-real violence: *Pulp Fiction* and other visual tragedies. *Social Identities, 1*, 333-354.

Gresson, A. D. III. (1995). *The recovery of race in America*. Minneapolis, MN: University of Minnesota Press.

Isaacs, H. R. (1975). *Idols of the tribe: Group identity and political change.* New York: Harper and Row.

PART I

INTRODUCING
THE BELL CURVE

1 WHO SAID IT CAN'T HAPPEN HERE?

JOE L. KINCHELOE · SHIRLEY R. STEINBERG

We live in an era of the spectacular, the hyperreal. In such a time the logic of profit privileges the outlandish, leaving the cautious in the publicity wilderness of scholarly endeavor. Books on race, intelligence, public and educational policy, socioeconomic class, social behavior, family issues, testing, poverty, the workplace, and affirmative action are not uncommon in the late twentieth century. How often, however, have such books "broken through" to the *Larry King Show, Meet the Press,* presidential news conferences, or the covers of mainstream news magazines? In the Age of the Spectacle, an age so anaesthetized by the constant bombardment of images via electronic visual media, it takes something extravagant to grab attention. The publishing business is not immune from such pressures: What will we have to do to engender interest in our less-than-outlandish response to the work of the late Richard Herrnstein and the recalcitrant Charles Murray? Without the hyperbolic ambiance of the *National Enquirer, Measured Lies* may not make our hometown newspaper. Maybe a few choice excerpts will tease the mainstream press: "IQ's of apes dramatically increased by massive intake of banana daiquiris;" or "daily masturbation substantially increases SAT scores." Not a good idea, our academic colleagues admonish us.

The editor of *The Bell Curve,* the Free Press's Adam Bellow, certainly recognized these social dynamics, as he marketed the book as electronic/print spectacle. We wonder how Editor Bellow sleeps at night, knowing he has both successfully legitimated some of the culture's most ugly ways of seeing and resuscitated the zombies that inhabit the netherworld of Euro-consciousness. It would be tempting to oppose the book by simply ignoring it, but the zombies are loose stalking the landscape from Oklahoma City to our backyards in Pennsylvania with its scores of white militias. Bellow is no dolt, he knows that *The Bell Curve* blurs the lines between scholarship, pseudo-science, amusement, and Elks Club banter. He also knows that such a recipe sells—the more controversial the better. Despite the packaging and the hype, there is nothing new in *The Bell Curve*. Its claim to reveal the hidden and taboo is just another marketing lie, for the book presents only a refried social Darwinism left over from the nineteenth century. Indeed, *The Bell Curve's* most provocative characteristics may be its shallowness and unoriginality—no aspect of its controversiality involves the discovery of an untraveled road or the mapping of a previously uncharted territory. Ho-hum, as the wise philosopher put it, "been there, done that."

Meanwhile, back at the Peoria K-Mart *The Bell Curve* continues to sell. As the theoretical torch bearer for the right-wing insurgency of the 1990s, the book speaks to white Americans suffering from the economic vicissitudes of the last two decades. The book's ability to assume center stage, to capture a popular audience for racial prejudice is chilling for those dedicated to a pluralistic democracy. The late Spiro Agnew would have been proud of the "liberal media's" response to Herrnstein and Murray. Despite their "measured lies," scholarly gaffs, and sycophantic pandering to white racism, the media legitimated their standing as respected scholars who offered merely "another important perspective" on the problems of the day. Lap dog correspondents, however, rarely reported the financial backing of the filthy rich and ultra-conservative Bradley Foundation or Murray's comfortable position with the equally conservative American Enterprise Institute. These cozy fiscal affiliations do not sit well with the authors' immodest proclamation of their intellectual bravery, their venture into the no-man's land of ethnic mental differences. Like CIA operatives Herrnstein and

Murray pursued their dangerous fieldwork, literally hiding it on planes and trains from a public apparently ready to neutralize them in the name of political correctness. Murray, after Herrnstein's death, paints a portrait so exciting, one might think a Hollywood movie is a possibility—Hoffman as Herrnstein? Redford as Murray?

AS OBJECTIVE SCIENTISTS WE HAVE TO LEVEL WITH YOU

In their own eyes Herrnstein and Murray are not only heroic but they are also fair—merely objective men of science doing their job. For example, Murray repeatedly claims that the book is not, for the most part, about race. One does not have to read far to discover the book is obsessed with differences in intelligence between different races and classes of people. Yet the denials continue unabated, constructing a public portrait of the authors as wounded but well-meaning characters unafraid to pursue the truth no matter what its personal costs. Thus, even as they announce intractable black and Latino inferiority to the world, they distance themselves from charges not simply that they are racists but that *The Bell Curve* is primarily about race. Earnest House and Carolyn Haug (1995) write that 239 of the book's 552 pages (43 percent) explicitly concern comparisons of black, Latino and white intelligence and its effects. Indeed, even when African Americans and Latinos are not specifically mentioned, *The Bell Curve* is hard at work justifying the genetic arguments which support the contention that Whites are innately superior. To argue that the book is not primarily about race is duplicitous.

So egregious is the deceit of the authors that we as critics find it difficult to find a comfortable idiom for response: are we too strident, too excessive in our disgust?; are we too understated, too dispassionate in our attempt to convey the degree of deception involved?; how do we engage scholars and the public in an analysis of both *The Bell Curve* as a piece of scholarship and the implications it holds for the future of Western culture? *Measured Lies* is our response to that question, our effort to inform our readers of the profound issues Herrnstein and Murray raise about race and class in American society, the nature of the public political conversation, the dynamics of knowledge production and distribution, the future of democracy, and the efficacy of conventional approaches to the sciences of human psyche. We find it phenomenal that a naked ideological treatise on *human worth* can be received by the mainstream media as a work of disinterested scholarship. As a society, unfortunately, Americans have difficulty with what it is that "objective" science does and how it does it. Wrapping itself in the flag of neutrality, *The Bell Curve* was consciously designed as a public relations ploy to "market" (as Cathy Lugg puts it in this volume) particular political ideas. Certainly, there is nothing wrong with advocacy, unless it deceitfully denies its existence. We are not advocates, Herrnstein and Murray maintain, we are mere messengers from the objective laboratory of hard science. We're sorry if the message upsets you, they whisper, but don't blame us.

As educational, cultural, and psychological scholars, we make no pretense to objectivity. We have learned that there are always multiple interpretations of educational, cultural, and psychological texts. For example, what does it mean that Karen scored low on her IQ test: is she genetically predisposed to low intelligence?; is English not her first language? has she been raised in an economically disadvantaged environment with little overlap between her cultural experiences and those rewarded by schools and standardized tests? Indeed, such questions are complex and depending on one's values and concerns can be answered in a variety of ways. But Herrnstein and Murray let us know that when the smoke clears an *objective* scientific analysis will produce only one correct answer: Blacks and Latinos are intellectually and morally inferior to Whites. Only through significant ideological manipulations of data could such a conclusion even be suggested. As Phil Carspecken argues in this volume, theoretical assumptions are a part of all scientific work. To contend that this is not the case, is to engage in a hoax that views human beings outside of the cultural context that has shaped them.

Hidden theoretical assumptions about Herrnstein and Murray's science are consumed unknowingly by readers. Worshipping at the graven image of scientific value freedom, Herrnstein and Murray are unaware of what they attend to and what they ignore. What definition of intelligence, for example, do we employ to study cognitive ability and its distribution within a society? Do we use Howard Gardner's theory of multiple intelligences (1983), Joe Kincheloe and Shirley Steinberg's postformal intelligence (1993), Robert Sternberg's notion of practical intelligence (1979), or Charles Spearman's concept of g, that views intelligence as a specific entity residing inside the head (Herrnstein and Murray use Spearman's)? The definition we choose holds profound consequences for who will test well or poorly, who will gain social rewards and who will not. The definition we choose also depends upon our theoretical presuppositions: How important is the social and cultural context in shaping the individual? Do we value the ways other cultures define and express intelligence or do we focus exclusively on the way *our* culture operates in this domain? Do we believe that the mind is so complex that all variables cannot be controlled in empirical studies thus negating statistical analysis of what has been labeled intelligence? Make no mistake, all scientists, psychometricians in particular, hold political opinions that influence their views of intelligence and their answers to these questions. The fallacy of objectivity undermines *The Bell Curve* at every step, rendering Herrnstein and Murray blind to their own presuppositions. Trapped by its own adulation of empirically-produced, objective facts, the culture of objectivity fails to acknowledge the historical and social context that gave birth to it.

CAPTURING THE HIGH GROUND: HIT AND RUN SCHOLARSHIP

In her response to Herrnstein and Murray's chapter five, Joyce King labels their pseudo-objective psychometrics a "hoodoo social science." Taking the concept of hoodoo from the spiritual history of West Africa, King uses it to signify a science of deception. Not only do Herrnstein and Murray use white culture as a benchmark for quality, but they also covertly employ white cultural knowledge as the basis on which standardized measures of achievement are based. Only a hoodoo science could utilize standards developed by one cultural group to determine the worth of the members of another group. Proclaiming that race and culture are irrelevant in psychometrics, the authors produce data that (they argue) justifies a range of policies— especially policies that undermine the efforts of the non-white and poor to gain financial and social stability. Ever presenting themselves as well-meaning and benevolent figures, Herrnstein and Murray scramble for the high ground after these revelations. Just because, they generously contend, African Americans are not as intelligent as Whites, this is no reason to discriminate against individual Blacks. Such understandings among the white population will not hurt African American's chances for success, the authors assure us. With anti-racist proclamations such as these, who needs the Ku Klux Klan?

We admit to our disdain not only for the form of social science employed by the authors but also for the disingenuous style they use to present their findings. Herrnstein and Murray's is a hit and run scholarship, as they *hit* readers with a mass of evidence in support of an extreme position regarding race and class only to *run* away from what they have implied at the last possible moment. Thus, the style is cowardly as it engages readers in support of an outlandish position, while providing Herrnstein and Murray with what CIA operatives call "plausible deniability." Always set up an operation, the ploy demands, in such a way that if the covert action becomes unpopular or fails, operatives can distance themselves from it. "No, we're not saying that Blacks are inferior," Murray opines on the national TV talk shows; the book, however, tells a different story— plausible deniability in action. One wishes for an honest position—at least previous advocates of qualitative genetic differences between races such as Arthur Jensen and William Shockley didn't run away from their noxious positions. As the victim lays bleeding on the sidewalk, Murray is the scholar who claims, "I didn't know the gun was loaded."

IQ AS SINGLE-BULLET THEORY

Whatever the social malady, Herrnstein and Murray tell us, low IQ is the cause: bad parenting, poor school performance, poverty, crime, teenage pregnancy, accidents in the workplace, divorce, etc. . . . Indeed, according to the authors, IQ shapes almost everything including not simply cognitive matters but moral issues as well. Thus, when Herrnstein and Murray claim that a mental revolution has taken place in America that designates class placement on the basis of IQ, there is cause for panic. Although they present no convincing evidence to support such a dramatic claim, the authors portray a Manichaean class structure with the smart and *virtuous* occupying the upper provinces and the dumb and the *malevolent* occupying the lower. My god, some racially fearful white readers may think, an army of dim-witted but violence-prone Blacks and Latinos are coming to get us. Success and failure, the single-bullet theory continues, are more and more determined by the genes we inherit; at the bottom of the flesh pile, the unlucky inferior stock wallows with no hope of upward mobility. The privileged are absolved of any responsibility for this wretched refuse. Because IQ is *the* scientifically validated measure of social worth, there is nothing the genetically privileged can do outside of managing the inferior in a custodial state.

The point *The Bell Curve* makes is very clear: collective stupidity and corruption *not* racism and class-bias produce poverty, crime, and social despair. To make such an argument the authors must convince readers that all is right with the world. The American division of wealth is merely a manifestation of genetic justice, nothing more—social psychologists years ago labeled this the "just world phenomenon." IQ and the general intelligence it represents exist outside of history and based on income statistics, housing patterns, and job distribution, people are both doing the work they should be and receiving, for the most part, the rewards they deserve (Merelman, 1986). Because post-Fordist capitalism produces a state of Darwinian nature, a true meritocracy exists; and when this happens cream rises to the top and impurities collect at the bottom of the social milk pail. Where is sociology in this analysis? Do Herrnstein and Murray understand that psychological and hereditarian concepts alone cannot explain the complex process by which socioeconomic stratification takes place? Questions about socioeconomic context are not new. To read *The Bell Curve,* however, one would never know that a critical sociological or social psychological tradition exists. That a best-selling book on "intelligence and class structure in American Life" could be written and published in the mid-1990s without such acknowledgment is extraordinary.

POWER AND THE USE OF IQ

It is in the interests of those who own and manage America's businesses and industries to "regulate" the workers they employ and the citizens who support or reject governmental economic policy. A significant portion of the educational reforms proposed and enacted over the last fifteen years have involved producing graduates who (as Michael Apple argues in this volume) can help meet the needs of the economy. In this context business has entered into partnerships with schools around the nation. A consistent thread running through many of these alliances involves employers preaching a doctrine of neoclassical free enterprise economics to a captive audience of students. As part of an amazingly successful cultural education effort, corporate leaders and their political allies produce positive cultural representations in conjunction with images of a just world catalyzed by free market economics. Because of their success, corporations in the late 1990s are freer to pursue larger profit margins, union-busting, lower minimum wages, reduced environmental regulations, and lower corporate taxes. IQ and other forms of testing cannot be removed from the larger dynamic of corporate power and its effort to regulate the population.

For example, IQ in schools is used to "track" students into academic or vocational tracks. Operating on the assumptions of Herrnstein and Murray's decontextualized psychometrics, students are deemed capable or incapable of academic work. Rarely is much attention granted to the social baggage students bring to the test— who they are, where they come from, their personal histories and lived experiences, their linguistic backgrounds (all factors that significantly affect how they "test"). Those who score poorly are relegated to the Siberia of schooling, tracked into vocational programs that too often prepare them for dead end jobs. This tracking holds harmful consequences for low IQ students and the school in general, as (contrary to the conventional wisdom) it undermines the achievement of lower track students without improving upper-track students' performance (Oakes, 1985; Grubb, et. al., 1991; Beck, 1991). If IQ's complicity in this subversion of marginalized students' attempt to use education for socioeconomic mobility wasn't enough, Herrnstein and Murray up the ante even further. Not only does IQ accurately reveal the intellectual capacity of students, they argue, but it also indicates an individual's wisdom, maturity, thoughtfulness, judgment, and even prudence. In their hit-and-run modus operandi the authors imply that through the miracle of psychometrics scientists understand the connection between intelligence and the *moral dimension* of individual behavior. As a result of this "breakthrough," America can now begin to formulate social policy. Tomorrow belongs to the successful test takers.

Drawing upon their absolute faith in testing, Herrnstein and Murray attempt to point out the causal relationship between IQ and job performance. Various studies have demonstrated a correlation between workers with high IQ and workers who score high on written multiple-choice tests on "workplace knowledge." Obviously, a significant gap exists between scoring high on a written test about the job and competence on the job. Herrnstein and Murray's understanding of the connections between IQ and job performance is based on two military studies. Flagrantly distorting the findings of the study by Schmidt and associates and the investigation conducted by Maier and Hiatt, Herrnstein and Murray claim support for their view of IQ and work performance—support that simply is not a part of the studies in question. Indeed, Maier and Hiatt, for example, found when hands-on work sample tests were used instead of written job knowledge tests that after four or five years of experience low IQ workers actually outperformed those with high IQs (Kamin, 1995). Profound implications attend these findings. What IQ measures may have little to do with an individual's capacity to perform vocationally or academically in different contexts. These portentous contextual dynamics, however, are virtually ignored by Herrnstein and Murray and their brand of number-crunching psychology. Moreover, what Herrnstein and Murray portray as the exacting measurement of the causal relationship between IQ and job performance upon closer examination is a magician's illusion. For example, job performance assessment is almost always based on supervisor ratings that can't escape issues such as interpersonal chemistry between supervisor and employee. Such human dynamics are shaped by non-quantifiable intangibles such as an employee's style, affect, and conventionality—hardly the components of an exact objective empirical science.

The power of IQ and other tests to shape the lives of men and women in this society is dramatic. If Herrnstein and Murray are able to convince their fellow citizens that they are correct and that IQ fairly and accurately portrays the worth of individuals, African Americans, Latinos, and poor Whites face a psychic, economic, and political disaster. Contrary to the misleading picture the authors paint, the viewpoints promoted in the book, if taken seriously, will explode the dreams of millions of oppressed people in America. As educators, we cannot imagine a stronger disincentive to our non-white students than to be told that they are genetically inferior to Whites and there is nothing they can do about it. "Don't worry, be happy" might become an apt motto for The Predominantly Poor and Black Charles Murray Elementary School. At the very least, as Herrnstein boasted before his death, *The Bell Curve* will destroy racially preferential admissions in the university. Such an effect, when combined with the authors' championing of a nineteenth century social Darwinism that justifies selfishness and cruelty toward the occupants of the lowest rungs of the social ladder, lays the foundation for a *Bladerunner*-like twenty-first century replete with race wars and blood in the streets. Meanwhile, Murray continues to romp in the primordial ooze of racism hawking a primitive hereditarianism that is not too far removed from the head bump readers of phrenology. This ancestor of positivist psychometrics also claimed to be an exacting and objective science.

HERRNSTEIN AND MURRAY'S BLACK MAGIC— AND THE SOCIAL AND ECONOMIC VANISHED

Herrnstein and Murray are neo-rationalists in their belief that the thoughts and contents of the mind are more important than environmental controls upon the body and the emotions and feelings they engender. In this context the cultural is irrelevant— Herrnstein and Murray's black magic involves their effort to erase the cultural, social, and economic as influences on the human mind. In this manner they continually attempt to take a social and historical dynamic and turn it into a natural process. Indeed, this prestidigitation has ancient origins—since the time of Plato, theories of intelligence have been used to justify socioeconomic disparity. The "dregs" at the bottom have always been said to be deficient and/or pathological. Like their elitist forebears, Herrnstein and Murray blame the poor for being poor. It is an academic and logical outrage to separate environmental factors from any effort to measure ability or intelligence.

It doesn't take a sociologist to uncover the strange alchemy that occurs when a culturally different and/or poor student encounters the middle class, white culture–grounded practice of school and the conservative wing of the testing psychology establishment. This middle class mind-set often views poverty as a badge of failure. One African American child absorbed this lesson in her first experiences in school, as evidenced by her response to the question, what is poverty? Poverty, she said, is when you aren't living right. Herrnstein and Murray seem to be oblivious to the psychic toll of such lessons and the ways they move marginalized young people to reject the academic world and the experiences that surround it as a matter of self-protection.

In this context teachers and students of educational sociology come to understand that children from lower socioeconomic and non-white homes do not ascribe importance to school work in the same way as do upper-middle-class white students. Poor and racially marginalized children often see academic work and the information and skills tests seek as unreal, as a series of short-term tasks rather than something with long-term significance for their lives. Important work is something you get paid for after its completion. Without such compensation or long-term justification, these students display little interest in the "academic." This lack of motivation and its consequences involving reduced understanding of certain knowledge forms and discursive formats is interpreted by many educators and psychologists as a lack of intelligence. Poor performance on standardized tests scientifically confirms the "inferiority" of such students.

Unfortunately, this happens every day. Too many educators and psychologists (though certainly not all) mistake culturally different and lower socioeconomic class manners, attitudes, speech, and school performance for a lack of intellectual ability. Some teachers and counselors report that they place some students in low-ability tracks because of their cultural or class backgrounds. Their rationale involves the marginalized student's social discomfort around students from a higher status/ability background. These students should be with their own kind, they maintain. Herrnstein and Murray agree and worry that the presence of such students will subvert the quality of education received by more intelligent students. Such beliefs constrict the educational establishment's view of the human capacity for development and the understanding of multiple dimensions of human diversity. Herrnstein, Murray, and their ideological compadres miss these social complexities. As they reduce intelligence to one's performance on an IQ test, they ignore the unique and creative accomplishments one is capable of in diverse venues and contexts.

Research on the educational performance of low-status groups in other countries provides important insight into the shortcomings of *The Bell Curve*. In Sweden, Finnish people are viewed as inferior—the failure rate for Finnish children in Swedish schools is very high. When Finnish children immigrate to Australia, however, they do well—as well as Swedish immigrants. Koreans do poorly in Japanese schools where they are viewed as culturally inferior; in American schools, on the other hand, Korean immigrants are very successful. The examples are numerous, but the results generally follow the same pattern: racial, ethnic, and class groups who are viewed negatively or as inferiors in a nation's dominant culture tend to perform poorly academically. Herrnstein and Murray don't want to understand that power relations between groups must be considered when individuals' abilities are analyzed. Without the insights derived from such environmental understandings brilliant and creative people from marginalized backgrounds will continue to be relegated to the vast army of the inferior and untalented. To speak of a custodial state for such people as outlined in *The Bell Curve* is morally unacceptable in any society. Unfortunately, the unthinkable has been thought—"intellectual cleansing" can happen in America (Oakes, 1985; Nightingale, 1993; DeYoung, 1989; Block, 1995; Zweigenhaft and Domhoff, 1991; McLaren, 1995; Kincheloe, 1995).

THE WAGES OF STUPIDITY

As the rich and poor grow farther apart in terms of the distribution of wealth, Herrnstein and Murray correctly warn of great danger to the social fabric. Indeed, it is rare for mainstream figures to broach the subject of socioeconomic class in the public conversation. Confusing correlation for cause, the authors blame the growing economic disparity on the mushrooming IQ gap. The implicit theoretical understanding of how society operates and changes is, in a word, primitive. As they designate IQ as sole determining agent of social inequality, the authors fail to examine the effects of the ascendancy of business and corporate power in the last two decades, the accompanying decline in labor organizations, the emergence of global competition, the flight of American industry to poor countries, and the subsequent loss of manufacturing jobs in America. Herrnstein and Murray's view of social change neglects not only these essential factors but fails to comprehend the complex nature of opportunity. Assuming that everyone has access to social mobility, they absolutely dismiss studies that display the relationship between socioeconomic circumstance and success. They fail to comprehend that parental socioeconomic background rigs the roulette table of success in favor of individuals with particular white and middle class privileges—advantages that include both familiarity with individuals who control political power, knowledge, and job opportunities and comfort with dominant cultural ways of interacting and operating.

Herrnstein and Murray's ignorance of the socioeconomic domain sabotages any contribution they might have made to the understanding of the interrelationships of class, race, intelligence, mobility, and justice. Decontextualizing the distribution of wealth from larger social and cultural issues, the authors ignore the fiscal changes that have taken place since the end of American post–World War II economic growth in the early 1970s. The rise of Western Europe and Japanese economics, the displacement of American workers as a result of the success of Fordist rationalization and automation strategies, the decline in corporate productivity and profitability, and the beginning of an inflationary trend opened a new reality for American workers—blue collar workers in particular. Simply put, opportunities for jobs with a secure future for men and women without college degrees significantly declined. Given the limited access individuals from racially and economically marginalized groups possess, pressures on them to compete for long-term stable employment increased. The number of steelworkers was cut in half in less than a decade. The ranks of rubber workers were decimated. In 1970, 26 percent of American workers had jobs in the manufacturing sector; by the early 1990s that percentage had fallen to 18 percent and by the year 2000 it will fall to 12.5. Not only has the federal government failed to provide support to the victims of this decline, but it has encouraged an American corporate migration to the so-called "Third World" (Rubin, 1994, p. 223).

The industrial manufacturing path to socioeconomic mobility was often closed to African Americans, but as a result of union reforms and the civil rights movement such jobs did begin to open up in the late 1950s and 1960s. The decline in American manufacturing beginning in the 1970s has been devastating to poor black and latino communities, as one of the few avenues for mobility has been closed. While many have argued that the loss has reduced the number of employed role models for young African American men, a more important effect has been the dissolution of job connections and employment networks for young black and Latino men and women. When unemployed individuals don't live near successfully employed people, then the grapevine through which one worker tells another about a job opening and recommends him or her to the employer is destroyed.

Much to the horror of African American and Latino young people, the loss of these connections, coupled with the loss of manufacturing jobs, has helped turn inner city neighborhoods into hopeless wastelands. To non-white workers and their children such changes have undermined the possibility that they will ever possess secure jobs. The forty-hour-a-week position that pays a livable wage and provides health and retirement benefits is becoming a dinosaur, a relic of a previous age. Indeed, one of the fastest growing types of employment in the last decade of the century is so-called contingent work—part-time, low-benefit, low-pay work. There are nearly 34 million of these "disposable" workers in the American workforce of the 1990s, constituting already about one-third of all U. S. workers. Because of such economic trends, the average take-home pay of employed black men in the 1990s is so low that it would take the salary of four of them to enter the middle-class mainstream. Proponents of social justice and economic democracy must challenge the simple-minded and mean-spirited blame of the "stupid poor" championed by Herrnstein, Murray, and their political supporters. Instead of attempting to find new and sensational ways of blaming victims, the friends of democracy need to join the struggle to challenge corporate and governmental policies that contribute to these deteriorating economic conditions. Such sobering realities, not some pseudo-scientific notion of genetic inferiority, are the causes of the polarization between black and white and rich and poor. Left unchecked they will destroy the American dream of socioeconomic mobility (Coontz, 1992; Ellwood, 1988; Giroux, 1993; Haymes, 1995; Johnson, 1991).

INTELLIGENCE AND ECONOMIC STRATIFICATION

A central feature of Herrnstein and Murray's thesis concerning the cognitive stratification of American society involves the notion that jobs in a high-tech economy are becoming more and more intellectually demanding. The unquestioned assumption here is that the contemporary economy rewards highly intelligent people who because of their superior ability are better workers. Neither Herrnstein, Murray, or most of their critics question this assumption. What types of skills are required in American workplaces in the 1990s? Do intelligent workers increase productivity and quality of services and products? The answers to such questions are not as simple as Herrnstein and Murray might assume.

The American economy in the late twentieth century is an amalgam of Fordist (mass-production industry) and post-Fordist (specialized, shorter, and more flexible production runs using computerized technology) dynamics. Some analysts have concluded that post-Fordist jobs always demand higher worker skills and intelligence than the boring and repetitive assembly-line jobs of Fordism—but such is not necessarily the case. What Herrnstein and Murray fail to take into account is that the impact of technological change has always been paradoxical. Some employers use the same technologies in significantly different ways; some ways do require greater worker skills, others "deskill" employees. While this need for higher skill, highly intelligent workers is a part of the changing post-Fordist economy, such jobs will account for no more than thirty percent of the workforce by the early twenty-first century. The U. S. Labor Department reports that the growth in high-skill jobs has already stagnated. The remaining years in the century will see most job growth in fast-food restaurants, small retail stores, custodial work, and service establishments. Studies conducted at the Bureau of Labor Statistics have found that many college graduates are not getting high-skill jobs. As the creation of high-skill jobs has stagnated, 568,000 college graduates work as sales clerks, 475,000 as secretaries and typists, and 125,000 as bartenders, waiters, and waitresses. Where is this cognitively-segregated, high IQ–rewarding economy that the authors portray?

There is further evidence that Herrnstein and Murray focused on the wrong planet. Another example of the deskilling trend within the American labor market involves the rationalization and standardization of professional jobs—Stanley Aronowitz (1992) calls this the proletarianization of professionalism. The term, proletariat, refers to the lowest class of citizens in a community. Thus, proletarianization indicates the debasement of what once were high skill positions in a way that strips skills from professional practitioners. The medical profession would seem to be one of the last professions to experience rationalization and deskilling, but the last decade has witnessed just such a trend. Physicians find themselves under increasing external controls by managers and bureaucrats who are not medical doctors. These controls bring with them a predictability that removes diagnostic analysis from the everyday lives of doctors. In these situations doctors no longer rely on personal medical judgment to determine procedure in a case—rules, regulations, or the demands of technology make decisions for them. Thus, even high-status, high-skill professions like medicine are not exempt from these deskilling tendencies (Block, 1990; Weisman, 1991;

Ritzer, 1993). A two-tier workforce is emerging just as Herrnstein and Murray contend, but cognitive differences are not the cause of the stratification. Indeed the United States is not the most economically unequal of all industrialized countries because we have dumber poor people than the rest of the world.

CULTURAL CAPITAL AND ACCESS TO SHRINKING NUMBERS OF HIGH-SKILL, HIGH-PAYING JOBS

We are dedicated to the task of understanding the subtle processes that work to create class and race stratification in America, that undermine the educational and economic mobility of the non-white and the poor. Why do individuals from such groups often fail to gain access to the core jobs that respect human dignity and provide a livable wage? Parents, concerned citizens, teachers, social workers, and business people dedicated to the struggle against economic injustice must understand such dynamics in order to counter the charges of inferiority made against African Americans, Latinos, and the poor of all races made by Herrnstein, Murray, talk radio commentators, and government leaders in the late 1990s. We have learned much about the insidious process, but little of it finds expression at the public level. Differences in academic and economic achievement are not simply the result of primary effects such as deficiencies in intelligence but more of secondary effects such as poor and minority students' cultural capital and social practices resulting from particular cultural experiences.

Cultural capital involves ways of dressing, acting, thinking, or of representing oneself. For example, the knowledge one would need to deport oneself gracefully in an expensive restaurant is a form of dominant cultural capital. Thus, style, manners, courtesy, language practices, moving, and socializing are all forms of culture capital. Teachers and workplace managers often identify the possession of dominant cultural capital as an innate quality that emanates from an individual's "inner essence." However, such traits are culturally determined and are inseparable from the cultural and socioeconomic class backgrounds of the people who exhibit them. Thus, students and workers who don't possess the cultural capital of the dominant culture are in trouble. They are viewed as rude and uncouth, not the type of people a more "cultured" person would want to have around. Those without cultural capital are not the type of students whom middle-class educators want to represent their school; they are not the type of workers who will get promoted. Schools will privilege those students who exhibit the dominant cultural capital—they are the school leaders, the applicants who will obtain the core jobs with high-skill and high-pay. In this context, therefore, the mediocre wealthy student with dominant cultural capital will get the prized job over the brilliant student without it.

As long as we view human beings from the same frames as do Herrnstein and Murray, we will condemn those individuals who come from the margins of society. Psychometricians often dismiss the effects of cultural capital and its relation to test scores, IQs, and supervisory assessments. They fail to understand that the factors used to assess human worth reflect not as much an individual's innate ability as they mirror the values and identity of the school or workplace in which the assessment takes place. Such an argument threatens Herrnstein, Limbaugh, and Gingrich's decontextualized "logic"—a mind-set that attributes the economic, social, and educational failure of the poor and non-white to laziness, a lack of motivation, and mental deficiency (McLaren, 1994; Aronowitz and Giroux, 1991; Kincheloe, 1995). In this manner culture is connected to dominant power—our cultural background plays a major role in determining our access to social, political, and economic rewards. Many of us who have taught in American schools have listened at faculty meetings to colleagues warn us not to expect too much from a particular group of students, maybe those Laotian immigrants or those kids from up at Highland Park. Those kids are inferior to "our" kids, the monologue continues, they just don't have what it takes. In all of these ways a socioeconomically decontextualized education perpetuates racial and class-based inequality, all the while draping the pathology in the language of Herrnstein and Murray's cognitive psychology.

RUN FOR YOUR LIVES, THE PEOPLE WITH
THE LOW IQS ARE COMING: DYSGENESIS

Low IQ black parents, Herrnstein and Murray tell us, are reproducing at an alarming rate bringing our (read, white) collective intelligence down. Genetically inferior people, the story of dysgenesis maintains, will capture the cities and terrorize the good intelligent citizens. To control them "we" will have to devise a custodial state—not in hopes of some future improvement but for purposes of our own safety. The white fear of dysgenesis contributes to a climate of racism that justifies the arguments of *The Bell Curve*. Indeed, the 1990s have witnessed a legitimation of a racist pseudo-science that changes the public conversation about race in contemporary America. In this context the debate over the book transcends merely the book itself—it becomes a struggle about the future of race relations in North America and western societies in general. In this sense it becomes a battle for America's soul.

Not to worry, it is obvious where Herrnstein and Murray's allegiance falls—few readers mistake the political role *The Bell Curve* occupies in this larger cultural debate. With all the ambiguities concerning the evidence that connects genes with the complexity of the intellect, it is amazing how quickly the authors validate notions of genetic racial superiority and inferiority. Obviously, there is an agenda here, an attempt to prove a larger point. Even though they recognize the problems with the definition of race that they use (a cultural stereotype not a strict biological concept), Herrnstein and Murray push on. Why can't the differences in test scores between African Americans and Whites be interpreted as the results of racial discrimination that black Americans have faced over the centuries? The answer is obvious:

Herrnstein and Murray are attempting to make a larger argument about social, economic, and educational policy in the United States, and black and Latino inferiority is central to their case.

The book is structured around Herrnstein and Murray's attempt to promote policies that put an end to any form of help to the poor. Having "established" the inferiority of Blacks, Latinos, and poor Whites, the authors lay out their policy agenda in chapters 19 and 20. The ending of governmental programs designed to help the needy is the logical response to the white myths of our time—that the system is rewarding the dark-skinned incompetents while concurrently victimizing the fair-skinned. The authors express their sorrow about having to reveal the unfortunate truth, but then, of course, proceed to fan the flames of white racism. Like racists of the past they invoke the baseline fallacy that generalizes about all people in a category on the basis of one unrepresentative example. The welfare cadillac with its implication that many welfare recipients live in the lap of luxury is an example of the baseline fallacy. Herrnstein and Murray invoke the fallacy in their effort to justify the end of affirmative action, as they tell stories of poor whites losing jobs to underqualified, economically prosperous Blacks. All of this is merely a part of the larger strategy to elicit white complicity in self- (or dominant group–) justification. Dominants are taught to think of themselves as superior to subordinates in order to justify their control over them. A sense of justice is restored only by degrading the subordinate. This is the job of *The Bell Curve*—to provide a pretty package for an ugly white supremacy. Herrnstein and Murray's scientific justification of white power is racism in a tuxedo.

THE END OF RACISM: THE GREAT WHITE DENIAL

For too long, Herrnstein and Murray argue, minority groups in the United States have used racial discrimination as an excuse for their failures. Racism, they argue, no longer exists. Indeed, the history of white racism in America has been greatly exaggerated. As this book was going to press, Herrnstein and Murray's ideological nephew, Dinesh D'Souza, was hawking his own snake-oil racism in the form of his book entitled, *The end of racism.* Like his uncles, D'Souza dismisses the existence of discrimination in an effort to garner support for right-wing political policies. In place of discrimination and racism the authors all substitute a so-called distribution model— another way of saying that intelligence is distributed unequally with Whites and some East Asians getting a lot of it and Blacks and Latinos getting little. Social failure is not the fault of the culture, it is the sole responsibility of the individual. Racism is simply not a part of the contemporary cultural landscape and, if we believe D'Souza, its historical reality in America has always been exaggerated. According to D'Souza slavery wasn't so bad for African Americans, racial segregation was created to protect Blacks, and only a small percentage of the black population was lynched (Raspberry, 1995). So what's the big deal? Such scholarship comes from the same sewer that produces Holocaust-denial tracts. That it is so eagerly swallowed up by the American public indicates that something else is happening: Many white Americans are in a state of denial. Herrnstein, Murray, D'Souza and many others are here to validate and exploit that denial for specific political purposes.

To believe *The Bell Curve* we must close our eyes and cover our ears. Despite the pronouncements of the Labor Department, there is no racial discrimination in the workplace, no job displacement, no glass ceilings that bar minority promotion to the highest levels of management. We must work hard to ignore the racial dynamics of rising underemployment that continues to grow faster with African Americans than with all other demographic categories. The disparities between predominantly black and predominantly white schools must be disregarded to maintain Herrnstein and Murray's illusion, and we must be sure not to read Jonathan Kozol's *Savage inequalities* (1991). We must forget what we know about the effects of being labeled as "abnormal" or "inferior" and the resulting dehumanization that accompanies it. We must look the other way when confronted with cross-cultural examples of discrimination such as the fifteen point IQ difference between Protestants and Catholics in Northern Ireland—a society where Catholics have faced a battery of unfair social practices (Herbert, 1995). Even though we are blind to such evidence of discriminatory effect, we are attentive to every detail of attempts to redress the effects of oppression. Whenever a Black or Latino gets a job on the basis of affirmative action, we charge reverse discrimination and scream that minorities are acquiring outrageous advantages.

Herrnstein and Murray's message is clear: both Whites and Blacks must learn to live with the reality of racial inequality. Because Blacks and Latinos really are inferior, Whites are not responsible for non-white failure. Whites have been framed for a crime they didn't commit, a crime that was never really committed. Indeed, if any discrimination exists in America, it is a racism toward Whites themselves. It is this belief that has evoked the white anger that shapes the political landscape in contemporary America. And it is the voice of the angry white working and middle-classes that *The Bell Curve* seeks to validate scientifically and stroke emotionally for political effect. Whites are victims of a political correctness (pc), the argument goes, and in this context white anger is quite justified. Given the circumstances, it is only fair that Whites begin the process of recovering white supremacy before the multiculturalists allow for the complete destruction of what white Americans of the past worked so hard to create. *The Bell Curve*'s subtitle could have been "I'm OK, You're OK With Our Racism." Indeed, these are bad times for white people, Herrnstein and Murray maintain—*The Bell Curve* is an appeal to Whites to save "our" society from non-white-induced dysgenesis.

THE POLITICAL BENEFITS OF THE
RECOVERY OF WHITE SUPREMACY

Herrnstein and Murray have resided at the center of power in neo-conservative American society. It was no fluke that Murray was President Reagan's favorite social scientist: Murray whistled the tune Reagan and his fellow conservatives liked to hear. While we want in no way to promote some simplistic conspiracy theory about Herrnstein and Murray plotting with Newt Gingrich in some hidden locale, it is true that elements of the authors' work fit well with larger political strategies developed by right-wing politicos over the last 25 years. The recovery of white supremacy (see Gresson, 1995 for an expansion of this concept) is certainly in the interests of corporate and right-wing political leaders who are, of course, overwhelmingly white. The economic and political advantages of this white recovery were specifically outlined by political analyst Kevin Phillips' *The new Republican majority* published in 1970. Struggling to retain corporate profit margins of the 1950s and 1960s, many business leaders and their political allies deployed the rhetoric of white recovery to gain the electoral cooperation of their natural adversaries, the (in this case white) working class.

So strong were the white working class's racial concerns that they were induced to support economic and political policies (e.g., trickle-down Reaganomics) contrary to their own interests. Employing the disguised racial codes of the welfare state, drugs, crime in the streets, family values, and the liberal assault on Western/Judeo-Christian values, right-wing and later centrist political candidates began the process of creating "favorable business climates" characterized by lower corporate taxes, reduced governmental regulations, lower wages for workers, higher public expenditures for defense-related business contracts, and so on (Amott, 1993; West, 1993). It's not difficult to trace this political and economic trajectory over the last three decades of the twentieth century. Nixon used busing as a racial code as early as 1968. Quickly the Republican Party became adept at using the language of white recovery to woo white voters away from the labor- and black-identified Democrats. Understanding the effectiveness of the strategy, the Democrats would eventually get into the game in the 1992 election with Bill Clinton's appeal to the middle class (read white people). The Republicans, however, perfected the politics of white recovery using it to divert white voter attention from the politics of the workplace and economy. Ronald Reagan with the help of advisors Mike Deaver and Roger Ailes was the master of the racially encoded recovery, as demonstrated by his ability to elicit worker support of a no-tax business policy and government grants to corporations.

Lacking Reagan's charm George Bush was forced to up the racial ante in his 1988 campaign, employing black visual imagery in the picture of rapist Willie Horton. In this manner Bush linked the recovery rhetoric to his political persona. This racial imagery worked so well that by 1990 the TV ads of North Carolina Republican Senator Jesse Helms, in his campaign against a black challenger, could make overt references to minorities taking white working-class jobs— all the while denying racial intent. Of course, such encoded references to white victimization by minorities had nothing to do with reality— job loss in North Carolina involved corporate flight to poor countries with cheap labor. Such flight was made possible by tax-incentives passed by the business-friendly Senator Helms and his corporate-financed colleagues in government. The success of such strategies kept raising the racial ante—racial scapegoating works. How far can we go? conservative candidates began to ask. What are the most effective ways of conveying racial codes? By the early 1990s such questions prepared the American political landscape for more radical and daring racist encodings. David Duke, former Ku Klux Klan and Nazi Party leader, pushed the racist envelope. The work of Nixon, Reagan, Bush, and Helms had plowed the ideological and cultural terrain so as to make it more acceptable to racist seeds (Marable, 1992). It is in this context that the political dynamics of *The Bell Curve* can be better understood. Herrnstein and Murray took the recovery of white supremacy to the scientific level—"proving" once and for all the innate intellectual and moral inferiority of those who would challenge white power.

BAD SCIENCE IN A SHAKY PARADIGM

Not only is *The Bell Curve* weak science marked by unreliable sources, the dismissal of problematic data, logical non sequiturs and misguided purposes, it emerges from a crumbling paradigm often deemed inadequate for the complex study of human intelligence. As Patrick Slattery argues in this volume, Herrnstein and Murray perpetuate the myth of modern science that the universe is totally knowable and controllable. Their cognitive science is reductionistic in that it asserts that complex psychological phenomena can best be appreciated by reducing them to their constituent parts and then piecing these elements together according to causal laws. The cognitive psychology they employ is the product of the Cartesian-Newtonian paradigm. The word, paradigm, comes from the Greek word for pattern. A paradigm is a pattern, a scheme for understanding the nature of the world. Just as Isaac Newton saw the physical world in terms of predictable mechanical forces in a clockwork universe, Herrnstein and Murray perceive the psychological world in terms of predictable generalizations that can be derived by isolating intelligence and studying its variables in a controlled setting (IQ testing).

While the classical scientific paradigm developed important methods for studying the physical world, it has often failed in its attempt to study the human world, its psychological features in particular. Caught in this Cartesian-Newtonian web, scientists find themselves able to gather copious data about matter and energy but unable to increase their insights into the minds that put such information to use. The discourse of classical science with its obsession with measurement has shaped cognitive psychology and the education it supports. Education formulated in this context has devoted exaggerated attention to the development of ever more precise systems of measurement and the application of such measurement to the mind of the learner. As a result, many educators and much of the public itself can't think of intelligence in any terms other than the quantitative. To arrive at this numerical picture of intelligence the psychologist measures an individual's ability in isolation from her life experiences and the natural setting in which she operates. In this controlled context attention to circumstances surrounding the object of study are viewed as contaminants that subvert the validity of a study. The study of intelligence, we would argue, is always contextually contingent. Any research study that locks the subject of the study within the confines of a laboratory, or is satisfied with partial photographs of isolated events at a particular point in time, insults the subject by denying its complexity.

DEFERRING TO THE AUTHORITY
OF A FRIGHTENING SCIENCE

When *The Bell Curve* is viewed as a signifier of power, an entire range of insights into its "packaging" can be exposed. The length of the book, the imposing black background and gold lettering, the gratuitous statistics, and the 57 pages of references all contribute to the creation of the illusion of authority. Counting on the public's fear of numbers, Herrnstein and Murray hold their lay readers hostage—tied and gagged by statistics. At its best the scientific tradition the authors invoke has been out-of-date for decades. Herrnstein and Murray's view of intelligence, Cameron McCarthy and his co-authors argue in chapter 16, is taken from the most conservative behavioral science tradition of psychology. Indeed, theirs is a "Middle English" of scientific research that in its avoidance of social, cultural, political, and economic issues surrounding intelligence ignores the most compelling social psychological work of our time. At the end of the twentieth century, for example, few natural scientists analyze genetic and environmental influences as if they were mutually exclusive dynamics. In the late 1990s most researchers have reached the conclusion that the central task of the psychology of intelligence involves appreciating the complexity of genetic and environmental influences. In this context Herrnstein and Murray's absolutist pronouncements on genetic inferiority and superiority can be read as little more than expressions of a scientific false bravado.

Buried in the cacophony of the authors' bluster is the realization that the attempt by social science to apply physical scientific strategies to the analysis of human behavior has failed. Social activity is much too ambiguous to be "controlled" in laboratory experiments. Strict behavioral measurements don't work with humans. Blinded by their science, Herrnstein and Murray are indifferent to alternative explanations of the correlations they uncover. As Slattery maintains, controlling IQ is inappropriate, misleading, and impossible. The authors deploy science to *undermine* the public's understanding of the subtle dynamics of human cognition— indeed, popular confusion is in the interests of the right-wing groups who have supported and in turn are supported by Herrnstein and Murray's work. Moreover, the authors' mind game of confusion helps conceal the value assumptions on which hereditarian psychometrics is based—assumptions that are essential to elitist and antidemocratic political policies. When psychologists look for difference in performance rather than *different types of performances,* they will inevitably find some areas where rankings can be devised. For their lower performance in some isolated but measurable domain (probably produced by a complex assortment of social, economic, political, environmental, and hereditary factors), these individuals will be deemed incapable of high-skilled, high-status, or high-paid academic and/or vocational endeavors. Thus, they will be relegated to the dregs of the society. Despite all the ambiguities and all the evidence to the contrary, Herrnstein and Murray are more than willing to recommend such human sorting.

THE DISCURSIVE DYNAMICS OF
HERRNSTEIN AND MURRAY'S PSYCHOLOGY

A discourse is defined as a set of tacit rules that regulate linguistic practices such as what can and cannot be said, who can speak with the blessing of authority and who must listen, and whose educational perspectives are scientific and valid and whose are unlearned and unimportant. The discourse of Herrnstein and Murray's brand of psychology is marked by particular rules and assumptions that too often fail to be exposed and analyzed in the public arena. Hereditarian psychology demands that an infallible definition of intelligence be accepted before any analysis can begin: intelligence is the quality that intelligent tests test. The decontextualized reductionism of this definition demands that intelligence be viewed as a single entity capable of being expressed as a number that is distributed unequally in the population with white people possessing more than non-whites, the rich more than the poor. As Jo Anne Pagano argues in chapter 10, *The Bell Curve* "works" only if we accept a circular definition of intelligence. Failing to justify this definition, Herrnstein and Murray appeal simplistically to the authority of longevity: if it wasn't true, it would have been abandoned long ago. The theory of spontaneous generation of maggots in spoiled meat held sway for centuries as well, but it was also unfounded.

Once we begin to expose and challenge the discursive assumptions of hereditarian psychology, that which IQ measures becomes more and more clear. Understanding that social dynamics shape both the mind itself and the ways we perceive the mind, we learn that we cannot separate peoples' IQs from the historical circumstances of the social groups to which they belong. Thus, hereditarian psychology measures the social circumstances of various groups—the status of the group, its self-esteem, its power relative to other groups, its economic success, its acceptance in the larger community, etc. . . . In this context Brigitte Berger (1995) argues that IQ tests measure what she calls "modern consciousness"—a coterie of abilities that enable one to negotiate the complex cultural terrain of contemporary life with its technological innovations and rationalistic bureaucracies. Often referred to as "modernism," this Western way of seeing the world emerged in the seventeenth and eighteenth centuries. Buoyed by Rene Descartes, Sir Issac Newton, and Sir Francis Bacon's delineation of the scientific method, modernism was marked by impulses to centralize, concentrate, and accumulate—the faster and more efficiently the better. Modernism laid a foundation that allowed science and technology to transform both the physical world *and* the Western psyche.

The better IQ test takers can operate in modern Western society, the higher their scores will be. Take the variable of time, for example. Modern Western societies have been trapped in a time warp of speed that dramatically affects perceptions of intelligence. While premodern cultures may have associated haste with waste, modern cultures believe that speed reflects alertness, power, and success. Pondering, reflecting, or musing might be valued in some cultures, but not in the culture of the modern West. In a study involving male undergraduates in college, Robert Knapp and John Garbut (1965) found that the individuals who scored the highest on standardized tests were those who placed the most value on speed. Students from traditional, indigenous, and agrarian cultures tend not to place as high a value on speed as urban, white, and mainstream ones. Thus, for *cultural* reasons, not *cognitive* ones, traditional, indigenous, and agrarian students do not tend to score highly on standardized measurements of ability.

In addition, researchers have discovered a correlation between one's socioeconomic class and one's perception of time. To conservative psychometricians such correlations remain hidden, as they reduce variables and refuse to examine social, cultural, and economic influences on the test taker. With such information psychologists are better able to account for IQ increases when individuals, for example, migrate from rural to urban areas or when they move from the lower-middle to the middle class. In these circumstances the individuals in question have repositioned themselves closer to the pulse of modern consciousness. Using Berger's analytical framework, we appreciate the distance experienced by most poor people in general and poor African Americans and Latinos in particular from this modern consciousness. Cultural features such as proximity to Western modernism are virtually infinite in number, but Herrnstein and Murray are undaunted by their implications. Robert Hendrickson argues in chapter 23 that the authors, who use the Scholastic Aptitude Test (SAT) and the American College Testing (ACT) examination as accurate measurements of cognitive ability, express a faith in the validity of such tests that is not held even by the tests' manufacturers. In this way Herrnstein and Murray push the envelope of the discourse of cognitive psychology to a level that makes even enthusiastic champions of IQ tests nervous.

IQ IS TO INTELLIGENCE AS *WHEEL OF FORTUNE*
PUZZLES ARE TO POETIC GENIUS

Don't use IQs as a measure of a fixed, intractable notion of intelligence, Alfred Binet warned after inventing the first practical IQ test in 1905. No sooner than the words were out of Binet's mouth, psychologists deployed the tests for just that purpose. As perceptions of intelligence mutated into what the tests measured, the mental characteristics attributed to intelligent people followed closely behind. Students and other individuals who failed to conform to the tyranny of the IQ definition, whatever the reason, were often dismissed as incompetent. From Herrnstein and Murray's psychometric perspective intelligence is viewed merely from one limited frame of reference. The intellectually gifted in this discursive context learn to view reality from a "correct" frame—a way of seeing that too often removes that being observed from its multiple contexts. Such an approach may serve to exclude the brightest among us. Where would Albert Einstein have ended up if he had been tested and tracked accordingly? What would have happened to Van Gogh, Magritte, Duchamps, or Georgia O'Keefe if they had been forced to paint the picture *correctly?*

Einstein once described intuition as a sacred gift and rationality as a servant. Modern science along with Herrnstein and Murray's psychometrics have worshipped the servant and profaned the sacred gift. In Einstein's personal case it is difficult to follow the rationality of his work in physics, for unpredictable, non-linear, even non-rational expressions are common in his scientific theorizing. Indeed, the nature of his genius did not lend itself to the measurements of an IQ or other standardized tests. Such instruments would not have picked up those cognitive qualities that set Einstein apart from his fellow physicists. Intuitively understanding the limits of reason and logical linearity, realizing that scientific discoveries were not made by a logical series of successive steps, Einstein's mental functions did not lend themselves to efficient measurement. To understand his brilliance a more in-depth observation would have been necessary, a more journalistic description would have been required to convey what social and psychological dynamics were at work in Einstein's brain. A short-answer or multiple choice convergent-answer instrument would have been unable to account for Einstein's ability to perceive relationships between ostensibly unrelated entities, to transfer knowledge gained in one domain to a completely different context, to apply information to the practical solution of problems in the everyday lived world. These abilities—the building blocks of genius—are irrelevant to IQ tests not to mention school success in general.

THE BELL CURVE, TEACHING, LEARNING, AND JUSTICE

The way intelligence is understood exerts a dramatic impact on schooling, teaching, and learning. Classrooms that accept Herrnstein and Murray's right-wing psychometric views are organized in a way that differs dramatically from classrooms that view intelligence in line with the qualities associated with Einstein's genius. (We have discussed these qualities in detail elsewhere; Kincheloe and Steinberg, 1993; Kincheloe, 1995). The classroom supported by Herrnstein and Murray reduces student learning to the notion of replication rather than interpretation. Here students "know" only when they can display a decontextualized fragment of data at the bidding of the test. Assuming that the most significant aspects of school performance and cognitive activity can be quantitatively measured, the psychometric discourse discourages students and teachers from connecting their lived experience to academic knowledge. Students learn to lay aside their creative and interpretive predispositions and focus on what data will be included on the examination, regardless of its relationship to the meaning of the subject matter or to their attempts to make sense of the world. In this context students are rewarded for their ability to present testmakers with what they have been taught in the exact manner it was first presented to them. The ability to engage information critically, creatively, or synthetically is often irrelevant, even, it could be argued, harmful to the quest for high evaluations (Slattery, 1995; Pinar, 1994; Maher and Rathbone, 1986; Bozik, 1987; Lawler, 1975; Gallager, 1992; Hanson, 1994).

In the name of rigorous science Herrnstein and Murray's psychometrics, like a category five hurricane, leaves destruction in its wake. The discourse of testing trivializes the curriculum, focusing attention on educational dynamics that are not necessarily important but that lend themselves to quick and easy measurement. Professional prerogative is stolen from teachers who are forced to make curricular decisions not on the basis of their professional evaluations of student needs but on the demands of a test. In this context the standardized test becomes "the tail that wags the dog," as the exam (not the teacher) determines what is taught and learned (Kincheloe, 1991; Rivlin, 1971; House, 1978). The *social* relationship of the student to the school, the teacher, the curriculum, and the tests is irrelevant in Herrnstein and Murray's educational psychology. A student's membership or lack of such in what Jean Lave and Etienne Wenger (1991) call "a community of practice" exerts a profound impact on how he or she performs in testing situations in particular and school in general. Any evaluation of student progress and potential must ask: how integrated is a child into mainstream education's discourse community? School activities, tasks, functions, and understandings are inseparable from wider cultural relationships that grant them *meaning*. If a student lives outside these wider cultural relationships, it becomes extremely difficult for her to understand why the school requires particular tasks to be performed or why certain knowledge is important. A cultural outsider may feel bewildered by the demands of the school. Growing up in the mountains of rural Tennessee, I (Joe Kincheloe) witnessed dirt poor but savvy mountain children capable of brilliant out-of-school accomplishments fall victim to their cultural exclusion from the discourse community of schooling. "What is she talking about?," such students often asked in regard to the teacher's explanation of an assignment. Needless to say, such students—no matter how brilliant—typically performed poorly in my school.

Herrnstein and Murray exhibit little compassion for those excluded from the educational discourse community—such students are mere pebbles in the great sea of the low-IQ incompetent. Here is where Herrnstein and Murray confuse high IQ with cultural advantage. Such an error is the direct result of Herrnstein and Murray's social decontextualization of the study of intelligence. Unable to realize the academic benefits gained through access to the school's discourse community, the authors unabashedly continue to equate high intelligence with people who are most like them—white, privileged, and profoundly immersed in the discourse community of education. Such understandings provide great insights for those committed to the promise of a democratic system of education. Indeed, egalitarian reform of American education may have to begin with the identification of those students who reside both within and outside the discourse community of the school. For the outsiders democratic intervention would not involve "remedial" drill and recitation but a cultural immersion into the assumptions and codes of the discourse community. Democratic reformers well understand the ways biology and environment limit our choices and performances, but, unlike Herrnstein and Murray, they maintain that progress is possible. Individuals can with facilitation achieve far beyond what the dismal pseudo-science of Herrnstein and Murray allows.

We argue in this book that there is reason for hope. Ignoring literally scores of studies that document the benefits of educational intervention, Herrnstein and Murray would rob the poor and non-white of future promise. An entire school of psychological analysis has emerged over the last two decades that views the development of higher orders of thinking around sociocultural interaction (Bohm and Edwards, 1991; Gardner, 1983, 1991; Hultgren, 1987; Kincheloe, 1993; Lave, 1988, 1995; Raizen, 1989; Vygotsky, 1978; Walkerdine, 1984, 1988; Wertsch, 1991; Wexler,

1992). With these compelling psychological understandings at our fingertips, democratic educators and citizens find it incumbent to respond to the assertions of *The Bell Curve*. Our response is meant to put these pseudo-scientific dalliances behind us so that we might turn our attention to the important work of educating students of all races, ethnicities, creeds, and socioeconomic classes for personal fulfillment and social justice. One of the first steps of such a project involves rethinking educational psychology in a manner that appreciates the cultural dimensions of intelligence, that expands the guidelines for what can be labeled as intelligence.

Viewing cognition from this vantage point, we are drawn to the validation of a variety of thinking styles. We don't have to look very far to find forms of intelligence dismissed by psychometricians. Different forms of intelligence surround us. If we read *Frames of mind: The theory of multiple intelligences* (1983) by Howard Gardner (dismissed by Herrnstein and Murray as a radical who doesn't present his findings in the language of statistics), or observe individuals that schools have labeled as "slow," more likely than not we will discover fascinating and sophisticated forms of intelligence. Educator John Goodlad (1992) writes eloquently of the brilliance of the individuals he encounters in his everyday life outside the academy and the humility he experiences in their presence. When we avoid Herrnstein and Murray's cognitive reductionism, a new world is opened to us—in the strangest places we uncover forms of valuable thinking. In no way are we attempting to romanticize the unschooled. Our point is simple: as our democratic psychology embraces unrecognized manifestations of intelligence, it challenges the reductionism and mechanism of *The Bell Curve*'s psychometrics. Indeed, our democratic psychology confronts the status quo as it rejects the evaluation of students against a single standard of higher-order cognition. Threatened by the expansion of the definition of intelligence, right-wing advocates of elitism will be agitated. They will frame our arguments as examples of the breakdown of academic standards, the vulgarization of society. When Herrnstein and Murray assert their theory of dysgenesis or Dinesh D'Souza (1991) claims that an appreciation of cultural diversity

undermines traditional academic excellence, they all express an ethno-
centric and privileged fear of losing control of the cultural discourse,
of losing their "natural" right to define "quality."

THE LENGTHS TO WHICH ONE WILL GO:
HERRNSTEIN AND MURRAY'S SOURCES

How far are Herrnstein and Murray willing to go to protect their
race, their elitist psychological discourse, their exclusionary definition of quality? We are tempted to answer this question by saying,
"whatever it takes," after examining the sources used to produce *The
Bell Curve*. The authors are not afraid to employ the work of
self-proclaimed white supremacists and eugenicists. Securely connected to the scientific racism establishment and its pantheon of
white supremacists, Herrnstein and Murray provide new data to
support the establishment's concern that racial integration undermines the status of whites. At the center of the racist establishment
rests the Pioneer Fund founded in 1937 by Wycliffe Draper to
promote the procreation of the progeny of white families living in
America before the Revolutionary War. The Fund financially supports research that "proves" that African Americans are disproportionately poor because of their genetic inferiority. Over the
last decade the Fund has contributed 3.5 million dollars to researchers cited by Herrnstein and Murray. Closely tied to eugenics
advocates in Nazi Germany during the years following its founding,
the Pioneer Fund lost credibility after the revelation of the Nazi
eugenicists' Final Solution. But, not to worry, the organization is
back in the 1990s (Linklater, 1995; Sautman, 1995; Muwakkil,
1995; World News Tonight, November 22, 1994).

The Pioneer Fund is an exciting place to be in the 1990s
with the election of legislators who support many of the
organization's views and who turn to it for pertinent information on
pending legislation. Fund Director Harry Weyner has endorsed the
brilliance of *The Bell Curve,* as well he should. A sizable number of

the sources utilized by Herrnstein and Murray were produced by Pioneer Fund recipients. Embedded in right-wing political circles, the Pioneer Fund's most favored political organization is the Federation of American Immigration Reform (FAIR). It was this organization that helped California Governor Pete Wilson formulate support for Proposition 187. The work of the Fund extends into many arenas, as it funnels money and information into studies of non-white immigrant IQs, anti–school desegregation battles, and research that connects crime and race. The "scholarship" supported by the Pioneer Fund is uniformly racist, as it attempts to prove once and for all the inferiority of African Americans and Latinos. When confronted with his association with the organization, Murray deflects such inquiries by charging his questioners with intellectual witch hunting.

Besides the Pioneer Fund another cornerstone of the scientific racism establishment is *Mankind Quarterly*—a white supremacist journal financed by the Pioneer Fund. *Mankind Quarterly* was founded in 1960 by Robert Gayre, a British anthropologist. A long-time Nazi associate, Gayre claims to be a leading expert on issues of race and genetics. Herrnstein and Murray must have accepted his claim for they used five articles published in *Mankind Quarterly* and seventeen scholars who had published in it as sources in *The Bell Curve*. In order to understand the tradition Herrnstein and Murray represent it is important to examine the groups with whom they collaborate. Contributors and advisors to *Mankind Quarterly* include Corrado Gini who was leader of Fascist Italy's eugenics program; Ottmar von Vershauer who mentored German Nazi scientist Josef Mengele, the "angel of death"; and present editor Roger Pearson who is so right-wing he was kicked out of the ultra-conservative World Anti-Communist League. In the second volume of the journal, Editor Gayre provided important insight into its ideological leanings when he contended that the Nazis' crimes should not force us to give up racial scholarship that proves that some races are superior to others. Given his racial perspectives, it is not inconsistent that Gayre was an early supporter of South African apartheid.

Another god in the racist pantheon Herrnstein and Murray employ as a source is Philippe Rushton, a Canadian psychologist who has received world wide attention for his racial theories. Rushton's portrait of African Americans (he calls them Negroids) includes their stupidity, small brains, big penises, sexual promiscuity, criminal predispositions, and inept parenting. Rushton is known particularly for his argument that brain size and penis size are inversely proportional. Only "Caucasoids" meet all 21 items on Rushton's "Criteria for Civilization" checklist, while African Americans score poorly on his "Personality and Temperament Traits." To prove his contentions about the races, Rushton has conducted research at shopping malls, where he asks men from different racial groups to specify the distance their semen travels during ejaculation. The farther the distance, he argues, the lower the individual's intelligence. Obviously, serious research methodological problems emerge in this context. How many men know with precision such statistics? The last time we tried to find out, we forgot to bring our tape measure. Obviously, there is room for comedy in this context, but Herrnstein and Murray don't "get it." Responding to questions about Rushton and his research, the authors claim time and again that he is not a crank, that his work grants convincing insights into the nature of racial differences. Rushton returns the compliment lauding *The Bell Curve* as a work of great scholarship that will alter the manner in which we understand human beings (Childley, 1995; Easterbrook, 1995; Kamin, 1995; Linklater, 1995; Pearson, 1995; Sautman, 1995; World News Tonight, November 22, 1994).

Other deities or sub-deities in the racist pantheon include Michael Levin, a professor at City University of New York, who has argued that white people should fear and avoid African Americans because blackness is a danger sign. After some well-publicized announcements proclaiming that some forms of racism are justified, Levin received a 124,000 dollar grant from the Pioneer Fund to continue his good work. Herrnstein and Murray cite Levin's work in *The Bell Curve* along with another member of the pantheon, Richard Lynn. A regular contributor to *Mankind Quarterly*, Lynn is used extensively (21 different citations) by Herrnstein and Murray in their attempt to prove that the slave history of African Americans is not the cause of their alleged low intelligence. The authors use Lynn's work in 1991 as proof that the average African IQ is 75. No analysis of the cultural dynamics involved in arriving at this figure is mentioned. Another member of the pantheon cited by the authors is British anthropologist, Roger Pearson. Along with the famous Nazi anthropologist Hans Gunther, Pearson formed the Northern League in 1958 for the purpose of encouraging Teutonic solidarity. Not surprisingly the organization developed close ties with neo-Nazi groups and the alliance with Pearson as its spokesperson called for racial purity. In 1966 Pearson wrote extensively about the possibility of Teutonic racial suicide if "inferior tribes" were not exterminated. (Space prohibits further delineation of the racist scholars utilized by Herrnstein and Murray in *The Bell Curve).* Who said it can't happen here (Miller, 1995; Sautman, 1995)?

FASCIST RUMBLINGS

On a number of levels Herrnstein and Murray's work hints at the development of a home-grown, American style Fascism. Stephen Haymes recognizes this theme in his analysis of chapter eleven and uses Toni Morrison's speech at Howard University to help formulate his critique. Using the alleged black inferiority and predisposition to violent criminal activity to justify forms of social control, Herrnstein and Murray advocate a behavioral, psychology-based social policy. A careful reading of *The Bell Curve* and the sources it draws upon reveal a positioning of African Americans and Latinos as internal enemies who present a threat so profound that extraordinary action is required. A central theme of the book commented upon by many reviewers involves the rhetorical device Herrnstein and Murray deploy to flatter the reader (white) and demonize the "other" (the non-white). *We* work hard, lead moral lives, and hold to historical cultural values; *they* are worthless and immoral and deserve nothing from us. We have no choice—we must develop better, more efficient, even more forceful forms of social control. We hate to raise the question, but just what are we going to do with our inferior co-habitants? Build more prisons? Hire more policemen? Devise anti-immigration policies? Untie the hands of the police? Nullify civil liberties in specific circumstances? Discourage reproduction of inferior genetic stock? Positive responses to such questions, we believe, move us in an anti-democratic direction.

Herrnstein and Murray's social vision, their view of what constitutes a good society, contributes to the discordant Fascist rumblings being heard in late twentieth-century America. As Debbie Britzman and Alice Pitt document in chapter 26, the authors are obsessed with order—indeed, Herrnstein and Murray's enthusiasm for ubiquitous IQ testing is based on the efficiency of testing as an ordering device. In typical hit and run fashion the authors dance around the issue of a custodial state but paint a revealing picture of a predominantly white police force controlling predominantly black Washington, D.C. It is hard in this context to refrain from imagining Herrnstein and Murray smiling approvingly as newly-promoted Officer Mark Fuhrman uses his muscle and savvy to control restless African Americans. Everyone understands his or her place in Herrnstein and Murray's dream world, a cosmos much like the world before the Civil Rights Movement *nearly* destroyed it.

The virtuous and talented deserve their privilege in this new/old World. Everyone who "makes the grade," who embraces the authors' notion of family values and a conformist form of citizenship, will thrive in this "psychotopia." This virtuous and talented will have to divest themselves, however, of soft-hearted notions of egalitarianism and the democratization of social institutions. Like those individuals on the extreme left of the cognitive bell curve, the elite too will have to learn to live with inequality in Herrnstein and Murray's new world (Walden III?). Education will improve its ability to acculturate us to the justified inequality of the psychotopia. Taking Herrnstein and Murray's suggestion, the schools of the future will transfer monies spent on the slow students to the gifted.

Educational psychologists will become increasingly adept at defining and specifying the boundaries of normality and abnormality for the purpose of tracking and segregating individuals along these lines. Voucher programs, fervently supported by Murray, will extend class and race segregation by neglecting schools for the poor and rewarding elite private schools and their privileged clientele. One of the most important objectives will involve adjusting African American, Latino, and poor students to the understanding that the American dream of upward mobility is not for them. *The Bell Curve* is the social blueprint for the Fascist future—it cannot be ignored in hopes it will just go away.

References

Amott, T. (1933). *Caught in the crisis: Women and the U.S. economy today.* New York: Monthly Review Press.

Aronowitz, S. (1992). *The politics of identity: Class, culture and social movements.* New York: Routledge.

Aronowitz, S. and Giroux, H. (1991). *Postmodern education: Politics, culture, and social criticism.* Minneapolis, MN: University of Minnesota Press.

Beck, R. (1991). *General education: Vocational and academic collaboration.* Berkeley, CA: NCRVE.

Berger, B. (1995). Methodological fetishism. In Jacoby, R. and Glauberman, N., eds., *The Bell Curve debate: History, documents and opinion.* New York: Random House.

Block, A. (1995). *Occupied reading: Critical foundations for an ecological theory.* New York: Garland.

Block, F. (1990). *Postindustrial possibilities: A critique of economic discourse. Berkeley, CA: University of California Press.*

Bohm, D. and Edwards, M. (1991). *Changing consciousness.* San Francisco: Harper.

Bozik, M. (1987). Critical thinking through creative thinking. Paper presented to the Speech Communication Association: Boston.

Childley, J. (1995). The heart of the matter. In Jacoby, R. and Glauberman, N., eds., *The Bell Curve debate: History, documents and opinion*. New York: Random House.

Coontz, S. (1992). *The way we never were: American families and the nostalgia trap*. New York: Basic Books.

DeYoung, A. (1989). *Economics and American education*. New York: Longman.

D'Souza, D. (1995). *The end of racism: Principles for a multicultural society*. New York: The Free Press.

Easterbrook, G. (1995). Blacktop basketball and *The Bell Curve*. In Jacoby, R. and Glauberman, N., eds., *The Bell Curve debate: History, documents and opinion*. New York: Random House.

Ellwood, D. (1988). *Poor support: Poverty in the American family*. New York: Basic Books.

Gallager, S. (1992). *Hermeneutics and education*. Albany, NY: SUNY Press.

Gardner, H. (1983). *Frames of mind: The theory of multiple intelligences*. New York: Basic Books.

Gardner, H. (1991). *The unschooled mind: How children think and how schools should teach*. New York: Basic Books.

Goodlad, J. (1992, February 19). Beyond half an education. *Education Week, 22*, pp. 34, 44.

Giroux, H. (1993). *Living dangerously: Multiculturalism and the politics of difference*. New York: Peter Lang.

Gresson, A. (1995). *The recovery of race in America*. Minneapolis, MN: University of Minnesota Press.

Grubb, N., Davis, G., Lum, D., Phihal, J. and Morgaine, C. (1991). *The Cunning hand, the cultured mind. Models for integrating vocational and academic education*. Berkeley, CA: NCRVE.

Hanson, F. (1994). *Testing, testing: Social consequences of the examined life*. Berkeley, CA: University of California Press.

Haymes, S. (1995). *Race, culture, and the city: A pedagogy for black urban struggle*. Albany, NY: SUNY Press.

Herbert, B. (1995). Throwing a curve. In Jacoby, R. and Glauberman, N., (eds.), *The Bell Curve debate: History, documents, and opinion*. New York: Random House.

House, E. and Haug, C. (1995). Riding *The Bell Curve:* A review. *Education Evaluation and Policy Analysis, 17* (2), pp. 263-72.

Hultgren, F. (1987). Critical thinking: Phenomenological and critical foundations. In Thomas, R., ed., *Higher order thinking: Definition meaning and instructional approaches.* Washington, D.C.: Home Economics Education Association.

Johnson, W. (1991). Model programs prepare women for skilled trades. In Wolfe, L., *Women, work, and the school: Occupational segregation and the role of education.* Boulder, CO: Westview Press.

Kamin, L. (1995). Lies, damned lies, and statistics. In Jacoby, R. and Glauberman, N., eds., *The Bell Curve debate: History, documents, and opinion.* New York: Random House.

Kincheloe, J. (1995). *Toil and trouble: Good work, smart workers, and the integration of academic and vocational education.* New York: Peter Lang.

Kincheloe, J. (1993). *Toward a critical politics of teacher thinking: Mapping the postmodern.* Westport, CT: Bergin and Garvey.

Kincheloe, J. and Steinberg, S. (1993). A tentative description of post-formal thinking: The critical confrontation with cognitive theory. *Harvard Educational Review, 63* (3), pp. 296-320.

Knapp, R. and Garbut, J. (1965). Variations in time descriptions and need achievement. *Journal of Social Psychology, 67,* pp. 265-81.

Kozol, J. (1991). *Savage inequalities: Children in America's schools.* New York: Crown Publishers.

Lave, J. (1988). *Cognition in practice.* Cambridge, MA: Cambridge University Press.

Lave, J. and Wenger, E. (1991). *Situated learning: Legitimate peripheral participation.* New York: Cambridge University Press.

Lawler, J. (1975). Dialectical philosophy and developmental psychology: Hegel and Piaget on contradiction. *Human Development, 18,* 1-17.

Linklater, M. (1995). The curious laird of nigg. In Jacoby, R. and Glauberman, N., eds., *The Bell Curve debate: History, documents, and opinion.* New York: Random House.

McLaren, P. (1995). *Critical pedagogy and predatory culture: Oppositional politics in a postmodern culture.* New York: Routledge.

McLaren, P. (1994). *Life in schools: An introduction to critical pedagogy in the foundations of education.* White Plains, NY: Longman.

Maher, F. and Rathbone, C. (1986). Teacher education and feminist theory: Some implications for practice. *American Journal of Education, 94* (2), pp. 214-35.

Marable, M. (1992). Race, identity, and political culture. In Dent, G., ed., *Black popular culture.* Seattle, WA: Bay Press.

Merelman, R. (1986). Domination, self-justification, and self-doubt: Some social, psychological considerations. *Journal of Politics, 48,* pp. 276-99.

Miller, A. (1995). Professors of Hate. In Jacoby, R. and Glauberman, N., eds., *The Bell Curve debate: History, documents, and opinion.* New York: Random House.

Muwakkil, S. (1995). Timing is everything. In Jacoby, R. and Glauberman, N., eds., *The Bell Curve debate: History, documents, and opinion.* New York: Random House.

Nightingale, C. (1993). *On the edge: A history of poor black children and their American dreams.* New York: Basic Books.

Oakes, J. (1985). *Keeping track: How schools structure inequality.* New Haven, CT: Yale University Press.

Pearson, H. (1995). Breaking ranks. In R. Jacoby and N. Glauberman, eds., *The Bell Curve debate: History, documents, and opinion.* New York: Random House.

Phillips, K. (1970). *The new Republican majority.* New York: Anchor Books.

Pinar, W. (1994). *Autobiography, politics and sexuality: Essays in curriculum theory, 1972-1992.* New York: Peter Lang.

Raizen, S. (1989). *Reforming education for work: A cognitive science perspective.* Berkeley, CA: NCRVE.

Raspberry, W. (1995, September 23). Only racists will cheer this. State College, PA. *Centre Daily Times.* p. A2.

Ritzer, G. (1993). *The McDonaldization of Society.* Thousand Oaks, California: Pine Forge Press.

Rubin, L. (1994). *Families on the faultline: America's working class speaks about the family, the economy, race, and ethnicity.* New York: HarperCollins.

Sautman, B. (1995). Theories of East Asian superiority. In Jacoby, R. and Glauberman, N., eds., *The Bell Curve debate: History, documents, and opinion.* New York: Random House.

Schmidt, F., et. al. (1988). Joint relation experience and ability with job performance. A test of three hypotheses. *Journal of Applied Psychology, 73,* 46-57.

Slattery, P. (1995). *Curriculum development in the postmodern era.* New York: Garland.

Sternberg, R. (1979). The nature of mental abilities. *American Psychologist, 34,* pp. 214-30.

Vygotsky, L. (1978). *Mind in society: The development of higher psychological processes.* In Cole, M., et. al. Cambridge, MA: Harvard University Press.

Walkerdine, V. (1984). Developmental psychology and the child-centered pedagogy: The insertion of Piaget into early education. In Henriques, J., Hollway, W., Urwin, C., Venn, C., and Walkerdine, V., *Changing the subject.* New York: Metheun.

Walkerdine, V. (1988). *The mastery of reason: Cognitive development and the production of rationality.* London: Routledge.

Weisman, J. (1991, November 13). Some economists challenging views that schools hurt competitiveness. *Education Week, 9* (11), 1, 14-15.

Wertsch, J. (1991). *Voices of the mind: A sociocultural approach to mediated action.* Cambridge, MA: Harvard University Press.

Wexler, P. (1992). *Becoming somebody: Toward a social psychology of school.* London: Falmer Press.

West, C. (1993). *Race matters.* Boston: Beacon Press.

World News Tonight with Peter Jennings (November 22, 1994), ABC News Transcript #4232.

Zweigenhaft, R. and Domhoff, G. (1991). *Blacks in the white establishment.* New Haven, CT: Yale University Press.

PART II

SITUATING
THE BELL CURVE

2 DOMINANCE AND DEPENDENCY: SITUATING *THE BELL CURVE* WITHIN THE CONSERVATIVE RESTORATION

MICHAEL W. APPLE

There have been scores of reviews of Richard Herrnstein and Charles Murray's recent volume *The Bell Curve*. It is easy to demonstrate that its claims both in genetics and on the nature of intelligence are at best shaky and at worst simply untenable. I do not wish to recapitulate these criticisms in this chapter, though I very much agree with them. Rather, I want to situate *The Bell Curve* as a phenomenon within the social and educational upheavals within this society currently and in the past. This is a time when conservative groups have recognized that in order to win politically, you must win in civil society. Thus there is a complicated politics of common sense now going on in which dominant groups are attempting to redefine what we actually mean by democracy, equality, and the common good. In order to understand the reasons behind the wide circulation of ideas such as those embodied in *The Bell Curve*, we also need to understand the larger processes involved in the reconstruction of common sense (Apple, 1993). This shall be my agenda for this chapter. I can but point to the historical and current tendencies and dynamics involved. But an outline of what is going on should be readily visible. In order to accomplish my goal, I shall need to move back and forth in time.

I shall need as well to move back and forth between education and other institutions and between cultural and economic dynamics, detailing the broader conservative restorational politics in educational and other parts of society. In the story I wish to detail, class, gender, and racial dynamics all play a large part.

BETWEEN NEOLIBERALISM AND NEOCONSERVATISM

Many of the rightist policies now taking center stage in education and nearly everything else embody a tension between a neoliberal emphasis on "market values" on the one hand and a neoconservative attachment to "traditional values" on the other (Whitty, Edwards, and Gewirtz, 1993). From the former perspective, the state must be minimized, preferably by setting private enterprise loose; from the latter, the state needs to be strong in teaching *correct* knowledge, norms, and values. Schools are either too state-controlled and/or they don't mandate the teaching of what they are "supposed" to teach. It's a bit contradictory, but the rightist agenda has ways of dealing with such contradictions and has managed to creatively stitch together an alliance that unites (sometimes rather tensely) its various movements.

This new hegemonic alliance has a wide umbrella. It combines four major groups: 1) dominant economic and political elites intent on "modernizing" the economy and the institutions connected to it; 2) largely white working-class and middle-class groups that mistrust the state and are concerned with security, the family, and traditional knowledge and values and who form an increasingly active segment of what might be called "authoritarian populists"; 3) economic and cultural conservatives who want a return to "high standards," discipline, and social Darwinist competition; and 4) a fraction of the new middle class who may not totally agree with these other groups, but whose own professional interests and advancement depend on the expanded use of accountability, efficiency, and management procedures that are their own cultural capital.

The sphere of education is one in which the Right has been ascendant. The social democratic goal of expanding equality of opportunity (itself a rather limited reform) has lost much of its political potency and its ability to mobilize people. The "panic" over falling standards, dropouts, and illiteracy, the fear of violence in schools, and the concern over the destruction of family values and religiousity have all had an effect. These fears are exacerbated, and used, by dominant groups within politics and the economy that have been able to shift the debate on education (and all things social) onto their own terrain—the terrain of traditionalism, standardization, productivity, marketization, and industrial needs. Because so many parents *are* justifiably concerned about the economic and cultural futures of their children—in an economy that is increasingly conditioned by lower wages, capital flight, and insecurity—rightist discourse connects with the experiences of many working- and middle-class people.

Behind much of the conservative restoration is a clear sense of loss of control over a number of things: economic and personal security, the knowledge and values that should be passed on to children, what counts as sacred texts and authority, and relations of gender and age in the family. The binary opposition of we/they becomes important here. "We" are law-abiding, "hard working, decent, virtuous, and homogeneous." The "theys" are very different. They are considered "lazy, immoral, permissive, and heterogeneous" (Hunter, 1987, p. 23). These binary oppositions distance most people of color, women (that is, "feminists"), gays and lesbians, and others from the community of worthy individuals. The subjects of discrimination are now no longer those groups that have been historically oppressed, but are instead the "real Americans" who embody the idealized virtues of a romanticized past. The "theys" are undeserving. They are getting something for nothing. Policies supporting them are taking away our way of life, most of our economic resources, and creating government control of our lives (Hunter, 1987, p. 30).

As with much of the ideological agenda behind such criticisms, the issues in education are the removal of schools from state and bureaucratic control, the enhancement of privatization and marketization, and the reconstruction of a people's character based largely on individual entrepreneurial values or on fundamentalist interpretations of "Christian morality."

Though my tone may be negative when discussing these seemingly unremitting attacks on the state, on schools, on the public sphere in general, and on the "other," this should not be interpreted as an assumption that everything that the government does "in the public interest" in education or anything else is always wise. Indeed, it is possible to argue that because of ideological conflicts, insufficient resources, and their own interests and internal structures, governments often are organized to generate failure. In fact, some analysts have argued provocatively that, paradoxically, one of the conditions of government expansion (a very sore point with conservatives, as you know) is that it must fail to reach its goals. Though overstating his case, Ian Hunter discusses government as programming its own failure and doing so as a "condition of its ongoing and truly remarkable inventiveness" (p. 134). Governments often have ever-reaching horizons, goals, and spheres of interest (equity, equality of opportunity, and so on) that under the current distribution of power and resources simply cannot be met. Yet in order to maintain its own legitimacy and the continued need for all of its offices, programs, and personnel, the state must be seen to be striving to meet these goals and must continually measure itself against them. Thus "demonstrating its own failure in this way is the means by which government opens up new tracts of social life to bureaucratic knowledge and intervention" (p. 134). It should not be a surprise, then, that not all of these forms of knowledge and intervention are necessarily in the long-term interests of those who are the subjects of them. And here, intuitions of conservatives seem to have an element of insight.

This is *not* to say, however, as the New Right does, that what is public is bad and what is private is good, that the very idea of government regulation is a threat to freedom. Rather, it is to remind us of the connections among resources, power, institutional interests, failure, and, hence, continued bureaucratization and expansion. It is clear that this very sense of bureaucratization, inefficiency, and expansion underpins many of the attacks on schools and the state.

Consider the current calls for educational reform surrounding the ties between education and (paid) work. A large portion of current reform initiatives are justified partly by wanting to enhance the connections between education and the wider project of "meeting the needs of the economy." This increasingly powerful economic critique of the educational system is grounded in a number of challenges. The system is basically antientrepreneurial. It is horribly wasteful. And at a time of severe international competition, schools are failing to produce a labor force that is sufficiently skilled, adaptable, and flexible (Whitty, Edwards, and Gewirtz, 1993). Attached to this sense of schools as producers of "human capital" is an equally crucial cultural agenda concerning the sets of social logics that should guide our daily conduct.

For both neoliberals and neoconservatives, the educational task here is "not only [to] encourage members of a market economy to think of themselves as individuals in order to maximize their own interests." This is a crucial goal, but the task goes considerably further. People also need to be encouraged to accept that it is entirely acceptable for there to be winners and losers in the system (Whitty, Edwards, and Gewirtz, 1993). Genetic explanations—most of which cannot be evaluated by the general public—assist this acceptance in powerful ways, as does claiming that a process such as this is "wealth creating."

Part of this position on the distribution of wealth—that inequality is a good thing and more inequality is an even better thing—can be found in a quote from Keith Joseph, a former minister of education for Margaret Thatcher:

> The relief of poverty has not in the past been thought to require an equal society and it is difficult to find any necessary connection between them today. On the contrary, everything in the experience of this country since the last war has combined to demonstrate that you cannot make the poor richer

by making the rich poorer. You can only make the poor richer
by making everyone richer including the rich. (Honderich,
1990, p. 196)

Friedrich Hayek, one of the economic theorists relied upon
by conservatives, stated the case even more bluntly:

> If today in the United States or Western Europe the relatively
> poor can have a car or a refrigerator, an airplane trip or a radio,
> at the cost of a reasonable part of their income, this was made
> possible because in the past others with larger incomes were
> able to spend on what was then a luxury. The path of advance
> is greatly eased by the fact that it has been trodden before. It
> is because scouts have found the goal that the road can be built
> for the less lucky and less energetic. . . . Even the poorest today
> owe their relative material well-being to the results of past
> inequality. (Honderich, 1990, p. 197)

Of course, these empirical claims are subject to evidence.
We must indeed ask, in the United States and Britain of the New
Right, whether as the rich got richer the poor got less poor? The
answer to this would be nearly laughable were it not for the disastrous
consequences of such redistribution upward, for that is indeed what
has happened: the lives of so many people have become increasingly
insecure and even desperate (Apple, 1993).

Like the neoliberal position with its romantic vision of the
market, the neoconservative agenda also has its interesting contradictions. While it may seem clear that such conservatism lends its
support to that which is "traditional" in society, it should be just as
clear that its allegiance is more than a little selective. It does not
support *all* that is traditional in society.

One of the distinguishing features of the neoconservative
position is its vision of character. There is a clear preference for
incentive systems rather than the encouragement of social altruism
(Honderich, 1990), though the latter is sometimes mentioned in its

bag-of-virtues approach to moral education. Yet the tradition of altruism has just as deep roots in our nation, and its expression needs to be expanded, not contracted. Selfishness is simply another form of the possessive individualism that has been one of the more destructive parts of social policies institutionalized in Western nations over the past two decades.

When they criticize the educational system, commentators of the neoconservative persuasion often are very concerned about the supposed lack of values found among, say, inner-city children. Yet perhaps this is not the primary place we should focus. Rather, we need to ask critical questions about the values of those groups of people—groups with considerably more power and money—that have made the political and economic decisions that segregated these communities economically and racially. In essence, rather than studying the poor, we might justifiably study the nearly "pathological detachment" of the affluent and of their allies in government and neoconservative intellectual and policy circles (Kozol, 1991).

Even with these variations of emphases in some of the multiple but overlapping tendencies within the conservative movement, many of those within it seem to agree on one thing. It is an agreement whose class, race, and gender history is certainly not innocent. It is an agreement that enables us to better understand the circulation of material such as *The Bell Curve.*

CREATING A GOLDEN AGE

In nearly all English-speaking countries, though certainly not only these countries, the various factions of the Right have forced the relationship between the market and the common good onto the political stage. Among the most influential of these ideas have been the following: that the welfare state, and the social contract that stands behind it, has not been a "good thing" for the economy because "we" simply cannot afford it; that it has limited the exercise of free democratic choice because of entrenched, mainly professional, interests; and that it is destructive to the character of the poor because it makes "them" dependent (Lewis, 1991).

Nearly all of the literature supporting this position invokes an earlier "golden age" before the welfare state, when policies were economically and morally sound, when normative and institutional structures were stable, and when class, gender, and racial harmony prevailed as "we" moved toward "progress." The state was not needed for the common good. The debate over government's role in both creating and maintaining the common good in education and elsewhere is as old as government itself. A very long history lays behind the conflict over, say, workfare and learnfare in the United States and the demand that "unworthy" people should not get "something for nothing." A history rooted in the "workhouse test" that played such a significant part in how the United States often deals with the poverty caused by economic dislocations. Earlier relief systems often were based on a conscious attempt to separate the "deserving" poor from the "undeserving" poor. They were also usually characterized by a distinct lack of shyness in blaming the poor for their fate.

In Jane Lewis's words:

> The nineteenth century poor law, which operated in England and parts of the United States, Canada and Australia, aimed firmly to distinguish between the poor and the pauper. Claimants were offered the "workhouse test" to determine whether or not they were truly destitute, the idea being the conditions within the workhouse would be less favorable than those of the lowest paid laborer. If a claimant were prepared to accept relief on such terms, then s/he might be reckoned to be truly destitute. . . . The principle was clear enough. What the nineteenth century system of welfare provision aimed to do was effectively to segregate the pauper from the market, incarcerating him or her in a workhouse where men were deprived of the vote (if indeed they qualified for one under the limited franchise) and where such work as was offered ([often] stone

crushing for men and oakum picking for women) would not interfere with the local labor market. (Lewis, 1991, p. 329)

In essence, the poor were as Lewis referred to them, a "race apart." They could be incarcerated, deprived of basic rights of citizenship, and treated as not worthy of personhood. The relationship of these ideas to class dynamics is clear. Yet there has always been a connection between these policies and race and gender as well, with biologized and moral explanations usually lying just beneath the surface.

Take the Victorian ideals of gender and the family, for example, as they were institutionalized at the turn of the century in a number of nations. For Victorians, like many of today's conservatives, social problems disappeared when the family was strong and effective. Such a family—husbands who were reliable breadwinners and wives who were efficient managers in the home—cared for the old and infirm and socialized children into "the habits of labor and obedience" (Lewis, 1991, p. 331). Women's paid work was frowned upon because it might damage male work incentives. Yet the Victorians were of two minds when it came to poor women, especially those who were alone. While they wished to encourage and/or enforce male labor market participation and were attached to the idea that the "proper" role of women was in the home, applying the same standard to the increasingly large numbers of, say, widowed, deserted, or unmarried mothers presented them with a dilemma. And here an intricate moral hierarchy entered to complement the effects of the even earlier losses of poor people's personhood, respect, and citizenship rights.

Government officials had a decision to make. Were these women to be treated as mothers or workers? On the whole, they chose the latter. Here the moral hierarchy entered in new forms. Widows were counted as "more deserving." They usually were allowed to keep as many children as they could support through their paid labor, usually one or two. The rest were taken to the workhouse or to orphanages. "Deserted wives" who had the courage (and it did take immense courage) to seek help and to declare officially that they indeed were destitute were treated much more harshly. Government authorities were deeply suspicious of collusion between spouses. Working-class men might be living off of "their women's" benefits. "Unmarried mothers" were seen as morally reprehensible. Often the only relief available to them was entering the workhouse.

All too much of this is redolent of current rightist discourse around the poor and especially poor women. This constructs an image of, for example, the poor African American man who lives off "his woman's" welfare check; of morally uncontrollable poor women; of poor unmarried women who drop out of school and have baby after baby simply to get more money. This distressingly biased and empirically problematic image of the poor is what stands behind many of the social and educational policies of the conservative restoration today (Burdell, forthcoming). The answer for the rightist coalition is to revivify their image of the traditional family, to force a form of slavery or indentured servitude on poor people of color and the poor in general, and to create a vision of the poor once again as totally the cause of their own conditions. Volumes such as *The Bell Curve* provide "scientific" legitimacy for such positions. Back to the future?

The *image* of the family (not the reality, which is and has been very varied throughout the history of the United States) (Coontz, 1992a) plays a central part in this ideological drama. Just as in earlier times, the discourse of the family can be used for many social purposes. In this case, as before, its use is more than a little retrogressive.

For example, for the neoconservative and authoritarian populist Right it is the family's role—a role defined by genetic, moralistic, and religious "givens"— to act as a "guardian of social stability within an aggressively competitive economy" (Arnot, 1991, p. 15). How are we to minimize the state? Part of the answer is to maximize the family. In Arnot's words, "By rehabilitating the family, [we] could break down the 'scrounger state' and through a 'moral crusade' counter the effects of permissiveness and arguably feminism" (Arnot, 1991, pp. 15-16).

It is evident from this discussion that there clearly are patriarchal elements and intentions within the conservative restoration; but what is behind a good many of its policies is not only an antifeminist stance. It always must be remembered that the guiding set of principles for a significant portion of this agenda is to increase profits by raising productivity, cutting costs, weakening the collective organizations of paid workers, and disciplining workers through a fear of unemployment. Given the need of capital for the paid labor of women, the Right could not pursue just a policy of returning women to the family and domestic labor. It had to integrate women aggressively into the paid labor market. Yet the process through which this integration occurred was carried out under the "worst possible terms" for these women (Arnot, 1991, pp. 25-26). Protection was reduced; unemployment rates remained high; child care was not provided by the state; domestic burdens actually were increased as the state withdrew its support of social services and programs and then threw its responsibilities onto a private sector that never totally compensated for the loss. For working-class women and women of color, the cumulative effect of these policies was devastating. Their opportunities were severely restricted and the kinds of work available to them were indeed "under the worst possible conditions." An understanding of gender, *and* race, *and* class is essential then to understand both the contradictory intentions and effects of the conservative restoration.

These intentions and effects at times appear contradictory; for example, the proper role for women is at once to be recruited into the paid workforce for economic reasons *and* to stay at home in order to reproduce the "traditional family." But, overall, the rightist alliance has effectively created the conditions that give it increasing hegemonic power over policies and over even how we talk about what is right and wrong in the economy, social welfare, politics, and, as many readers know all too well from personal experience, education. The discourse of the alliance combines two kinds of language: of children as "future workers," of privatization and market choice for "consumers," of business needs and of tighter accountability and control on the one hand, and of "Christian" values, the Western tradition, the traditional family, and back to the "basics" on the other. These two languages, spoken simultaneously, have created such a din that it is hard to hear anything else. Putting these two kinds of language together, as the rightist coalition does, gives it immense power. It threatens to become truly hegemonic. In the process, it both creates and marginalizes those "others" who do not fit inside either its aggressively competitive and individuating market or its limited yet universalizing moral universe.

CONSTRUCTING DEPENDENCY

So far I have focused largely on a number of the crucial historic and current social dynamics such as gender that have constructed the terrain upon which the conservative restoration operates. As I noted, behind these dynamics is an attempt to create biological and moral explanations—rather than structural ones—for those populations that remain "uncompetitive." This is part of a larger process in which dominant groups export the blame for the consequences of their own decisions away from themselves and onto those groups who suffer the most from these decisions (Apple, 1995). A key element in these explanations is how the issue of dependency is construed. And, once again, the United States has a powerful historical legacy that makes it easier for *The Bell Curve* to find a ready audience. Let us take race as a starting point here.

As Cornel West reminds us, the enslavement of Africans— over 20 percent of the population of the nation at the time—"served as the linchpin of American democracy." Thus, it is not an overstatement to suggest that "the much-heralded stability and continuity of American democracy was predicated upon black oppression and degradation" (West, 1993, p. 156). Slavery as a legally sanctioned act may be over, but the racial structuring of this country is worsening every day.

For decades new patterns of segregation have been clear and growing, as European Americans have moved to the suburbs and abandoned the inner cities. One result of this is that urban areas, in essence, have become "reservations," with majority black and Latino/Latina populations and declining or disintegrating tax bases. Local governments in these urban areas are less and less able to meet even the basic needs of their citizens. In concert with these trends, the nation as a whole is steadily moving toward a politics centered around the suburban vote. The growth of suburbanization enables white middle-class voters to fulfill communitarian impulses by taxing themselves for direct services (e.g., schools, libraries, police), while both ignoring urban decay and remaining fiscally conservative about federal spending. This is an ideal situation for suburbanites since it allows them to shield their tax dollars from going into programs that benefit the poor and racial minorities. And as conditions in these inner cities worsen significantly, the structural relations that concretely tie suburban benefits to urban disintegration—in a manner so reminiscent of the history of stable democracy and economic progress being bought at the cost of black slavery and exploitation—lead us to blame the poor for being too "dependent." This is not a new phenomenon for the United States in any way and complements my earlier discussion of gender and the workhouse test.

Historically, the United States has been especially hospitable to the development of the belief that dependency is "a defect of individual character." Given the fact that this country lacked a strong legacy of feudalism and aristocracy, the widespread popular sense of reciprocal relations between lord and "man" was underdeveloped. The older preindustrial meanings of dependency as an *ordinary, majority condition* that were widespread in, say, Europe were very weak here, and pejorative meanings were much stronger. Thus, whereas in the colonial period dependency was seen largely as a voluntary condition (except for the slave) as in being an indentured servant, the American Revolution "so valorized independence that it stripped dependency of its voluntarism, emphasized its powerlessness and imbued it with stigma" (Fraser and Gordon, 1994, p. 320).

In their investigation of the very idea of dependency and its social uses in the United States, Nancy Fraser and Linda Gordon suggest the following.

> The American love affair with independence was politically double-edged. On the one hand, it helped nurture powerful labor and women's movements. On the other hand, the absence of a hierarchical social tradition in which subordination was understood to be structured, not characterological, facilitated hostility to public support for the poor. Also influential was the very nature of the American state, weak and decentralized in comparison to European states throughout the nineteenth century. All told, the United States proved fertile soil for the moral/psychological discourse of dependency. (p. 320)

Currently there is increasing stigmatization of dependency. "All dependency is suspect, and independence is enjoined on everyone." Yet it is wage labor that is the identifying sign of independence. In essence, "the worker"—one who is "self-supporting"—becomes the universal subject. Any adult who is not perceived to be a worker carries an immense burden of self-justification. After all, we all "know" that this economy and this nation have removed the barriers to work for anyone who really wants it. This is not a neutral description of reality. It smuggles in a considerable number of normative claims, not the least in its assumption that "the worker" has access to a job paying a living wage and is also not a primary parent.

There are two major results of this. The first is to increase the already strong negative connotations associated with dependency. The second is to increase even more its individualization. Both results are ideally suited to an articulation of the connections between race and gender and dependency that have played such a strong role in constructing dominant discourses in the nation's history. As I noted, the view of dependency as a character trait was already beginning to be widespread in the early years of the nation. This sense is given more power currently now that the legal barriers (formal and legally recognized overt segregation) have been supposedly ended. With the changes in coverture (the legal status of women in marriage) and Jim Crow brought about by the successful struggles by women and African Americans, it now has become possible for some groups to argue that equality of opportunity really exists; that it is individual merit, nothing else, that determines outcomes. Fraser and Gordon put it in the following way:

> The groundwork for that view was laid by industrial usage, which defined dependency so as to exclude capitalist relations of subordination. With capitalist economic dependency already abolished by definition, and with legal and political dependency now abolished by law, postindustrial society appears to some conservatives and liberals to have eliminated every social structural basis of dependency. Whatever dependency that remains, therefore, can be interpreted as the fault of individuals. That interpretation does not go uncontested, to be sure, but the burden of argument has shifted. Now those who deny that the fault lies in themselves must swim upstream against the prevailing semantic currents. Postindustrial dependency is increasingly individualized. (p. 325)

In this scenario, the poor did get poor the old-fashioned way: they earned it. They are dependent and therefore are "the other," either by reason of their individual character traits or by reason of their collective genetic endowment as in *The Bell Curve*. Either way, as in the case of suburbia, it's not "our" problem.

We now face a situation in which "economic dependency" has become a synonym for the immense *creation* of poverty by the economic apparatus of this society. It is as if a new "personality disorder" called moral/psychological dependency is in the air. Once again, those who are poor are talked about as morally and genetically inferior. Talk of dependency as a fully *social relation of subordination* has become all too rare (Fraser and Gordon, 1994, p. 331). In the process, power and domination become invisible.

CONCLUSION

In this chapter, I have suggested that one of the best ways to understand *The Bell Curve* is to place it back into the larger context of transformations of educational, political, and economic institutions. I have argued that the politics of its reception are strongly related to historical dynamics that have played a large part in this nation's past and current treatment of gender, race, and class—and of the poor in general.

Changing the reception of a work such as *The Bell Curve* requires a thorough-going reconstruction of our understanding of how this society operates. One of the keys is at the level of common sense. People need to stop thinking—as the Right does—of the poor as "others" and instead need to substitute a vision of "us." This change needs to be accompanied by a restriction of market models of human activity to their appropriate, and very limited, boundaries. All people should reassert the significance of positive freedom based on human dignity, community, and the realization of democracy in all of our institutions (Katz, 1989).

This requires a rejection of arguments such as those found in Herrnstein and Murray's work. Instead, it necessitates the reconstruction of the discourse about poverty and welfare, a reconstruction that seeks to regain a sense of ethics and community. Michael Katz (1989) argues that such a reconstitution needs to be based on five general tenets:

1. Reawakening our sense of moral outrage at the deadly persistence of homelessness, hunger, absent or inadequate health care, and other forms of deprivation rather than a pseudo-scientific search for genetic explanations.

2. Defending and enlarging the principles of human dignity, community, and the realization of democracy in concrete events in our daily lives, rather than the increasing emphasis on social Darwinist policies in the public arena.

3. Reinventing ways of insisting on and talking about poor persons not as "them" but as *us*.

4. Restricting market models to very limited spheres so that social justice—not profit and loss—provides the dominant lens through which we examine social and educational policies.

5. Strategically connecting these progressive points to other widely shared American values, such as liberty, by showing how poverty undermines families (of many kinds), community, the economy, and so on.

While each of these points requires the development of detailed policies and sources of revenue, among the other major requirements are creative resources (something in abundance among *all* parts of the American population) and political will. The *fundamental* questions, however, are about "the basis of community, the conditions of citizenship, and the achievement of human dignity." In even starker terms, these questions are simply and profoundly about our definition of America, just how much we as citizens are willing to do to realize it, and who shall be engaged at all levels in deciding this.

The spread of a rightist common sense will no doubt make this difficult. Yet it is not naturally preordained that the populist sentiments shared by many people must be organized around conservative social movements. The urge to have power over one's life, to actually be listened to by the state, to care deeply about one's cultural roots and traditions, can provide the basis for a less authoritarian and more socially just formation as well. Thus, studying the Right, as I have done here, may be more important than may be realized. Those on the Right have recognized how important it is to build social movements that connect the local with the global. They have been more than a little successful in reorganizing common sense by engaging in a truly widespread educational project in *all* spheres of society—in the economy, in politics, and in the media and cultural apparatus. There are lessons to be learned here. The Right has proven that long term engagement in cultural politics can be effective. Those of us who decry the authoritarian tendencies in their message could do worse than to study the ways in which such messages seem to connect successfully with the hopes, fears, dreams, and despairs of many people. Taken together, the commissioning, writing, publishing, and massive publicity campaign accorded to *The Bell Curve* provides a case study of how this is done.

I am not asking us to copy some aspects of the Right, in their cynical, well-financed, and often manipulative politics. Rather, I am saying that something important has gone on here, something that is, in essence, one of the largest "educational" projects we have seen this century. Transformations of common sense take time and organization and commitment; but they also must connect with people's daily lives if they are to be widely successful. These are not inconsequential points. They speak to the need to engage in the long-term project of building such connections in more progressive terms. Needless to say, there is work to be done. Otherwise, *The Bell Curve* will mark the success of rightist common sense again. We cannot afford to allow this to happen once more.

References

Apple, M. (1993). *Official knowledge: Democratic education in a conservative age*. New York: Routledge.
Apple, M. (1995). *Education and power*, 2nd ed. New York: Routledge.
Apple, M. (1996). *Cultural politics and education*. New York: Teachers College Press.
Arnot, M. (1991) Feminism, education and the New Right. Paper presented at the American Educational Research Association: Chicago.

Burdell, P. (In press). Teen mothers in high school. In Apple, M., ed., *Review of Research in Education, 21*. Washington, D.C.: American Educational Research Association.

Coontz, S. (1992). *The social origins of private life*. New York: Verso.

Coontz, S. (1992). *The way we never were*. New York: Basic Books.

Fraser, N. and Gordon, L. (1994, Winter). A genealogy of dependency. *Signs, 19*.

Honderich, T. (1990). *Conservatism*. Boulder, Co.: Westview.

Hunter, A. (1987). The politics of resentment and the construction of middle America. Ms., Department of Sociology, University of Wisconsin, Madison.

Hunter, I. (1994). *Rethinking the school*. St. Leonards, Australia: Allen and Unwin.

Katz, M. (1989). *The undeserving poor*. New York: Pantheon Books.

Kozol, J. (1991). *Savage inequalities*. New York: Crown.

Lewis, J. (1991, Autumn). Back to the future: A comment on American New Right ideas about welfare and citizenship in the 1980s. *Gender and History, 3*.

West, C. (1993). *Race matters*. New York: Vintage Books.

Whitty, G., Edwards, T. and Gewirtz, S. (1993). *Specialization and choice in urban education*. New York: Routledge.

3 THE BELL CURVE DEBATE AND THE CRISIS OF PUBLIC INTELLECTUALS

HENRY A. GIROUX · SUSAN SEARLS

Ever since the birth of our nation, white America has had a schizophrenic personality on the question of race. She has been torn between principles of democracy and a self in which she sadly practiced the antithesis of democracy. The white backlash of today is rooted in the same problem that has characterized America ever since the black man landed in chains on the shores of this nation. The white backlash is an expression of the same vacillations, the same search for rationalizations, the same lack of commitment that have always characterized white America on the question of race.
—Martin Luther King, Jr., 1968, p. 68

INTRODUCTION

Writing a year before he was assassinated, Martin Luther King, Jr. was keenly aware that the principles of democracy were at odds with the reality of racism. King recognized that the most explosive issue facing white America was its refusal to address its role in a history steeped in racism—a history of the Middle Passage, slavery, Southern Reconstruction, segregation, and urban ghettoization—that has crippled the nation since its inception. Bearing witness to centuries of oppression, King consistently sought to make visible the ways in which racism was invariably reproduced through a crisis of leadership in which white America could neither confront the legacy of its white supremacist doctrines nor, when individual conscience burned, take a firm and unequivocal moral stand against racial injustice.

What King could not foresee was that as the close of the century drew near, whiteness as a racial category in the United States would become more visible and hence the subject of scrutiny, and as a form of social identity it would become more fragile and less a guarantee of economic or moral superiority. Economic restructuring, rising unemployment, and the downward mobility of many Americans coupled with attempts by people of color to write themselves into the history of the United States generated a conservative backlash among many Whites, who defined themselves as under siege, as public discourse and space became more pluralized and racially diverse. In the current crisis of leadership and democracy, Martin Luther King's insights about racism take on a new urgency as race becomes one of the defining principles of a new conservative backlash that has emerged in the 1990s.

While, in its endless quest for rationalizations and scapegoats, the old racism unabashedly employed racist arguments, the new racism offers a two-pronged argument that, on the one hand, refuses to acknowledge that the issue of race is at the heart of its policy-making (as in welfare cutbacks, the end of school lunch programs, the call for orphanages) and, on the other hand, offers rationales for policy changes that claim to be color blind (as in the call to end affirmative action). In the first instance, the new racism articulates and legitimates a range of ideologies and practices that deeply affects both the privileges at the heart of the construction of whiteness and the racist practices that bear down heavily on the lives of people of color—while denying that race matters. For instance, Newt Gingrich denies that race has anything to do with the slash-and-cut polices at the heart of his Contract with America, and yet the policies produced by such legislation affect most drastically poor Blacks and the urban poor. Similarly, in his defense of *The Bell Curve,* Charles Murray has consistently denied that the book is primarily about race since only 1 of its 21 chapters center on arguments about black intellectual inferiority. However, as the 8 chapters of part II discuss Whites alone, this demonstrates that a third of the book is organized around questions of race—unless one is willing to make the argument that whiteness is not a racial category. Further, the denial that race is central to *The Bell Curve* is contradictory coming from an author who has legitimized his work by arguing that it provides a language for "a huge number of well-meaning Whites [who] fear that they are closet racists [and] tells them they are not. [This book] is going to make them feel better about things they already think but do not know how to say" (Murray, 1994, p. 50). Clearly, Murray's defense of white America is an argument for privileging whiteness as a racial construction. The authors of *The Bell Curve* make no apologies for arguing "that society is and must be stratified by intelligence, which is distributed unequally among individuals and racial groups and cannot be changed in either" (Reed, 1994, p. 660).

In the second instance, in efforts to end the alleged reign of special interest groups, national leaders propose changes in public policy that disproportionately affect African Americans and other minority groups. According to Gingrich, criticisms of societal injustices such as racism, what he calls "our newfound sense of entitlement and victimization," are "exactly wrong" and so corrosive to the "American spirit." Appealing to a racially coded sense of nationalism and patriotism, Gingrich offers this pedagogical lesson from his new book, *To Renew America:* "when confronted with a problem, a true American doesn't ask: 'Who can I blame this on?' A true citizen asks, 'What can I do about it today?'" (Gingrich, 1995). For Gingrich, civic leadership has nothing to do with social responsibility and social justice, since these demand some notion of social criticism and ongoing struggle. For Gingrich social criticism represents a kind of whining and pessimism that "celebrates soreheads and losers jealous of others' successes" (Gingrich, 1995). Of course, the soreheads are feminists, critical multiculturalists, environmentalists, civil rights activists, critical educators, and all those others who believe that dissent is central to any reputable notion of citizenship. Senator

Robert Dole appeals to a similar kind of numbing logic when he attacks affirmative action. Dole argues that "The race counting game has gone too far" and that it is time for the federal government to "get out of the race-preference business" (Jackson, 1995, p. 15). Nor, it appears, can President Bill Clinton support the conditions that foster equality and fair treatment. Ignoring the Glass Ceiling report issued by the United States Labor Department in 1994, which found massive racial and gender disparities in the workplace, Clinton panders to the Right: "First of all, our administration is against quotas and guaranteed results" (Jackson, 1995, p. 15).

As we will demonstrate, the new racism works through the power of the judicial and legislative processes and legitimates and rationalizes its policies through the use of public intellectuals who make racism respectable in their talk radio programs and through the wide-circulation of magazines, national newspapers, television, and other forms of media culture. Housed in and financed by right-wing foundations, the new conservative public intellectuals are enormously skillful in mobilizing racial fears and class resentment and in undermining the basic principles of democracy and equality.

Any analysis of *The Bell Curve* by Richard J. Herrnstein and Charles Murray has to be addressed within the crisis in democratic vision, moral leadership, and ethical conviction that has been spawned by the rise of the new racism and its growing defense by a number of conservative public intellectuals. In part, the popularity of *The Bell Curve* and the debate it has engendered needs to be placed within a context that signals its historical continuity with a line of pseudoscientific reasoning and moral ambivalence that defines white America's response to race.

RACIST SCIENCE AND THE DENIAL OF HISTORY

That Charles Murray and Richard J. Herrnstein have acute political timing is evinced by the ocean of publicity spurred by the publication of *The Bell Curve* in the fall of 1994. Capitalizing on the resurgence of racism and racist exclusions in contemporary U.S. culture at the same time it flames racist expression and provides scientific and philosophic justification for it, *The Bell Curve* was heralded an "important" and "brave" book. Indeed *The Bell Curve* and its pseudoscientific claims set the agenda for discussions on welfare, crime, affirmative action, and civil rights on public affairs programs such as *Larry King Live, Nightline,* the *MacNeil/Lehrer NewsHour,* the *McLaughlin Group, Charlie Rose, Think Tank, Primetime Live,* and *All Things Considered* (Naureckas, 1995). The "controversy" made the covers of *Newsweek* and the *New York Times Magazine* and was reviewed in such prominent and respectful newspapers as the *Wall Street Journal,* the *New York Review of Books,* and the *New York Times Book Review.* In addition, journals such as *The New Republic* and *Discover* devoted almost entire issues to the debate.

The publication of *The Bell Curve* and the wide-ranging publicity it has received raises questions about the range of cultural, pedagogical, and social conditions that contributed to its widespread success and the relevance of such a book in the current political arena. Of course, the diverse set of factors contributing to the book's success cannot be abstracted from the particular ideological interests that it legitimates. Although a few brave reviewers of *The Bell Curve* have exposed the contorted statistics, contradictory data buried in appendixes, unsupported and illogical claims, research funding by a neo-Nazi organization, "scholarly sources" including eugenicists, racists, and advocates of far-Right agendas, the "fact" of racial differences supported by statistics that register large "behavioral" disparities between Blacks and Whites in the areas of crime, welfare dependency, and teenage pregnancy undergird the call for social change.

While it is not our intention to repeat these arguments, we want to situate the popular reception of *The Bell Curve* in a broader context in order to understand how racist culture is both produced and legitimated by public intellectuals in the United States. Against the popularity of *The Bell Curve,* it seems reasonable to ask how mainstream commentators would have treated a book that relied on statistics drawn from neo-Nazi sources to support the claim that the

Holocaust never happened. In fact, when such books do get published, they often are denounced as anti-Semitic and dangerous in their whitewashing of the Nazis' genocidal crimes. Yet when *The Bell Curve* appeared, few reviewers in the mainstream media denounced the text as a racist tract or even questioned its basic propositions regarding the measurability of intelligence, the causal relationship between intellectual ability and race, or the hereditarian justification of inequality. Pseudoscientific babble as an apology for black intellectual inferiority along with the advocacy of policies designed to justify the existence of an "inferior" black underclass seemed to warrant little, if any, critical attention as an attack on the very nature of democracy itself. In addition, the book's widespread popular support provides an opportunity for educators and others to consider pedagogically and politically how racist cultural divisions are being legitimated. We believe that underlying *The Bell Curve* is a racist agenda that is fundamentally at odds with any viable notion of democracy. Educators must respond to it by considering its implications for political and moral leadership. We are not arguing that the book be censored as much as suggesting that educators and other cultural workers attempt to understand and confront those economic, political, and social conditions that provide the pedagogical and political contexts for the book's success.

In many ways, *The Bell Curve* suggests not only what Edward S. Herman has called "the renewed acceptability and/or tolerance of straightforward racist doctrine" (Herman, 1994, p. 24), it also points to the refusal of the dominant liberal press and conservative press, the White House, and numerous academics and public intellectuals to denounce the ever-increasing popularity of racist discourse as dangerous to the very precepts and principles of democracy in the United States. This is not to suggest that critical commentators have failed to denounce *The Bell Curve*. On the contrary, the book has been treated as a racist tract by many reviewers in the academic press. But very few commentators have gone further and linked the racist assumptions that fuel the book to an attack on the most fundamental principles of democratic public life. Thus, some reviewers can denounce the book's racist ideology while supporting policy recommendations that are equally undemocratic but do not employ the discourse of race to legitimate themselves. Conservative and liberal commentators such as Mickey Kaus, Rush Limbaugh, and Nathan Glazer separate themselves from the racism of *The Bell Curve* but support policies that are similar in their effects on the black underclass and urban poor.

The editors of *The New Republic* announced unapologetically, in an issue devoted entirely to discussing *The Bell Curve*, that the "notion that there might be resilient ethnic differences in intelligence is not, we believe, an inherently racist belief" (p. 9). The *New York Times Magazine* ran a review of *The Bell Curve* and two other books on heredity and race in which the author, Malcolm Browne, argued that Herrnstein and Murray's basic premises were really important to society, especially to a democratic society. With no wrong intended, Browne argued that the authors under review, all of whom offered a hereditarian justification for racial inequality, were actually exercising a healthy form of truth-seeking in their plea for "freedom of debate and an end to the shroud of censorship imposed upon scientists and scholars by pressure groups and an acquiescing society" (Browne, 1994, p. 45). The liberal-oriented *Chronicle of Higher Education* gave Charles Murray major coverage as a reputable scholar and argued that whatever evidence exists on race and intelligence "is open to widely varying interpretation, and how researchers read the data often suggest as much about their politics as anything" (Coughlin, 1994, p. A12). In spite of the falsifications and misrepresentations of scholarship, the use of neo-Nazi research, and the racist implications of his writings, the liberal establishment praises Murray as a serious, albeit conservative, scholar rather than denouncing him for reproducing a legacy of racist science that supports a racially divided and hierarchically ordered society.

The popularity of *The Bell Curve* points in part to a number of important considerations at work in American society that must be acknowledged by critical educators who wish to fight against the perpetuation of a racist culture and its deeply antidemocratic practices.

First, it must be recognized that *The Bell Curve* represents a significant manifesto in what appears to be a developing and dangerous antidemocratic movement that uses pseudoscience and racial fear as a rationalization for white supremacy. Critical agency is reserved for those who are white and privileged, and the "valued places" of mindless work, deadend jobs, and grueling labor are allotted for those who happen to be black and of less intelligence. In this scenario, low IQ is linked causally with social pathology, suggesting that societal intervention is unproductive because inherited intelligence fixes one's level of accomplishment and agency. Hence the new counterculture rationalizes racist thought and practice without having to evoke the critical language of ethics, democracy, or compassion. In fact, these categories become irrelevant in the new beehive state imagined by Herrnstein and Murray. The force of such an argument and its interconnecting links to elitism, the market economy, and the emerging discourses of mean-spiritedness are well captured by Lee Siegel.

> Herrnstein and Murray's fantasy of a beehive society, in which mobility is frozen and stations assured, crops up across the political spectrum. So does their notion of aristocracy. At a time of collapsing boundaries—social, cultural, psychological—accompanied by new fragmentations, a pseudo-aristocracy based on genetic transmission simulates a sense of real aristocratic birthright and stability. And a pseudo-science nicely fits the modern, rationalist habit of mind, while also answering the need for comfort beyond reason's sterile categories. At the same time, the genetic "edge," the Darwinian struggle to survive, and the fiction of biologically inevitable social strata all mesh neatly with the dominant market ethos of untrammeled competition, no less than they did in Dickens's day. (p. 28)

Second, the massive public attention that conferred upon *The Bell Curve* a halo of academic respectability suggests a crisis of moral leadership within American society that is as pedagogical as it is political. Civic leadership appears to have lost its ethical referents for sustaining, defending, and struggling over the principles of social justice, equality, and freedom. In the current seats of power, both in the nation's capital and the major cultural apparatuses of our society, intellectuals casually reject democracy as unworkable and embrace the laws of the marketplace as the most dynamic principles driving society. Within such a context, there is no language to define schools, for instance, as democratic public spheres, to cultivate democratic relations, or to educate the young in the discourse and practice of critical citizenship. Against the democratic imperative that grounds citizenship in social responsibility, the new conservative public intellectuals speak in a language that shuns human compassion, legitimates excessive individualism and greed, and encourages racial conflict. Echoes of such a discourse exist in the attack on welfare mothers, calls to dismantle public schooling, and Herrnstein and Murray's claim that "there is nothing [people with low cognitive ability] can learn that will repay the cost of teaching" (Herrnstein and Murray, 1994, p. 520). This is more than self-serving cynicism, it is an emerging worldview that considers democracy dangerous and racism acceptable.

Third, the popularity of *The Bell Curve* signals the rewriting of history by omitting the legacy of slavery and racism in the United States. In this case, the history of the eugenics movement and its disparaging attempts to fashion a theory of scientific racism appears to have been lost in the mainstream discussions of *The Bell Curve*. Neither Arthur Jensen's nor Cyril Burt's discredited research has been called into question in popular discussions of the book. Except for some academic reviews, few theorists have revealed the bogus research that Herrnstein and Murray relied on. Although much of the research they used was provided by the Pioneer Fund, which has been described by the *London Sunday Telegraph* as a "neo-Nazi organization closely integrated with the far right in American politics," Herrnstein and Murray were consistently labeled as "serious scholars" by the American press (Naureckas, 1995, p. 13). Richard Lynn, heavily quoted in *The Bell Curve*, has been less than subtle about his own scientific insights on race. In a 1991 article, "Race Differences in Intelligence: A Global Perspective," he concluded, forsaking all scholarly integrity, "Who can doubt that Caucasoids and the Mongoloids are the only two races that have made any significant contribution to civilization?" (Rosen and Lane, 1994). Another pillar of research for Herrnstein and Murray's hereditarian defense of inequality and racism can be found in the work of J. Philippe Rushton. Rushton, whom many liberals have defended as a worthy scholar, was censured by Western Ontario University for conducting a survey in a local mall (for which he used Pioneer Fund money) where he asked 150 participants— a third were black, a third were white, a third were Asian—questions regarding the size of their penis and how far they could ejaculate. But Rushton has done more than try to correlate the size and use of sex organs with racial groups; he also has suggested that "'Negroids' are genetically programmed for sexual behavior that spreads the deadly AIDS virus" (Miller, 1995, p. 169).

Racist and bogus research aside, Charles Murray is a fellow at the American Enterprise Institute. He typifies the new breed of conservative intellectuals in this country who are heavily financed and educated within public spheres that are aggressively ideological, right-wing, and primed to develop and shape public policy. However, it would be disingenuous to view *The Bell Curve*'s attack on democratic principles such as egalitarianism and social justice as an isolated event on the American landscape or as a brief lapse of consciousness in a nation that has consistently fought for racial justice. Neither is the case. In what follows, we explore the current social and political contexts that have created the conditions for a favorable reception of *The Bell Curve* as an accurate depiction of the phenomenon of intelligence and a legitimate commentary on race relations in America.

AMERICA'S TURN TO THE RIGHT

The November 1994 elections that ushered in Republican majority rule in Congress do not represent the beginning of a political and cultural revolution as much as they signaled that one had already taken place. The shift to the ideological Right—and the circulation and affirmation of its particular constructions of (racialized) Otherness—is everywhere apparent on the national landscape. Rising conservatism is visible not only in the nation's capital but on the airwaves, in the media, in the judicial system, in education, in the workplace, and in the home. Moreover, the Right has won new allegiances among youth and minority communities.

One of the most disturbing signs of the times is the entrenched nature of right-wing talk radio across the country. Rush Limbaugh is estimated to reach 20 million people a week for a daily monologue of welfare trashing punctuated by the angry cry of the white male. Hosting New York City's WABC Radio Network is Bob Grant, a racist who has nonetheless emerged as an important figure in regional politics. According to Jim Naureckas, a reporter for *Extra! magazine,* Grant repeatedly describes African Americans as "savages," arguing that the United States has "millions of sub-humanoids, savages, who really would feel more at home careening along the sands of the Kalahari or the dry deserts of eastern Kenya—people who, for whatever reason, have not become civilized"(Naureckas, 1995, p. 20). His solution to the problem, frequently promoted on air, is the "Bob Grant Mandatory Sterilization Program." Yet Grant has received call-ins on his program from Senator Al D'Amato, New Jersey Governor Christine Todd Whitman, New York City Mayor Rudolph Giuliani, and New York Governor-elect George Pataki to thank him for his support in their elections. WABC, where Grant and Limbaugh go back to back, claims to be the most successful radio station in America.

In San Francisco, former liberal talk radio KSFO went conservative virtually overnight. The station's hosts and callers have described themselves as "beleaguered revolutionaries" in the new right-wing countercultural movement (Tierney, 1995, p. A10). Jack Swanson, the operations director at KSFO, compares the station's new format to the first "Gay Talk" show 15 years earlier, saying: "We're letting the last group [conservatives] out of the closet" (Tierney, 1995, p. A10). Attesting to the increasing influence talk radio wields, Jonathan Freedland reports that according to one poll "44 per cent of Americans regard talk radio as their prime source of political information" (p. T2). What is more, other "attitude surveys suggest that the firebreathers of AM radio are merely saying what everyone else already thinks" (Freedland, 1995, T2).

On issues related to criminal justice, politicians meet the public outcry to get tough on crime with such policies as the "Three Strikes and You're Out!" demanding life imprisonment for the three-time offending criminal. Some politicians are backing a two strikes policy while others are willing to throw away the key with one violent felony conviction. Doing his share, Newt Gingrich promises $10 billion to make new prisons in his Contract with America. Meanwhile, the media, with its obsession on events such as the O.J. Simpson murder trial, remains bent on forging the link between black men and criminality.

One of the most important issues of the political campaign of 1994 was immigration and how America's changing racial and ethnic demography affected the "core values of the country" (Chideya, 1994, p. 75). In efforts to exclude the racial Other, the passing of California's *Proposition 187* effectively barred illegal immigrants from going to public school and prevented them from receiving nonemergency care in hospitals. California's governor, Pete Wilson, effectively outlawed positive discrimination policies at the state level, and President Clinton has agreed to review affirmative action policies to see if they in fact work.

The Supreme Court has considered right-wing allegations that enough is enough when it comes to forcing schools to desegregate. Supreme Court Justice Antonin Scalia argued that "societal discrimination" is discrimination that courts have no power to remedy. He insists that it is not fair "to impose on a school district the obligation to remedy discrimination not of its own making" (Cole, 1995, p. 43). More recently, the Court has declared that certain affirmative action programs are unconstitutional. Demonstrating not only its refusal to "remedy" discrimination but its capacity to perpetuate its legacy, the Court moved to invalidate a black-majority congressional district in

Georgia, a decision the *Boston Globe* termed "a landmark ruling that could slash the number of minorities in Congress and local governments" (Puga and Kranish, 1995, p. 1). Other rulings include a decision to allow the Ku Klux Klan to erect a wooden cross in a public square in front of the state capitol in Columbus, Ohio, on the grounds that the display constituted private religious speech fully protected by the First Amendment.

Public schools also have come under fire in the Republican-controlled Congress. The GOP budget proposal would not only eliminate funding for President Clinton's Goals 2000 education program but would also reduce or eliminate federal monies for more politically popular programs. Federal programs facing the chopping block include Head Start, a program designed to prepare young children, predominantly poor and non-white, for school; low-income college prep programs such as Upward Bound; and Pell Grants, which help low-income families pay for college tuition. Such cuts, disproportionately affecting children of color and the poor, not only reflect complicity with social scientists who, using racist logic, make similar proposals on the grounds that federal aid can do little to help the cognitively disenfranchised (who also happen to be poor and often black), but also demonstrate how the logic of the market overwhelms the imperatives of a democratic society. Other issues facing the nation's educational system concern prayer in schools and the relative "waste" of the school lunch program. Advocates of school "choice" see victory on the horizon in their quest to turn public schools over to the logic of the market and to make parents into consumers of education. Absent from national agendas are concerns with improving the conditions or quality of education per se.

The conservative backlash is also visible at the cultural level. Increasingly, there exists a growing culture of violence in the United States that exhibits an indiscriminate rage, if not outright violence, against those deemed as the racial Other, especially African Americans. This is obvious not only in the rise of police brutality against urban black youth, the high levels of incarceration among young black men, or the violent attacks on black college students across the

United States, but also in the popular reception of racist films such as *Pulp Fiction,* hate talk radio programs, and the demonization of black youth in media culture. The culture of racist violence is also evident in the discourse of right-wing public intellectuals. Intellectuals such as Dinesh D'Sousa (1995) have become apologists for a form of racism that parades as a legitimate voice for a universal white culture that defines itself as both under siege and willing to fight back in defense of its power and privileges.

Needless to say, Herrnstein and Murray's *Bell Curve* fits well with current political agendas. Worried about the "cognitive capital" of the country, they suggest that Latino and black immigrants are putting downward pressure on the distribution of intelligence and conclude that there is a need to rethink current immigration policy. Funding for educational programs such as Head Start come under fire when it is "proven" that special programs to improve intelligence have had negligible and short-lived effects. (Curiously, in efforts to resolve other funding issues, they advocate federal support for programs that enable "all parents, not just affluent ones" to choose the school that their children attend.) Further, Herrnstein and Murray set out to prove that the underlying assumption of affirmative action—that ethnic groups do not differ in abilities that contribute to their success academically or professionally—is simply wrongheaded.

While few politicians and pundits seek to embrace Herrnstein and Murray's genetic determinism, many found the concluding chapters of *The Bell Curve* useful in justifying newly proposed cutbacks to federal programs. *Crossfire's* Patrick Buchanan, of course, did not miss a beat: "I think a lot of data are indisputable. . . . It does shoot a hole straight through the heart of egalitarian socialism which tried to create equality of result by coercive government programs" (Naureckas, 1995, p. 15). Indeed, Herrnstein and Murray not only offer a "compelling" social theory to legitimate the conservative pursuits of the state, but also provide a potent, if skewed, critique of the political philosophy of egalitarianism in order to redefine state interests.

While Herrnstein and Murray support the notion that people are equal in terms of the rights that should be afforded them, they contend that people are different in all other aspects. For them, the egalitarian ideal of contemporary political theory "underestimates the importance of differences that separates human beings" as it simultaneously "overestimates the ability of political interventions to shape human character and capacities" (Herrnstein and Murray, 1994, p. 532). According to their logic, the discourse of egalitarianism is at odds with the discourse of rights that grants people the freedom to behave differently, which would necessarily lead to social and economic inequalities—inequalities that egalitarianism in turn attempts to suppress. What lies ahead of the nation if it continues to accept the main tenets of the welfare state? In short, the "coming of the custodial state." Herrnstein and Murray explain, "by *custodial state,* we have in mind a high-tech and more lavish version of the Indian reservation for some substantial minority of the nation's population, while the rest of America tries to go about its business" (p. 526).

As a form of resistance to the uniformity that the state must impose in the interests of so-called social justice, Herrnstein and Murray condemn "egalitarian tyrannies" on the charge that they are "worse than inhumane. They are inhuman" (p. 533). Their solution to this social democratic nightmare is a society in which all members occupy "a valued place"—whether IQ has destined them to manage a UniMart or head a multinational corporation—and presumably that they know their place and stay there. The rigidity of the proposed castelike system in many ways masks as it reconfigures the centuries-old dream of much of white America for a racially homogenous society. And of course, members of such a society would not be expected to value other members' positions in quite the same way; that wouldn't be *discriminatory,* "a once useful word with a praiseworthy meaning" (p. 533). The irony of Herrnstein and Murray's modest proposal, as David Theo Goldberg insightfully argues, is that people "assume value . . . only in so far as they are bearers of rights, and they are properly vested with rights only in so far as they are imbued with value" (Goldberg, 1993, p. 37).

It would seem logical to assume that the resurgence of racism at a time when conservatives and liberals alike have insisted upon the urgency of moral reform and the return of "values" would appear deeply contradictory and troubling to most minds. Herrnstein and Murray, however, have a different worry, one that pits the principles of equality and social justice against the discourse of "truth": "The ideology of equality has stunted the range of moral dialogue to triviality. In daily life—conservation, the lessons taught in public schools, the kinds of screenplays or newspaper feature stories that people choose to write—the moral ascendancy of equality has made it difficult to use concepts such as virtue, excellence, beauty, and—above all—truth" (Herrnstein and Murray, 1994, p. 534).

THE CRISIS OF MORAL LEADERSHIP AND DEMOCRACY

The desire for truth and value brings us to Nathan Glazer's commentary on *The Bell Curve*. As a prominent neoconservative, Glazer ponders the viability of the cognitive development of non-Whites. He notes that Herrnstein and Murray do not specifically argue against efforts to improve the education of Blacks; however, in his view, closing the gap between Blacks and Whites remains a vexing possibility: "In a few cases, in our large cities in particular, greater resources are put into the education of Blacks than Whites. But the kind of difference that might help close the gap is hardly imaginable. And politically, it would be impossible. How could one argue that the holding back of improvement of white intelligence so that Blacks could catch up is morally legitimate, or would improve society?" (Glazer, 1994, p. L6). Glazer invokes rights discourse, like a kind of zero-sum game, to argue that black improvement necessarily impinges on the possibility of white improvement insofar as disparities in intelligence foster unequal allocation of resources in education. (We are left to imagine which inner cities provide greater resources for black youth.) For Glazer, the scientific weight of Herrnstein and Murray's analysis coupled with the moral imperatives of truth and the political philosophy of rights sanctions a departure from the principle of equal division and social justice. The necessary end of egalitarianism, as it has been argued morally and rationally, is nonetheless a bittersweet moment for this supposed lover of the truth and the common good: "Our society, our polity, our elites, according to Herrnstein and Murray, live with an untruth: that there is no good reason for this inequality, and therefore society is at fault and we must try harder. I ask myself whether the untruth is not better for American society than the truth" (Glazer, 1994, p. 16).

There is more at stake here than Glazer's efforts to ground his racist and antidemocratic arguments in the acceptable sociopolitical discourses of science and philosophy; there is also a failure of moral leadership and an arrogance characteristic of a new breed of right-wing public intellectuals that turns its back on the poor and offers no language for challenging racism, discrimination, and social injustice.

As we have argued, the lack of vision and meanspiritedness that informs the conservative notion of leadership is not limited to *The Bell Curve* and its defenders; it also can be found among those who occupy honored positions in government, higher education, and other important public spheres. In a recent essay in *Newsweek,* Newt Gingrich argues that the most important elements of being an American are to be found in personal responsibility and individual ability. But these are not merely elements in a larger ethic of responsibility, they are the *only* elements. As such, they are transfigured into a notion of citizenship that eschews a moral focus on suffering and abstracts individual agency from social responsibility. What is one to make of Gingrich's claim that entitlement is just another form of victimization, that social criticism is an escape from personal responsibility, or that Captain John Smith's 1607 statement "'If you don't work you won't eat' [serves as] a guiding principle of social life" (Gingrich, 1995, p. 26). In Gingrich's model of leadership, generosity and trust become synonymous with the entrepreneurial spirit, and school reform offers an opportunity to "comb through our educational system and laws to clean out the barriers to starting businesses and creating new wealth" (Gingrich, 1995, p. 26). The notion that generosity and trust might not be calculated exclusively in market terms or that schools might be important in creating a critical citizenry rather than merely a workforce for the global economy is lost in this model of leadership.

From Martin Luther King, Jr., to Václav Havel we have alternative models of leadership that embrace the necessity for substantive democracy. King and Havel, living in different times, point to a notion of leadership and a responsibility for public intellectuals that allows them to "identify with humanity, its dignity, and its prospects" (Havel, 1995, p. 37). For Havel, public intellectuals represent the conscience of society and in doing so, they,

> build people-to-people solidarity. They foster tolerance, strug-
> gle against evil and violence, promote human rights, and argue
> for their indivisibility. They care about the fate of virgin forests
> in faraway places, about whether or not humankind will soon
> destroy all its nonrenewable resources, or whether a global
> dictatorship of advertisement, consumerism, and blood-and-
> thunder stories on TV will ultimately lead the human race to
> a state of complete idiocy. (p. 37)

We began this chapter with a quote from Martin Luther King, Jr., and we want to conclude with his passionate reminder that "We are now faced with the fact that tomorrow is today. We are confronted with the fierce urgency of *now*" (King, 1968). This urgency is signaled in the current threat to democracy posed by the rise of racist discourse, the attacks on equality and social justice, and the growing indifference to human suffering and misery. *The Bell Curve* is not *the* problem; it is symptomatic of a larger and more dangerous crisis of democracy in the United States—a crisis made increasingly visible as the intellectual storm troopers spread their messages of hate, greed, and racism through the airwaves, newspapers, halls of government, and other public forums across the nation.

References

Browne, M. (1994, October 16). What is intelligence and who has it? The *New York Times Book Review*, 45.

Chideya, F. (1994, November). Letters. The *New York Times Book Review*, 75.

Cole, D. (1995, January 23). "Hoop Dreams" and colorblindness. *Legal Times*, 43.

Coughlin, E. (1994, October 26). Class, IQ and heredity. *The Chronicle of Higher Education*, A12.

D'Sousa, D. (1995). *The end of racism*. New York: The Free Press.

Editorial. (1994, October 31). The issue. *The New Republic*, 9.

Freedland, J. (1995, January). The right stuff. *The Guardian*, 31, T2.

Gingrich, N. (1995, July 10). Renewing America. *Newsweek*.

Glazer, N. (1994, October 31). The lying game. *The New Republic*, 4 (163), 15-16.

Goldberg, D. (1993). *Racist Culture*. London: Blackwell.

Havel, V. (1995, January 22). The responsibility of intellectuals. *The New York Review of Books*, 37.

Herman, E. (1994, December). The new racist onslaught. *Z Magazine*, 24.

Herrnstein, R. and Murray, C. (1994). *The Bell Curve: Intelligence and class structure in American life*. New York: The Free Press.

Jackson, D. (1995, July 7). The rhetoric of job freeze out. The *Boston Globe*, 15.

King, M. L., Jr. (1968). Racism and the white backlash. *Where do we go from here: Chaos or community?* Boston: Beacon Press.

Miller, A. (1995). Professors of Hate. In Jacoby, R., and Glauberman, N., eds., *The Bell Curve debate*. New York: Times Books.

Murray, C. (1994, October 9). Cited in DeParle, J. Daring research of "social science pornography?" The *New York Times Magazine*, 50.

Naureckas, J. (1995, January/February). Racism resurgent: How media let *The Bell Curve*'s pseudo-science define the agenda on race. *Extra*, 20.

Puga, A. and Kranish, M. (1995, June 30). Supreme Court rejects black-majority district. The *Boston Globe*, 1.

Reed, A., Jr. (1994, November 28). Looking backward. *The Nation*, 660.

Rosen, J. and Lane, C. (1994, October 31). Neo-Nazis. *The New Republic,* 14.

Siegel, L. (1994). For whom the bell curves. *Tikkun, 10* (1), 28.

Tierney, J. (1995, February 14). A San Francisco talk show takes right-wing radio to a new dimension. The *New York Times,* A10.

4 THE APE'S IQ

ALLEN SHELTON

Honored members of the Academy! You have done me the honor of inviting me to give your Academy an account of the life I formerly led as an ape.

— Franz Kafka, "A Report
to the Academy"

The epigraph is taken from a short story by Franz Kafka. In it an ape is giving a lecture to a scientific gathering, a typical Kafka touch. Written in Prague toward the end of World War I in 1917, the story is a long way from the burgeoning IQ complex in the United States where 1.75 million men were tested as part of the war effort. Kafka never mentions the war or IQ directly; instead, as in his better-known story "The Metamorphosis," he uses the fantastic to critique the mundane. In the place of the dutiful son, Gregor Samsa wakes up in his bed as a bug with six squirming legs sticking out of the covers. In "A Report to the Academy," Kafka reverses the transformation. A young ape mounts a full-speed assault to become a man. The change is stretched out over five years, requiring self-discipline and a series of instructors, but in the end the ape still looks like an ape. Neither story has a happy ending. Gregor is slowly crushed by an apple sinking into his back. The ape is tormented by the wild looks of his chimpanzee companion and the realization that the possibility of returning to his life as an ape is growing smaller and smaller. To change back, the ape says to the Academy, "I should have to scrape the very skin from my body" (Kafka, 1971, p. 250). Still the ape has succeeded in something. He is a man with a respectable IQ at the "cultural level of the average European" (Kafka, 1971, p. 258).

Just how far the ape has come is one of the things *The Bell Curve* purports to measure. IQ is a measurement technology through which individuals and ethnic and national groups can be graphed. The bell curve is not completely flexible but follows a 60 percent genetic determination, according to Herrnstein and Murray. Individual IQ is predominantly a product of one's ethnic genetic background, the authors argue. That leaves 40 percent to socialization—like schools, teachers, parents, movies, books, baseball games, art museums, and milk-shakes. But apparently these are the unimportant factors in determining IQ or what turns out to be one's place in society. The genetic code is determinant. Kafka's ape is lucky then, since he finds himself at the center of a relatively exclusive bell curve. Instead of European it could have been African, which for Herrnstein and Murray would have placed him lower on the universal bell curve and made him less of a "man." It is the experience of less and more that makes IQ such a dangerous technology. Stephan J. Gould (1981) describes it as "the mismeasure of man." Michel Foucault (1979) would describe it as the measure of the man and mean that IQ is part of a new disciplinary apparatus that organizes bodies from the inside out. The brain, like the public space or the soul, is a critical disciplinary site through which power is deployed. The ape knows it. He feels it in the nagging insecurity of not being smart enough.

However fantastic Kafka's story is, it parallels what was going on in less fantastic places like the courthouse, the hospital, and the school. The army's testing fed right back into these institutions and vice versa. New kinds of individuality were being sculpted. What Foucault (1979) saw in the disciplining of the body in the penal system, Frederick Taylor was putting into practice in scientific management across the industrial edge. The IQ was a continuation of this process beneath the skin in the cerebellum. Like bodies in the time-motion studies, intelligence was cinematically cut and sutured to be more efficient. Erroneous elements were omitted. The ape's story is not so farfetched; rather it is a model for what was happening around the United States and Western Europe with the disciplining of labor and the development of the IQ state. Intelligence was suddenly quantifiable, and the state was squarely behind the new clinical categories. Legal decisions were made. People were being made up.

> In 1927 Oliver Wendell Holmes, Jr., delivered the Supreme Court's decision upholding the Virginia sterilization law in Buck v. Bell. Carrie Buck, a young mother with a child of allegedly feeble mind had scored a mental age of nine on the Stanford-Binet. Carrie Buck's mother, then 52, had tested at mental age seven. Holmes wrote, in one of the most famous and chilling statements of our century: "We have seen more than once that the public welfare may call upon the best citizens for their lives. It would be strange if it could not call upon those who already sap the strength of the state for these lesser sacrifices. . . . Three generations of imbeciles are enough." (Gould, 1981, p. 335)

These new kinds of individuals were part of the expansion of the state. A market was created for schools and hospitals as disciplinary sites. Simultaneously, the IQ state opened up another dimension to the division of labor. The army's tests, like Taylor's time-motion studies, were designed to create a more efficient labor force. Now Herrnstein and Murray want to instigate a series of policy changes based on how IQ is spread across the bell curve. No new individuals are on the scene. No idiots. No imbeciles. Groups are to be eliminated through new immigration laws, welfare reform, and revised criminal codes. Ethnic groups replace the individual as the target category. The goal of the project is a return to America before the IQ fall, a time for which Herrnstein and Murray have a profound nostalgia. Beneath their nostalgia is a new leviathan, an *X-File* state dealing in intelligence. The IQ state is a racist cinema sunk as deep as sex into the body, heralding the interior as the new frontier for expansion. Freud was only a dabbler. IQ allows for and sustains new technologies that eliminate reflection, and replace thinking with productivity. Kafka's ape stands in front of the audience like a bestial Frankenstein, the first of his kind to make the move into the Academy as a spectacle. Herrnstein and Murray recognize the inefficiency of this and would reverse the switch, turning certain groups back into apes. For them, it is the only way back to the state that they love and the America they revere.

However dubious the ape's admission into the Academy was, it did complete the transformation. He was a man. Herrnstein and Murray's book, *The Bell Curve*, raises serious doubts about what being "a man" requires. More IQ is needed. And what IQ means here is not intelligence in the ordinary sense of the word, or even in the extraordinary sense such as Einstein's brain powering a city from a jar, but IQ as social class sunk deep down into the bones, the muscles, and the sentimental structures of an individual. The proxy for this deep structure is the genetic determination of cognitive ability. The ape would have just made it as a waiter dressed in a tuxedo and bow tie, which emphasizes that genetics are inevitably experienced from either side of a social relationship. A large amount of the controversy surrounding this book originates in the tense border between social classes and whether the borders should be electrified like a line across Texas or a swank Los Angeles neighborhood, or exposed and reconfigured for a more equitable distribution of goods and services. The IQ controversy is not new. IQ is the new sign in the ascension of a displaced discipline. Herrnstein and Murray have delivered a report to the Academy from the other side of Kafka's ape. They want the old America back.

Kafka's story is part of a genre that is common enough along the borders where cultures meet, particularly when that context is marked by racism and violence. *The Bell Curve* is never far away from that genre itself in the way the borders are dramatized between an essentially white affluent class and everyone else. Fear and violence permeate the book from the opening acknowledgments, which quiver nervously on the page in a strange parody of an e.e. cummings poem, to the repressed fear in the concluding chapter, which hides behind slaveowner Thomas Jefferson for moral support. Kafka's story imitates the captive's tale. Instead of from Tarzan's point of view, Kafka writes from the ape's, from which the captivity and the proper discipline and training produce a lyricism coaxed out by coercion.

A CAPTIVE'S MIMESIS

> Research has shown that apparently trivial matters such as the use of chairs with desk arms, instead of conventional desks, can have significant effects upon performance.
>
> —Akhurst, 1970, p. 115

Kafka's ape is shot somewhere on the Gold Coast. He is hit once in the shoulder and again in the hip. He is thrown into a three-sided cage in the bottom of a boat headed for Europe. With all avenues of escape blocked—the cage is so small it cuts into his back—the ape makes a decision. Escape as an ape is impossible, but movement as a man is possible. He watches his captors and imitates them. He learns how to spit. No drug is administered to make him smarter. Jane Goodall does not make an appearance. There is no brain transplant. Kafka defines intelligence as an act of mimesis, copying one's captors. Here "A Report to an Academy" begins to reframe the stories Herrnstein and Murray tell in *The Bell Curve*. IQ is a peculiar kind of intelligence, a peculiar kind of mimesis exchanged between individuals in opposing networks. Critics often have pointed to the racial bias in IQ tests, but the exchange does not just follow a white-to-black circuit. It is more pervasive. Racism is just one of the big circuits. Discipline is another that cuts across bodies differently. Discipline does not necessarily discriminate on skin color, but character. IQ allows the movement into a new kind of racism based on character, intelligence, and access to the medias that simulate intelligence. The

IQ state is now a mediated state, controlling and dispensing what Stephen Pfohl (1992) graphically scripts as "inFORMation." Gould saw the beginnings of this in his critique of the army's use of the IQ test. It tested culture, not intelligence. It still tests culture, but culture as it is projected out of the intersection of institutional sites, medias, and, most importantly, access to the critical hookups in the new information economy.

Originally the IQ was a private affair reminiscent of what transpired on Freud's couch in Vienna. World War I and the army changed that. The army administered mental tests to 1.75 million recruits. Whereas Freud and his office provided plenty of clues as to what to say—his office was stuffed with antiquities, Persian rugs, paintings, and Freud's pet chow laying beside the couch acted as cue cards for the analysis—but in a pinch whatever happened to pop into one's head would do. The army made it harder. The tests were often given "in cramped barracks with no furnishings at all, and inadequate acoustics, illumination, and lines of sight" (Gould, 1981, p. 205). The only mimesis possible was what was already inside one's head or in the sterile surroundings. This is why Gould points to the cultural bias. Defenders of IQ argue that intelligence is inside the head in genes and only secondarily in socialization. They have it all wrong. Intelligence is public. It is between heads and objects. It is in a system of actants (Latour, 1993), or half-alive objects backing-up the person. Intelligence is squeezed out of objects. No wonder Magnavox is smart, very smart. It sits in very smart living rooms.

The testing situation further deteriorated once the labyrinth-like questions were unleashed. Punctuating the test were bursts of discipline. Stop. Begin. Attention. Ask no questions. It is not surprising that Gould concludes that the army IQ test measured familiarity with American language and culture, not innate intelligence. Added to that list should be something called the discipline quotient, or the capacity to be disciplined and provide the appropriate mimesis. Kafka was not far from wrong. Intelligence is the imitation of discipline, and the army tests were introductions to the reconstruction of the individual. The war did not just produce new technologies, it produced new kinds of individuals. The concept of total war is matched by total intelligence, the total state, the total individual. IQ is a sign of the new discipline that, like sex, reorganizes the individual and how institutions work. Sexuality is the public side of intelligence. A history of intelligence needs to be written in Foucauldian terms. In the following account, Michael Taussig records a captor's or a host's version of mimesis that swings, like the dancer's hips, between sexuality and intelligence. Dancing is not a measurable IQ quality. Count Harry Kessler is the author. On February 28, 1926, he brought Josephine Baker, the famous African American cabaret dancer, from Paris, to dance for his dinner guests. A space was cleared in his library. Josephine was turned loose. The eyes were turned on her for another kind of report to the academy.

> Josephine Baker was as though transformed. When, she implored, will the part be ready for her to dance? She began to go into some movements, vigorous and vividly grotesque, in front of my Maillol figure, became preoccupied with it, stared at it, copied the pose, rested against it in bizarre postures, and talked to it, clearly excited by its massive rigor and elemental force. Then she danced around it with extravagantly grandiose gestures, the picture of a priestess frolicking like a child and making fun of herself and her goddess. Maillol's creation was obviously much more interesting and real to her than the humans standing about her. Genius (for she is a genius in the matter of grotesque movement) was addressing genius. Suddenly she stopped and switched to her Negro dances, spicing them with every sort of extravagance. The climax was reached when Fried tried to join in the clowning and she caricatured, ever more preposterously, ever more dizzily, any and every movement he made. Where Fried was just ungainly, with her it became a wonderfully stylish grotesquerie which struck a balance between what is depicted in an ancient Egyptian relief frieze and the antics of one of George Grosz's mechanical dolls. Now and again Luli Meiern also improvised a few movements,

very delightful and harmonious; but one twist of the arm by
Josephine Baker and their grace was extinguished, dissolved
into thin air like mountain mist. (Taussig, 1993, p. 69)

Between Kafka and Count Kessler, a force field is generated.
What is meant by intelligence is interwoven with race, gender, class,
and sex. Kessler's books and art objects are matched by Baker's
dancing as an alternative to the institutional grid. Herrnstein and
Murray are less generous in this estimation of what intelligence is.
"We confess to reservations about using the word intelligence to
describe such factors as . . . musical abilities, kinesthetic abilities or
personal skills" (Herrnstein and Murray, 1994, p. 20). Intelligence is
more like the music produced by pressure across the person in which
each square inch gives up a different note on a timed sequence.
Baker's grace is no match for a stopwatch. "The majority of tests are
timed within very exact limits. For this reason a stopwatch should be
used and where possible it should be calibrated against a time piece
of known accuracy. Watches with a sweep second hand have been
used successfully in an emergency, but are not to be recommended"
(Akhurst, 1970, p. 117).

A STATE OF EMERGENCY

Gregor's transformation into a bug happened overnight in Kafka's
short story. Josephine Baker's transformation had an historical
time-beat with an escape plan in it. She left St. Louis for Paris for
more movement and for what I would define as intelligence based on
a different configuration of objects and individuals. Paris gave
Josephine Baker's dancing a stage linked with the modernist explo-
sion. Not so much less racist than St. Louis, but differently racist.
Whereas simulations of black women's bodies were cookie jars in
Missouri, in Paris they became modernist art housed in museums—a
different valorization allowing a different kind of movement. Movement is the key. The ape's change took five years but, as he described

it, there was still "a tickling at the heels" that made his life a hell. Everyone feels it, "the small chimpanzee and the great Achilles alike" (Kafka, 1971, p. 250).

The tickling is a chronic state of anxiety yielded up by the measure of the individual. For the ape it is particularly acute. He is under constant surveillance. Each minute action takes on monumental significance. What is comic book-like in Kafka, Gould sums up as "the mismeasure of man." Gould (1981) is talking about IQ tests and what the surveillance blownup in an IQ test is connected to. A kind of discipline is measured. In Gould's ironic phrase, a sexism swirls around the use of "man," and in Kafka's short story the ape is part of a thinly veiled racism. Both are intertwined with an equation of intelligence with white men. Unfortunately, this tendency is continued in two of the commentaries on *The Bell Curve*. In both *The Bell Curve Wars* and *The Bell Curve Debate*, women are decidedly underrepresented. The IQ state is not a lessening of sexism and racism but an intensification of them as it fully realizes Ralph Ellison's image of "the invisible man." Sexism and racism flourish in the optical unconscious blown up by the IQ technologies.

None of the anxiety is so distant that it is not felt. If you have been to school, you have felt the tickling of the bell curve. At the beginning, to set up the oedipal gene pool, I should note that my mother and my grandfather taught mathematics. I had not done well in the subject. I had gotten a D in high school geometry. The teacher made me come in early every day to work problems untill the class bell. So, I was prepared to do badly in statistics. It was part of a family drama. The classroom reminded me of a large waiting room in a court house. I sat at the end of a long Formica table next to the window. The professor called out each name like an announcement. The expression on his face did not change but the students' did. It was clear he was handing back the tests in the order of the score. The weekend before the exam I had put up a fence to keep a Belgian mare and foal in the upper pasture. The foal had gotten spooked and run through a barbed wire fence. It stood there like a toy horse wrapped in wire ribbon, snags of rusted barb wire kinked around its legs. The foal could not move. The horse had been lucky. There were only a few deep gashes around the throat. I was the last name called out. At the top of the exam without any flourish was the number 6. For any good Pentecostal the number is significant: 666 is the mark of the beast. As nonchalantly as I could I turned the page. The second was cut up in red ink. I folded the paper lengthwise and stuck it in my notebook. I stared straight ahead. I remember thinking "So this is how it feels to be hit between the eyes with a baseball bat," and I made a mental note, a wooden bat like the professionals use. The professor stepped back to the board and mechanically drew a large bell curve from end to end. He plotted each score on the board. My six was by itself on the wrong end of the tail. My classmates each snuck a look. I was part of the lecture, what Kafka called a report to the Academy.

While it may not be altogether fair to connect my experiences with the 845-page book, the world is, as they might put it, intercorrelated. I don't remember taking an IQ test but my mother assured me that I did. I took the test on a marine base in southern California, near the ocean, near an old mission, and near Herbert Marcuse, who was still teaching in San Diego then. Vietnam was still festering. I did well. My mother tells me I am very bright but she will not tell me my score. Like sex, IQ is another family secret. I do remember taking the standardized exams: the SATs, the ACTs, and the GREs, which are interconnected with the IQ. These tests played into a recurrent nightmare I had about getting into heaven. I would have to pass a test like the GRE to get next to God. Apparently my fantasy is not so wrong. IQ is the new great divide between happiness and unhappiness. Herrnstein and Murray argue that a new cognitive elite is emerging who have happier marriages, make better citizens, have better job satisfaction, enjoy the arts more, and are less likely to commit a crime. No wonder Kafka's ape located himself at the center of the bell curve. It was like joining an exclusive new country club as a waiter.

Walter Benjamin goes further in his analysis. The anxiety is not a sensation limited to extraordinary transformations or the sudden realization that your brains have been knocked out by a baseball bat in a classroom. It is a chronic state, the very sensation that defines the modern period. Benjamin himself was ideally situated to pick up these sensations. He was a German Jew living in exile in Paris during the 1930s. His personal life opened him up like a clairvoyant. His typewriter clattered at night. He was a chubby Kafka. But his diagnosis is more than experiential, it has an historical dimension. This Kafka read Marx.

> The tradition of the oppressed teaches us that the "state of emergency" in which we live is not the exception, but the rule. We must attain to a conception of history that is in keeping with this insight. Then we shall clearly recognize that it is our task to bring about a real state of emergency, and this will improve our condition in the struggle against Facism. One reason why Facism has a chance is that in the name of progress its opponents treat it as a historical norm. The current amazement that the things we are experiencing are "still" possible in the twentieth century is not philosophical. This amazement is not the beginning of knowledge—unless it is the knowledge that the view of history which gives rise to it is untenable. (Benjamin, 1969, p. 257)

The feeling is not as esoteric as it might seem. It is as close as caffeine heating up your muscles or the kind of tension surrounding a test at school. The state of emergency is contagious. Whole portions of my biography are infected with the tension. Institutions like coffeehouses are dedicated to the anxiety. What the ape felt is commonplace. What he felt is the tingling of the nervous system or the chronic state of emergency that binds the modern world together.

ONE-DIMENSIONAL INTELLIGENCE

A Klee painting named "Angelus Novus" shows an angel looking as though he is about to move away from something he is fixedly contemplating. His eyes are staring, his mouth is open, his wings are spread. This is how one pictures the angel of history. His face is turned toward the past. Where we perceive a chain of events, he sees one single catastrophe which keeps piling wreckage upon wreckage and hurls it in front of his feet. The angel would like to stay, awaken the dead, and make whole what has been smashed. But a storm is blowing from paradise; it has got caught in his wings with such violence that the angel can no longer close them. This storm irresistibly propels him into the future to which his back is turned, while the pile of debris before him grows skyward. This storm is what we call progress.   —Benjamin, 1969, pp. 257-258

Benjamin wrote these lines 17 years after Kafka's death. Within a few months the angel would get Benjamin. He committed suicide on the Spanish border running from the Nazis. No less than Kafka, he died like a dog at the end of his leash. In his writing on the eve of the Nazi Holocaust, the angel flutters malevolently close to the wreckage, his muscles clearly seen beneath a thin white gown. It was at this point that Benjamin's personal tragedies merged with the coming of the Nazis. What Benjamin felt and saw was the splintering of his own nervous system in sync with the goosestep. Opened up like a clairvoyant, Benjamin must have felt like he was writing with razors stuck beneath his fingers. Benjamin's dramas, like those surrounding the bell curve, are part of my own small biography. I can think them, I can see the outlines of them in little scenes spread across the writing of this paper. I tried to take an IQ test. I called the Education and Psychology departments at Drake University in Des Moines, Iowa. It is a swank school. The student's pay nearly $20,000 a pop per year. "Impossible," I am told, "no facilities. See a clinical psychologist." For something so omnipresent, it seemed hard to get in direct touch with the IQ complex, but that is precisely the point. Around the hard edges of the bell curve are layers of ambiguity. I have no idea where fact and fiction separate. My own tentativeness turns on me and envelopes me in a dull cocoon. For Benjamin the feeling was finally sharp. For me it is like trying to remember a nightmare while driving down the interstate, the radio mixing indiscriminately with my memories. I have no confidence in my memories or my ability to cut through into the IQ state. That is the effect of the IQ state on most of us. Hegemony does not burn, it aches in such a way that you cannot be sure where the pain is coming from.

Pain is the first step in thinking through the murk. Benjamin had made an art of it, using his own pain like a long needle to probe the chronic state of emergency before the situation worsened. A photograph taken in 1938 outside his friend Brecht's house in Denmark showed Benjamin as "an old man at 46, in white shirt, tie, trousers with watch chain, a slack, corpulent figure looking tentatively at the camera" (Benjamin, 1979, p. 7). Missing from the photograph is the angel mussing his hair. His personal situation was exasperated by the lack of steady institutional support. Benjamin and his typewriter floated in an intellectual free zone in his Paris apartment. He was what Deleuze and Guattari (1987) describe as a nomadic writer, a pirate or guerrilla thinker working the edges for enough money to eke out a living. I would guess that most writers in this volume have a position within the university system. Benjamin's principal support came through the journal of the exiled Frankfurt School. Increasingly that support was thinning. The editors had problems with what Benjamin would describe as profane illumination in his own work. Benjamin first used the term to contextualize the surrealist's project as materialized seeing. In his work *One Way Street,* Benjamin developed the concept further by using street signs, advertisements, and phrases as explosive thinking devices to shock the tangible into talking. "Today," wrote Benjamin (p. 89) "the most real, the mercantile gaze into the heart of things is the advertisement." It was a radical point. Profane illumination abandoned the normal institutional frames for criticism. For Benjamin as for the surrealists, the razor would do. There was no need, necessarily, for Nietzsche.

There is a lesson here for how to read *The Bell Curve.* There is no need for statistics. There is no need for Harvard schooling. The

book can be dismantled using a pocket calculator, an assemblage—
Levi's, Doc Marten's, a J. Crew T-shirt, advertising slogans, an
Absolut Vodka ad, a memory, a relationship, anything will do. Hack
at the book, pierce it, set glasses of iced tea on it. Imagine a colony of
ants living in it and call up E. O. Wilson for advice. He teaches at
Harvard. The core of the book is in the pain coiled up in the authors'
stomachs, which slips like a tapeworm into the reader's own, and
back to the pain knotted up in the subject of the book, those outside
the cut-off point on the curve. Normal thinking cannot approach
this. It is too one dimensional. It is too much a part of the problem:
For instance, the authors assembled in *The Bell Curve wars* are drawn
from a powerful triangle of universities, magazines, and publishers
headquartered in the northeast—Harvard, *The New Republic,* and
Brandeis. Two authors are from Stanford and Michigan. These are
not nomadic intellectuals, but state intellectuals. What they say is
amplified by their intellectual affiliations. Harvard talks as a privileged site in both *The Bell Curve* and in *The Bell Curve wars,* which is
why in an otherwise enviable essay Orlando Patterson, a Harvard
man, can take Herrnstein to task for falling away from the Harvard
values. The shame is that Herrnstein and Murray pull away the polite
mask of a civil hegemony manifested in privilege and show its teeth.
Harvard is as much a part of the problem as IQ. The IQ state does
not just deal in racial and sexual divisions, but in social class.

   Even more than the castle in Kafka's writing, IQ is what
Michael Taussig would identify as a part of a culture of terror. The
myths surrounding the IQ form the equivalent of a space of death in
which signifiers and signifieds mix, netting the individual in webs of
fact and fiction. One-dimensional thinking cannot challenge the
castle-like intensity in which the IQ state has settled into the
imagination and institutional nexuses in the United States. Critiques
need to be pushed toward absurdity to break down what appears to
be reasonable. One should situate one's own biography, as Kafka's
ape did, on the bell curve and get in touch with the dull ache in the
back of the head. Push the angel aside and practice crude think-
ing/profane illumination without repeating the tragedy of both Kafka

and Benjamin thinking alone. Think in packs outside privileged institutional sites. Follow the ape's example. Shock the Academy.

References

Akhurst, B.A. (1970). *Assessing intellectual ability.* New York: Barnes and Noble, Inc.

Benjamin, W. (1969). *Illuminations.* New York: Schocken Books.

Benjamin, W. (1979). *One way street and other writings.* New York: Verso.

Deleuze, G. and F. Guattari. (1987). *A thousand plateaus: Capitalism and Schizophrenia.* Minnesota: University of Minnesota Press.

Foucault, M. (1979). *Discipline and punish: The birth of the prison.* New York: Vintage.

Foucault, M. (1990). *The history of sexuality, volume I: An introduction.* New York: Vintage.

Fraser, S., ed. (1995). *The Bell Curve wars: Race, intelligence, and the future of America.* New York: Basic Books.

Gould, S. (1981). *The mismeasure of man.* New York: W.W. Norton & Co.

Herrnstein, R. and Murray, C. (1994). *The Bell Curve: Intelligence and class structure in American life.* New York: The Free Press.

Jacoby, R. and Glauberman, N. (1995). *The Bell Curve debate: History, documents, opinions.* New York: Times Books.

Kafka, F. (1971 trans.). *The complete stories.* New York: Schocken Books.

Latour, B. (1993). *We have never been modern.* Cambridge, MA: Harvard University Press.

Pfohl, S. (1992). *Death at the Parasite Cafe: Social science (fictions) and the postmodern.* New York: St. Martin's Press.

Taussig, M. (1992). *The nervous system.* New York: Routeledge.

Taussig, M. (1993). *Mimesis and alterity: A particular history of the senses.* New York: Routledge.

PART III

RESPONDING TO
THE BELL CURVE:
CHAPTER BY CHAPTER

5 THE SET-UP: CROCODILE TEARS FOR THE POOR

PHIL FRANCIS CARSPECKEN

Chapter 1 of The Bell Curve *is entitled* "Cognitive Class and Education, 1900-1990." Since the 1950s, argue Herrnstein and Murray, "cognitive ability," as measured by the Scholastic Aptitude Test (SAT) and IQ scores, has begun to supplant race, gender, religion, class of birth, and other factors as the core determinant in university admissions. Universities have become more stratified themselves, with elite institutions boasting mean student scores at the very top of the SAT and IQ distributions. Greater geographic mobility and more "democratic"university admission policies are supposed to be the causes of these trends. The chapter argues as well that a partitioning effect has occurred, such that students sharing a certain ranking in the overall distribution of SAT scores are unlikely to meet students with scores a few percentiles higher or lower. There is little overlap between the various strata.

Furthermore, they argue that these trends are reorganizing United States class structure, raising "new barriers between people that may prove to be more divisive and intractable than the old ones" (p. 29). Why is this so? Because, argue Herrnstein and Murray, when students leave universities with their degrees in hand, they enter occupations that also have become both stratified and highly partitioned along cognitive lines. Social class is becoming based more and more on cognitive ability, as indicated by the distribution of SAT and

IQ scores. Higher education, always *one* of the sorting mechanisms that determine which youth will come to occupy which class position in society, is becoming *the* central determinant of social stratification, according to *The Bell Curve.*

UPPER-CLASS PARTITIONING

Why do Herrnstein and Murray believe this is a disturbing trend? In chapter 1 the argument emphasizes upper-class partitioning. "When people live in an encapsulated world, it becomes difficult for them, even with the best of intentions, to grasp the realities of a world with which they have little experience but over which they also have great influence, both public and private" (p. 50). The cognitive elite, as the authors call them, are merging with the economic and politically powerful elite. They are becoming a ruling class, totally out of touch with those they effectively rule. This is upper-class partitioning: the segregation of a ruling class from those they rule.

Certainly a society in which a ruling elite is out of touch with those they rule is not a good thing. It is hoped that few would disagree with Herrnstein and Murray on this point. But what is really new about this state of affairs? When I moved to England in the 1980s, many people told me that the English upper-class only became aware of how terrible life was for the English working class during World War II, when German bombing forced people of all classes together in the subways. Upper-class partitioning is hardly a new state of affairs in most societies, the United States included. So what is different in Herrnstein and Murray's picture? Haven't we always had a ruling class of economically and politically powerful people, well partitioned off from less privileged groups? If, for the sake of argument, we grant Herrnstein and Murray their thesis that the economic elite is now becoming a cognitive elite as well, why should this disturb readers *more* than would learning about previous forms of elite rule in the United States?

LOWER-CLASS PARTITIONING

To understand what is supposed to be new and especially dangerous in the formation of a cognitively based class structure, we have to examine other chapters of *The Bell Curve*. And when we do, a message delivered much less explicitly in the opening sections of the book turns out to be the central message of the book. To readers of *The Bell Curve*, upper-class partitioning will not come across as the real problem. Herrnstein and Murray seem to stress the dangers of upper-class partitioning in chapters like the first one mainly in order to claim humanist credentials. Of course it is bad to have a society in which the ruling elite does not have any real communication with lower strata; Herrnstein and Murray must be good guys to show such concern. But then partitioning and elite rule has long been the case anyway. Cognitive partitioning is not going to make the upper class any less connected with groups below them than they always have been.

So what is the real message? First of all, Herrnstein and Murray are careful to *include the reader* within their brighter (but not necessarily brightest) cognitive strata. This is done repeatedly throughout the book as a sort of reassurance to the reader that the mere act of reading a book like theirs puts one well "above the average." The effects produced by this strategy are not likely to cause readers to worry about a cognitive elite existing *above* them, because we readers are, after all, at least *almost* up there ourselves, aren't we? The information and arguments of *The Bell Curve* are meant to be alarming, but not so as to awaken readers to the fact that they have a ruling elite above and partitioned off from them.

Chapter 1 argues that higher education is producing a cognitive elite. In later chapters, especially those in part II, the *correlate* of upper-class, cognitive partitioning emerges as the real issue to cause alarm. Universities are extracting the cognitively most able from all social classes, leaving a population of "dull" people in the lower classes. Dull people do stupid things, like take drugs and commit crimes. This is what is meant to be alarming: *lower-class partitioning.* Readers are invited to be alarmed about the behavior of groups they do not, according to *The Bell Curve,* belong to.

In part II, Herrnstein and Murray muster all sorts of statistical information to argue that people of the lowest cognitive abilities are basically incompetent as citizens. They are the ones with the highest unemployment. Why? Because they are too dull to get and keep jobs. They are the ones with the highest crime rates. Why? Because they are too dense to understand that crime is morally undesirable, too undeveloped to exercise restraint over their dangerous impulses. They are the ones with the largest number of single-parent families, the highest number of drop-outs, the worst parenting skills. Why? Because they are stupid. Though my words are harsher than those carefully chosen by Herrnstein and Murray, they basically convey the message of the book as a whole.

Thus the real significance of chapter 1 turns out to be other than what the authors emphasize explicitly on its pages. The problem is not, per se, the way in which new university admission policies concentrate the most cognitively able citizens into an elite social class. It is rather the correlate that supports the brunt of their sociological critique. By extracting the "brightest" from all tiers of society, higher education is leaving a large group of incompetent people in our lower strata. Without "smart" peers to guide them, these people are escalating crime rates, draining the government of resources in the form of welfare checks and other services, having more children and raising them poorly to produce new, numerically larger, generations of deviants and ne'er-do-wells. Since they mate with each other and since cognitive ability is supposed to have a high genetic component, these people are probably just getting stupider as well.

For many readers, this will be the central message of the book. This is what is new. Here is an argument, supported with all sorts of charts and graphs, that social problems actually are caused by low intelligence. Lower classes in society are increasingly becoming the location of our stupidest citizens, so social problems can be expected to be on the rise. Anyone intelligent enough to read the book is not one of *them,* not a member of the lowest cognitive classes.

Thus anyone reading the book is invited to blame social problems on the personal qualities of lower-class people. Chapter 1 is meant to explain the sorting mechanism involved: Greater "democracy" in university admission policies is creaming off the most competent of our citizens, leaving society with several tiers of dangerously dull people at the bottom of the class structure.

THE CUSTODIAL STATE

Herrnstein and Murray, however, attempt to maintain their claim to humanist intentions by emphasizing their worries about how the lowest classes in our society will be *treated* by the new elites. The elite can be expected to lose tolerance for lower-class behaviors and establish greater policing and surveillance policies. A "custodial state" looms in the near future; a state that provides services to those too incompetent to serve themselves and thus takes on a paternalistic, maternalistic quality. At the same time, this will be a state that monitors, confines, and polices lower-class activities in violation of true democratic values.

The truth is that many within our present elite classes would no doubt welcome increased custodial policies if there were some ideological justification for them. *The Bell Curve* goes far in providing such justification by linking crime and other negative social behaviors to low intellect. While Herrnstein and Murray state their desire to avoid a custodial state, all their suggested "solutions" in chapter 22 are blatantly weak, based on outdated social theory of Hobbes, Locke, and Jefferson. The solutions could not possibly have any effect on readers other than to keep the authors of *The Bell Curve* looking good. It provides *nothing* in the way of viable social policy.

So, let us be clear about the role chapter 1 plays for *The Bell Curve* as a whole. It is really an argument that higher education has become the basic mechanism for determining U.S. class structure. Higher education, now that it is much more "democratic," extracts the most intelligent from all levels of society, leaving an underclass and a working class of people who share dangerously low levels of intellect. Thus many readers of the book might wonder: "Custodial state? Hum, never thought of that before. Regrettable, but maybe not such a bad idea. After all, people in the lowest strata cannot look after themselves, doesn't the book make this a statistically proven fact? And only those who act in criminal ways would be punished: What else can be *done* with such people?"

FACTS AND THEORY

We already have something approximating a custodial state, and publications like *The Bell Curve* could well speed the trend along by giving it legitimacy. The book is really a long argument for blaming the victim. But *The Bell Curve* is flawed as a work of social science. While the flaws show up already in chapter 1, they work their major damage in those chapters that discuss lower-class behavior. The flaws are seen most easily in the *theory* Herrnstein and Murray use to frame their factual displays. Theory is an essential part of all science, social science in particular. Yet *The Bell Curve* reads primarily not as a theoretical work but rather as a factual and descriptive piece of social science, with inferences tied closely to the facts. Few purely theoretical discussions can be found within its pages, though portions of the introduction give a cursory discussion of "intelligence" and its measurement.

The bulk of the theory used by Herrnstein and Murray to frame their arguments and give meaning to their statistical displays is either totally unstated or grossly understated. Most readers will imbibe Bell Curve theory as "ground" rather than "figure." Consequently, most readers will imbibe Herrnstein and Murray's social theory unconsciously, ignorant of its naive and flawed nature, unaware that social theorists have largely rejected the social models implicit to *The Bell Curve*.

Social theory concerns itself with the primary concepts employed necessarily by all social sciences, including psychology, economics, political science, and sociology. No social science can even begin its empirical investigations without first theoretically framing its objects of inquiry and without employing some sort of epistemology (theory of how valid knowledge is acquired).

What is Herrnstein and Murray's social theory? I think it can be roughly divided into two main domains: one concerning the concept of "intelligence" and the other concerning Herrnstein and Murray's model of society.

INTELLIGENCE

The first theoretical domain is the one that will jump out at most critical readers. The concept of "intelligence" is given a cursory discussion in the book's introduction, where the authors acknowledge but attempt to diffuse alternative ideas about intelligence developed by other psychologists. Because this area is so contentious and because Herrnstein and Murray really gloss the issues in a very cursory way, it is this theoretical domain that has attracted attention from most of the book's critics.

Is there such a thing of which *The Bell Curve* refers to as general intelligence (g)? If so, can it be measured by tests? Herrnstein and Murray, of course, answer yes to these questions. Once one answers "yes," a host of secondary, empirical questions follow. Herrnstein and Murray ignore some of these, but take on others, including the following:

- *Do tests contain bias?* Herrnstein and Murray say no and offer some support for their view. Many, myself included, would object saying that the way in which culture might influence testing skills is extremely subtle. Researchers seem to have only scratched the surface in this area. Performance fears and inhibitions, both greatly conditioned by culture and personal life experiences, can reduce test performance skills enormously in ways that are extremely difficult to control for. Many people have "math anxiety," for example, that blocks their mathematical reasoning whenever they are put on the spot. Fears, inhibitions, the effects of internalized labeling, and so on are little understood to date. Clearly they could have subtle and differential effects, making a person feel blocked on some test questions and confident on others. Moreover, bias in a broader sense is built into the limited concept of intelligence Herrnstein and Murray employ.

- *Are differences in* g *caused mainly by environmental factors or genetic factors or a mixture of both?* Herrnstein and Murray think that genes explain about 60 percent of the variation in *g.* This claim is responsible for much of the damage done by *The Bell Curve,* as it implies genetic inferiorities within minority populations and the lower classes generally. The idea that genetics are a significant determinant of intelligence has been attacked widely and famously by such authors as Stephen J. Gould. Other chapters in this collection take it on directly.
- *Can* g *change over the course of a lifetime?* Herrnstein and Murray argue that it does not change for most people. Given the ambiguity of the bias question, I very much doubt that sufficient research has been done on the question of changing intellectual abilities to warrant so firm a position.

These three secondary, partially empirical questions all must be answered in the way Herrnstein and Murray answer them if their book is to come anywhere near to supporting its major theses. Only if there is such a thing as *g,* only if it can be measured by tests, only if the tests are designed to capture all human capabilities we would wish to include in the concept of intelligence, only if *g* has a strong genetic basis, and only if *g* cannot change during a lifetime will the concept of "cognitive class" make sense. Yet each of these questions is rife with legitimate controversy unresolved by Herrnstein and Murray's presentation.

The next question, also secondary to the question of what "intelligence" is and whether it can be measured is, to my mind, even more important, yet it receives virtually no principled discussion in *The Bell Curve:*

> • *Does "low* g*" result in low moral consciousness, poor decision making in basic areas of life, and low self-restraint?* Herrnstein and Murray do not take on this question where they should. Yet it is absolutely central to all they have to say about the undesirable behaviors of the lower classes. They provide many chapters that correlate low IQ with crime, drug addiction, poor parenting, and other negative behaviors of moral significance. They suggest, for example, that higher unemployment among the lowest classes is the result of less intelligence. This is an unbelievably ridiculous idea. What is intelligent about sticking with a demeaning, underpaid, absolutely stifling job? As another example, Herrnstein and Murray even suggest that low IQs lead to a greater number of job accidents because duller people are no doubt more accident prone. This is such an absurd notion, it made me wince when reading it. Have these guys ever worked within the dangerous environments of a factory floor or ever worked a job so lowly paid and so undignified as to make claiming a disability a most desirable and intelligent thing to do?

The general idea is that low IQ means less self-restraint, less ability to plan basic life activities, and lower moral consciousness. This idea is conveyed through the display of correlations: Low test scores are correlated with membership in the lower class, which is correlated with probabilities for engaging in negative social behaviors. Correlations are presented in a way to suggest causes. But then in other chapters of the book Herrnstein and Murray explicitly state that having high intelligence is not the same as having "wisdom" or being predisposed to moral behavior. So low g is supposed to cause general incompetence in all areas of life, including those areas demanding a moral consciousness, while high g is supposed to be quite independent of wise and moral behavior. Someone should tell the authors that you can't have your cake and eat it too. If crime rates, child abuse, drug dealing, and other negative behaviors are lower for the more privileged classes, and yet this cannot be explained by cognitive ability, then something other than whatever an IQ test measures must be at work in *all* classes.

This area, the *causal* connection of g to behavior and moral reasoning, is one of *The Bell Curve*'s greatest vulnerabilities in terms of empirical support. The authors make contradictory claims about it, yet deliver the bulk of the book's central message on the assumption that low g will give rise to bad behavior. The confused way in which Herrnstein and Murray treat the relationship of their g concept to social behaviors generally is related to their flawed social theory—the second major theoretical domain I mentioned earlier.

Let me summarize these points about the first theoretical domain of *The Bell Curve*. Chapter 1 supports the overall arguments of *The Bell Curve* mainly through the claim that higher education is extracting intelligent people from all tiers of society, leaving a "dull" underclass and working class. The chapter offers no support at all to this central argument if the concept of intelligence Herrnstein and Murray employ is flawed. Even if their concept of intelligence was granted validity, a large number of secondary, more empirical questions must be answered in one and only one way for chapter 1 to support the book's main conclusions. If intelligence tests, for example, *do* contain bias, then the basic logic of the book is undermined. If g has nothing to do with the bulk of social behaviors discussed by Herrnstein and Murray, then the extraction of students with high SAT scores from all social tiers is *not* a cause of our growing social problems.

INTELLIGENCE AND SOCIETY

The second theoretical domain actually has strong linkage to the first, but it has not been well exploited, to date, by critics of *The Bell Curve*. On what core concepts do Herrnstein and Murray rest their depiction of society and social dynamics?

Let's take chapter 1 as the illustrative case. Chapter 1 claims that as higher education admission policies become more meritocratic, intelligent people from all tiers of life choose to enter universities in order to reap the social rewards that a degree can bring. We have a market model of higher education and a rational choice model of the human being.

Later chapters of *The Bell Curve* extend the same core imagery of markets and choices to other social sites. Why do young females of the lower classes have higher rates of pregnancies? Because their lower intellect predisposes them to poor choices in sexual matters. Why do they then sign on for social welfare benefits? Because their low cognitive ability makes them unaware of what a poor choice being a welfare dependent is (!). It is a model of rational choices, made within various markets of opportunity and constraint, the sum total of which equal "society." Low *g* becomes a factor in social dynamics when it is equated to poor decision-making skills and when society is modeled as a grandiose marketplace.

Social theorists have long understood that market models of society do not work. Only in some social domains within modern society do we find market-like conditions putting the human capacity for planning and choosing at a premium. Economic behavior is one example, of course, because it is from economic behavior that the market model originates. Other examples include decision-making behaviors within governments and the highest tiers of corporations. But there are many social domains in which people operate more according to their skills at constructing a social identity, conforming to or innovating upon cultural values, negotiating social norms, and articulating inner states verbally, musically, or artistically *much* more than they operate as planners and choosers from clearly defined options. The family is such a domain. Intimate relationships are another. So is much of the behavior exhibited by students from kindergarten to twelfth grade (K-12). So is community life.

In fact, earlier forms of human society were integrated primarily through their cultural milieu, within which each social act *integrated* planning, goal seeking, value claiming, aesthetic references, and identity constructions. The formation of markets as *major* socially integrating processes is a modern phenomena. In fact, markets are just a special case of the development of systems of social action in which objectified options and the value, identity, and moral implications associated with them become fixed outside the actor's volition. The actor is left with nothing but her capacity to make rational choices from a set of given (but socially constructed) conditions.

In modern societies such systemic integrating social processes have come to dominate in economic transactions and within the governmental and legal spheres. "Culture" becomes frozen in such spheres because actors are forced to make choices from a set of system-generated options. Culture is left in spheres such as the family, the early years of schooling, community life, religious institutions, and the social/informal (non—goal-driven) domains of the workplace. But systemic social processes, like the economic institutions of modern society, have begun to "push"on the realms that may still be described as cultural, influencing values and beliefs within non market social domains. Advertising and the media industry generally, both driven by economic forces, have influenced cultural realms in the direction of consumerism, for example. Educational policy decisions taken at governmental levels have pushed the idea that "excellence" in education means the production of an adequate workforce for American industry, resulting in more prestige for the sciences and less for the humanities. A system based on profit making and technological industries is exerting pressure on cultural realms of life, pushing values, identities, and norms that support a complex capitalist structure. A core feature of that structure is class stratification, which is determined first by the economic organization of society. Selection mechanisms, such as higher education, evolve secondarily in response to economic imperatives. Cultural milieu becomes pushed and influenced to produce values supporting systemic imperatives; the central thrust of *The Bell Curve* is a good example of this.

In sum, a more accurate view of society gives us a picture of human beings making complex kinds of acts within diverse sets of conditions. Only some areas of a person's life pose conditions approximated by the market and rational choice model. In most social spheres it is the human concern with value issues and personal identity, with caring for others and artistic expression, that take primacy. All these dimensions to social behavior have related motivation complexes within the psychology of individuals, and each dimension is employed with greater or lesser skill by individuals according to their respective talents and capacities.

IQ scores have little to do with the vast bulk of human intelligence. A psychological model like that of Gardner's (which Herrnstein and Murray dismiss in their introduction) is consequently much closer to human reality than that used by Herrnstein and Murray.

So, back to chapter 1. What is most interesting in the data displays of this chapter is not captured in a rational choice and market model. What ought to be of most interest to social scientists includes the following:

- The social construction of higher education as a type of market, due to economic imperatives outside the volition of actors; outside "culture."
- The increased use of testing to determine university admissions.
- The highly limited span of human capability reflected by the SAT and IQ tests.
- The cultural trends that have generalized the selection mechanisms of SAT and IQ scores to popular concep-

tions of "intelligence." These trends, of course, legitimate the stratification of higher education and help with blaming-the-victim strategies when it comes to social problems.

- The rise of a particular social "science," psychometrics, as a selection device for a highly stratified society.
- The correlation between those limited human capacities reflected by IQ scores and the sort of human skills deployed in a techno-capitalist society.
- The cultural processes involved in *producing* a relatively small pool of college applicants with identities and value orientations preparing them to compete in a higher education market. The market model Herrnstein and Murray use in chapter 1 does explain university attendance, given a pool of applicants. But the formation of this pool of applicants itself must be studied, and this will require a careful examination of nonmarket, largely cultural and social domains such as families, neighborhoods, and K-12 schools.

Explorations of these questions will lead to conclusions very different from those of *The Bell Curve*. Higher education has become a type of market in a way that sustains class inequalities. The "science" of testing serves this market by maintaining its legitimate appearance to the public. To serve all those who merit services seems to be democratic, but if "merit" means the ability to perform well on tests that are relevant to only a small band in the continuum of human capabilities, obviously real democracy is undermined. The "science" of testing, applied to university admissions, also draws attention away from both the manner in which our social system has organized work and the differential rewards it distributes to workers. A system that runs on profit accumulation for the owners of increasingly technological industries is both legitimated and sustained through testing practices. Such a system has little interest in human capacities for caring, for artistic expression, for moral consciousness and wisdom. Rather it favors person-to-world forms of reasoning (not person-to-person or person-to-self) and to this end has made people objects to study and classify.

Intelligence is defined narrowly in terms that best meet system requirements; all other human potentialities are devalued, removed from the concept of "intelligence." Social problems, so obviously a product of such system factors as work organization and job markets, are given the appearance of personality traits so victims can be blamed for their socially imposed misery. These are the interpretations that ought to follow from the data presented in chapter 1 and the other chapters of part I.

Herrnstein and Murray argue that environments play about a 40 percent role in the determination of g. I will leave this contentious claim aside and ask a question they have not posed. What is the effect of environment on other human potentialities, such as caring for children, understanding one's self, constructing positive intimate relations, understanding other people, becoming wise? Such things are not easily studied, but it obviously would be extremely important to investigate them in order to explain much of the data in *The Bell Curve*. My own qualitative studies of social life have convinced me that most important social behaviors are *highly* influenced by social environments and culture. They are *little* affected by whatever an IQ test measures. Trust levels, time constraints, work conditions, economic resources, all greatly affect the social activities that Herrnstein and Murray discuss as social problems. Class structure and the quality of work appear to be the core determinants of such things, not one's skills at taking IQ tests.

CONCLUSIONS

The admissions policies of universities, based more and more on test results, are not going to increase social problems by creaming off our most competent and wise citizens. Rather, they are just a new chapter in an old book: a new way of classifying and labeling and stratifying people that ignores or devalues the bulk of human potentialities.

I find the most condemning feature of *The Bell Curve* is its acceptance of cultural beliefs that clearly are generated by a social system in great need of change. That it accepts the widely distributed idea that intelligence is the same thing as IQ score is condemning. That it accepts the gross misdistribution of social goods across a highly stratified class system is condemning. That it fails to see psychometrics as itself a system phenomena, an objectification and truncation of human beings in the service of perpetuating and legitimating inequalities, is condemning. That it fails to consider the highly complex cultural processes at root in the formation of a pool of college applicants is condemning. Most repulsive is the equation at the heart of its central message: low scores on "intelligence" tests = low "intelligence" = low moral consciousness and general incompetence.

In summary, who wants to live in *any* of the societies depicted in *The Bell Curve?* I do not merely mean the authors' custodial state, I also mean their vision of an alternative. Who wants to live in a society in which the requirements of profit making within technological industries determine the very way we define human capability? Who wants to live with an occupational structure that rewards those able to actualize imperatives of the system and ignores those able to question the moral value of the system itself? Who wants to live in a society that has objectified so much of human culture into markets, destroying traditional forms of life for large numbers of people, denying them meaningful work environments, and then blaming them for the social problems that, not surprisingly, arise?

Can't we instead image a society that puts culture ahead of profit, that organizes work so that all people might develop themselves through it, that recognizes a huge as-yet uncharted span of human potentialities we can include in the concept of "intelligence?" Within *Bell Curve* imagery such a society cannot be imagined. But outside this imagery more benevolent societies are easy to picture, based on our everyday experiences with other human beings. It is hoped that books like the present one will help to break *The Bell Curve* spell, to restore the possibility of more humane visions.

Reference

Herrnstein, R. and Murray, C. (1994). *The Bell Curve: Intelligence and class structure in American life.* New York: Free Press.

6 FOR WHOM *THE BELL* TOLLS: A COGNITIVE OR EDUCATED ELITE?

YVONNA LINCOLN

Charles Murray has done it again—found politically convenient and misleading uses for inaccurately analyzed and/or displayed data—and found a colleague to help him with this bit of statistical legerdemain. I label it "statistical legerdemain" because the analyses are sometimes false and misleading and other times they are simplistic and consequently misleading. Chapter 2, "Cognitive Partitioning by Occupation," appears to proceed very much as the other chapters do. My own deconstruction of this chapter will follow two paths: the internal logic of the argument and reconstructing counterevidence to indicate that Herrnstein and Murray's analyses are at best inadequate statistics and, at worst, deliberate avoidance of methodical historical research that would create alternative explanations for their "findings."

THE LOGIC OF THE BASIC ARGUMENT

Herrnstein and Murray's basic argument is that there has been a partitioning of occupations since before World War I and, most particularly, since World War II. This partitioning, they argue, is almost solely and uniquely the product of the formation of a "cognitive elite" in the United States. They note that in 1950 highly intelligent people were dispensed throughout society and occupations; in the 1990s that group is concentrated within a small number of occupations that are screened for IQ. The arguments they go on to make resemble the old correlational conundrum many of us "cognitive elite" studied in a beginning logic class, viz., (1) Polio outbreaks occur when the highest per-capita consumption of Coca-Cola takes place, therefore (2) Coke causes polio.

It is no doubt true that a wide variety of IQ levels occupied a wide range of occupations in the early part of this century and, indeed, until recently. It is equally probable that increasingly, most professional occupations today require a somewhat higher average IQ than in previous years. I also shall stipulate that increasing the levels of educational opportunity and attainment have extended to some proportion of students the potential for achieving a professional occupation that was not possible for their grandfathers and grandmothers. But what cannot be stipulated is the causal relationship between those statistics. High correlation between consumption of Coca-Cola and the incidence of polio may simply mean that the season is summer and that more children are exposed to more of all manner of infectious diseases and other accoutrements of summer—including the drinking of soda pop on a hot day. Whether occupational status is "caused" by IQ (and the experts cannot even agree what an IQ test measures, let alone what it's contribution is to human functioning) is not proven by Herrnstein and Murray's analyses; those variables, IQ and occupational status, exist in a correlational relationship to each other, not in a causal relationship to each other. (For a deconstruction of the misuse, abuse, and ignorance of statistical application in Herrnstein and Murray's work, see House and Haug, 1994.) Not only are IQ and occupational status not causally related, it is highly probable that their correlation is itself mediated by a third variable, years of education. Tumin's (1985) analysis would almost certainly support my assertion.

THE HISTORICAL EVIDENCE CONTRADICTION
OF *THE BELL CURVE'S* FINDINGS

If I and others (such as House and Haug, 1994) find the statistical logic faulty (impugning causality when there is only a correlation), what other explanations can be adduced for the relationship between an increasing separation between high-status professional occupations and lower-status positions and between the projected IQs of those who hold such positions? Four interrelated historical factors and forces speak to this issue.

The first historical force has been the creation of primary and secondary labor markets in the United States and in the West, in general. This historical force has generated what is now called the "proletarianization of the workforce" (Morgan, 1986) in the West. Its result has been slow but accelerating segmentalization of the workforce, with a concomitant "deskilling" of laborers and a generalized degradation of the skills needed for any work (Braverman, 1974; Wood, 1982).

Primary and secondary labor markets are the creation of capitalist industrialization and the accompanying development of a wage labor system. In a system of fixed costs (that is, factories, machinery, power, raw goods, transportation), there is little room for economic upturns and downturns to affect deeply the flow of production. In such a system, the largest variable is *labor*. But not all labor is created equally. Some labor is more valuable than other forms of labor. The recognition of this truism led to "segmentalization," or the creation of wage markets comprised of *primary labor*, or "career-type jobs that are especially crucial, or which call for a high degree of skill and detailed knowledge" (Morgan, 1986, p. 284), and *secondary labor*, a labor force of "lower-skilled and lower-paid workers in offices, factories, and open-air work [such as construction]" (p. 285).

In the secondary labor market, the most elastic of the labor markets, the homogenization of the workforce in order to increase flexibility on the part of corporations has led to its deskilling (Gordon, Edwards, and Reich, 1982) and to the monotony and alienation of workers from their work so ably documented by Terkel (1982). These processes of segmentalization (even within occupations) and deskilling have continued unabated since before World War II (Berger and Piore, 1980; Gordon, Edwards and Reich, 1982; Piore, 1979).

The second historical force has been the relocation of the manufacturing base of the United States to the developing nations. In part, this relocation of the manufacturing base to countries with lower, or no, corporate taxes has been a successful search for cheaper wage labor markets on the part of multinational corporations. The relocation has not been without its costs for the developing nations, however (see, for example, Gladwin and Walter, 1980), since ecological degradation, worker exploitation, and corporate avoidance of accountability have followed in its wake. But the main issue has been the loss of manufacturing and heavy industry jobs for American workers. As a sad Bruce Springsteen song is paraphrased, a father tells his son that the jobs are going and will never come back. While Robert Reich (1983) argues that this loss will aid developing nations to bootstrap themselves via the creation of an economic base and that the United States will become an information and service-sector economy, it does little to sustain a strong middle class in the United States at the present time. This loss of mainstay manufacturing jobs has further eroded the middle class (alongside tax breaks for the very wealthy, coupled with a growing reluctance to engage the social question of a growing underclass), taking overseas those relatively well-paid positions and not replacing them within an increasingly divided, segmentalized labor force. Thus workers with a high school education find themselves with fewer and fewer choices about jobs, forced into a sharply deskilled labor market, and unable to compete for primary labor market positions that are themselves increasingly specialized. The transfer of the middle-class labor markets to foreign countries has thus created, at least in part, the "occupational partitioning" of which Herrnstein and Murray speak.

The third historical force has been the strengthening of the social class reproduction capabilities of the capitalist system, accompanied by the internecine and alienating struggles of the working class. The former situation was in part foretold by Karl Marx but with consequences unanticipated by him: the failure of workers to unite to end the control of the means of production and capital markets on the part of a narrow group of individuals. As the wage labor markets have segmentalized and become degraded, secondary labor jobs require fewer and fewer skills. As this has occurred, the workforce has been increasingly comprised of less-educated individuals, contributing to the compartmentalization, division, and partitioning of which Herrnstein and Murray speak. This situation is hardly a function of IQ, however, but rather a function of globalizing labor markets (transferred overseas), available jobs for the high school educated, and the increasing numbers of individuals able to enter college (and who can thus increase what Melvin Tumin (1985) called their "life chances," or abilities to enter the ranks of professionals in the primary labor markets).

The long-range outcome of this international job transfer and labor movement has been to reinforce and reproduce the class system in the United States (and other countries where this has occurred (Clegg, 1981; Clegg and Dunkerley, 1980). Those with the least education or opportunity are offered the least-skilled jobs; in turn, those are the same individuals who traditionally have had access to the least economic or educational opportunity, having come from (or dropped out of) schools that have been described as "factories for failure" (Rist, 1973). As Herrnstein and Murray quite accurately surmise, these workers, occupying the lowest-status jobs, are largely poor Whites, African Americans, and minorities. As they quite incorrectly deduce, the relegation to low-status jobs may have quite literally nothing to do with IQ but rather with educational opportunity and quality of schooling.

The fourth historical force is what Robert Michels (1949), a French sociologist, called the "iron law of oligarchy." The oligarchic theory predicts that under capitalism, capital, professional knowledge, and power will increasingly rest in the hands of a small number of individuals. Large corporations (or, indeed, organizations of any kind, but especially bureaucracies and quasi-bureaucracies) will create a primary labor market of a very narrow number of individuals who will hold virtually unbridled power over vast amounts of capital and very large numbers of secondary labor market workers. This narrowing of the number of decision-making professionals also has continued unabated for four or five decades and, indeed, has have accelerated coincidental to the rise of the great multinational corporations.

One "take," therefore, on the Herrnstein and Murray data, in addition to labeling their analyses as misleading if not downright false uses of data, is that labor markets—all labor markets, both primary and secondary—have been shifting in the West. That shift has been primarily responsible for the accelerating trends that Herrnstein and Murray discern between occupational status and the status of the poor and noncollege educated. In addition to the shifts in labor markets and the concomitant segmentalization of the labor force, the manufacturing base of the United States has relocated to developing nations, the historical patterns of the "iron law of oligarchy" (wherein capital and power become concentrated in the hands of a narrower and narrower number of individuals in the corporate world) and a social class system has reproduced, unchecked, due to the corporate attempt and need to create an "interchangeability of skills in the workplace" (Morgan, 1986, p. 378).

While Herrnstein and Murray do not ignore the fact of changing labor markets, their lack of sophistication—or their disingenuousness—about those markets has created an argument that once again blames the victims and that feeds the contemporary mood by providing a superficial and spurious, but widely legitimized, argument for derailing efforts to increase our commitments to the poor, minorities, and the marginalized. Rather than dealing with the consequences of corporate interests' creation and sustenance of a permanent underclass, they have chosen to ignore substantial bodies of research on labor, the creation of a managerial class via the appearance of a wage labor system, the growing phenomenon of "corporatism" (Benson, 1975), and the class-reproductive capabilities of capitalist bureaucracies such as the modern corporation and multinationals. That their arguments are racist, class-based, and contributory to intolerance and prejudice is well masked, even to numbers of the "cognitive elite" who will and have read the book without strong "deconstructive" skills, with little statistical expertise, and with a strong bent already toward seeing life in terms of *them* and *us*. As Herrnstein and Murray see race and socioeconomic status so clearly, it is odd, to say the least, that they also missed or chose to ignore significant troves of data on historical forces at work in the marketplace or the wage labor market.

And so I am left with two ineluctable conclusions: First, it may be true that IQ and occupations are related, but I and other readers are uncertain as to how, since the figures are not causally inferential but merely correlational, and in any event, Herrnstein and Murray have manipulated various forms of tests and test scores to arrive at IQ, when the tests are probably not comparable—a statistically and conceptually fraudulent task. The second conclusion regarding occupational stratification or partitioning is that, among the variables that might account for the correlation they have described (a statistically spurious set of operations), one of the largest set of arguments, the research on the historical effects of corporatism in the West, has been ignored or sidestepped. The influence of the historical forces associated with the rise of capitalism, wage labor markets, managerialism, and the class structure reproduction effects of the modern corporation all have been downplayed in the effort to paint low IQ (and indirectly, race and socioeconomic status) as determinants of occupational status. Ignored too have been the effects of consistent segregation, continued unequal schooling, tax laws that reinforce the privilege of the privileged, and the social "scapegoating" that attends economic downturn, loss of jobs and worker dislocation, structural unemployment, and political swings to the right. A disturbing socioeconomic decontextualization here induces the naive reader to accept pernicious biological determinism.

Herrnstein and Murray are probably guilty of a crime yet to be named but that I will call "statistical misconduct." Another generation down the road will regard their work with the same combination of intellectual disgust and fascination as we now hold for the proponents of the racially biased eugenics movement so popular in scientific and educational circles at the turn of the century (Selden, 1988).

References

Benson, J. K. (1975). The interorganizational network as a political economy. *Administrative Science Quarterly, 20,* 229-249.

Berger, S. and, Piore, M. J. (1980). *Dualism and discontinuity in industrial societies.* New York: Cambridge University Press.

Braverman, H. (1974). *Labor and monopoly capital.* New York: Monthly Review Press.

Clegg, S. (1981). Organization and control. *Administrative Science Quarterly, 26,* 545-562.

Clegg, S. and Dunkerley, D. (1980). *Organization, class and control.* London: Routledge and Kegan Paul.

Gladwin, T. N. and Walter, I. (1980). *Multinationals under fire.* New York: John Wiley and Sons.

Gordon, D. M., Edwards, R. C., and Reich, M. (1982). *Segmented work, divided workers.* New York: Cambridge University Press.

Herrnstein, R. J. and Murray, C. (1994). *The Bell Curve: Intelligence and class structure in American life.* New York: The Free Press.

House, E. R. and Haug, (1995). Riding *The Bell Curve:* A review. *Educational evaluation and policy analysis,* 17, (2), 263-272.

Michels, R. (1949). *Political parties.* New York: The Free Press.

Morgan, G. (1986). *Images of organization.* Thousand Oaks, CA: Sage Publications.

Murray, C. (1984). *Losing ground: American social policy 1950-1980.* New York: Basic Books.

Piore, M. (1979). *Birds of passage: Migrant labor in industrial society.* London: Cambridge University Press.

Reich, R. (1983). *The next American frontier.* New York: Times Books.

Rist, R. (1973). *The urban school: A factory for failure.* Cambridge, MA: MIT Press.

Selden, S. (1988). Biological determinism and the normal school curriculum: Helen Putnam and the NEA Committee on Racial Well-Being, 1910-1922. In Pinar, W. F., ed., *Contemporary curriculum discourses,* pp. 50-65. Scottsdale, AZ.: Gorsuch Scarisbrick.

Terkel, S. (1982). *Working.* New York: Avon.

Tumin, M. M. (1985). *Social stratification: The forms and functions of inequality,* 2nd ed. Englewood Cliffs, NJ: Prentice-Hall.

Wood, S., ed. (1982). *The degradation of work? Skill, deskilling and the labour process.* London: Hutchinson.

7 IQ as COMMODITY: THE "NEW" ECONOMICS of INTELLIGENCE

RICHARD CARY

MOTIVE:
RESEARCH AND DEVELOPMENT
FOR CORPORATE COLONIALISM

Motives as well as methods must be closely questioned in a critical reading of *The Bell Curve*. Herrnstein and Murray advance the notion that since intelligence determines efficiency, big business should be free to hire exclusively on the basis of IQ. In the third chapter, titled "The Economic Pressure to Partition," their thesis is simply put: Although education and other variables such as age, health, and job complexity influence work proficiency, the most important determinant by far is general intelligence, that is, the capacity scientists call *g* that IQ tests purport to measure. The authors hypothesize that the higher a person's IQ, the better job performance can be expected.

Herrnstein and Murray amass what they hope will be enough statistical evidence in support of this hypothesis also to qualify as a compelling scientific rationale to overturn the 1971 Supreme Court decision, *Griggs v. Duke Power*, 401 US 424 (1971). A legal cornerstone of affirmative action, this ruling proscribes discriminatory hiring practices based on general qualifications such as IQ tests and stipulates that hiring criteria must relate to specific job skills. Herrnstein and Murray argue that this legal fetter of social responsibility costs "the economy" billions of dollars annually. Their reading of selected research on this issue gives the conclusion that general intelligence is the best predictor of job performance. It follows that if big business could only use IQ as a criterion for hiring, it could be assured of hiring the most productive workers and thereby increase profits *without appreciably increasing production costs.* Profit without investment is a capitalist's dream come true, a dream so enticing that concerns about negative social, ethical, and legal consequences are silenced. IQ thus conceived becomes an economic commodity.

The tacit purpose of the book is to further the interests of corporate America, despite the inevitability of exacerbating the problems of racism. Herrnstein and Murray's narrow definition of what constitutes the economy reveals one subtle way this purpose is served. By covertly equating the economy with the economy's corporate sector, Herrnstein and Murray grant priority to the interests of the corporate establishment while subordinating the interests of the rest of society, which also participates in the economy.

To carry out this agenda, the authors erect a facade of indisputability from selected results of quantitative social science research. A detailed look behind this facade reveals that Herrnstein and Murray's strategies include questionable assumptions, fortuitous inaccuracies, systematic exaggerations of statistical evidence, misinterpretations of the meaning of that evidence, and inappropriate rejection of research findings that contradict their claims. The authors' evidence comes from studies aimed at developing increasingly efficient tests for predicting workers' productivity. A review of this research base reveals that the tone of certainty achieved in the third chapter is demonstrably counterfeit. The present examination also reviews the statistical methods of correlation and meta-analysis to demonstrate how Herrnstein and Murray exploit quantitative research methods to create an economics of intelligence dedicated exclusively to the interests of big business. That they do so without counting the costs to other interests indicates that Herrnstein and Murray disengage social science from the moral dimensions of the issue. Other concerns focus on accuracy, fairness, and quality of scholarship, not only of the authors, but also of the research they cite.

EXAGGERATED COSTS OF NOT HIRING TOP DOWN ON IQ

Herrnstein and Murray's main stratagem is to present estimates of the cost of regulations that prevent American big business from hiring exclusively on the basis IQ tests. These alarmingly high estimates are misleading and, in some instances, inaccurate. The authors do not actually calculate estimates themselves. They cite figures from another study. Hunter and Hunter (1984) estimated losses to employers at a minimum of $13 billion and a maximum of $80 billion in 1980. In contrast, a 1989 study fixed the range far less, at $1.5 to $10 billion in 1980 dollars. This major study, titled "Fairness in Employment Testing: Validity Generalization, Minority Issues, and the General Aptitude Test Battery" was commissioned by the National Research Council and edited by Hartigan and Wigdor.

Even the minimum figure Herrnstein and Murray cite from the Hunter and Hunter study is exaggerated. The $13 billion was a preliminary estimate later adjusted for inflation (Hartigan and Wigdor, 1989, p. 240). The corrected figure is $10.75 billion. Although this may be dismissed as a minor discrepancy on such a large scale, fair practice in the presentation of quantitative evidence demands that evidence be accurate and complete. This is one of a series of inaccuracies that seem to operate inexorably in Herrnstein and Murray's favor.

Herrnstein and Murray also indulge in a less-than-subtle ploy that, in one sense, is aggressive advocacy but in another seems to be deceptive manipulation. They refer to the costs estimates as "losses to the economy." Use of the term "losses" implies that American business actually had $80 billion in hand but let it slip through its fingers due to unwise hiring procedures imposed by a meddlesome government bureaucracy bent on restricting free enterprise. The term "losses" is not widely used in productivity prediction research. Hartigan and Wigdor (1989) refer to these amounts as "gains." Hunter and Hunter (1984) use the term "productivity differences." The term's change of valence, apparently reversed for the purpose of bolstering their argument, sparks suspicions about the authors' credibility.

To further bolster their arguments, Herrnstein and Murray accept Hunter and Hunter's larger cost figures and reject the smaller amounts of the Hartigan and Wigdor group. Superficially, this seems to be an effective tactic, for the higher the estimate, the louder the cry of alarm that can be raised. The greater the "losses," the more likely it is that extreme measures enacted as remedies, no matter how draconian, will appear justifiable, find acquiescence, and gain acceptance as a commonsense solution to a dire business problem. However, Herrnstein and Murray's degree of confidence in the Hunter and Hunter figures is unwarranted. Hunter and Hunter made an assumption that resulted in systematic overestimation of the correlation between IQ test and job performance by as much as 25 percent to 35 percent, a very large error (Hartigan and Wigdor, 1989, p. 170). Specifically, in their calculations of cost estimates, Hunter and Hunter used a formula that assumes employers hire at random in the entire population. This means that everyone in the United States is an applicant for each and every job opening, which is absurd. Employers hardly run nationwide lotteries to fill jobs. Some criteria are virtually always established: grades, references, age, physical abilities, interviews, even IQ scores. Moreover, people self-select for jobs according to their own estimates of their abilities, interests, and aspirations. It is counter-intuitive to believe that these criteria can be construed as random procedures operating like the standard normal curve, a.k.a. "the bell curve."

In fact, the standard normal curve does not realistically describe applicants for jobs. If it did, the formula for calculating the costs of not hiring top down on IQ would not work. Since the mean of the standard normal curve is zero, the mean IQ test score of job applicants would therefore be zero. Using zero for the value called for in the formula results in gains of $0.00, or in Herrnstein and Murray's term "losses" of zero. Hartigan and Wigdor (1989) suggest this challenge to Hunter and Hunter's assumption.

Another problem with estimates of financial gains is that if American business accepts Herrnstein and Murray's plan to hire applicants with the highest IQ scores, it should also ask what these applicants were doing prior to their successful job search. Did they hatch from a nest of convenient assumptions? More likely, given their high ability, they worked at other jobs. If indeed they worked previously, then it must be recognized that gains to the economy would be offset by corresponding losses in productivity in the jobs that the able workers vacated. There is also the cost of training replacements. Hunter and Hunter, and therefore Herrnstein and Murray, ignore this inconvenience. Their naive reliance on figures crunched indiscriminately from a mathematical formula founded on untenable assumptions continues the misuse of quantitative methods characteristic of knee-jerk naive positivism, the unquestioned belief that science can answer all questions.

EXAGGERATED ASSOCIATIONS BETWEEN IQ AND PRODUCTIVITY

If exaggerated cost estimates are to produce their desired effect, Herrnstein and Murray's case must include research-based evidence of a strong relationship between IQ and job performance. They make the claim often that a strong relationship exists. However, the authors' attempts to support this assertion fail because they misinterpret research results. From their readings of job performance prediction research, Herrnstein and Murray characterize the correlation between general intelligence and productivity as strong, consistent over time, consistent across all income levels, and consistent across all job skill levels from menial to professional. These interpretations are misleading. For example, the authors place great emphasis on the claim that intelligence is a strong predictor of job performance at all levels of job complexity (p. 65). However, they cite research findings that indicate precisely the opposite. They provide a table on page 73 (adapted from Hunter and Hunter, 1984) that lists correlation coefficients indicating strength of relationships between test scores and measures of performance on jobs of five different complexity levels. This table contains figures that directly contradict their claim. Specifically, the test/performance correlation for the most complex job category, management, is $r = .58$; for the least complex job, loading and unloading machinery, $r = .23$. Yet they conclude from comparing the two correlation coefficients that the test/performance correlation is strong regardless of job complexity. This is nonsense. A correlation coefficient that is less than half of another r is not comparable to it and therefore not indicative of a consistently strong relationship. The relationship is neither strong nor consistent: It differs by more than half between complexity levels.

INTERPRETING CORRELATION COEFFICIENTS

The Pearson Product-Moment correlation coefficient is a measure of the degree of relationship between two quantitative variables. Although other types of correlation coefficients exist, the Pearson is the most frequently used in research. Other types are mathematically related to the Pearson r and are interpreted essentially the same way. Correlation coefficients can vary between + 1.0 for a direct correlation and - 1.0 for an indirect correlation. Direct correlation means that if a person obtains a high score on one measure, he or she would be expected to have a high score on the other measure. Herrnstein and Murray offer the stock example of height and weight: Taller people usually weigh more. Indirect correlation is the inverse. A high score on one measure is accompanied by a low score on the second measure. An example is number of errors on an exam and grade. The strength of the relationship is indicated by how close the correlation coefficient is to 1.0, regardless of the sign. A value of $r = .00$ indicates no relationship at all between the two variables. A correlation coefficient of $r = .80$ or above normally indicates strong association. A value of $r = .50$ usually indicates a moderate relationship. An $r = .20$ usually is considered weak. It should be cautioned, however, that there are no absolute rules for determining the strength of a particular coefficient in practical applications. It depends on the seriousness of the circumstances. Criteria for tests of the reliability of airplane engines, for example, should be held to the very highest standards. An important point concerning interpretation of correlation coefficients should be underscored: Correlation does not conclusively prove causality. This places a serious limitation on job performance prediction research, which relies almost exclusively on correlation.

It also should be noted that a correlation coefficient is not a percentage. To interpret a correlation coefficient correctly, it should be squared. The resulting value, called the coefficient of determination, indicates the percentage of common variance between two correlated variables. Common variance refers to the percentage of the differences in one set of scores that is attributable to differences in a second correlated set of measures.

MISINTERPRETING CORRELATION COEFFICIENTS

Herrnstein and Murray's claims deteriorate when the coefficients on which they are based are interpreted correctly. The coefficient of determination for their evidence (*the* $r = .58$) that intelligence and job performance are strongly related for the most complex jobs is only $r^2 = .336$. This means that only 33.6 percent of the difference in workers' job performance in complex jobs is accounted for by intelligence differences among the workers. This leaves a large amount of job performance variation unexplained, 66.4 percent to be exact. In other words, almost two-thirds of the differences among workers' productivity is *not* related to differences among them on IQ. For low-complexity jobs, intelligence differences account for only about 5 percent ($r = .23^2$). Typically in quantitative research, a figure of 5 percent is regarded as occurring by chance and not indicative of any true relationship between variables. Herrnstein and Murray clearly exaggerate the strength of these figures. Correlation of $r = .58$ indicates only moderate association. The correlation coefficient $r = .23$ is actually relatively weak. To Herrnstein and Murray, however, $r = .23$ looms strong. In fairness, it should be reemphasized that the enlightened attitude on interpretation is to leave to the reader the responsibility of evaluating the strength of a statistic within a reasonable range in the applied context. Herrnstein and Murray stretch this range beyond credibility.

STATISTICAL EVIDENCE OR HARDCORE LEGERDEMAIN?

The linchpin of Herrnstein and Murray's statistical evidence of the relationship between IQ and job performance is a single number, the correlation coefficient $r = .4$. Three questions emerge: (1) how did this value of r originate?; (2) what *does* $r = .4$ mean with regard to IQ tests and productivity?; and (3) how do Herrnstein and Murray use this figure to support their thesis? The answers seriously undermine their case.

Herrnstein and Murray conclude that the overall correlation coefficient for the relationship between scores on tests of cognitive ability and job performance measures is $r = .4$ (p. 72). They portray this figure as indicative of a strong relationship with "large economic implications." However, they studiously avoid using the widely accepted coefficient of determination, r^2, to interpret the strength of the correlation coefficient. The reason for their aversion is immediately apparent why when the value $r = .4$ is squared. The result, $r^2 = .16$, means that only 16 percent of the variation in workers' job performance is related to scores on intelligence tests. Contrary to Herrnstein and Murray's claims, this evidence does not creditably establish a strong relationship between general intelligence and job performance. In fact, this association is relatively weak by most standards. Certainly $r = .4$ is too weak to use as a basis for calculating the costs of not hiring top down on IQ and promoting the reversal of affirmative action programs when doing so has the dire consequences of furthering racism and its attendant problems. Herrnstein and Murray's exaggeration of the strength of the correlation between IQ and job performance is the primary basis for skepticism about their work.

A second basis is the curious provenance of the correlation coefficient $r = .4$. The correlation coefficient $r = .4$ appears to derive from the meta-analytic study of productivity prediction research by Hunter and Hunter (1984). The meta-analysis integrated the results of 425 studies of performance prediction that used the General Aptitude Test Battery (GATB), a test used by the U.S. Labor Department. The average correlation coefficient for all studies was $r = .45$. Herrnstein and Murray accept Hunter and Hunter's work but lower their overall figure to $r = .4$. In a footnote, they mention that unspecified "corrections" were applied. Consistent with their failure to substantiate other claims, no further details are provided.

The difference of 0.05 in the two correlation coefficients may seem negligible in the abstract. However, since Herrnstein and Murray ascribe profound economic implications to the correlation between IQ and job performance and are willing to risk the consequences of increased racism, they should be precise, not cavalier with numerical data. A pattern emerges in the third chapter which suggests that the authors are precise when it is favorable to their case and less so when precision is detrimental. This capriciousness is evident in the reasons they give for accepting Hunter and Hunter's meta-analysis and their corresponding rejection of the conflicting results of another meta-analysis of research on the same topic, the Hartigan and Wigdor study. These are the same two studies on which Herrnstein and Murray based estimates of the costs of not hiring top down on IQ.

The two studies produced dramatically different correlations between test score and job performance. Hunter and Hunter found a moderate correlation coefficient of $r = .45$ between the GATB and work performance. The Hartigan and Wigdor committee found a weak correlation coefficient of only $r = .25$. This is a large difference. It should be recalled that the correlation coefficient, when squared, gives the percentage of variation in one set of scores that is due to the other variable. The results of the Hunter and Hunter meta-analysis mean that scores on the GATB, the major cognitive ability test used by the U.S. Department of Labor, account for only about 20 percent of the differences in workers' proficiency. The Hartigan and Wigdor committee found that cognitive test scores account for only about 6 percent. Although neither measure indicates a strong relationship between general cognitive ability and work performance, the larger of the two coefficients works more in favor of Herrnstein and Murray's agenda by permitting larger estimates of the costs of not hiring top down on IQ.

Using the equation for calculating gains from hiring (top down on IQ to be cited), the use of the smaller r value would yield much smaller dollar estimates. As we have seen, a central feature of their argument is the estimate that the costs of not allowing corporations to hire unilaterally top down on IQ tests reach as high as $80 billion. Accepting the correlation coefficient of $r = .25$ from the Hartigan and Wigdor meta-analysis would deflate this cost estimate considerably. Hunter and Hunter's cost estimate was calculated by the formula from Brogden (1946):

$$G = (r)(s)(A)$$

where $G =$ dollar gain per worker per year due to hiring top down on test score; $r =$ correlation between test and performance; $s =$ standard deviation of yearly productivity in dollars; and $A =$ average test score of applicants hired standardized.

QUESTIONING CLAIMS BASED ON META-ANALYSIS

Herrnstein and Murray's preference for the higher correlation found by Hunter and Hunter is no mystery. However, a review of the reasons they offer for rejecting the Hartigan and Wigdor committee's results and an examination of the basics of meta-analysis reveal that the bases for their confidence in the Hunter and Hunter study are unsound. The purpose of a meta-analysis is to integrate the accumulated findings, many of which may differ, of all studies on an issue in order to determine what the research means as a whole. The purpose is the same as a narrative review of literature. Meta-analysis offers greater precision. Herrnstein and Murray present the methodology of meta-analysis as if it were one unified set of established procedures. Instead, however, there are at least three distinct approaches to meta-analysis. Although there are methodological controversies among the adherents of each, all three are valuable research tools. Each has been used successfully to gain increased understanding by integrating research findings on a variety of issues.

The initial methodology, developed by Glass and others in the 1970s, defines meta-analysis broadly as an "attitude" that accepts the legitimacy of combining quantitative results of individual studies and analyzing their accretionary meaning. A variety of statistical tools may be used to summarize, integrate, and interpret the group of research findings. Glass and his associates used meta-analysis to study the research on such topics as the effects of class size on academic achievement and the effects of psychotherapy compared to the effects of psychotherapeutic drugs. In 1981 Glass, Barry McGaw, and Mary Lee Smith published a detailed account of their approach, *Meta-analysis in Social Research.*

Meta-analysis begins with the identification of an issue on which study outcomes markedly disagree. The researcher subsequently locates all possible studies, including fugitive studies, theses and dissertations, and even those of questionable quality. To exclude any study a priori is to open the meta-analysis to the same sources of error described as mortality in experimental designs and has the same effect as ignoring a sizable population segment in a survey. Also, including all possible studies increases the power of the meta-analysis in the same way that increasing the sample size increases statistical power and generalizability in experiments. The subjects in a meta-analysis are the studies themselves. The data are the outcomes of each study, usually group means in experiments or correlation coefficients in correlational studies. A meta-analysis does not, as is sometimes believed, reanalyze the original data of the studies. To be comparable, study outcomes are transformed to the same scale. The quantitative outcome of an experiment becomes an effect size, or *ES*. The *ES* is determined by finding the difference between the experimental group mean and the control group mean and standardizing this difference by dividing it by the control group standard deviation. The formula is

$$\underline{ES} = \frac{\overline{X}_e - \overline{X}_c}{S_c},$$

where $\overline{X}_c$ = control group mean, $\overline{X}_e$ = experimental group mean, and S_c = standard deviation of the control group.

This puts the study outcome in standard score form so it can be compared readily to results from other studies that may have used different measures. For correlational studies, the Pearson Product Moment correlation coefficient is the effect size.

When all *ES*s are transformed and assembled, there usually are considerable differences among *ES* values. The meta-analysis begins the task of determining the cause(s) of this variation. The researcher wants to determine if the variation in *ES* values is the result of influences extraneous to the variables under study or to the variables themselves. For example, in Glass's meta-analysis of the effects of class size on student achievement, it is feasible that at least part of the *ES* variation might have been due to variables such as parental income, per-pupil expenditure, geographic region, or to study characteristics such as quality controls and year the study was published. However, Glass was interested only in the effects of class size, not these extraneous variables. In Glassian meta-analysis, the causes of *ES* variation are actually determined quantitatively, not merely assumed. The researcher records and codes the values of any theoretical variables and any study characteristics in each study that may plausibly contribute to *ES* variation. Determination of the extent of variation due to extraneous variables is then made quantitatively, usually through regression analysis. Knowing the causes of *ES* differences allows the researcher to exclude the effects of causes that have nothing to do with the variable under study. For example, if Glass had found that the *ES* variation in his study was due to parental income and per-pupil expenditure, he could have made adjustments to separate the effects of class size alone on academic achievement. In productivity prediction research, extraneous variables such as gender, age of the worker, motivation, workplace safety, and salary may significantly affect measures of performance. If the researcher is interested in determining the influence of IQ on productivity, the effects of extraneous variables must be separated from the effects of IQ. When extraneous variation is accounted for and adjustments made, in theory, the average *ES* value may be regarded as true.

There proved to be some sources of bias in Glass's methods, however. To counter these problems, a second approach to meta-analysis was developed by Larry Hedges and associates during the 1980s (Hedges and Olkin, 1985). Hedges's work removed some sources of bias and established a sound mathematical basis for meta-analysis as an inference-sufficient methodology. This means that the quantitative outcomes of meta-analysis can be correctly generalized from the study to the population. In theory, certain conditions must be met for an inference to be valid. One of these is homogeneity of variance, the assumption that the variances of the populations from which samples are drawn are equal. All but the smallest departures from equal variance can produce large errors in quantitative research. Statistical methods are available to test homogeneity of variance. One of Hedges' contributions was incorporating these methods in meta-analysis to allow more confident inferences.

A third methodological approach to meta-analysis was developed by John Hunter and Frank Schmidt and described in their 1990 *Methods of Meta-analysis*. This is the same John Hunter who coauthored the 1984 meta-analysis of job performance prediction research that Herrnstein and Murray rely on so heavily. Hunter and Schmidt's method of meta-analysis is similar to the Glass and Hedges versions. Study findings are expressed as *ES*s or as correlation coefficients, but Hunter and Schmidt do not stipulate that all possible studies should be located. Another exception, perhaps the most significant departure from the other practices, is that Hunter and Schmidt preemptively exclude *ES* variation before data analysis by mathematically transforming *ES values* to eradicate *assumed* variation. Hunter and Schmidt refer to possible extraneous causes of variation as "artifacts" and to the transformations of ES values as "corrections."

Hunter and Schmidt's practice of changing data is controversial. Some methodologists believe that transforming data to remove variation is itself a source of error and should be performed only when the effects of an extraneous variable are precisely known, not merely presumed. This practice may obscure subtle interactions, suppress meaningful diversity, and suggest greater certainty than is warranted. Also, eliminating some of the ES values because they might vary is tantamount to the a priori exclusion of studies, which is contrary to accepted procedures. In a meta-analysis, the goal is to find out what the accumulated research says, not what *part* of the research says. Researchers who wish to make a valid inference to a population know that no segment of the population should be excluded. To do so creates an error that inevitably changes the outcome.

The purpose of this critique is not to resolve these issues. Rather, it is to reveal how Herrnstein and Murray ignore significant implications of these methodological issues in their choice of the Hunter and Hunter figures over those of Hartigan and Wigdor, whose study provided a less advantageous basis for exaggerated cost estimates. Herrnstein and Murray present the Hunter and Hunter study as methodologically correct and the Hartigan and Wigdor study as methodologically flawed. Despite claims to the contrary, however, neither study is completely flawed nor completely infallible. It is interesting to note that John Hunter served as an advisory liaison to the Hartigan and Wigdor study that produced results contrasting with those of his own earlier study.

CORRECTING FOR ARTIFACTS: LEVELING MOUNTAINS OR MOLEHILLS?

According to Herrnstein and Murray, they prefer the Hunter and Hunter figures because they were corrected for artifacts and therefore more sources of error were controlled than in Hartigan and Wigdor's study. Herrnstein and Murray place great emphasis on correction of one artifact in particular, range restriction. They attribute the difference between the findings of the Hunter and Hunter study and the Hartigan and Wigdor study to this artifact. As usual, they present no data to support their speculation.

Range restriction can indeed be a source of error in correlational research. If a set of measures has little room to vary, for mathematical reasons, its correlation coefficient with another set of measures will be attenuated. Correlation coefficients quantitatively express the degree to which differences in one variable are associated with differences in another variable. An example of how range restriction operates is the relationship between weight and Sumo wrestling ability. In the general population, there is a broad range of weight and, in all likelihood, a broad range of Sumo ability. Mathematically, a high correlation coefficient is possible. In professional Sumo circles, however, virtually all wrestlers are large and have high ability levels. Since there is little variation, correlation coefficients will be small and misleading.

Range restriction is also a problem in productivity prediction research. All applicants are given a test that the company hopes will predict the most productive workers. The highest-scoring workers are then hired. Researchers later measure their job performances and correlate them with test scores. The problem is that successful applicants, i.e., those hired, are compared to the entire group of applicants, including unsuccessful ones. The entire group has a broader range of IQ scores than the hired applicants, whose scores are higher and distributed over a more restricted range.

The purpose of the range restriction correction is to nullify mathematically the effects of this inequality between the two groups. Unequivocally, the most mathematically sound way to calculate this correction factor is to compare the ratio of the standard deviation of test scores for all applicants to the standard deviation of scores of the hired workers. Hunter and Hunter do not correct this way. Instead of using the standard deviation of the GATB scores of the applicants in the studies in their meta-analysis, they use the standard deviation for everyone in the entire population who ever took the GATB. As noted earlier, this substitution makes the untenable assumption that the entire U.S. population applies for every job opening. This assumption would be plausible only as a last resort if a study report does not include standard deviation data. The Hartigan and Wigdor committee recommends that in the absence of such data, researchers should use the standard deviation(sd) of scores of qualified job applicants grouped on the basis of similar job types.

More important, as the Hartigan and Wigdor committee found, the correction method adopted by Hunter and Hunter artificially inflates the correlation coefficient between test and job performance by 25 percent to 35 percent (p. 170). This tendency to inflate the value of r erroneously is the most serious methodological flaw in Herrnstein and Murray's case. If Hunter and Hunter's finding of $r = .45$ is deflated by 35 percent, the corrected figure would be about $r = .29$, which approximates the figure from the Hartigan and Wigdor study. This deflated r dramatically reduces Herrnstein and Murray's cost estimates and deflates some of the anti-affirmative action hysteria and tunnel-visioned ardor for easy profits that their claims elicit.

The importance of range restriction as a source of error is subject to question. While range restriction can cause some problems in a correlational study and in a meta-analysis, it does not account for enough ES variation to merit the importance Herrnstein and Murray attribute to it as the sole basis for rejection of the lower findings. There are other sources of error in research, only some of which can be mathematically corrected. These include (1) sampling error, (2) differences in the reliability of the testing instrument, (3) instrument validity differences, and (4) human error, such as typographical, transcriptional, and computational mistakes. Instrument validity and human errors are, in practice, uncontrollable. However, mathematical adjustments are available for sampling error and instrument reliability. Of all the sources of error, sampling error by far contributes the most extraneous variation. In fact, one of the most prominent developers of meta-analysis estimated that sampling error accounts for more than 90 percent of the extraneous variation in *ES* and, further, that ignoring correction for range restriction would probably not change the outcome of a meta-analysis. Who was this prominent methodologist? It was none other than Herrnstein and Murray's *eminence gris,* John Hunter (Schmidt, Hunter, and Caplan, 1981). Also, in their 1990 book on meta-analysis, Hunter and Schmidt state that artifact correction in meta-analysis typically produces only slight changes in *ES* sets and should be considered to yield approximation rather than precision (p. 179).

Other questions should be raised in regard to corrections for influences of extraneous variables. In performance prediction research, although researchers typically correct for instrument reliability and range restriction, they seldom correct for sampling error. This leaves their research open to the greatest error. Not correcting for sampling error makes Glass and Hedges's stipulation of including all possible studies in meta-analysis even more critical. This practice, which Hunter and Hunter did not use, minimizes the effects of sampling error because the larger the sample, the more closely it matches the population. The more closely the sample approximates the population, the less error the sample contains.

Another concern with the Hunter and Hunter meta-analysis is their assumption that all dependent variables, the operationally defined measures of job performance, are linearly equatable and may therefore be included in the same *ES* set for analysis and interpretation. In productivity prediction research, indicators of job performance are measures such as work sample analyses, error rates, supervisors' ratings, peer workers' ratings, and so on. It is not defensible to treat these measures as linearly equivalent. For example, supervisors have an interest in increasing productivity and rate employees accordingly. Peer workers, on the other hand, may not be as ambitious. Not wanting to be compared unfavorably to a highly productive fellow worker, they could conceivably find faults and express them in ratings.

NOTHING ELSE IS AN IQ TEST

Another weakness in Herrnstein and Murray's assessment of productivity research is the claim that tests purporting to measure vocational abilities are, to use their phrase, "tantamount to intelligence tests" (p. 75). They provide no data to support this claim, as usual. The GATB, which the U.S. Department of Labor uses to assess workers' employability, the Armed Forces Qualification Test (AFQT), and the Armed Services Vocational Aptitude Battery (ASVAB) are three of the most important tests in job performance prediction research. Scores on these tests constitute an enormous database. The ASVAB, for example, is administered to all recruits entering the armed forces. These tests are composed of subtests, each of which tap a different skill or ability. An overall test score and scores for each subtest are computed. Herrnstein and Murray believe that the *overall* score is equivalent to an IQ test (p. 75). They allude to a number of studies, uncited as usual, that conclude that these three tests measure general intelligence, *g*. Presumably such studies report high correlations between scores on them with scores on an established IQ test. Correlation between two tests is a measure of their congruent validity, or the degree to which they measure or discriminate the same characteristics. Congruent validity is determined if the tester is interested in developing a less expensive or less time-consuming means of gathering information. Congruent validity data is most likely to be readily available if indeed the three vocational tests are equivalent to IQ tests. However, in their third chapter, Herrnstein and Murray specify no congruent validity data between IQ tests and any of the three vocational abilities tests in their arsenal.

Even if they provided data, other concerns remain. One is that since correlation does not prove causality, even a high correlation between two tests does not establish their absolute equality. Another difficulty with equating overall vocational abilities test scores and IQ tests is that the former are composed of some subtests that are far too specific and experience-based to constitute valid measures of general intelligence. The ASVAB's subtests, for example, include tests for "electronics information" and for "auto and shop information." Both subtest scores are mathematical components of the overall ASVAB score that Herrnstein and Murray regard as tantamount to IQ. The primary purpose of the three tests is to sort out workers for industry and the military, not to find intelligence quotients. Scores on the three tests are not designated IQ scores by the military or others. The *Eleventh Mental Measurements Yearbook* (1992), edited by Kramer and Conoley, the venerable catalog of tests, does not list among its tests of intelligence and scholastic aptitude any of the three tests that Herrnstein and Murray regard as "tantamount to IQ tests."

POOR REPORTING

Another problem with Herrnstein and Murray's book, especially their third chapter, is that it contains poor reporting. *The Bell Curve*, strictly speaking, is not social science research. It is commentary based on scientific research. Nevertheless, this commentary should reflect the commitment to objectivity and fairness that science holds as its ideal. However, as I have shown, the authors indulge in the ploy of excluding data contradictory to their ideas, often on questionable pretexts. Failure to provide details to substantiate their claims is a hallmark of at least poor writing, if not devious argument as well. For example, they reduce the body of job performance prediction research to three interpretations that they present as widely recognized conclusions. These are (1) job performance is predicted better by broad-based intelligence tests that measure specific job skills; (2) the reason intelligence tests predict job performance is that they measure *g*, that is, general intelligence; and (3) the higher correlations between intelligence tests and job performance that have been found since 1980 have profound economic consequences. These conclusions are drawn from published quantitative studies that report specific numerical values to describe relationships observed between the variables alluded to in the three statements. Herrnstein and Murray, however, fail to cite the figures to support their claims. They have chosen to state the three conclusions "qualitatively" because, although unnamed experts in the field agree that the three relationships exist, these experts often disagree about the numbers (p. 71). Lack of consensus about the numbers is a preposterous reason to exclude specific figures. Researchers arrive at differing results in every field of inquiry. Appraisal of equivocal findings is part of research of any type. The fact that Herrnstein and Murray fail to substantiate their claims in detail is poor reporting. Further, the fact that they appear actually to believe that a such a specious reason absolves them from routine scholarly obligations indicates a patronizing disingenuousness that must stem from insecurity about the validity of their claims. It suggests a deceptive tendency to obscure details that, if not suppressed, might contradict their strained interpretations.

The book is also riddled with inaccuracies, at least one of which ironically highlights its arrogance. In an appendix jocularly titled "Statistics for People Who Are Sure They Can't Learn Statistics," Herrnstein and Murray explain basic concepts in statistics, including correlation. They also provide shorter, one-topic instructional windows in the text and in footnotes. In the explanation on page 674 of the components of the Pearson formula, there is an error that explains why some people are sure they can't learn statistics, especially from Herrnstein and Murray. Following their explanation for the formula will produce a correlation coefficient of $r = 0$ each time, every time. The explanation of the terms in the formula fails to explain the symbol for the designation of the averages for the variables to be correlated, X and Y. The symbol, a line directly above each term, is correctly printed in the formula. However, for readers unfamiliar with statistics, the error in the explanation is a potential source of bewilderment and frustration.

Herrnstein and Murray also neglect the statistical significance of the correlation coefficients from the studies on which their interpretations are based. Statistical significance is a mathematical way of determining the degree of confidence that a study's numerical outcomes did not occur by chance. Significance data were undoubtedly reported in many, if not all, of the original studies that

Herrnstein and Murray could have used. Their failure to cite or to mention the degree to which they considered these data in their conclusions is a departure from the norms of good writing and fair scholarship. It raises suspicions that statistical significance data might have countervailed their claims.

CONCERNS ABOUT PRODUCTIVITY PREDICTION RESEARCH

The methods of productivity prediction research are subject to criticism. Virtually all productivity prediction studies use the same design and statistical analysis tools. Typically, a group of applicants is given an ability test intended to predict which applicants will become the best workers. The performances of those hired are later quantified by a variable such as supervisor's ratings, work sample analyses, error rates, and so on. These measures are statistically correlated with test scores yielding an indication of how accurately the test predicts job performance. In theory, a high positive correlation indicates that applicants with high scores will likely be proficient workers and applicants with low scores will tend to be poor workers. A test with a high correlation to work performance can be a profitable tool for employers.

One problem is that correlation coefficients are not the strongest statistical tools. Measures of any two variables can be plugged into the statistical formula. Even though computed correctly, the resulting correlation coefficient may or may not be meaningful. Statistical evidence can be produced to establish a relationship between virtually any two variables, no matter how implausible their association. Moreover, correlation usually is deployed early in the development of a field of inquiry to identify potential relationships among variables for further study by more precise methods. Correlation is an entry-level method, not an endgame.

Another limitation of this body of research is its virtually exclusive use of univariate designs. Typically, a productivity prediction study correlates a single variable that measures job performance with a test score that putatively measures ability. Job performance variables are studied one at a time, as if they operated in isolation. This reductionistic practice paints a simplistic picture. Reality, to the extent that it is composed of people's behaviors and experiences in social contexts, is a complex of phenomena teeming with variables that constantly change and interact. Many factors could influence job performance: salary, health, age, time of day, and so on. Multivariate statistical methods are available to study how several variables operate simultaneously to affect a measurable outcome such as job performance. While multivariate methods are by no means golden paths to truth, they offer greater sophistication to productivity research, by making it more sensitive to the complexities of its real-world context. This capacity would make its findings less vulnerable to misinterpretation by showing that categorical statements based on univariate correlation are instead conditional due to the highly interactive nature of the variables in job performance. No research is perfect; it is clear, however, that Herrnstein and Murray have placed too much confidence in inquiry conducted with limited methods and tools.

It also should be asked whose interests are favored in productivity prediction research. Job performance prediction studies are unquestionably aimed at increasing corporate profits. This is their only purpose and, most would agree, a legitimate one. However, there is a meretricious air to the masquerade of mercantile research and development as disinterested social science. Especially in this present case, wherein quantitative methods are used to address an issue that has such significant moral implications. Social science has a broader agenda than increasing corporate profits. Its agenda focuses instead on increasing basic understanding of human experience and developing more altruistic applications for its findings.

THE BELL CURVE AS A SYMBOL OF SCIENCE'S AUTHORITY

Herrnstein and Murray assume the authority of science to be so certain and so absolute that questions of its legitimacy are silenced. They hope the guise of objective social science imbues their case with this aura of indisputability. The authors long for the old regime, naive positivism's halcyon days when science was exalted as the single source of authorized knowledge. The bell curve is a symbol of its former status. It is polysemous—not a singular sign. The challenge of the new perspective is to discover the array of meanings that a symbol signifies. Although it has entered the popular animus as a symbol of science's entrenched power and procrustean misfeasance, the bell curve is a useful tool. It permits calculation of the odds of occurrence of a conceivable event. But as an intellectual tool, it cannot escape its status as a text, a theoretical construct, mindcraft contrived for prediction. Like all texts, it is open to question.

THE BELL CURVE'S UNRESOLVED DISSONANCE WITH THE MORAL DIMENSION

In separating the enterprise of science from its connection to morality, Herrnstein and Murray forfeit considerable advantage. A science contextualized in the whole of human affairs, a science cognizant of the conjunction of facts and values can be more powerful and useful than fetishistic obsession with results from purported value-free, objective methodologies. Herrnstein and Murray's approach to this complex issue reconfigures it in simplistic, absolute terms. They tacitly impose a false dichotomy that forces a choice between scientific understanding of IQ and productivity and the moral ramifications of that understanding. Their presumption that science, not moral and legal forms of knowledge, has final authority to designate answers removes the issue of the role of intelligence in job performance from the human context where it actually occurs. It also removes the concept of justice from this arena of lived experience. A fixed hierarchy of knowledge with science ascendant is the shibboleth of the cult within the academic community and its environs that limits its perspective to naive positivism. This group has acquiesced to the depredations of corporate colonialism. Their narrow vision not only denies connections between the moral and the scientific dimensions of an issue, it vitiates each domain. This distorted vision recognizes no possibility of integrating science and ethics in the context of human experience. This is the ultimate reason *The Bell Curve* fails, not the many flaws in its argument from quantitative evidence.

References

Brogden, H. E. (1946). On the interpretation of the correlation coefficient as a measure of predictive efficiency. *Journal of Educational Psychology, 2,* 171-183.

Glass, G. V., McGaw, B., and Smith, M. L. (1981). *Meta-analysis in social research.* Beverly Hills, CA: Sage.

Hartigan, J. A. and Wigdor, A. K., eds. (1989). *Fairness in employment testing: Validity generalization, minority issues, and the General Aptitude Test battery.* Washington, D.C.: National Academy Press.

Hedges, L. and Olkin, I. (1985). *Statistical methods for meta-analysis.* Orlando, Academic Press.

Herrnstein, R. J. and Murray, C. (1994). *The Bell Curve: Intelligence and class structure in American life.* New York: The Free Press.

Hunter, J. E. and Hunter, R. F. (1984). Validity and utility of alternative predictors of job performance. *Psychological Bulletin, 96,* 72-98.

Hunter, J. E. and Schmidt, F. L. (1990). *Methods of meta-analysis.* Newbury Park, CA: Sage.

Kramer, J. J. and Conoley, J. C., eds. (1992). *Eleventh mental measurements Yearbook.* Lincoln, NE: The Buros Institute of Mental Measurements.

Schmidt, F. L., Hunter, J. E., and Caplan, J. R. (1981). Validity generalization of results for two occupations in the petroleum industry. *Journal of Applied Psychology, 66,* 261-273.

8 IN THE NAME OF SCIENCE AND OF GENETICS AND OF *THE BELL CURVE:* WHITE SUPREMACY IN AMERICAN SCHOOLS

LADISLAUS SEMALI

My response to chapter 4 of The Bell Curve focuses on the most fundamental claim of the book: that people are slotted into places that fit their intelligence or cognitive ability. These claims are not absolute science and are by no means new to the academy. They have emerged at different times in history. The issues: Who is intelligent and who is not? How does intelligence vary with race? Are non-Anglo students less intelligent than Anglo students? What Herrnstein and Murray affirm as "intelligence," many scholars have recognized as an attempt to reinforce notions of white supremacy and white prejudice about black inferiority. Research studies comparing the races in cognitive abilities have been undertaken during in the past 75 years, and some of the findings remain as controversial today as when the studies were first undertaken. By the same token, parents and students constantly are being confronted with the dilemmas and contradictions of social stratification and educational marginalization, especially when schools tend to reward cognitive ability by dividing up the school cohort into categories of "gifted" and "non-gifted" students. What does it mean to be gifted? Many schools in the United States have used this term to justify, to privilege, and to give the best teachers, equipment, and curriculum to so-called gifted students. The basic tenet: We are not all equally intelligent! Most scientists and neurologists who study the electrical and chemical marbles of the brain say that little is truly known about the origin or character of intelligence. *The Bell Curve* claims to know a great deal. Its fundamental claim is that intelligence can be measured accurately by the IQ test and that Africans, African Americans, and other non-Whites fall short of Asians and white middle-class people.

Leading education researchers now say that standard IQ tests are far too narrow; that logic and language are only two kinds of intelligence. There are others—spatial intelligence, interpersonal intelligence, among others. Recent neurological research on the development of the brain, however, attests that the brain is constantly changing, especially when exposed to environmental stimulation. These findings pose the biggest challenge to the most fundamental claim of the book: While the environment may have an effect, intelligence is largely genetic and largely fixed in a person by the age of 16 or 17. Moreover, African Americans as a group are permanently set at a lower level of intelligence than Whites. Blacks score an average of 15 points lower than Whites on those standard IQ tests. Therefore, the book suggests, welfare and job training programs should reconsider spending money to change people who cannot be changed, which is an unproven assertion.

Questions regarding intelligence across racial lines are disturbing, yet they have come back to haunt our civilization even as different forms of multiculturalism have gained entry into American schools. Many scholars who believed that questions of race and intelligence had been put to rest were unprepared for genetic explanations of racial intelligence seeping into journals and books of the academy. The return to this debate has been fueled by a frenzy of the mass media and has served as a flagpost for years of losing crusades by individuals such as Arthur Jensen, William Shockley, and Cyril Burt who attempt to justify inequality in the American society by attributing it to hereditary characteristics and thus to support insidious "racial policies" that acclaim white racial superiority and genetic inferiority of all non-Whites. Herrnstein and Murray have resurrected in *The Bell Curve* old claims that were unfounded then and that are unfounded now. In short, what they purport is but a narrow biological determinism of the worst kind—a kind of genetic fundamentalism related to the nineteenth century imperialist racism, the kind that has prevailed on the African continent since the first colonizers set foot on African soil in the sixteenth century. In this chapter, my task is to uncover the fallacy of Herrnstein and Murray's arguments and to show that their claims are racist and based on unfounded misconceptions. I examine the origins of the misconceptions about Africans and origins of white prejudice about black inferiority. In addition, I draw largely from historical examples from Africa to expose the underlying racist campaign by these authors aimed at non-white populations, especially Africans on the African continent and African Americans in the United States. I show how current racist attitudes reflected in textbooks and in the production of images in the media and popular culture that position Africans onto dominant Whites, can to some degree be attributed to early misconceptions about Africa.

The anecdotes summed up in chapter 4 are daunting: The claims advanced in the weak and dated statistics from the Bureau of the Census (1975), the Bureau of Labor Statistics, and the National Longitudinal Survey of Youth (NLSY), which form the basis for the authors' claims to justify inequality by attributing it to innate, and therefore supposedly ineradicable, differences in intelligence. Herrnstein and Murray use the metaphor "Steeper Ladders, Narrower Gates" in the title of chapter 4 to capture their central thesis and send a clear warning to entrepreneurs: The value of intelligence in the marketplace is rising. As the title suggests, Herrnstein and Murray contend that the key to explaining all inequality and all social problems in the United States is stratification by a unitary entity called intelligence, or "cognitive ability," measured of course in IQ. This claim has surfaced repeatedly over the past 75 years only to be refuted each time as unfounded class, race, and gender prejudice. Herrnstein and Murray see rigid IQ stratification operating throughout every sphere of life: school, work, including choices of whom to mate with; where to live, shop, play, worship, send children to school, and even propensity to crime. But little evidence is given that intelligence is solely responsible for such social behavior.

KEY ARGUMENTS

Herrnstein and Murray put two distinct signatures to their claims. First, Herrnstein makes his old claim that IQ stratification is becoming ever more intense in a postindustrial world that requires cognitive ability over all else. Second, they propose a world in which people will be slotted into places that fit their cognitive ability, in which each of us will be respected for what we actually are and can be. Their fears come out in what they consider a crucial issue when they ask: How much good would it do to improve education for the people earning low wages? The authors of *The Bell Curve* doubt that by having youths stay in school for a few extra years would only modify their economic disadvantage. They claim this is so because the job market has been rewarding not just education but intelligence. That prosperity is reserved for those "lucky" enough to be intelligent. Their conclusion is that American successes and failures within the economy, are a matter of the inherited genes.

The Bell Curve's message about the inevitability of existing patterns of inequality rests on a series of existing claims concerning intelligence. These claims could be summed up as follows:

- Human intelligence is reducible to a unitary, core trait that is measurable and reliably expressed as a single numerical entity, IQ,
- IQ increasingly determines (or is correlated with) socio-economic status and behavior,
- IQ is distributed unevenly throughout the population in general and by race in particular,
- Cognitive ability is given and "substantially" fixed by genetic inheritance.

These claims, together with the overall themes embedded throughout the book, conjure up lots of skepticism about the veracity of facts, the application of data, and claims of absolute science. I will focus my comments on the myth of white supremacy. However, suffice it to say, that the argument against test scores and how they measure IQ are well known. I concur with the arguments advanced by Stephen J. Gould and others who characterize Herrnstein and Murray's idealist fallacy, simply, that there is no evidence to show that tests themselves are self-evidently measures of innate abilities that can be arrayed hierarchically. Furthermore, Adolph Reed, citing Gould's *The Measure of Man* dismisses the statistical and logical sophistry of Herrnstein and Murray's opus of tough love for poor people (Reed, 1994). Herrnstein and Murray consistently bend backward to give the benefit of the doubt to research whose conclusions they find congenial, and they dismiss, misrepresent, or ignore that which contradicts their vision. For instance, they decline to engage the work of Harvard psychologist Howard Gardner or Yale's Robert Sternberg, among others, who argue for multiple fields of intelligence that are not hierarchically organized. They don't mention the work of Gardner's colleague David Perkins.

While writing this chapter, I heard *ABC News* announce the results of research by Professor Mary Frasier at the University of Georgia who has challenged the whole idea of "giftedness" in the state's schools. Typically, only about 1 percent of school-age students are reckoned as "gifted." Nationwide, there are about 2 to 3 percent of "gifted" students of any race. In Atlanta, Georgia, Professor Frasier found that students must have an IQ score of 130 to qualify as "gifted." In this category about 17 percent were minorities and 26 percent were white. These discrepancies led Frasier to examine closely IQ scores, which are by and large believed to be used as a cover for segregation. Besides, many students who would have qualified as "gifted" are never tested. Frasier pursued this research and attempted to develop other holistic criteria important to consider besides IQ. Contrary to the claims advanced by Herrnstein and Murray that individuals are "hardwired" from birth, Frasier's research advocates for alternative methods of evaluating students' ability levels in a fair manner and with unlimited chances to everyone irrespective of race or ethnicity.

The consequences of segregating students into "gifted" and "nongifted" camps have been disastrous in the classrooms as well as at the workplace. Parents are unhappy about this elitist way of educating children. Some believe that having separate classes for the so-called advanced students is psychologically harmful and eliminates the chances of peer teaching and challenges for students emanating from a mixed learning environment. Many parents and educators believe such segregation is a tool legitimated by science as accurately measurable and an efficient way to sort the populations according to cognitive ability and therefore able to predict who will be successful in education and who will not. From elementary schools to colleges and universities, where thousands of students have learned the misconception that IQ differences are related to race, schools have fostered the belief in white supremacy.

Recent studies indicate that claims of white supremacy take different forms. The emerging class awareness in America has been identified as the guild "oligarchy" or simply white "elites." The most remarkable thing about our own American oligarchy is the pretense that it doesn't constitute anything as definite as a social class. Some observers indicate that Americans prefer to assign good fortune to individual merit, saying that we owe our perches in the upper percentiles of income and education not to our "connections" but solely to our own IQ, virtue, brio, genius, "sprezzatura," chutzpah, gumption (Lind, 1995).

> Had we been switched at birth by accident, had we grown in a ghetto or barrio or trailer park, we would have arrived at our offices at *ABC News* or the Republican National Committee or the ACLU in more or less the same amount of time. The absence of black and Hispanic Americans in our schools and our offices and our clubs can only be explained, we tell ourselves, not by our extrinsic advantages but by their intrinsic defects. Compared with us (and perhaps with middle-class

East Asian immigrants), most blacks and Hispanics must be disproportionately lazy, even disproportionately retarded. What other explanation of their failure to rise can there be? America, after all, is a classless society. (Lind, 1995)

This characterization of the American elite epitomizes a crisis in the war between the "have" and the "have-not" class as well as denial of the existence of anything but middle class in America. The denial of racism, sexism, and class is indicative of a Western European phenomenon: living with contradictions. How difficult is it to see that the effects of stratification can work in subtle and indirect ways that persist through momentary parity of income? For instance, the child of a first-generation middle-class African American or Hispanic family is likely to have fewer social resources—given the effects of ghettoization and discrimination in access to sources of personal capital (mortgages and other bank loans, accumulation of capitalizable home equity, investment opportunities, inherited wealth, and so on)—than her white counterpart, and is likely to shoulder an additional burden of everyday racial discrimination. Herrnstein and Murray presume that in measuring patterns of variation in IQ scores in a way that neutralizes the effects of selected aspects of environment, they can distill the part played by heredity in determining cognitive ability. They ignore environmental and social conditions and choose to be insensitive to this level of complexity as they do when they compare Jews to Blacks and middle-class East Asians. The case of Africa and the cultural roots of African Americans provides ample examples of such insidious insensitivity.

MISCONCEPTIONS ABOUT AFRICA

The truth about Africa has been distorted among non-Africans. For centuries, starting with perceptions of the "Dark Continent," the worldview of many non-Africans, particularly Europeans, was clouded over with myths and stereotypes, and Africa was misconceived then as now with all the myths and stereotypes intact. Some of the simplest myths are most common: lions in the jungles, the isolated Dark Continent, inferior savages, a race of Negroes—heathens developed only by the grace of God and the white man—and a land of turmoil, incapable of self-government. Because these myths and stereotypes are alive today in the schools' curriculum (however unintentional the distortions and omissions may be), in the hands of unaware and unskilled teachers, the curriculum continues to feed the racist doctrines and practices of white supremacy. Raised on a diet of westernized history, Tarzan books and films, and sensationalized news media, many students in the United States believe Africa to be a primitive land of hot, steamy jungles inhabited by wild animals and savages. In truth, less than 10 percent of the African continent is covered with forests, much like parts of Pennsylvania or Washington. Of course, lions live in grasslands in national parks, not in jungles. Nearly half of the African continent consists of grassy savannah, and approximately one-third is desert.

However, unequal representation of news and events of non-Western societies persists. African media outlets on the continent lack the technology and speed to generate reports or images of its people fast enough for the world beyond their borders. The African continent is often misunderstood because of Western media's dismissal of it as backward and therefore unworthy of coverage. What is not portrayed is that Africa is a diverse continent, both of reemerging democracies and of troubled areas with leftover vestiges of colonialism, and is made up of many countries, climates, geographies, histories, and peoples. And yet Western media portray Africa as just one massive civil war, a famine-torn place with a few pyramids in the north, racial struggle in the south, and some lions and elephants in between.

What is omitted from the curriculum leaves many American students not only hungry for knowledge beyond their own borders but equally afraid of the unknown and the unlike. Few students get to learn about achievements of the early West African kingdoms of Ghana, Mali, and Songhai, the clove empires of Zanzibar and Kilwa on the east coast of Africa, and the rich kingdom of Benin, or Kanem Bomu in the heartland (Toppin, 1969). The prosperity and power of the great West African empires, which covered an area almost as large as the United States, arose from the agricultural base of the Niger River Valley yet it is barely taught in American social studies curriculum. Africa's record of achievement is not limited to large kingdoms, however. But, little is acknowledged in North America about the elaborate social and political systems, complex religions (frequently dismissed as animism), effective health care practices (for example, the herbal-psychological services of the traditional healer), and advanced expressions of music and art that developed in African villages as well as in large empires (Airhihenbuwa, 1994). In spite of anthropologists' findings that the greatest genius of the African peoples was their capacity for social organization, textbooks continue to perpetuate myths about so-called primitive people of the Congo forest and the Kalahari desert as representative of the diversified societies found on the continent. The question that needs to be asked is: Why do American textbook writers continue to adhere to these misconceptions? Where did these myths come from? Who stands to benefit from this misinformation? Since school knowledge is socially produced, deeply imbued with human interests, and deeply implicated in the unequal social relations outside the school door, it is not surprising to see this campaign of unfounded myths about Africa and the Africans continue.

ORIGINS OF MYTHS

How and why did these myths develop about Africans and their descendants in the diaspora? Basil Davidson, a renowned writer on the history, culture, and politics of Africa, has brilliantly documented the myths of inferiority about Africans (Davidson, 1994). First was misinformation. Competition among the emerging European nations and houses of commerce led to practices of secrecy lest rivals benefit from knowledge gained through the early explorations of lands unknown to Europe. Hence myths grew out of deliberate misinformation provided by early European explorers. Second was the blatant dishonesty: of literary hacks who concocted all sorts of nonsense for a gullible public. Still prevalent today, one finds inaccurate and distorted news reels put together by major American news networks on Africa, whether it is about warlords in Somalia, civil war in Rwanda or the outbreak of the *Ebola* virus. As surmised by an editor of a metropolitan newspaper in America, there is more and better reporting on Africa in one weekly airmail issue edition of the British *Manchester Guardian* than in all the American national press combined (Wiley, 1976). Third was the need to justify the slave trade in the minds of Christians and the enlightened. Assurances that slaves were heathen savages, who would benefit by becoming Christianized and civilized, became the basic rationalization. Many philanthropic organizations operating in Africa in the colonial days to the present continue to base their mission on this rationalization. Not all of them are genuine or altruistic. Some use the claimed "primitive" conditions of Africa as a basis for their *raison d'être*, they collect charitable articles and funds, which are tax exempt in their home countries, in the name of Africa, but only a small percent of what is collected actually reaches those most in need. Almost two-thirds of the charity goes to administrative costs and overheads. It is important to remember also that soon after the partition of Africa in 1885 at the Berlin Conference, Europeans launched into an era of imperialism and the quest for new lands from which to exploit natural resources. To control the new colonies, in this case the African colonies, traditional history, culture, and sources of group identity had to be suppressed, subjugated, and replaced (at least temporarily) by the colonialists' culture, history, and doctrines of white supremacy.

OUTCOMES OF MISCONCEPTIONS

All these are examples of a larger system of representation and production of images in the media and school texts that position Africans in relation to dominant Whites. In many cases American students depend on the media, more so than on textbooks or the classroom, for their understanding of existing relations of dominance and subordination in the world. Today many textbooks continue to draw from outdated information about the African nations. For example, while introducing the African athletes at the Olympic games in Barcelona, the sports anchor used information from a dated almanac to retell the histories of the countries from which the athletes came. Besides using antiquated statistics and anecdotal information, demeaning comments were circulated over the airwaves about the alleged cannibalism practiced by dictators such as Idi Amin of Uganda and Bokassa of Central African Republic as well as other trivial incidents that were of no consequence or relevance to the Olympics. It is important to emphasize that rapidly changing events on the African continent may make maps and other content obsolete even in relatively new texts. In addition to outdated content, most current textbooks that attempt to present Africans to elementary and secondary school students prefer to emphasize exotic and irrelevant information about race and overemphasize small groups with insignificant populations—such as the Mbuti (alias Pygmies), the San (Bushmen), and Khoi (Hottentots)—who continue to be regarded as the primitive people of Africa. It is unclear how those nicknames made it to American textbooks, since those names are nowhere used by local people. Rather, these names were concocted by Europeans to describe the difference between self and others. Many young Americans come to believe that many or most African people live like these exotic, small atypical groups because so much of the curriculum is devoted to their study. Thus the unsophisticated non-African reader who comes across illustrations and texts that show Africans in the bush perceives the particular conditions and "unfamiliar" behavior and evaluates the people as uncivilized, promiscuous, and *inferior.*

Another result of ignorance about Africa is that it feeds the doctrine of white supremacy and the belief that African Americans as a group are inferior because they are genetically related to Africans. Myths and theories from the past that were used to justify slavery continue to serve as a rationalization for inferior schools, substandard homes, low-paying jobs, and so on. Often dismissed by the general comment, "That is the way all of them are" these segregating practices of the past consistently continue to reemerge in our society as a form of oppression and subjugation of Africans. Herrnstein and Murray's work in *The Bell Curve* legitimizes this longstanding rationalization, finds ways to get gullible Americans to believe their bigotry, and schemes to reassert white supremacy in the name of science. It is important for American children and youth to understand the basic human characteristics they share with the various people of Africa. Unfortunately, *The Bell Curve* does not foster or provide this understanding.

AFRICANS AND *THE BELL CURVE* DOCTRINE

The point of *The Bell Curve* is not profound; it is to advance a reactionary, racist, and otherwise antiegalitarian ideological agenda by dressing it with a scientific patina. After acknowledging that genetic variations among individuals within a given "race" are greater than those between "races," Herrnstein and Murray persist in maintaining that racially defined populations must differ genetically in significant ways because otherwise they wouldn't have different hair texture or skin color. And besides, they say, there must be differences between races because races are defined by groups of people whose characteristics differ. What Herrnstein and Murray have done in chapter 4 and throughout the book is to drive a wedge between the races in a world whose people are growing closer and more interdependent due to a global economy. This is a reminder of the old campaign of cultural racism that pervades Western society. To justify the treatment of the African slave and later of the African American citizen, white society encourages an army of propagandists to prove "scientifically" the inferiority of black people. While this ideology of racism was applied to all people of color with whom European-American society came into contact, its severest application was against African Americans. The reasons are simple: Because they were the most physically different from Whites, because their numbers were the second largest to Whites, and because of their geographical and social proximity to Whites, Blacks have been perceived as the greatest threat.

By dwelling on such trivial human traits as skin color, Herrnstein and Murray have successfully resurrected Carl von Linné's classification of *Homo sapiens*. Western society has tended to accept this classification of *Homo sapiens*, along with the erroneous assumption that mental, behavioral, and sociocultural tendencies are determined by a few visible biological traits and the belief that Western Europeans are superior to all others. One commonly held belief in the United States is the inferiority of the implements, handcrafts, agriculture, economics, music, art, religious beliefs, traditions, language, and history of non-Anglo European people; another is that these people have distinctive cultures apart from that of mainstream white Americans (Jones, 1981). School texts and educational media have presented negative myths and stereotypes about Africa and Africans and have presented a distorted view of past and current history that reinforces the doctrine of white supremacy. The myths are based on beliefs that members of another race are inferior, that the inferior person's behavior, morality, and intellectual qualities are determined by genetics, and that this inferiority is a legitimate basis for inferior social treatment. These distinctions are arbitrary and pervaded with contempt, especially when applied to Africa and the Africans. Put simply, the myths are summed up in a dichoto-mized fashion: America is rational. Africa is not. America is democratic. Africa is not. America is virtuous, moral, and on the side of good and right. Africa is vicious, immoral, and on the side of evil. Such dichoto-mization harbors prejudice and unfounded misconceptions about distant and faraway societies.

CONCLUSION

The bitter debate engendered by *The Bell Curve* is not isolated. A similar debate has been carried on in the popular press and in several widely reviewed books that has overshadowed the progress made in multicultural education during the last two decades, a debate that perpetuates harmful misconceptions about theory and practice in multicultural education. Consequently, it has heightened racial and ethnic tensions and trivialized remarkable accomplishments in theory, research, and curriculum development.

Current efforts in American schools to introduce multicultural curricula should, therefore, be encouraged. A critical multiculturalism should be more reflexive with respect to the relationship between different social groups in the United States and the relationship of developments in the United States to the rest of the world. This would mean, for instance, that we begin to see the issue of racial inequality in global and relational terms in the context of what Immanuel Wallerstein calls "world systems theory" (Wallerstein, 1990). The links between America's development and the underdevelopment of the poor countries of the world and the links that African Americans have had in terms of their intellectual and political engagement with the people of Africa must be emphasized. This will not be achieved by emphasizing exoticism and cultural differences associated with so-called primitive humanity. Certainly Herrnstein and Murray's fantasies do not help students in their important journey of learning about other cultures.

References

Airhihenbuwa, C. (1994, Fall). Health promotion and the discourse on culture: Implications for empowerment. *Health Education Quarterly*, *21* (3), 345-353.

Davidson, B. (1994). *The search for Africa: A history in the making.* London: Currey.

Jones, J. (1981). The concept of racism and its changing reality. In Bowser, B. and Hunt, R., eds., *Impacts of racism on white Americans.* Beverly Hills, CA: Sage.

Lind, M. (1995). To have and have not, notes on the progress of the American class war. *Harper's Magazine.*

Reed, A. (1994, November 28). Looking backward. *The Nation,* 654-655.
Toppin, E. A. (1969, March 6). The forgotten people. *The Christian Science Monitor.*
Wallerstein, I. (1990). Culture as the ideological battleground of the modern world system, in Featherstone, M., ed., *Global culture: Nationalism, globalization and modernity.* Beverly Hills, CA: Sage.

9 BAD LUCK, BAD BLOOD, BAD FAITH: IDEOLOGICAL HEGEMONY AND THE OPPRESSIVE LANGUAGE OF HOODOO SOCIAL SCIENCE

JOYCE E. KING

Psychology manages to lose sight of man [sic], with the effect (politically) that having been lost sight of, he cannot assert the demands of his nature against the social system that encloses him. This conjuring trick is achieved by the process of reification, that is, the reduction of human realities to the order of things.
—David Ingleby, 1972, p. 57

But what if the numbers are faulty because the assumptions that went into their creation are flawed? Suppose that they are socially determined rather than genetically comprised.
—Earl Lewis, 1995, p. 21

The real question is, what is the present value and distribution of the stream of income that has been coercively and wrongfully diverted from Blacks to Whites through slavery and discrimination to produce lopsided income and wealth distributions by race, and, in doing so, has robbed too many Blacks of the skills they need to perform effectively.
—Richard America, 1994, p. 1

"What was Tanya Harding doing *in the Olympics? She's poor white trash."*
—Overheard, at a California campus, 1994

It has been noted that "hegemony cannot do its work without the support of ideology" or worldview: the complex of meanings, ideas, significations, social practices, "rituals and representations *that we tend to accept as* natural and common sense " (McLaren, 1989, p. 176). Insofar as hegemony is a "struggle in which the powerful win the consent" and unknowing participation of those who are oppressed, this "battle for domination" is fought at the level of cultural forms, the social construction of identity/subjectivity, and the mobilization (or elimination) of desire (Donald and Hall, 1986). Given the role of conceptual whiteness (Wynter, 1992b) in the U.S. cultural system (and globally), ideological hegemony also depends on the folklore of white supremacy (Murray, 1970) not just to oppress black people but to induce white people to accept the lower social position of the white working and underclass—and those perceived as "poor white trash"—as "natural" as well.

This commentary on *The Bell Curve* is concerned primarily with Chapter 5. However, I will argue that in this neo-Reconstruction period the aim of *The Bell Curve* on the whole is to rearticulate the ideology of white supremacy/racism (Omi and Winant, 1994) in order to dismantle the gains of recent struggles for justice and to disguise dominating power relations and the reconstitution of the U.S. economy. That *The Bell Curve* argument attempts to put a veneer of scientific respectability on the myth of white superiority for these ideological purposes is why I am calling it hoodoo social science.

HOODOO SOCIAL SCIENCE/IDEOLOGY/HEGEMONY

The *Dictionary of African-American Slang* defines *hoodoo*, "an early African-American religion with origins in West African spiritual life," as "the spirit or essence of everything . . . magic; a conjurer; charm; jinx; spell" (Major, 1994, p. 240). Like the process of ideological hegemony, hoodoo can serve positive or negative functions, in contrast to vulgar stereotyped images of the more familiar, much-maligned term *voodoo*. As used in this chapter, hoodoo refers to "conjuring tricks"; it connotes a form of deception, as in Major's example: "Andrew going 'round here swearing up and down he can fix anybody—make a wife leave a husband, make a child turn on a mother—like he got the fit of hoodoo" (p. 240).

Traditional religious practices like hoodoo may seem to be at odds with the normal methods and thought of Western science. In spite of certain undeniable differences, both involve complex systems of thought, worldviews, "intellectual and experiential insights" (Suzuki and Knudtson, 1992) as well as specialized theoretical and empirical knowledge. Horton (1967) suggests that the traditional African religious expert, the diviner or healer, and the Western social scientist are both engaged in social analysis: diagnosing the cause of certain societal "afflictions." Both "are making the same use of theory to transcend the limited vision of natural causes provided by commonsense" (Horton, 1967, p. 54). The efficacy of both systems of knowledge/practice also depends on prior belief and commonsense assumptions that are founded on a preanalytic worldview (Suzuki and Knudtson, 1992).

This is where ideological hegemony comes into view in certain aspects of explanatory or theoretical thinking in Western science. For example, in a penetrating analysis of "Ideology in the Human Sciences" Ingleby (1972) observed that "to the extent that the human sciences are taking over from religion the function of providing man [that is, humans] with a self-image, they should be seen in the same light as religious myths" (p. 57). In other words: "it is through its potency as myth that [the] psychological model of man can be seen as serving ideological interests" (p. 57). Likewise, *The Bell Curve* argument, founded on the faulty premise of the IQ myth, by justifying the ideology of white supremacy/racism, puts the "fit of hoodoo" on the unsuspecting lay public and the believing social science professionals and academicians.

The Bell Curve argument serves the ideological purposes of hegemonic or hoodoo social science by conjuring up bad luck and bad blood as the alleged cause of social "afflictions" such as poverty that are attributed to the genetic defectivity/inferiority of poor people themselves. This allegation serves to legitimate and maintain the hegemony of the dominant group and the upward mobility of the relatively few "subalterns" permitted to move up the social scale in recent years. Among the conjuring tricks or "magical rites" employed in chapter 5 are oversimplified conceptualization and flawed statistical comparisons that are used to enthrall people into believing that being poor, or "poor white trash," is just a matter of bad luck.

According to Anthony Giddens (1979), ideology works in the following ways: (1) sectional (for example, class) interests are presented as universal; (2) societal contradictions are denied or transmuted, and (3) the present is naturalized or reified (p. 193). Notwithstanding another claim of Herrnstein and Murray that the "quest for human dignity" is "at the heart" of their thought (p. 551), *The Bell Curve* is fundamentally about the elimination of human possibilities in precisely these ways. This is because the paradigm or model of being human in which their thought is centered is based not on scientific premises but on the "founding superstition" of our culture: the "pre-analytic premise of metaphysical naturalism" (NHI, 1995, p. 4).

The Bell Curve paradigm and the statistical evidence Herrnstein and Murray present follow from the assumption that human beings are "purely biological" organisms in perfect (that is, natural) evolutionary continuity with organic species. Within this worldview, genes—not human agency, intention, and possibility—determine social behavior and "human destiny" (p. 4). Or as Herrnstein and Murray put it so simply: the bell curve "refers to a

common way that *natural* phenomenon arrange themselves approximately" (p. 556). The system of positivistic logic that permits this
belief that biology determines human destiny enables the corollary
conviction that human beings differ according to their different
degrees of "genetic value," or IQ. Herrnstein and Murray also
assume that "intelligence is a well-understood construct" (p. 1).
Equally problematic, therefore, is their assumption that there are
"accepted standards of what constitutes scientific evidence and
scientific proof" (p. 19) that cannot be called into question. Yet
racism has always been able to "come up with a scientific veneer"
(Mensh and Mensh, 1991, p. 28).

In addition, as the organization of the data presented in
chapter 5 demonstrates, Herrnstein and Murray contend that racism,
which is relegated to an artifact of the black experience, is not relevant
to understanding or explaining the economic and social status of
white people (p. 131). More will be said about this later. Suffice it to
say that the term "white supremacy/racism" (as Carlos Nelson and
Hermon George [1995] suggest) "makes clear the uniting of power
and racial bias which produce racial oppression" (p. 59). Nor does
this system rule out that certain groups, including white women,
nonelite white men and middle-class people of color, can be simultaneously exploited and privileged within this race-, class-, and gender-
based system.

The Bell Curve paradigm reifies and rationalizes the persistence of the social hierarchies of race, class, and gender and the
inhuman conditions of existence that increasing numbers of people—including white people and others—are enduring throughout
the world. This debased perception of humanity—is linked to the
suspicion that black people are "subhuman," which *The Bell Curve*
attempts to prove as a matter of uncontestable scientific truth—is so
well entrenched in the social science and humanities disciplines that
even critiques of the "IQ myth" such as Stephen J. Gould's *Mismeasure of Man* argue against it but from within the paradigm's accepted
beliefs about the distribution and *measurability* of whatever is meant
by "intelligence" (Mensh and Mensh, 1991).

DISAPPEARING ACTS: DENYING REALITY WITH "TABOO FACTS"

The point I am making is that, to the extent that *The Bell Curve* argument functions *ideologically* (and politically)—that is, hegemonically—to mystify rather than explain social reality, to justify the race, class, and gender hierarchy in American society in order to deny the reality of societal oppression, it serves the ideological functions of hegemonic or hoodoo social science. Such mystification cannot enable people to challenge dominating power relations and the cultural beliefs that sustain societal injustice. Rather, *The Bell Curve* loses sight of real human beings as it deflects attention away from actual relations of power and societal contradictions that need to be *explained* but that disappear behind a barrage of statistics and putative scientific reasoning. In typical hoodoo fashion, *The Bell Curve* paradigm employs a number of "conjuring tricks," including statistical associations that magically become causal relationships and a nostalgic narrative of the "reconstitution of American economics and politics" (Coontz, 1992, p. 254).

The concern of this chapter is not to argue that *The Bell Curve* represents bad science, however. Ingleby (1972) was correct to emphasize this point when he stated that "we are not primarily interested in outrages—in scientists who tell lies, in rigged experiments" (p. 53). As he explained: "Generally such behavior turns out to be an act of deviance, a violation of accepted norms: more important, and more difficult is the task of showing how these norms themselves serve or reflect political aims" (p. 53). One such accepted norm to which the authors of *The Bell Curve* claim allegiance is following the "inner logic of science," on which they rely to bring forward research questions that reveal "taboo facts." Actually, the "facts" *The Bell Curve* presents obscure unpleasant social and contradictory economic realities such as job displacement, employment discrimination, the glass ceiling, and the like. The reassertion of white racial superiority and women's place in a traditional gender role (with a husband and in the house) rationalizes white poverty and justifies women's economic exploitation. The IQ myth is a diversion from this reality. The statistical facade of "taboo facts" *The Bell Curve* presents does not make it less so. But, as Earl Lewis asks, What if the numbers they present are faulty because the social problems in our society are "socially determined" not "genetically comprised"? Given the system of white supremacy/racism in which scientists are socialized, in which science as a social activity is practiced and from which it, therefore, is not immune, the inner logic of science alone cannot answer this question. "Scientists, no less than lay people," Andrew Hacker (1992) points out, "have political dispositions" (p. 27).

BAD LUCK/BAD BLOOD: THE REIFYING LANGUAGE OF OPPRESSION

Interestingly, Herrnstein and Murray frequently use the unscientific commonsense notion of "luck" when describing the purported causal connection among genes, "intelligence," social behavior, and poverty (and other social problems). Within *The Bell Curve* paradigm genes are a matter of luck and poverty is a consequence of bad blood, or genetically determined human *in/capacity* for social success (for example, avoiding poverty—presumably through moral, that is, middle-class behavior). This choice of language reveals a great deal about the model of human difference that displaces and debases human agency in *The Bell Curve.*

According to *The Bell Curve* argument, the "cognitively fortunate" few have become more prosperous, while those who inherit inferior genes from their parents and who are thus not so well "endowed" are thus destined (condemned, rather) to live out the inexorable consequences of their bad blood and bad luck. "Through no fault of their own," so *The Bell Curve* argument goes, these unlucky people share the similar fate of poverty because of *their* "bad luck in the genetic draw" (p. 130). Suggesting that bad luck and bad blood explain societal inequity in this way represents just one instance of the "oppressive language" in *The Bell Curve* that serves to legitimate the status quo by obscuring the relations of power that are largely responsible for it.

In her acceptance speech upon receiving the Nobel Prize for Literature in Stockholm, Toni Morrison (1994) exposes the role that language plays in societal oppression. Morrison described oppressive language this way: She said it "drinks blood, laps vulnerabilities, tucks its fascist boots under crinolines of respectability and patriotism" (p. 17) and—I would add—"accepted standards" of scientific evidence. Morrison's critical appraisal of language and its mis/use is instructive and worth quoting further: "Oppressive language does more than represent violence; it is violence; does more than represent the limits of knowledge; it limits knowledge. Whether it is obscuring state language or the faux language of mindless media; whether it is the proud but calcified language of the academy or the commodity-driven language of science . . . or language designed for the estrangement of minorities, hiding its racist plunder in its literary cheek—it must be rejected, altered and exposed" (p. 16). By reducing social power relations and their consequences to simplistic notions of bad luck and bad blood, the oppressive language in *The Bell Curve* reifies race, class, and gender domination. This choice of language belies a flawed perception of humanity and social reality. It represents another conjuring trick of hoodoo social science that reduces "human realities to the order of things" (Ingleby, 1972, p. 57). What, after all, are poverty, white supremacy/racism, class and gender oppression if not forms of violence against the human spirit that often result in social if not physical death and psychic annihilation? The argument that bad luck and "bad" blood (genes) are responsible for such human suffering is the epitome of bad faith.

WHITE SUPREMACY/RACISM AND BAD FAITH

Thus, the debasement of humanity is accomplished in *The Bell Curve* through the refusal of the authors to recognize how social forms and institutionalized social practices and structures oppress people (McLaren, 1989). Instead they construct oversimplified conceptualizations and regression analyses that mystify societal complexities. For example, in chapter 5, entitled "Poverty," which opens part II, "Cognitive Classes and Social Behavior," Herrnstein and Murray present their "best estimate of how much intelligence has to do with America's most pressing social problems" (p. 117). The authors limit the discussion of poverty to Whites—to "make it easier" they say, "to focus on the evidence without constantly having to worry about racism, cultural bias in the tests, or other extraneous issues" (p. 315). Herrnstein and Murray justify their refusal to perceive poverty in relation to "broad system causes" by suggesting that, because much of the literature "focuses on poverty among Blacks and its roots in racism," it does not apply to poverty among Whites (p. 131). Given the emphasis on white people in the book's largest section, it is worth noting, as Richard America (1994) points out, however, that Whites continue to benefit not from luck but from the "lopsided income and wealth distributions" that characterize U.S. society (p. 1). Saying this is not to deny, however, that the societal hierarchy also "wrongly and coercively" extracts wealth and privilege from the exploitation of others, including nonelite Whites, who in spite of their racial advantage are exploited on the basis of their class or gender. Because, for Herrnstein and Murray, genetically transmitted low intelligence causes or sits at the core of many of our social problems, they refuse to perceive the actual mechanisms of unequal power, including the nonneutrality of normal social scientific inquiry.

I categorically reject the specious premise of *The Bell Curve* argument: that science has demonstrated that human intelligence, like height or weight, is a measurable normally distributed natural law like thing in itself. The *system* of white supremacy/racism, including the belief in inherent white superiority, on which *The Bell Curve* argument is founded, is not *extraneous* but *most* central to understanding and resolving the problems in America and the world today. The refusal of Herrnstein and Murray to face this reality, while claiming to search for a way we can all live together and find "valued

186   Joyce E. King

places in society," is another instance of the element of bad faith in
The Bell Curve.

Philosopher Lewis R. Gordon (1995) has analyzed "antiblack racism" in the works of Jean Paul Sartre as a form of bad faith.
The attitude of bad faith can involve duplicity, dishonesty, and
self-deception. Gordon suggests that the Sartrean concept of bad
faith can be defined as fleeing a "displeasing truth for a pleasing
falsehood" (p. 8). Thus, constructing black people as inferior to
Whites is a "pleasing falsehood" of antiblack racism. This form of
bad faith is akin to Ralph Ellison's description of the way white
Americans seek to resolve, as if by magic, the dissonance or the
contradiction between America's democratic ideals and the reality of
how black people in America are treated. He observed that "Whatever else the Negro stereotype might be as a social instrumentality, it
is also a key figure in a magic rite by which the white American seeks
to resolve the dilemma arising between his democratic beliefs and
certain antidemocratic practices, between his acceptance of the
sacred democratic belief that all men are created equal and his
treatment of every tenth man as though he were not" (cf. Gordon,
1995, p. 78). In an essay review of Ellis Cose's (1933) *The Rage of a
Privileged Class,* Andrew Hacker (1994) emphasizes the persistence
and significance of this belief. Hacker writes:

> The ascription of *inbred* incapacity is the ultimate expression
> of racism, the one hardest to eradicate, not least because most
> people will deny they hold this view (my emphasis). It is a
> shackle that Americans of African origin have had to bear since
> they were first brought here as slaves. Could there have been
> something, Whites wondered that rendered the black race
> suitable for bondage? This suspicion has by no means disap-
> peared, even among those who wish they could rid themselves
> of it. (p. 459)

This element of bad faith in *The Bell Curve* enables the evasion of
"freedom and responsibility" in a humane world (Gordon, 1995); it

also contributes to the debasement of human agency and the elimination of human possibility.

"WHAT CAUSES POVERTY?"

Herrnstein and Murray concede that children of poor parents are more likely to become poor and vice versa or, in their words, that "rank hath its privileges." Even so, *The Bell Curve* argument is constructed in such a way that *only* the notions of either "nature" or "nurture," or some combination of such genetic and environmental factors, is thinkable. Actually, Herrnstein and Murray sidestep this debate by taking the *allegation* of biologically (and consequentially, racially) determined "intelligence" (or IQ) as given. Then they argue that presumed biological deficiency is the *crucial* factor that causes individual children to become poor as adults, not because of the social and economic background of their parents but because of their genes. Emphasizing the "stability of IQ over the life span" (p. 131) further supports the construction of "intelligence" as an unchanging personal "quality" of each individual.

Herrnstein and Murray give no consideration to the body of research regarding the various ways that school practices such as tracking, curriculum bias, disproportionate assignment to special education classes, disciplinary practices, low expectations of teachers, and other inequities reproduce unequal educational outcomes that accord with parental socioeconomic status (SES) or the presumed cognitive abilities of students (Anyon, 1981; McLaren, 1989). Such alternative explanations are outside the conceptualization of the hereditarian tradition (or belief structure)—which the authors conveniently dub the "classical tradition." Rather, within this tradition, educational attainment, like poverty, is not due to the effect of race or class-based schooling, but is posited as the result of a person's IQ. The statistical comparisons Herrnstein and Murray present as evidence to support this flawed formulation, *let you ask* questions such as:

(a) Imagine a person in the NLSY (data base) who comes from a family of exactly average socioeconomic background and exactly average age. What are this person's chances of being in poverty if he is very smart? Very dumb?

(b) Imagine a person in the NLSY who is exactly average in IQ and age. What are this person's chances of being in poverty if he came from an extremely advantaged socioeconomic background? An extremely deprived socioeconomic background? (p. 131)

Not surprisingly, the conclusion is: "Cognitive ability is more important than parental SES in determining poverty," though socioeconomic background is not "irrelevant" (p. 135). Focusing separately on measures of supposedly "identical" IQ and socioeconomic background, the marital status and economic status of women in the NLSY who became mothers, they reach the same conclusion. Unmarried white mothers who were "unlucky enough to have an IQ of only 85 . . . had a more than 50 percent chance [of being poor]—fives times as high as the risk faced by a married women of identical IQ and socioeconomic background" (p. 139). Also, whether a woman was separated, divorced, or never married at all "made no difference" in comparison to the results for married women. Thus, "IQ is extremely important," Herrnstein and Murray insist, "in determining poverty among women without a husband present" (p. 139).

"WHAT COULD BE PLAINER?"

In chapter 5 Herrnstein and Murray claim to want to "disentangle" the "comparative roles of cognitive ability and socioeconomic background in explaining poverty" (p. 132) to devise more appropriate policies. One thing is certain, however. *The Bell Curve* offers no knowledge that would enable people to confront the realities of an unjust social system. Instead Herrnstein and Murray insist that poverty; dropping out of school; unemployment, idleness, and injury; the "death of the traditional family" (including divorce and illegitimacy); welfare dependency; poverty or "malparenting" (which includes child neglect and abuse); crime and "growing incivility" as well as other indices of the lack of "middle class values" are the result of cognitive deficiencies. Yet Stephanie Coontz's (1992) *The way we never were: American families and the nostalgia trip* contradicts *The Bell Curve*'s interpretation of the "family crisis" in the United States and data regarding changing poverty rates and family composition. Using the kind of social and economic analysis that Herrnstein and Murray dismiss, Coontz concludes that "blaming our ills on family breakdown," as these authors do, "oversimplifies the issue and ultimately leads to a scapegoating mentality that is unfair and unhelpful" (p. 258). Thus, blaming mothers is equally problematic (King and Mitchell, 1995), because, Coontz argues, "The concentration of poverty in single-parent families during the past two decades was as much a result of gender discrimination, inflation, and government policy as of divorce or illegitimacy, while the increase in single parenthood itself was more often a *result* of economic slide than its cause " (pp. 260-261; author's emphasis). Coontz identifies the "three biggest predictors for family stress and disruption": income insecurity, job disruption and economic reverses. Among these economic factors are the decline in families' real incomes, wage stagnation, and an increase in low-wage jobs. In contrast to the traditional "role of gender" that Herrnstein and Murray reassert, Coontz concludes: "The main way . . . out of poverty for women as well as for men, remains work, not marriage" (p. 262).

"A PLACE FOR EVERYONE" OR JUSTICE FOR ALL?"

Coontz's conclusion that people need not only jobs but need access to the "social capital" of networks and support is not totally inconsistent with the recommendations regarding the need for community revitalization at the end of *The Bell Curve.* What Herrnstein and Murray advocate though with respect to the policy implications they discuss is a return to competitive individualism within the inherent limits of human capacity as determined by cognitive ability and the "natural" low wage for available jobs (p. 519). Thus Herrnstein and Murray anticipate the fulfillment of the pessimistic prophecy/predictions of hegemonic hoodoo social science: a society in which there is complacent, uncontested acceptance of a natural "place for everyone" in the social hierarchy of genetically predetermined wealth, rank, and privilege, primarily for white men. Coontz, on the other hand, emphasizes our human potential for altruism and cooperation; she underscores the capacity of people to be transformed through their efforts to overcome adversity and through participating in social struggles for justice. It is hoped that human potential and justice for all, not the ideological hegemony of white supremacy/racism, will prevail. As W.E.B. DuBois (1920, p. 29-30) observed, "the discovery of personal whiteness among the world's peoples is a very modern thing." If, despite the conjuring tricks of *The Bell Curve,* white people can accept the truth that "We are all cousins and all, originally, children of Africa," there may be reason for optimism (Hudson, 1995, p. 7).

References

America, R. (1994). The reparations question. *Poverty & Race, 3* (2), 1-2, 4.

Anyon, J. (1981). Social class and school knowledge. *Curriculum Inquiry, 11,* 3-42.

Coontz, S. (1992). *The way we never were: American families and the nostalgia trap.* New York: Basic Books.

Cose, E. (1993). *The rage of a privileged class.* New York: HarperCollins.

Donald, J. and Hall, S. (1986). Introduction. In Donald, J. and Hall, S., eds., *Politics and ideology.* Philadelphia: Milton Keynes, Open University Press.

Giddens, A. (1979). *Central problems in sociological theory.* Berkeley, CA: University of California Press.

Gordon, L. (1995). *Bad faith and anti-black racism.* Atlantic Highlands, NJ: Humanities Press.

Herrnstein, R. J. and Murray, C. (1994). *The Bell Curve: Intelligence and class structure in American life.* New York: The Free Press.

Hacker, A. (1994, April 14). The delusion of equality. *The Nation, 258* (13), 457-459.

Hacker, A. (1992). *Two nations: Black, White, separate, hostile, unequal.* New York: Charles Scribner's Sons.

Horton, R. (1967). African traditional thought and Western science. *Journal of the International African Institute, 37* (1), 50-71.

Hudson, J. B. (1995). Scientific racism: The politics of tests, race and genetics. *The Black Scholar, 25,* 3-10.

Ingleby, D. (1972). Ideology and the human sciences: Some comments on the role of reification in psychology and psychiatry. In Pateman, T., ed., *Countercourse: A handbook for course criticism.* Baltimore, MD: Penguin Books.

King, J. E. (1995). On race and education: A response. In Kincheloe, J. L. and Steinberg, S. R., eds., *Thirteen questions: Reframing education's conversation,* 2nd ed., 159-179. New York: Peter Lang.

King, J. E. (1992). Diaspora literacy and consciousness in the struggle against miseducation in the black community. *Journal of Negro Education, 61* (3), 317-340.

King, J. E. and Mitchell, C. A. (1990/1995). *Black mothers to sons: Juxtaposing African American literature with social practice.* New York: Peter Lang.

Lewis, E. (1995). The fallacy of positivist reasoning. *The Black Scholar, 25,* 21-24.

Major, C. (1994). *Juba to jive: Dictionary of African-American slang.* New York: Penguin.

McLaren, P. (1989). *Life in schools.* New York: Longman.

Mensh, E. and Mensh, H. (1991). *The IQ mythology: Class, race, gender and inequality.* Carbondale, IL: Southern Illinois University Press.

Morrison, T. (1994). *The Nobel lecture in literature, 1993.* New York: Alfred A. Knopf.

Murray, A. (1970). *The omni-Americans: Some alternatives to the folklore of white supremacy.* New York: DaCapo Press.

N. H. I. (1995, Winter). Final solution to the nigger question: Droppin' some science on *The Bell Curve. The Real News (3),* 3-4.

Nelson, C. and George, H. (1995). White racism and *The Cosby Show:* A critique. *The Black Scholar, 25* (2), 59-61.

Omi, M. and Winant, H. (1986, 1994). *Racial formation in the United States: From the 1960s to the 1990s.* New York: Routledge.

Suzuki, D. and Knudtson, P. (1992). *Wisdom of the elders: Honoring sacred native visions of nature.* New York: Bantam Books.

Wynter, S. (1992a). "No humans involved": An open letter to my colleagues. *Voices of the Diaspora, 8* (2), 13-16.

Wynter, S. (1992b). *Do not call us Negros: How multicultural textbooks perpetuate racism.* San Francisco: Aspire Books.

10 SPECULATION BASED ON SPECULATION: THE PROBLEM OF *THE BELL CURVE* AND THE QUESTION OF SCHOOLING

JO ANNE PAGANO

Knowledge confers social and economic power. That is, officially recognized and valued knowledge confers such power. In this we must agree with Richard Herrnstein and Charles Murray. Teachers, but not only teachers, distribute knowledge, and they certify that the students who pass through their classes have acquired or failed to acquire knowledge and to what degree they possess that knowledge. At the same time, by historical mandate and according to popular belief, schools and the teachers who work within them are charged with preparing the young to become responsible and committed participants in democratic structures. As Herrnstein and Murray draw out the policy implications of their position regarding schooling, it becomes clear that our embracing these implications will demand that we relinquish our commitment to democratic empowerment. Fortunately, their premises, their arguments, and their conclusions can be shown to be equally speculative, and their speculations deflect our attention from the real problems involved in educating all citizens of a society for responsible democratic participation.

Two speculative fantasies are central to all of the others leading to their policy recommendations. The first is that intelligence is so closely associated with genetic inheritance as to render any attempt at raising intelligence destined for failure. The corollary speculation is that this genetic capacity can be measured. The second speculation is that this genetic capacity determines, or at least limits, the quantity of official knowledge that we might predict a person to acquire. Therefore, genetic capacity determines, or limits, a person's access to social and economic power. It is clear as we read that the authors are aware that their speculations rest on shaky ground, that is, they are aware that their speculations rest on other speculations. For example, in chapter 6, "Schooling," the authors argue that recipients of GED diplomas should be treated differently from the population of high school graduates receiving diplomas through the officially sanctioned four-year process. They should be treated differently, the authors argue, because *as a group,* GED diploma holders fail to achieve the same success in the job market as the "typical" high school graduate. This observation is explained by the power of social class. GED diploma holders, *as a group,* are members of the lower class, and it is possible that lower class in its old-fashioned sense has an impact on how people behave." At the same time, the authors allow that "All of this interpretation is speculative" (p. 151).

We might well wonder what "lower class in its old-fashioned sense" might mean. But I think we know. Although the quantitative evidence provided leads to the conclusion that "lower class" simply means poor, the speculative interpretation leads us straight to the "old-fashioned sense." I believe that authors expect that the "old-fashioned sense" is part of the conceptual background that will allow readers of this text to concur in their speculative interpretation. For nowhere is socially class clearly defined. We can be sure only that the "lower class in its old-fashioned sense" performs less well on IQ tests and other standardized measures of achievement and that this performance differential is the cause of conditions that others might read as a result of social inequity. The chapters on college and on schooling are meant to provide evidence to the contrary by demonstrating that increased attendance at school has done little to mitigate that performance differential. Therefore, this performance differential must be an index of a genetically inherited debility. The effect of class "in its old-fashioned sense," becomes an effect on behavior, behavior that is genetically determined.

The substance of this book is all interpretive speculation; it is defensible only if we agree to the authors' definition of intelligence and acknowledge the explanatory power and empirical soundness of the "classicist" approach to the study of intelligence. Other contributors to this volume take up this issue in detail. I will simply point to the rhetorical sleight-of-hand the authors employed in their attempt to convince "nonspecialist" readers of the strength of this position. "Nonspecialist" is a word used by the authors to refer to those who dispute their position, although they do offer some grudging acknowledgment of Howard Gardner's professional standing. Dr. Gardner, however, becomes "an influential spokesman from the academy" for these nonspecialists (p. 18). In other words, he is their patsy, and the absence of quantitative data in his reported work should make us suspicious in any case.

Well, what is intelligence? On page 22, the authors claim that they have been convinced by Gardner "that the word *intelligence* carries with it undue affect and political baggage." That being the case, they tell us, they will clarify. Intelligence means cognitive ability. But isn't that precisely what Gardner and others deny? These authors will not trouble themselves to respond to that nonspecialist denial. Moreover, since *cognitive ability* is considered an uneuphonius phrase (this may not have occurred to us nonspecialist readers), we often give up scholarship so as to make the text readable. So do not get upset, gentle reader; intelligence is now to be understood "as just a noun, not an accolade." This claim is belied by the rest of the text, by the claim, for example, that intelligence has an effect on behavior. Lack of intelligence causes people to behave in ways that displace them from the socioeconomic reward structure despite the best efforts of those of us who are involved in their schooling. "Cognitive ability" provides a distinction without a difference.

One reason that the authors give for holding fast to their "classicist" position is that this position has persisted for over a century and across decades of "revisionist" and "radical" criticism. Say the authors of IQ tests, "If the tests had been fatally flawed or merely uninformative, they would have vanished . . ." (p. 6). The disingenuousness of that statement is mind-boggling. We can all think of beliefs, and even empirical claims, that have persisted for a very long time despite their being dead wrong. The language may seduce the "nonspecialist" reader into overlooking this objection, however. The authors take the "classic" position, while those who dispute this position are "revisionist" or "radical." It would be naive to take these as simply descriptions and not evaluations. The word "classic" carries much the same baggage as the word "intelligence."

In chapter 6, the authors say, "Low intelligence is one of the best predictors of school failure" (p. 143). One of the subheadings of this chapter is "What Does 'A High School Education' Mean?" Curiously, the text does not answer the question there. It is, however, answered in succeeding chapters, most specifically in chapter 18, "The Leveling of American Education." In chapter 6 we are led through a quick and dirty historical treatment of the increasing enrollments of lower-class children in secondary schools. The issue considered in chapter 6 is primarily that of dropping out. We are not surprised to learn that as the number of lower-class children attending high school increases, so does the dropout rate. Nor are we surprised to learn that dropouts are likely to score lower on IQ tests. Nor should we be surprised by the questions begged in the speculative interpretations and policy recommendations that succeed these data.

The question of the meaning of a high school education raised in this chapter is deferred to the end of the book to good rhetorical effect. In chapter 6 we are treated only to descriptions of school outcomes among the lower classes and correlations of those outcomes with socioeconomic standing (SES) and IQ performance. Up to this point the authors have assumed, without any real argument, that the purpose of schooling is to provide, plain and simple, job access and social power. Until the period beginning approximately after World War II, this purpose was largely achieved because those attending high school were intelligent. How do we know this? We know this because of their parents' social class status and their own performance on IQ and other standardized tests.

After World War II, and with increasing rapidity through the 1970s and 1980s, evidence of school crisis began to accumulate with increasing rapidity. For the authors crisis consists in the escalating dropout rate and the failure of economic success for those born to the lower classes. Chapter 6 does not reexamine school practice or even raise the difficult normative questions regarding the nature and purposes of schooling; rather its purpose is to confirm certain prejudices.

We have a long history in this country of ascribing economic and social success to virtue, talent, and the capacity for hard work. Anyone possessing the will and the heart may cultivate virtue, talent, and the capacity for hard work. We believe that education is designed to teach us to do so. Our beliefs regarding education are at the same time founded on certain "classical" paradigms that we associate with intelligence. Therefore, we come to believe that education leads to "intelligence." By a trick of association, economic and social success are taken as evidence of "intelligence." When I teach a course in the philosophy of education, I begin by asking my students to fill in the blank with a name in the following sentence: "(blank) is an educated person." My students do not disappoint. The list we compile is heavy with CEOs and celebrities and very light on intellectuals.

But now it seems, or at least perceived educational and economic crises indicate, that access to education does not lead to social and economic success. We will leave aside the question of equality in educational practice and the distribution of educational resources. We leave these questions aside because the authors insist that those who are genetically less intelligent simply cannot profit from education. Still, we insist on sending them to school with the more intelligent of our kids; as a result, we have turned out generations of ignoramuses not only among the lower classes but among the upper classes as well. Education has been "leveled" in a misguided attempt to produce silk purses out of sows' ears, to instill intelligence where there is none. Everyone suffers. The economy is shot. The Japanese and the Mexicans take advantage of us, and the lazy homeless, "the lower classes in the old-fashioned sense," won't stay out of our faces. We have a long history of tagging education as cause and cure. Now we add to education—intelligence.

Over and over again, the authors are careful to point out that their data refer to groups. They are scrupulous in noting that we can say nothing meaningful about the future of any individual by looking at group data. And yet all of their speculative interpretations and policy recommendations are based on group data. When I think of my work as a teacher, I do not think of my students as groups. I am interested in individual needs, dispositions, and talents, and in the previous experience of individuals. As far as I know only individuals have experiences. Groups do not. Individuals are intelligent; groups are not, in any meaningful or nonprejudicial sense. In any case, it should be noted that the authors concentrate their attention on the extremes of the bell curve in forming their speculations and not in the center, where even group differences are unlikely to make much of a difference.

All of us who teach know that an important factor in determining school success is previous experience with the official knowledge of the school curriculum and with certain cognitive operations and affective dispositions. Despite the authors' insistence on the heritability of intelligence and on the importance of the characteristics of groups in determining success, it turns out that even the venerable g has at least an experiential component. "G is a general capacity for inferring and applying relationships drawn from experience" (p. 4).

So far I have addressed only the question of social and economic purposes of education. These are the purposes that receive the most public attention. We have yet to consider the democratic purposes of education; we have yet to consider our need for a responsibly educated citizenry capable of analysis, imagination, and humane impulse. A citizen must have some understanding of the economy, of politics, of social structure. A citizen must be able to engage critically questions of social justice and individual moral commitment. Citizens must bring to their deliberations a historical critical consciousness that demands that they transcend the parochial.

I will not deny that the country is in a sorry state. I can even agree that education is implicated in the current situation. That a man like Jesse Helms could be elected to office is a sign of educational failure every bit as pressing as dropout rates, declining Scholastic Aptitude Tests (SAT) scores, and the size of the national deficit. I agree that the most successful of our students, *as a group,* are only slightly better prepared than the least successful for responsible democratic participation, which requires certain habits of heart and mind that should be the concern of schools. I do not agree that these habits of heart and mind can be achieved only by the few who should have more education.

The fact is that all adult citizens of a democratic society are entitled to vote. And so they should be. The fact is that many of them vote whether they are educated or not. The fact is that many of those who are successful in social and economic terms do not possess the intellectual habits and democratic disposition of citizens. This appears to me to have little to do with either intelligence or social class. The authors claim that more intelligent children have failed to realize their potential because we have attempted to provide the same education to all. How we can make some people less intelligent and claim that it is impossible to make others more intelligent escapes my understanding. I would like to see a study in which people were coached to take IQ tests in the same way that the wealthy, who already have high IQ's, we are led to believe, are coached to take SAT tests. This thought is provoked by the authors' suggestion that the correlation between IQ tests and SAT tests is natural.

It may be true that one of our mistakes is in trying to provide the same education to all. That depends on what we mean by the "same education." Writers as divergent from one another as John Dewey, Mortimer Adler, and William Bennett argue that the best education for anyone is the best education for everyone. This seems true to me when we look at the imperatives of sustaining democratic structures and practices. Still, previous experiences of individuals with differences in individual talent and disposition may require that we think of ways of achieving the same goals in ways tailored to those individuals.

The literature on individual differences in learning is enormous. We know that all people do not learn most effectively in the same way. We know, for example, that most people do not learn most easily by listening to other people talk and taking notes. Those of us who do learn easily in that modality have Ph.D.'s. Still we persist in a single modality of teaching. The lecture continues to be the standard mode of teaching in colleges and universities. John Goodlad and others have told us that 80 percent of students' time in public schools is spent listening to teachers talk. For those who come to school with certain kinds of experiences, this practice will be more or less successful.

During the early 1970s I taught in a Higher Education Opportunity Program (HEOP). My students were preparing to take the Graduate Record Examination (GRE). I was fortunate to be teaching in that program then. There was money, and there was institutional support for innovation. I and my colleagues did not take the standard approach to GRE preparation. That is, we did not focus our efforts on developing test-taking skills until the very end of the program. For most of our students, the program lasted for three semesters, during which time they passed through several levels of instruction at their own pace. We ignored the test preparation books. Students read books and stories. They studied math and history and science. They wrote papers and poems and stories and plays.

As a group, it is difficult to characterize the students. Some were African American and some from the Caribbean. There were some Italians, a French Algerian, and at one point for some reason, several Bulgarians. Many of them were white. Some were employed, and some were not. There were adults with families and young people living with parents. Some of them were "teenage mothers," and some were "convicted felons." Some scored at the third-grade level on the California Aptitude Test (CAT), and some at the twelfth. (It continues to seem odd to me to say that an adult reads at the third-grade level. Something must distinguish adult readers from third graders even if they get the same number of answers correct.) As a group they had two things in common: They were poor. They were frightened. I don't know what their IQs were.

I quickly came to understand that my students were victims of school experience. They would deal with difficulty by avoiding it. I remember putting algebra problems on the board and beginning to explain the method of solving them. This one went out to the hall for a drink. Another had to go to the bathroom. Several would physically turn away and stare at the back wall. As I walked around the room trying to help people with the work, I couldn't help but notice the hands shaking. Herrnstein and Murray tell me that it is likely that these students were in my GED class because they had low IQ's. They seemed to me as "intelligent" as the children of the wealthy and upper middle class who sit in my classes today. They did not have the confidence necessary for anyone to attempt learning anything.

When I was a child, I was much smaller than other kids in my classes. I couldn't run as fast or throw as far or jump as high. Nobody wanted to pick me for their team. By the time I reached high school, I was terrified of engaging in any physical activity in public. I knew before trying that I would fail and be laughed at or shouted at. I barely graduated from high school, having failed gym two years in a row. I used to spend gym period in the girls' room. By my senior year I was taking gym five days a week, still skipping class whenever I could, and still failing miserably at everything. I was unable to succeed in athletics because I avoided athletics. It seems obvious to me that competence requires practice and experience. It seems tragic to me that in literature class as well as in gym class, large numbers of students are being denied the opportunity for practice and experience even if no one intends to deny them that experience. We all try to protect ourselves from pain.

The official knowledge of school and of the IQ tests is founded on a set of experiences that require practice in certain other experiences. My GED students had failed at school and had left school because they found it humiliating and painful. Perhaps no one intended this. But no one asked what students already had to know and what experiences they required in order to learn what they were being taught. No one encouraged them to practice, and no one taught them how to practice.

"Confidence" and "self-esteem" are words uttered with a sneer in certain circles. Schools are in trouble because we worry too much about the self-esteem of low-IQ, lazy, old-fashioned lower-class students. But we can't teach people who won't come to school. And we can't make them come to school if we won't teach them.

Let's suppose that genetic endowment figures in the development of any talent—intellectual, artistic, or athletic. It's probably true that no amount of practice will result in my becoming an athletic star. However, there is no reason to suppose me incapable of learning to play tennis for pleasure just as my colleague does. Perhaps no amount of practice will result in my achieving musical recognition, but certainly I might learn to play the piano for the pleasure of myself and friends. Most people are neither tennis stars nor musical geniuses. That does not prevent their engaging in these activities with some degree of skill. Even if we were to demonstrate some upper limit for intelligence, most of us who fall at neither extreme should certainly be able to develop intellectual competence. This demonstration, of course, must wait on our developing an untautalogical definition of intelligence. For now, some continue to insist that intelligence is what IQ measures.

Reference

Herrnstein, R. J. and Murray, C. (1994). *The Bell Curve: Intelligence and class structure in American life.* New York: The Free Press.

11 LEAPS OF AN UNJUST FAITH: MISSING LINKS IN THE CAUSES OF LABOR FORCE PARTICIPATION

TOWNSAND PRICE-SPRATLEN

*In chapter 7, "Unemployment, Idleness, and Injury, "*Robert Herrnstein and Charles Murray evaluate the relationship between "cognitive classes" and labor force participation. Their intent is clear. The actual research, however, is far more shallow than their gingerly stated conclusions would suggest. Focusing only on the experiences of white males, they state that when considering questions of employment, that the state of the economy matters, but one must not ignore personal qualities. While this conclusion is certainly true, the analysis used to arrive at it warrants serious evaluation. I first consider the empirical, or data flaws in the chapter. Second, a few flaws in their model are discussed. Third, levels of context, potentially important to any analysis of labor force participation, are then discussed. Finally, I briefly outline a strategy, multilevel modeling, which, if used, could more effectively get at the authors' primary intent.

It is important to respond to "Unemployment, Idleness and Injury" for several reasons. First, the process of labor force participation is far more complex than the three tables and three figures in the chapter would suggest. And the veiled caution with which the authors present their final statements does not make up for their failure to consider at least a few of the factors to be presented. In addition, the fiction of the clarity of the IQ effect, present in sentences like, "In contrast to IQ, the role of parental SES is inherently ambiguous" (p. 160), is an explicit overvaluing of the role of "cognitive classes" in the employment question. Third, as they do throughout the text, in this chapter Herrnstein and Murray consistently fail to adhere to the simple adage that "correlation is not causation." As a result, they overstate the significance of their findings—potentially by a very wide margin. Because of the scholarly and political "echo" this bell has instigated anew, a detailed critique of chapter 7 is of critical importance.

PLACING VALUE ON A FLAWED MODEL

In their attempt to validate empirically the importance of cognitive ability in shaping employment outcomes, Herrnstein and Murray play rather fast and loose with data, to a degree that belies their valued reputations and distinguished academic careers. First, while acknowledging that an individual's job success is, in part, influenced by his or her background, the background index they use ridiculously oversimplifies this influence. Any number of factors in addition to an individual's parental socioeconomic status (SES) can affect the probability of being unemployed. Factors beyond the individual household, making up the neighborhood context, are essential to any analysis of individual employment outcomes—even in a sample made up only of white males. The proportion of neighborhood households with unemployed workers, persons on public assistance, or individuals employed in marginal jobs are all factors shaping the network of available opportunities to help prevent employment hardship. A single variable such as parental SES can in no way capture these important contextual influences. I'll expand on this issue later.

Second, as pointed out elsewhere in this volume, there is a great deal of "noise" in the cognitive classes used by the authors. This noise is a result of two factors: the extreme within-group variation among the classes and the ambiguities of heritability in cognitive class status. In other words, all Class II (all test takers from the lower-middle socioeconomic class) IQ scorers are not created equal. In fact, there is a great deal of difference among them, in terms of race, class, gender and geographical place, and these differences could influence the results. This variation is acknowledged in *The Bell Curve* but its possible effects are never dealt with in serious detail.

Third, through faulty inference, Herrnstein and Murray suggest relationships that may not be at all valid or, at least, may not be as valid as they suggest. Their initial table, for example, between cognitive class and months out of the labor force shows a nice, smooth trend line, with labor participation declining as class status declines. In prior chapters, they argue for the genetic heritability of these cognitive class statuses. Thus, because cognitive class is genetic, by inference, so too is the likelihood of labor force dropout.

The problem with this correlational sequence is that the sign of the predicted correlation between two factors can be predicted only under certain statistical conditions that their analysis does not meet. It is entirely possible to have a positive correlation between A and B, and another between B and C, and still have a negative (or zero) correlation between A and C. For example, height (A) and weight (B) are positively correlated (that is, taller people generally weigh more than shorter people). Weight (B) and calorie consumption (C) are also positively correlated, with heavier people generally eating more calories than lighter people. This does not mean that taller people (A) necessarily consume more calories (C). Just as in this example, the relationship among a high-class smart gene, an IQ score, and labor force success is similarly flawed.

Buried in the text on page 160 is an assertion that *should* in fact be the most important feature of the chapter: "we can also infer that all sorts of things besides IQ are important in determining whether someone stays at work." The role of social context is one of the things besides IQ that warranted much more attention by the authors.

MINIMIZING THE IMPORTANCE OF CONTEXT

Few would argue with the view that the environment that surrounds us contributes to our choices, which, in turn, can shape our success outcomes. Extending from my concern about the proper evaluation of "background" in shaping labor force outcomes, Herrnstein and Murray simply throw away the influence of surrounding environment in an offhand statement. By doing so, they imply that these many factors are far less relevant to their central question: the role of intelligence in getting and holding a job.

In brief, the view has been stated simply using two words: Context matters. Yet in *The Bell Curve* the influence of context is not only not tested, it is barely even acknowledged to exist. Addressing the decline over the last 40 years in the proportion of young white men having jobs, they tell the readers that forces, both macroeconomic and macrosocial, *that they decided not to bother to cover,* have been identified with this trend in employment. Why not try to cover some of these forces? At least a few are worth mentioning in some detail.

By not considering any contextual influences beyond parental SES, how can they possibly justify their conclusions about "what intelligence now has to do with getting and holding a job?" There is a large body of sociological research, ignored by Herrnstein and Murray, that evaluates numerous factors influencing the degree of difficulty in achieving even minimal employment success, and that invites the drawing of conclusions that, if taken seriously by the authors, might have tempered their own conclusions.

The authors' stated interest in changes over time would have been well served by at least a cursory consideration of the problem of "spatial mismatch" in urban employment. Since the late 1960s, there has been a growing geographic mismatch between where many African Americans reside and where jobs and job growth are located. The urban core, where the vast majority of African Americans live, has been hit hardest by the industrial transformation from goods-producing industries to the service sector that has been taking place over the last 30 years.

The reason this is so central to discussions about the causes of getting and holding a job is that structural changes, having nothing to do with individual intellect, play a critical role in shaping job outcomes. Whether it is the probability of being out of the labor force, length of unemployment, or any one of several others, context matters. This contextual influence is especially important in considering racial differences, which the authors conveniently avoid in chapter 7 by focusing solely on white males. Later in the book they use their "race-neutral" findings to challenge race-specific policy initiatives—a rather slippery choice that is not readily justified.

When race is brought into the discussion, the effects of spatial mismatch on labor force participation can be seen clearly. As one example, consistent with the first graph in the chapter, underemployment (the receipt of poverty-level wages or significantly reduced hours) has increased over time for both Whites and African Americans since 1970. However, due to shrinking opportunities related to the spatial mismatch, race differences in underemployment between African Americans and Whites have increased substantially. In other words, the pace of growing underemployment has been faster for African Americans. Worse yet, this race effect has increased regardless of age group, level of education, or macroeconomic shifts in the community. And the problem appears to be getting worse, not better. Yet in their analysis of employment outcomes in chapter 7, Herrnstein and Murray exclude such dynamics. Such omissions significantly alter the picture they present.

Also, this mismatch is made worse given sustained residential segregation. Residential segregation is the concentrated settlement of groups into separate neighborhoods based on a salient characteristic of difference. Typically, race is the primary characteristic. Segregation often limits African American access to more diverse environments of opportunity and to the wealth and well-being outcomes that can result from exposure to such environments. As Douglas S. Massey and Nancy A. Denton brilliantly point out in *American Apartheid*, "housing markets are central to individual social and economic well-being because they distribute much more than shelter; they also distribute a variety of resources that shape and largely determine one's life chances" (1987, p. 235). Thus the employment and economic consequences of sustained residential segregation should not be underestimated; independent of any other contextual forces, the level of segregation in an area has a negative impact on income and educational outcomes regardless of race. As might be expected, the negative impact is more pronounced for African Americans than it is for Whites.

Herrnstein and Murray might take the position that they were attempting to simplify the analysis by ignoring these contextual influences. While simplicity in research is sometimes worthwhile, the complexities of labor force participation demand a much more detailed analysis than chapter 7 provides. The use of multilevel modeling might have altered their findings. Multilevel modeling is a technique that allows a researcher to consider the influence of several different types of affects at the same time. An individual may be a part of a household, the household a part of the neighborhood, and the neighborhood part of a larger community. Measures of potentially important characteristics can be taken at each of these levels. By doing so, the relative importance of variables in these multiple levels can be determined.

In order for some of the preceding limitations to be addressed, researchers interested in improving on the Herrnstein and Murray analyses would do well to consider using some kind of multilevel modeling strategy. While the specifics of this analytical tool are well beyond the scope of this chapter, the use of such a strategy could begin to sort out some of the problems that their current three-variable model has.

A BELL WITH A SOUR RING—LEGITIMIZED INEQUALITY

The cultural context that has allowed *The Bell Curve* to achieve such enormous viability, both inside and outside of media and academic circles, must be addressed over the coming years. In the midst of an unsettled period of cultural insecurity, the need for solidifying "the Other" through racist regurgitation becomes all the more acute. It is in such times that the rebirth of legitimized inequality, ahistorical analyses, and contextual simplification are likely to be strongest—especially when broad access to commonplace expressions of the American Dream appear to be severely threatened. As I write these words, we are in such a time.

Under these circumstances, when analyzing labor force participation, initiating a dialogue that would specify the action-steps needed to move toward a sustainable justice and social equity is seldom defined as viable. Yet it is the essential missing link in eliminating the cultural insecurity that sparks the unjust spiral in the first place. It is my hope that we spend more time defining and refining the meaning and mission of sustainable justice and social equity, and less and less time considering strategies to further solidify injustice. May *The Bell Curve* serve as a contradictory starting point for such a dialogue to take place.

References

Herrnstein, R. J. And Murray, C. (1994). *The Bell Curve: Intelligence and class structure in American life*. New York: The Free Press.

Lichter, D. T. (1988). Racial differences in underemployment in American cities. *American Journal of Sociology, 93*, 771-792.

Massey, D. S., Condran, G. A. and Denton, N. A. (1987). The effect of residential segregation on black social and economic well-being. *Social Forces, 66*, 29-56.

Snijders, T. and Bosker, R. J. (1994). Modelled variance in two–level models. *Sociological Methods & Research, 22*, 342-363.

Taylor, H. (1995). Review symposium of *The Bell Curve, Contemporary Sociology, 24*, 153-158.

12 FAMILY MATTERS

ALAN A. BLOCK · DON STEPHENSON

Leo Tolstoy begins his novel, Anna Karenina, this way: "All happy families are alike but an unhappy family is unhappy after its own fashion" (1973, p. 13). This statement suggests Tolstoy's acknowledgment of the ultimate dilemma of life, perhaps even the motive force of life itself: Happiness is what we seek but its actual achievement represents a cul-de-sac. In fact, Tolstoy suggests, it is the *pursuit* and not the achievement of happiness (embedded in an original dissatisfaction) in which our individualities are produced. Happiness is inescapably the achievement of a conclusive product. This product, once achieved, is conceptualized as a form of stasis: It requires or, rather, it inspires no further movement. Happiness becomes an ultimate achievement. In this regard, happiness is conceived as a finite quantity. There is, after its attainment, only the immobility of stasis, of continuous habitual acting; nothing must change. Happiness looks the same everywhere; there is no specificity or individual agency.

Life, we must acknowledge, however, is premised on continual change; the happiness to which Tolstoy refers is death. In fact, *Anna Karenina* offers a portrait of the only type of family that exists—the unhappy family. *Anna Karenina* is a novel about the *unreality* of happy families and the *inevitability* of unhappy ones. Movement—life—is organized by a discrepancy between present position and desire; thought, or reflection, is premised on a dissonance between expectation and realization. In the novel the dynamics of an unhappy family work themselves out in the very particular manner of the personalities of those family members pursuing an evanescent happiness and as their individual actions in this pursuit produce events. In this regard, the unhappiness of the family must inevitably be after its own fashion. Unhappiness, for Tolstoy, is continually organized by the complex reactions of individuals to the exigencies of life and within a structure that is not of their choosing. Marx's great observation is an apt epigraph for *Anna Karenina*:

> Men make their own history, but they do not make it just as they please; they do not make it under circumstances chosen by themselves, but under circumstances directly encountered, given and transmitted from the past . . . And just when they seem engaged in revolutionizing themselves and things, in creating something that has never yet existed, precisely in such periods of revolutionary crisis they anxiously conjure up the spirits of the past to their service and borrow from them names, battle cries and costumes in order to present the new scene of world history in this time-honored disguise and this borrowed language. (1963, p. 15)

Families that are unhappy seek happiness and, hence, particular experience occurs as character and events transact in specific ways. The story of one family's particular unhappiness—that of the family of Karenina—is the subject of this novel; yet the greatness of *Anna Karenina* lies in its portrayal of the complex weave of life of which Russian society is comprised and by which it functions. The real subject of Tolstoy's novel is humanity in its variety, its passions, and its mortality. Or, in the words of a different popular culture, "Life is like a box of chocolates—you never know what you're going to get." *Forrest Gump* offered America support for its belief that regardless of ability and/or circumstance, anyone could achieve success. The immense popularity of the film speaks to the hopes and dreams (tinged with a debilitating sexism and racism though they are) of the American populace—to the human belief that in this world fulfillment is always possible.

What can we say? It is the argument of Richard Herrnstein's and Charles Murray's *The Bell Curve: Intelligence and Class Structure in American Life* (1994) that Tolstoy's observation about happiness and unhappiness in families is not true. Nor, these authors assert, is life like a box of chocolates: In many of the most important areas of life, what you are going to get is inextricably entwined with IQ scores, which the authors contend is primarily a function of genetic transmission. For the most part, chocolates come in boxes of singular assortment and you almost always know what you are going to get. Herrnstein and Murray argue in chapter 8 that unhappiness in families is very much organized by cognitive ability and education—and that the complexities of human personality play an insignificant part in the family drama. Family unhappiness can always be attributed to the same causes and will always appear the same. "Rumors of the death of the traditional family have much truth in them for some parts of white American society—those with low cognitive ability and little education—and much less truth for the college educated and very bright Americans of all educational levels" (p. 167). To paraphrase Tolstoy, Herrnstein and Murray would argue that *all happy families are alike because they are smart and an unhappy family is unhappy because it is dumb.* Herrnstein and Murray conclude that the American family in the more intelligent segments of the population continues to thrive (hence the importance and insistence on family values—*ours*, of course, and not *theirs*) and those families in the less intelligent continues to deteriorate. According to Herrnstein and Murray, in the lower IQ levels there is less marriage, more divorce, and more illegitimacies.

It is our view that the complexities of family life are denied in *The Bell Curve* and that the infinite weave of the intricate tapestry is reduced in this book to the polyestered texture of intelligence quotients. For the authors of *The Bell Curve,* those families in the lower quartiles are inevitably unhappy because of their deficient intelligences (and not the complex conditions of life that *The Bell Curve* reduces to intelligence). Conversely, those in the upper quartiles are—or at least ought to be—inevitably happy because of their superior intelligences.

Once again, simply stated, Herrnstein and Murray argue that those with low IQs marry less frequently; that the rate of divorce in families of low IQs is greater than those with high IQs; and that the rates of illegitimacy are higher for those with low than for those with high IQs. We will address each of these points in turn with regard to family matters; the larger issues of IQ and intelligence are the subject of other chapters in this book. Suffice it to say, we advocate that intelligence is not reducible to a single factor *g* and that IQ tests as presently constituted and because they are reducible to *g* must inevitably misrepresent intelligence. Even a theory of multiple intelligence as advanced in the work of Howard Gardner only begins to address the complexities of the human mind. The reduction of human complexity and potential in *The Bell Curve* flies in the face of all we know of human history, and the book's depiction of the family as organized not by human contingency in a difficult world but as a function of innate intelligence is insidious to the point of horror. The authors' espousal of the intractability of low IQ, taken to its logical conclusion, would necessitate a drastic program of eugenics and population control. In this chapter, then, we would like to address the issues in chapter 8 of *The Bell Curve* in the following ways: First, we reject the authors' reduction of human existence to statistical analysis. However, we address Herrnstein and Murray's statistical approach insofar as we might discover in it their ideological bias and the insidious speciousness of their techniques. Second, we look at the contradictions explicit in their analysis, contradictions that also expose the emptiness of their claims that intelligence is the key to understanding family behavior.

With regard to the rate of marriage in society, Herrnstein and Murray argue that low-intelligence individuals are disadvantaged in the competition for marriage partners. We note first that the language of *The Bell Curve* reduces marriage to a simple rivalry for partners. The complexities of human life and object relations are here reduced to a relatively simple contest for sexual mate. Second, human emotional response is reduced to a matter of IQ: Each category—initiative, romance, economics—examined in isolation. The everyday complexities that inevitably interconnect initiative, romance, and economics are discounted. The willing purchase of romantic boxes of Gump's chocolate is highly dependent on economic viability—a contextual factor ignored by Herrnstein and Murray.

Third, Herrnstein and Murray argue that percentages for marriages are highest for people in the middle of the intelligence distribution and then the distribution tapers off on both ends. We note the authors' own acknowledgment that 90 percent of the American public marry before the age of 40, but their analysis of marriage rates is based on those under 30. Nevertheless, even given the statistics they employ, they proceed to wander toward what sophomore psychology majors know to be the "mother load" of significant research findings: the comparison of extremes. A middle class high school graduate two standard deviations below the mean of IQ distribution has three in five chances of getting married. A high school graduate with the highest IQ scores has an 89 percent chance of matrimony. And though IQ did not make a difference in marriage rates in the college sample, the authors are willing to ascribe causation to the difference in IQ in the high school sample. Apparently, college is the great leveler. Further, we would like to note that it is not our experience that people with measured IQs of 70 or below (two standard deviations below the mean) have available the opportunity to attend college, though by law (PL 94-142) they *must* attend high school. Therefore, the statistic is heavily skewed and ultimately misrepresents the field it ascribes to portray; by the authors' own standards, the extremes marry less and the middle almost all marry. In addition, in many states, persons with an IQ of less than 70 are forbidden to marry. And perhaps we might further argue that people at the high end of the IQ spectrum may have less-developed adaptive behavioral skills and refuse to marry. In any case, the statistical argument (which is the only argument offered) in *The Bell Curve* appears to us terribly flawed.

Herrnstein and Murray argue that persons with low IQs have a higher divorce rate than those with higher IQs. Evidence shows, say the authors, that while smart people are more likely to get married, it is dumb people who are more likely to get divorced. The statistics are interesting. The standard for a successful marriage is defined as failure to divorce during the first five years of marriage. This measurement would seem a bit like jumping from a nine-story building and yelling "so far, so good" as you passed the fifth floor. Furthermore, the authors note that divorce rates in the bottom 75 percent of IQ distribution were the same—though in the upper 25 percent (two standard deviations above the mean, or an IQ of 130) couples were ten times as likely to remain married for at least five years as they were to seek divorce. What is being compared here?— especially since in the earlier section the marriage *rate* for those in the higher IQs was lower than for any other cognitive class. The question of what is being measured is even more relevant when not one paragraph earlier the authors acknowledge their inability to explain the expanding divorce rate in the United States. All we mean to do, the authors assert, is to correlate divorce with intelligence—as if correlation can even be used to attribute causation. As if, to offer a metaphor from the hallowed physics the authors misrepresent, correlation reveals anything other than the point of the view of the observer. Furthermore, this reduction of a complex causation to mere intelligence and to conclude with the catch-all and dismissive statement "and who knows what else" must demand that the argument in this section of the book be rejected. *By the authors' own admission,* divorce is too complex an issue to reduce to a single factor. Yet in the authors' analysis these intricate and myriad factors are noted and duly ignored.

Herrnstein and Murray assert that there may even be plausible reasons for expecting that cognitive ability will have an impact on the divorce rate. "One may hypothesize that bright people less often marry on whim, hence they have fewer disastrous short marriages" (p. 174). Needless to say, though we will say it, the authors present no evidence for this position. We cannot help think of the scores of films that portray the whimsicalness of romance endemic to those in the middle and upper middle classes, a social position that the authors earlier correlate with those of higher intelligence. Recall, if you will, Cary Grant's character in *Bringing Up Baby*. Or James Stewart as a patsy for the machinations of Barbara Stanwyck in *The Lady Eve*. Or perhaps we might consider the single mother in the perennial children's film, *Miracle on 34th Street*. How can we answer for these popular portrayals? What about whimsical Meg Ryan in *Sleepless in Seattle*? Now, we do not mean, as did Ronald Reagan, to mistake acetate for reality, but we wonder what social perspective was being worked out in these and many other films in American culture.

The authors suggest that the less intelligent the woman is, the more likely she is to give birth to an illegitimate child. They argue that the less intelligent a woman is, the more likely it will be that she does not think ahead from sex to procreation, does not remember to use birth control, does not carefully consider when and under what circumstances she should have a child. How intelligent a woman is may interact with her impulsiveness, and hence her ability to exert self-discipline and restraint on her partner in order to avoid pregnancy. We note several interesting themes here. First, the authors make no mention of abortion in their discussion of illegitimacy. In other words, according to *The Bell Curve,* the rate of illegitimacy has nothing to do with the availability of abortion; in its absence, abortion has been transmuted into a nonissue. This is, of course, no accident, because Charles Murray stands with the anti-abortion/pro-life segment of the conservative population. With the availability of abortion decreasing daily and with the violence at abortion clinics deterring clients, it is no wonder that illegitimate births are increasing and are seemingly centered in the lower socioeconomic classes, which also, Herrnstein and Murray note, coincidentally happens to be the segment of the population with the lowest IQ scores.

Second, the value judgment implicit in this entire discussion that a child born legitimately has greater value than one born out of wedlock retreats into the ideology of feudal Europe. The assumption in *The Bell Curve* is that a legitimate child is less of a burden on society, is born into a loving and caring home, and will therefore develop into a worthwhile and productive citizen whereas illegitimate children are merely a burden on society and often come to no good anyway—especially since intelligence is inheritable and most illegitimate children are born to women with lower IQs.

Finally, the authors attribute all inheritable characteristics of intelligence to the woman. Immaculate conception is, so to speak, reborn in *The Bell Curve*, also not surprising in a text that espouses the middle-class standards of family values where the woman controls all but the purse strings of the household. Furthermore, the belief that it is the intelligence or lack thereof in the woman which is responsible for illegitimacy by attributing deliberation to the woman before sex and procreation makes whole nations—such as China and India, for example—suspect of mass retardation. Thus it is no accident that the woman is afforded all of the control over procreation: In the conservative agenda men need not concern themselves with home care; it is home construction that rests in the male domain, and that obligation often does not require actually spending time there.

The reduction of family construction to the vagaries of intelligence reduces the wonderful complexities of life to a single line on a graph. We believe that the noun "matters" in the title of this chapter should be altered to a verb. It is in this context that a new public conversation about family should begin. The work of Herrnstein and Murray does disservice to scholarship, to "family values," to public policy, and to human value.

References

Herrnstein, R. J. and Murray, C. (1994). *The Bell Curve: Intelligence and class structure in American life*. New York: The Free Press.

Marx, K. (1963). *The Eighteenth Brumaire of Louis Bonaparte*. New York: International Publishers.

Tolstoy, L. (1973). *Anna Karenina*. (R. Edmonds, Trans.). New York: Penguin Books.

13 GENETIC RATIONALIZATIONS AND PUBLIC POLICY: HERRNSTEIN AND MURRAY ON INTELLIGENCE AND WELFARE DEPENDENCY

MARIA R. VIDAL

It is difficult for an empty bag to stand upright.
—Alexandre Dumas

Conservative policymakers, journalists, and scholars have been telling us for some time now that poor people, particularly those who are on Aid to Families with Dependent Children (AFDC) rolls, are promiscuous, immoral, violence prone, lazy, and uncommitted to American values regarding the importance of family, education, work, and self-sufficiency (Mead, 1986; Murray, 1984; Gilder, 1981). Now Richard Herrnstein and Charles Murray (1994) tell us that they are unintelligent. While earlier theorists have attributed these deviant and pathological behaviors said to be characteristic of the poor to an inheritance of a culture of poverty or to the effects of a permissive welfare state that discourages individual responsibility and encourages dependency, Herrnstein and Murray offer a new thesis. The authors of *The Bell Curve* place the blame on the low intellectual capacity bequeathed to individuals by genetically inferior parents.

Herrnstein and Murray argue that the lack of intelligence found among the poor is so profound that it frequently prevents them from making "good" choices with respect to education, work, childbearing, and family formation. Such inadequacy leads the unintelligent poor down the path to welfare reliance. In the introduction to chapter 9, entitled "Cognitive Classes and Social Behavior," the authors succinctly state their thesis that low IQ is a cause of irresponsible child bearing, inappropriate parenting behavior, unemployment, and—as an end result—poverty.

IQ AND WELFARE DEPENDENCY

Herrnstein and Murray set out to examine the relationship between welfare receipt and IQ utilizing data from the National Longitudinal Survey of Youth (NLSY). This is a study of American youth aged 14 to 22 years of age in 1979, the year marking the first wave of interviews. The NLSY contains detailed data regarding cognitive ability as measured by the Armed Forces Qualification Test (AFQT) and measures of social and economic outcomes. In their analysis, Herrnstein and Murray utilize data collected through the 1990 interview wave, but limited their study sample to a white-only subsample of women whose first child was born prior to January 1, 1989.

In their theorizing regarding the relationship between IQ and welfare dependency, Herrnstein and Murray draw distinctions between women they categorize as "chronic" recipients and those who receive welfare for a limited period of time. They define chronic welfare dependency as receipt of welfare income for five or more years. Employing this criterion, they found that 21 percent of the women had received AFDC assistance at some point and that 9 percent had become chronic recipients. When considering which women were more likely to seek welfare assistance within the first calendar year after the birth of her child, Herrnstein and Murray found that the IQ of the mother was significantly related to risk for welfare receipt for the study population as a whole, but that for women who had completed high school or more, IQ was not a significant predictor and that none of the college-educated women had received AFDC.

Among mothers whom they defined as chronic welfare dependents, they found IQ to be insignificant and observed that prebirth poverty status of the mother was a significant predictor regardless of her level of education. Furthermore, although the authors do not highlight this in their discussions, prebirth poverty and the marital status of the mothers was found to be highly significant in all analyses for both short-term and chronic welfare recipients. In fact, these two variables were found to be more significant than any others considered in their investigation, including IQ.

Interestingly, Herrnstein and Murray are not discouraged by these findings, which lend extremely limited support to their ideas regarding the strength of the relationship between IQ and welfare receipt among young mothers. Nor are they dissuaded by finding that the average IQ of the women studied were within the normal range (90 to 110), regardless of whether they: remained childless or were married at the time of the birth of their child, were unmarried and had a child but did not utilize AFDC, became short-term welfare recipients, or became long-term or chronic welfare beneficiaries.

SERIOUS SCHOLARSHIP OR SMOKE AND MIRRORS

A flurry of critiques followed Murray's 1984 publication of *Losing Ground: American Social Policy, 1950-1980,* many by social scientists who objected to his abuse and misuse of data (Bernstein, 1995). In this earlier book Murray argued that the expansion of the welfare state in the 1960s through the 1970s exacerbated social problems such as poverty, crime, school dropout, and unemployment and promoted childbearing outside of marriage and welfare dependency. The nature of his analysis and the manner in which data were presented in support of his thesis led many to question his honesty and the rigor of his scholarship. In *The Bell Curve* it appears as if once again Murray, this time in cahoots with Herrnstein, has been irresponsible and disingenuous in his analysis of data. As in *Losing Ground,* Herrnstein and Murray have tried to promote their social welfare policy agenda through a statistical shell game played with readers of *The Bell Curve.* Two of the gravest problems with their analysis lie in their handling of assumptions as fact and evading contradictory findings and arguments.

NOW YOU SEE IT, NOW YOU DON'T

Fundamental problems in Herrnstein and Murray's analysis are the lack of information presented and benefit of discussion afforded to the reader, the careful omission of contradictory evidence and/or writings, and the very limited and simplistic nature of their analysis. The authors carefully usher the reader around a constricted discussion of welfare dependency and IQ, exhibiting only supportive testimony and data.

In the last decade a plethora of research concerning poverty, AFDC utilization, and AFDC reform experiments has emerged. Unfortunately, Herrnstein and Murray do not provide readers with a review of this literature, nor do they place their work within the context of what other contemporary researchers have said about AFDC recipients and patterns of program use. For instance, they limit their discussion to very brief, passing comments regarding the important research of David Ellwood and Mary Jo Bane (1985) concerning lengths of stay on welfare and characteristics of AFDC recipient population. While presentation of research (Ellwood, 1988; Neisser and Schram, 1994) regarding the nature and consequences of low pay for low-skilled work and the lack of affordable child care and health care options for young families goes a long way in helping one understand why some turn to AFDC for support, this type of commentary is markedly absent in their discussion. By omitting a thorough and thoughtful exchange about what is known of the narrow employment and earnings prospects of young women with limited educational and work experiences, such as those who made up their study sample, Herrnstein and Murray misdirect the reader. Ironically, their own findings beg for this type of explanation, yet they choose to evade it because of the devastating implications it would have for their simplistic IQ and welfare dependency theory.

Not only do the authors obscure understanding by sidestepping the relevant literature, they also hedge when it comes to the results of their own study. First, the results of the analysis of their theoretical models are buried in an appendix rather than in the main text, which offers only a summary and interpretation. Unfortunately, the tables and figures that are found in the body of the book omit important information that should always be reported, such as frequency counts, levels of statistical significance, correlation coefficients, numbers of cases included in the analysis, and so forth. This leaves the reader unable to make a clear assessment of what is being presented and, therefore, vulnerable to the interpretations of the authors.

Furthermore, the authors grossly overstate their results. Most of the relationships between IQ scores and social behavior that Herrnstein and Murray explore throughout *The Bell Curve* indicate no systematic relationships or relationships that are very weak. In one brief moment of honesty the authors conceded that in their analysis, IQ accounts for at most 20 percent of the variance, typically less than 10 percent, and frequently less than 5 percent. Yet their modest, at best, findings do not prevent them from making forceful, sweeping conclusions. In short, Herrnstein and Murray discuss only those research results that support their IQ and welfare dependency theory, exaggerate the strength of their findings, and minimize or bury evidence to contrary.

POOR FAMILIES, WELFARE REFORM, AND THE RIGHT AGENDA

In a 1971 article appearing in the *Atlantic Monthly*, Herrnstein put forth the following proposition: "Because IQ is substantially heritable, because economic success in life depends in part on the talents measured by IQ tests, and because social standing depends in part on economic success, it follows that social standing is bound to be based to some extent on heritable differences" (Herrnstein and Murray 1971, p.10).

In 1984 Murray proposed a program that consisted of:

> Scrapping the entire federal welfare and income-support struc-ture for working-aged persons, including AFDC, Medicaid, Food Stamps, Unemployment Insurance, Worker's Compen-sation, subsidized housing, disability insurance, and the rest. It would leave the working-aged person with no recourse whatsoever except the job market, family friends, and public or private locally funded services . . . Billions for opportunity, not one cent for equal outcome. (pp. 227-28, 233)

And in 1994 Herrnstein and Murray came together in *The Bell Curve* to advance an agenda based on the combined themes of their earlier work. Herrnstein's "IQ equals destiny equation" and Murray's "sink-or-swim prescription" converge in the book's final chapter, "A Place for Everyone." Here the authors maintain that social statuses and hierarchies are the result of individual differences in natural intelligence and call for an understanding of equality based on individuals accepting their rightful place (based on cognitive ability) in society. Furthermore, they assert that government has no business in altering this natural order through intrusive policies aimed at eradicating inequality through "artificially manufactured outcomes," such as affirmative action and income transfer programs.

More direct to the point on welfare dependency issues and of out-of-wedlock births, the authors insist on the need to: restore stigma to bearing children outside of the context of marriage; once again make marriage the only legal institution responsible for exercis-ing rights and responsibilities regarding children; develop a social welfare system based on increasing self-reliance through finding one's own niche (that is, work and marriage) rather than providing cash supplements; and discourage births among the poor by eliminating support for poor women who have babies.

This welfare reform platform bears a striking parallel to that advanced by the Republicans in their *Contract with America* (1994). The Republican plan includes legislation that, if enacted, will: (1) limit AFDC benefits to a two-year maximum; (2) require that mothers establish paternity before receiving AFDC, food stamps, and public housing benefits; (3) deny benefits to parents under the age of 18; (4) deny an increase in AFDC benefits for any additional children born while the parent is receiving welfare; (5) exclude unmarried mothers under the age of 21 from AFDC, food stamps, and public housing programs (the age limit will be raised to 25 in 1998); (6) provide a $1,000 pro-marriage tax credit; (7) require that 50 percent of AFDC recipients work by 1996; and (8) require that single able-bodied food stamp recipients work off their benefit.

The similarity in tenor of both the Republican and the Herrnstein/Murray plan is not surprising, given that the writing of *The Bell Curve* was funded by a grant from the Bradley Foundation, which has been described as "the nation's biggest underwriter of conservative intellectual activity" and is currently funding William Kristol, former advisor to President Bush and director of the Project for a Republican Future (Eastbrook, 1994, p. 40). The resemblance between the two continues at the level of strategy: Republican politicians and Herrnstein and Murray have tried to legitimize their policy agenda through the creation of social myths under the guise of facts/science, moralizing, gross simplification of complex issues, and an overwhelming dose of denial.

In short, *The Bell Curve* is not a work of "objective" science offering insight regarding social issues. Rather it is a book with a political agenda. I agree with Stephen J. Gould's (1995) conclusion on this issue when he argues that *The Bell Curve* is less an academic treatise in social theory and population genetics and more a manifesto of right-wing ideology with its inhumane social and educational policy recommendation.

References

Bernstein, J. (1995, January/February). Welfare bashing redux: The return of Charles Murray. *The Humanist, 55,* 22-25.

Eastbrook, Gregg. (1995). Blacktop basketball and *The Bell Curve.* In Jacoby, R. and Glauberman, N., eds., *The Bell Curve Debate.* New York: Times Books.

Ellwood, D. (1988). *Poor support: Poverty in the American family.* New York: Basic Books.

Ellwood, D. and Bane, M. (1985). The impact of AFDC on family structure and living arrangements. *Research in Labor Economics, 7,* 137-207.

Gilder, G. (1981). *Wealth and poverty.* New York: Basic Books.

Gould, S. (1995). Mismeasure by any measure. In Jacoby, R. and Glauberman, N., eds., *The Bell Curve debate.* New York: Times Books.

Herrnstein, R. J. and Murray, C. (1994). *The Bell Curve: Intelligence and class structure in American life.* New York: The Free Press.

Herrnstein, R. (1971, September). IQ. *Atlantic Monthly,* 43-64.

Mead, L. (1986). *Beyond entitlement: The social obligations of citizenship.* New York: The Free Press.

Murray, C. (1984). *Losing ground: American social policy, 1950-1980.* New York: Basic Books.

Neisser P. and Schram, S. (1994, Winter). Redoubling denial: Industrial welfare policy meets postindustrial policy. *Social Text, 12* (4) 41-60.

Republican National Committee. (1994). *Contract with America: The bold plan by Rep. Newt Gingrich, Rep. Dick Armey, and the House of Republicans to change the nation.* New York: Times Books.

14 PARENTING IN THE PROMISED LAND

WILLIAM F. PINAR

> *Let us recall that the white man, in order to justify slavery and, later on, to justify segregation, elaborated a complex, all-pervasive myth which at one time classified the black man [sic] as a subhuman beast of burden.*
>
> —Eldridge Cleaver

The subject of parenting is a complicated one, studied by many specialists working in several fields (see Eekelaar and Sarcevic, 1993; Fantini and Cardenas, 1980; Hoffman, 1988; McLaughlin, 1976; Riesman, 1992). All agree upon its profound importance. Mario Fantini and John Russo (1980) observed: "The protection, nurture, and education of children by adults is fundamental to human life. . . . The experience of this role—parenting as it is now frequently called—is neither simply nor predominantly natural, as it inevitably involves both the child and parent in highly variable social and economic contexts" (p. xxix).

A mode of education, parenting cannot be understood apart from its various contexts, and like education, discourses on parenting create positions they pretend merely to describe. In recent years in the United States, discourses on parenting have become terrains on which political actors positions themselves and create "others." Currently, for instance, the right-wing displaces social responsibility for social problems onto private families and, more specifically, upon the presumed failures of parents (especially poor parents and black parents), in *The Bell Curve,* this responsibility is displaced onto genetic codes. In this brief chapter, a reaction to chapter 10, I wish to call parenting back from genes into culture, politics, and religion, concluding with the suggestion that the book itself is an instance of abusive parenting.

FIRST, FIND A GOOD MOTHER

Who's fit to be a parent? Mukti Jain Campion (1995) asks. Various right-wing players have insisted that contemporary problems of crime are rooted in unfit parenting. Worries regarding unfit parents do not remain identified with the ghettoes, however. Reports of "suppressed memory"—recently sensationalized in the media—leave even innocent parents slightly worried. There *are* the risks of abuse: psychological, physical, and sexual. If we suffer from "suppressed memory," are we able to trust our parenting? Whom can we trust: Harvard social scientists?

Perhaps we cannot trust our memories of our own childhoods. Could it be that we were so victimized that we invented a mythology of childhood that is now "gone with the wind?" Are we like the "Boys of St. Vincent?" If holy men can be unfit as parents, what about ordinary people? What is a good parent?

Studying the FulBe in northwest Africa, Paul Reisman (1992) explored the relationship between the development of personality and styles of parenting. In the West, he reminds us, there are two widely held assumptions regarding personality development: "The first is that one's personality influences the whole life course, for at every moment, it affects one's changes of success or failure. The second is that one of the most important factors shaping the personality is the way the parents raise the person from the very beginning of childhood" (p. 8).

Intelligence is, in many ways, expressed through the personality, itself a psychosocial, cultural, and gendered term. For the

Western educated classes, personality development is very much linked, especially early on, with the nuclear family and, in later childhood, with peer influences. For the FulBe, Riesman (1992) discovers, the mother is not socially isolated: "'finding a good mother' has less to do with choosing appropriate parenting behaviors than with linking the child to a particular type of social connectedness and set of relationships . . . the FulBe's distinctive sense of who they are grows out of the totality of their experience rather than from a single formative aspect of it" (p. 10).

What Riesman discovered in parents among the FulBe, namely that personality development is embedded in a set of connected relationships, does not disappear completely among the descendants of the Africans who were stolen across the Atlantic to North America. Indeed, the FulBe live in northwestern Africa, not far from Ghana and the Ivory Coast, the origins of many of those peoples who were brought against their will to this continent. James Comer (1980) locates the black legacy of kinship and social connectedness to this region of origin: "Most Afro-Americans are descendants of the people of the west African gold and ivory coast, around the Niger Delta and Dahomey. While conditions varied between groups, certain structural and functional elements were common or similar to all of them. A close-knit family or kinship was at the core of all political economic, and social organization (p. 45)."

Social power was hardly limited to the family; society itself was organized along what some would characterize as "collectivist" lines. Comer (1980) tells us:

> Among the Yoruba, a group significantly represented among present day Afro-Americans, each lineage had its own farmland. The land belonged to all members of the lineage; no man had to work for hire. All helped to provide or secure basic needs such as food, clothing, and shelter. The reverence of land, animals, and/or nature was more marked than in European societies. (p. 45)

Reverence for land, animals, and nature is slow to come to European Americans. Indeed, in our time, the Right has made environmental and animal rights efforts targets in their politics of reaction.

UNDER THE CIRCUMSTANCES

In terms of ancestral history as well as their North American experience, "The black family has not had the same experience as the white" (Comer, 1980, p. 43). This profound difference makes comparisons between white and black families especially difficult to draw. In the contemporary black family, we are told, "both African and slavery legacies exist" (Karenga, 1982, p. 211). However, "[slavery] never completely destroyed marriage and the family as important social institutions" (Blackwell, 1991, p. 112). When focusing on black parenting, then, comparisons with European American families are not especially helpful. Rather, it is essential to locate the black family historically, culturally, and, of course, racially, that is, in terms of American racial politics. As Comer (1980) observes: "A more fruitful approach is to simply ask how well the black family performs its adaptive task under given social circumstances" (p. 43).

"Under the circumstances," as Comer so understatingly summarizes the African experience of North America, the African American family has indeed performed "its adaptive task":

> For three quarters of a century after slavery many black families did the suppressive society's dirty work first and best. They prepared their children to accept a degraded position in the society. Parents crushed aggression in children, especially boys. . . . Harsh discipline observed in excess in many black families today is directly related to the black parents' need to "beat the badness out of the boy" . . . lest it cause him to forget his place with the white policeman. (Comer, 1980, p. 49)

Some writers have pathologized this particular adaptive strategy as insufficiently socializing (especially for black boys; see Madhubuti, 1990), but "it may well [have] provide[d] the single means of maintaining a black family unit in the midst of an overtly unsupportive, covertly hostile, and fundamentally pathogenic white society" (Cardenas, 1980, p. xvi).

There is an extensive literature outlining strategies for nurturing black children in a racist society. Step 1, as Clara McLaughlin (1976) advises, is: "Teach him to be proud of his blackness" (p. 211), which includes preparing "children to live and be among white people without becoming white people" (Hale-Benson, 1982, p. 46). Affirming one's African identity becomes essential, simultaneously as an act of self-affirmation, self-protection, and self-transformation: "Afrocentricity is . . . a process of individual transformation" (Shujaa, 1992, p. 258). In contrast to the myth of pathology and failure fabricated by right-wing strategists, the truth is: "black families place a strong emphasis on work and ambition" (McLaughlin, 1976, p. 52). Indeed, social problems such as crime are "contagious," spreading generationally, not familially (Crane, 1991). As Eldridge Cleaver (1968) theorized in his brilliant if sexist *Soul on Ice*: "The white man turned himself into the Omnipotent Administrator and established himself in the front office. And he turned the black man into the Supermasculine Menial and kicked him out into the field. The white man wants to be the brain and he wants us to be the muscle, the boy" (p. 162). And now that wages are due, there are few jobs in the city.

MALPRACTICE

On the subject of parenting, *The Bell Curve* is concise: "Smart parents tend to be better parents. People with low cognitive ability tend to be worse parents" (p. 232). Concise does not equal accurate, of course, and on this subject, as well as on others, *The Bell Curve* is mistaken, riddled with conceptual and methodological as well as interpretive fallacies (Karagiannis, 1995, pp. 113, 114). The flaws are profound and extensive enough that Ernest House and Carolyn Haug (1995) have judged: "If there were such a thing as social science malpractice, these authors would be at risk. . . . Herrnstein and Murray . . . infer from correlational data two unlikely explanations. . . . Their analyses and findings would not be acceptable in scholarly journals" (p. 263).

How could such a book be written, and why has it attracted such widespread attention? As the authors themselves note: "racism will reemerge in a new and more virulent form" (p. 525). Reactionary racial politics have typified national and many local elections since the decisive defeat of the Left in 1968 (Winant, 1990). Employing a stereotypical strategy attributed to the South—appealing to racism, homophobia, anti-intellectualism as well as to misogyny—reactionaries in the United States have so dictated the terms of mainline political discussion that Herrnstein and Murray can assert, apparently sincerely: "Cognitive ability is a function of both genes and environment, with implications for egalitarian social policies. . . . The irony is that as America equalizes the circumstances of people's lives, the remaining differences in intelligence are increasingly determined by differences in genes" (p. 91). These are brothers from another planet. During the past 30 years, America has done anything but equalize the circumstances of people's lives, and to speak of genetic content in such an environment requires a mystical faith in a world not present.

IN THE NAME OF GOD

Racism in America does indeed have a religious component. Fundamentalists have employed the Bible to justify racism, misogyny, anti-Semitism, homophobia, and child abuse, all in the name of the Father: "a central dynamic in religion is the scapegoating of an innocent individual— often a child— who is punished that the others may go free" (Capps, 1995, p. 50). Contemporary forms of

Christianity, particularly as they are expressed in fundamentalism and in the New Right's embrace of the American family (a "mythic," not real, entity, cf. Cardenas, 1980, p. xv), are implicated in this racist and classist employment of parenting in political discourse.

Theologian Donald Capps (1995) notes that "many religious ideas that children are taught cause them emotional torment and are therefore inherently abusive" (p. 51). For instance, Capps notes that: "the relationship of God to believers is reminiscent of the abusive relationship of parent to child" (p. 81). *The Bell Curve* as text, emulates a form of abusive parenting, the same kind teachers sometimes suffer, that which locates failure only in the child and more generally, blames the victims. As we know, teachers and parents often reproduce the worse—as well as the best—of what they themselves experienced as children.

David Bakan understood the story of Jesus in terms of the "infanticidal impulse" of parents toward their children (quoted in Capps, 1995, p. 97). So interpreted, the sacrifice of Jesus represents "the failure of God the Father to protect his Son, and thus, in Alice Miller's words, [functions to] *spare the parent"* (Capps, 1995, p. 117). The parents spared in our time are those who loot the nation, distort the Christian faith, and starve living children by cutting social programs as they murder physicians in the name of the unborn. It is their own history of abuse they seek to cover up, their own murdered "inner child" they deny, as they worship the great story of infanticide preserved in the New Testament. If God allows his own son to die, how great a sin can it be to allow the poor and black children of America to spend time on the cross?

REVELATIONS

The resurrection of children in an abusive society occurs every day, thanks to the spiritual strength of children and the love and support of many parents and teachers. Despite the racism that "sits at the center of American civilization" (West, 1993, p. 73), black parents struggle to point their children to the promised land. And for many, education remains the passage. Success in school, we know, depends on much more than intelligence.

When children fail in school, we know to look to the school as well as to the child, the family, and society. Studies of children who have experienced difficulty in school point specifically to those social conditions that have undermined the efforts of parents and children:

> Lower achievers' parents have experienced severe, psychologically debilitating events at earlier stages of their lives. Past (and contemporary) experiences in their own family of origin and in the marketplace have had a "trickle down" effect. . . . These parents have undergone repeated trauma, they have sustained immeasurable strain and pain, and they now have an impoverished human spirit. (Clark, 1983, p. 192)

Unfortunately, the school itself is often the site of psychologically debilitating events (Lomotey, 1990).

In the current political milieu *The Bell Curve* betrays the spirit of parents and children struggling to survive in an occupied land. The Right continues to assault the lower classes, especially the black lower classes, almost as if to see how far it can push, but also to deflect its own responsibility for what has happened in America these past (nearly) 30 years. Another reason, of course, is to fatten their wallets by reducing taxes (that is, impoverishing others). Even if the Right succeeds, it will fail: "Efforts to crush the symptoms of deterioration [of the black family]—crime, dependency, and so forth—will bring an end to the American social system as we now know it" (Comer, 1980, p. 53). (Though *The Bell Curve* was published 14 years later, we question any improvement.) Like the FulBe Riesman studied, all of us living in this occupied land are responsible for all of us: "the black family has permitted large numbers of its members to survive and thrive in the face of potentially negative social conditions. Whether it can continue to do so in the future will depend greatly on the behavior of the larger society" (Comer, 1980, p. 53). All this—repressive myths that position African Americans as beasts, the defense of infanticide, the cover-ups of the abusive parents disguised as patriots, loyalty to the fatherland, racialized and religious child abuse—does not constitute intelligence, except along the bell curve.

References

My thanks to Kofi Lomotey and Jim Garvin.

Blackwell, J. E. (1991). *The black community: Diversity and unity.* New York: HarperCollins.

Campion, M. (1995). *Who's fit to be a parent?* New York and London: Routledge.

Capps, D. (1995). *The child's song: The religious abuse of children.* Westminster: John Knox Press.

Cardenas, R. (1980). Foreword. In Fantini, M. and Cardenas, R., eds., *Parenting in a multicultural society.* New York: Longman.

Clark, R. (1983). *Family life and school achievement: Why poor black children succeed or fail.* Chicago: University of Chicago Press.

Cleaver, E. (1968). *Soul on ice.* New York: Dell Publishing Co.

Comer, J. (1980). The black family: An adaptive perspective. In Fantini, M. and Cardenas, R., eds., *Parenting in a multicultural society,* New York: Longman.

Crane, J. (1991). The epidemic theory of ghettos and neighborhood effects on dropping out and teenage childbearing. *American Journal of Sociology, 95* (5), 1225-1259.

Eekelaar, J. and Sarcevic, eds. (1993). *Parenthood in modern society: Legal and social issues for the twenty-first century.* Boston and Dordrecht: Martinus Nijhoff Publishers.

Fantini, M. and Cardenas, R., eds. (1980). *Parenting in a multicultural society.* New York: Longman.

Fantini, M. and Russo, J. (1980). Introduction: Parenting in contemporary society. In Fantini, M. and Cardenas, R., eds., *Parenting in a multicultural society,* (xxix-xxxvi). New York: Longman.

Hale-Benson, J. (1982). *Black children: Their roots, culture, and learning styles.* Baltimore and London: Johns Hopkins University Press.

Herrnstein, R. and Murray, C. (1994). *The Bell Curve: Intelligence and class structure in American life.* New York: The Free Press.

Hoffman, L. (1988). Cross-cultural differences in childrearing goals. In Levine, R., Miller, P., and West, M., eds., *Parental behavior in diverse societies.* San Francisco and London: Jossey-Bass Inc., Publishers.

House, E. and Haug, C. (1995). Riding *The Bell Curve:* A review. *Educational Evaluation and Policy Analysis, 17* (2), 232-272.

Karagiannis, A. (1995). *The Bell Curve:* A review. *McGill Journal of Education, 30* (1), 111-116.

Karenga, M. (1982). *Introduction to black studies.* Los Angeles: Kawaida Publications.

Lomotey, K., ed. (1990). *Going to school: The African-American experience.* Albany, NY: State University of New York Press.

Madhubuti, H. (1990). *Black men.* Chicago: Third World Press.

McLaughlin, C. (1976). *The black parents' handbook.* San Diego: Harcourt Brace Jovanovich.

Riesman, P. (1992). *First find your child a good mother: The construction of self in two African communities.* New Brunswick, NJ: Rutgers University Press.

Shujaa, M. (1992). Afrocentric transformation and parental choice in African American independent schools. *The Journal of Negro Education, 61* (2), 148-159.

West, C. (1993). *Race matters.* Boston: Beacon Press.

White, J. and Parham, T. (1990, 1984). *The psychology of Blacks: An African-American perspective.* 2d ed. Englewood Cliffs, NJ: Prentice-Hall.

Winant, H. (1990; 1989, March). *Postmodern racial politics in the United States: Difference and inequality.* Warwick, UK: University of Warwick, Center for Ethnic and Racial Studies. (First published in *Socialist Review, 20* [1], 121-147.)

15 RACE, REPRESSION, AND THE POLITICS OF CRIME AND PUNISHMENT IN *THE BELL CURVE*

STEPHEN NATHAN HAYMES

Therefore learn how to see and not to gape.
To act instead of talking all day long
The world was almost won by such an ape!
The nations put him where his kind belong
But don't rejoice too soon at your escape
The bowels he crawled from still is going strong.
—Bertolt Brecht

In Bertoldt Brecht's The Irresistible Rise of Arturo Ui (Brecht, 1990), he warns us that the culture of hate that created Adolf Hitler and Nazism is still with humankind. While reading chapter 22 in *The Bell Curve* on crime and intelligence, I was reminded of a recent speech delivered at Howard University by Toni Morrison, the renowned novelist and winner of the Nobel Prize in Literature. In that speech, Morrison is concerned about the contemporary manifestations of antiblack racism and its role in constructing a new brand of fascism in the United States. Morrison warns her audience that the country is advancing toward a pre-fascist culture; that the nation is being prepared to accept a fascist or "final solution" to national problems. She states:

"before there is a final solution, there must be a first solution, a second one, even a third. The move toward a final solution is not a jump. It takes one step, then another, then another" (1995, p. 760). Morrison, then, goes on to describe the ten steps that are sliding the United States toward a "final solution" to national problems. Although all the steps she identifies are relevant to my discussion, three directly pertain to my discussion regarding *The Bell Curve*'s explanation for crime in the United States: "Construct an internal enemy, as both focus and diversion. Pathologize the enemy in scholarly and popular mediums; recycle, for example, scientific racism and the myths of racial superiority in order to naturalize the pathology. Criminalize the enemy. Then prepare, budget for and rationalize the building of holding arenas for the enemy—especially its males and absolutely its children" (Morrison, 1995, p. 760).

Toni Morrison's description of the process leading to fascism provides a framework for understanding how *The Bell Curve*'s explanation for crime in the United States contributes to the making of a culture and politics of racial hate and vengeance in which "punishment" is a code word for racial repression. Rather than focusing on the why, Morrison's analysis focuses on the how of fascism. This shift is a reflection of the sense of urgency Morrison feels and her search for a practical way to halt our country's slide toward fascism. To begin with the how of fascism provides a way to unravel the process involved in constructing an internal enemy so necessary for fascism to thrive. The unraveling of the construction of an internal enemy is linked very closely to the biologizing of the enemy's alleged pathologies that predispose its members to criminal behavior. Robert Proctor points out that this hereditarian bias, "that nature is more important than nurture in the shaping of human character and institutions," was "one of the pillars of Nazi medical ideology" (p. 347). Drawing upon the eugenics movement in the United States, the Nazi racial hygienists followed the "claim that the science of genetics had shown that all human traits—normal or pathological, physical or mental—are shaped by hereditary factors" (p. 347). Nazi racial hygienists believed that "it was biology that we must look to to solve social problems" (p. 347). Proctor elaborates further on this point when he states: "Knowledge of (and control over) the human genetic future was the key to human destiny; racial hygiene would eliminate human disease—not just schizophrenia or flatfeet or epilepsy, but also criminality. The Nazis took major problems of the day—problems of race, gender, crime and poverty—and transformed them into medical or biological problems" (p. 357).

Like the Nazi racial hygienists, *The Bell Curve* also takes major problems of the day and makes them into biological problems, as in the case of crime discussed in the eleventh chapter. For the authors of *The Bell Curve*, the causes of criminality are the result of individual differences in "inherited" intelligence. Herrnstein and Murray contend that criminals are psychologically and biologically unique and that as a group they have low IQs. Is it accurate to claim that simply because Herrnstein and Murray support a psychobiological explanation regarding intelligence and criminality that they are making antiblack racist assertions that aid in the construction of an internal enemy? In describing the steps toward fascism, Morrison suggested those who pathologize the enemy recycle scientific racism and the myths of racial superiority in order to naturalize the pathology. By linking criminality to "innate" cognitive ability, do Herrnstein and Murray recycle scientific racism and the myths of racial superiority by pathologizing black people? And if so, how is this an attempt to provide a rationale for this country to blame its moral, social, economic, cultural, and spiritual crisis on black Americans, in order to legitimate their punishment and repression?

While being interviewed on *Nightline* and *C-SPAN Booknotes,* Murray responded to his critics' claim that the arguments presented in *The Bell Curve* are aimed specifically at proving the biological inferiority of Blacks. According to Murray the overwhelming discussion of *The Bell Curve* is not about race but class, a discussion that he claims Americans avoid, and of the book's four sections, only one deals specifically with racial differences in relation to "natural" cognitive abilities of Blacks and Whites. Although intentions cannot be proved, how Herrnstein and Murray choreograph their discussion leaves little doubt that they are not so innocent. Before looking at this in more detail, it is important to note that Herrnstein was supportive of the National Institute of Mental Health (NIMH) initiative, under the Bush administration, in which researchers used alleged genetic and biochemical markers to identify black children for biological and behavioral interventions, and whose director, Frederick Goodwin, publicly compared youth gangs to groups of "hyperaggressive" and "hypersexual" monkeys (*Observer,* 1992; Horne, 1992-93). Also, Herrnstein supported the use of biological indicators in determining judicial sentencing decisions (Bonn, 1988).

As for Murray, he is one of the premier intellectuals of the mainstream right-wing movement. He has been dubbed the ideologue par excellence of the 1980s antiwelfarism, and his book *Losing Ground* was Ronald Reagan's "bible." One of the defining features of the mainstream Right's racial project is its redefining of the themes of racial equality in terms of color-blindness. Ruth Frankenberg (1993, p.142) points out that color-blindness on the part of Whites represents "a mode of thinking about race organized around an effort not to 'see' or to not acknowledge" their racial privilege and power. Color-blindness, is "a double move toward 'color-evasiveness' and 'power-evasiveness'"; it represents a "polite language of race" that is deceitful when it comes to acknowledging the complicity of Whites with structural and institutional racial inequality. The color-evasiveness and power-evasiveness of Murray's color-blindness is expressed in his remarks on welfare reform in *Losing Ground:*

> My proposal for dealing with the racial issue in social welfare is to repeal every bit of legislation and reverse every court decision that in any way requires, recommends, or awards differential treatment according to race, and thereby put us back onto the track that we left in 1965. We may argue about the appropriate limits of government intervention in trying to enforce the ideal, but at least it should be possible to identify the ideal: Race is not a morally admissible reason for treating one person differently from another. Period. (p. 223)

Murray's color-blinded racial politics supports a reconceptualized understanding of racial equality based on "civic privatism" According to this reformulation, equality is the result of individual striving, merit, and deserved achievement, and discrimination, if intentional, is against specific individuals, not distinct groups. *The Bell Curve* is therefore an extension of Murray's (and Herrnstein's) mainstream right-wing color-blind racial politics; it is the rationalization of the idea of a color-blind, nevertheless racialized meritocracy— the false notion that social hierarchies represent the "natural" distribution of "innate" cognitive abilities. Herrnstein and Murray appeal to a romanticized version of the American political tradition, to the so-called founding fathers to justify their nonegalitarian view of equality. In Herrnstein and Murray's words: "Thomas Jefferson was thankful for a 'natural aristocracy' that could counterbalance the deficiencies of others, an aristocracy of virtue and talent, which Nature has wisely provided for the direction of the interest of society." Further elaborating, the authors declare: "The Founders were fully aware of how unequal people are, that they did not try to explain away natural inequalities" (p. 530). The authors' anxious efforts to rationalize inequality signals an uneasiness with social movements and policies that demand racial justice and democracy. It is a politics of fear; any transgression of the "natural aristocracy" is perceived as dangerous and threatening to monied white male privilege and power.

In *Losing Ground*, Murray is contemptuous of the civil rights movement. He perceives the radical and moderate wing of the civil rights movement as conspiring together to support violent urban transgression through its moral rhetoric of "blaming the system." Murray writes that "the riots and the militancy adjoined the moral monopoly that the civil rights movement enjoyed." He goes on to state: "Black leaders blamed the riots on Whites—or coextensively, The System. Stokely Carmichael and Rap Brown said it with a rhetoric as bloodyminded and as unapologetic as the rioters. Martin Luther King, Jr. said it with more elegance, thoughtfulness, and political astuteness, but said it nonetheless" (p. 30). From this Murray says that what distinguishes the "deserving poor" from the "undeserving poor" is that the former are hardworking and self-reliant, and blame themselves for failure, while the latter are lazy and dependent on welfare programs and blame the system. For Herrnstein and Murray, it is among the "undeserving" poor, the criminal, that lurks the would-be rebel, the potential transgressor of the system. We can see why the authors of *The Bell Curve* might be anxious about this potential of the "undeserving poor," as they say that their "central concern since writing [the] book is how people might live together harmoniously despite fundamental individual differences" (p. 528).

It is this fear that, I believe, motivates Herrnstein and Murray to not be interested in addressing the causes of black youth crime, but of to be horrified at the thought of black youth potentially transforming themselves into radical democratic activists who challenge the racial hierarchies that the authors are so intent on naturalizing and protecting. Andrew Hacker clues into what really lurks beneath white fear of "black crime." Hacker posed to white students the choice of carrying $300 in their wallet and having it taken by a white robber, or carrying $100 and having it taken by a black robber. The students gladly said they would pay the extra $200 to avoid a black assailant. White students feared that "the man in front of them would take another moment and do something horrible to repay the white race for what it has done to his people" (p. 46). Hacker concludes by stating: "So 'black crime' is not mainly about taking money or articles of value, or even about demands at gunpoint. For white Americans, it represents racial revenge, as if each robbery—or rape—is part of an ongoing insurrection. It is the same fear slaveowners had of being slaughtered in their beds. And compounding the dread is the sense that the man facing you has nothing to lose, that he has been in prison before, and the prospect of returning there does not frighten him" (p. 46). It is this point that Abu-Jamal describes, and that black political and cultural history documents, that threatens Herrnstein and Murray into constructing black urban youth as violent avengers, as menacing natural-born-criminals, as enemies of their philosophy of a place for everyone.

Herrnstein and Murray's aim in linking criminality to intelligence, and therefore to biology, is to rationalize a politics of repression against black urban youth. As mentioned earlier, the authors choreograph their discussion in such a way as to not call attention or appear to be talking specifically about black criminality and its rootedness in black physiology. For example, they preface their discussion of criminality and IQ by stating: "In the United States, where crime and race have become so intertwined in the public mind, it is especially instructive to focus on just Whites" (p. 244). Misleading readers by focusing on white men, Herrnstein and Murray create the illusion of disinterest in race. Despite the fact that race is at the center of their examination and is the primary category utilized to differentiate between people, the authors give the false impression that by exclusively focusing on white men, Blacks are no longer the implied referent. Herrnstein and Murray indicate that white males are involved in violent criminal behavior but quickly add that only a small minority actually are committing such crimes. They also claim that those white males involved in committing serious crimes are of low intelligence. Throughout the chapter on crime, Herrnstein and Murray do not even mention Blacks but imply that white male violent offenders are the exception within the total population of serious criminal offenders, neglecting the role of racism in arrest and sentencing. This leaves readers to question just who they see on the five o'clock news committing violent crimes. Herrnstein and Murray do not answer that question directly except in chapter 13, "Ethnic Inequalities in Relation to IQ," where they state: "In the national data, Blacks are about 3.8 times more likely to be arrested relative to their numbers in the general population than Whites. Blacks are also disproportionately the victims of crime, especially violent crime" (p. 338). From this they conclude that the differences in black-white crime is explained by IQ differences. Their assumption is that Blacks are more likely to be involved in violent crime because they are allegedly more likely to be of a "lower intelligence" than Whites.

By using intelligence as a "neutral" medium, Herrnstein
and Murray are able to claim surreptitiously that Blacks are biologically predisposed to violent criminal behavior, linking criminality
with race. Making this connection allows the authors of *The Bell
Curve* to use crime to talk covertly about the black body as being
menacing. In other words, Herrnstein and Murray link their explanation of crime with Western racial discourse. In that discourse, the
making of the African, as nonhuman or subhuman, an object, arises
out of making the African "black"; racial meaning is therefore
attached to the flesh. The black body is perceived as evidence of the
African's "natural and inherited inferiority." Historically, Western
science in collaboration with this perception has sought to give
validity to the claim that the African's black body is genetically
inferior and is therefore the body of a nonhuman or subhuman
"thing." This hereditarian bias of Western science regarding "race"
reduces the African to a body or, to quote Fanon, to the "fact of
blackness," constructing an antiblack racism that perceives Blacks as
mere objects of the environment, mere things among things. It is
through the ritualistic production of Blacks as things, as a menacing
black body, that they function as an internal enemy.

For example, in the chapter on crime, Herrnstein and
Murray frequently cite and rely heavily on Herrnstein's earlier
arguments in *Crime and Human Nature* (coauthored with James Q.
Wilson) that the "criminogenic" predisposition is significantly more
characteristic of Blacks than Whites. Wilson and Herrnstein's chore-
ography of race is as misleading as *The Bell Curve*'s. Wilson and
Herrnstein argue that social, cultural, and economic indicators are
ambiguous and not nearly as dependable as constitutional factors in
determining violent criminal behavior. They believe that "explanations of criminality should be based on an analysis of individual
psychology that incorporates both genetic predisposition and social
learning" (p. 19). They identified their theory as eclectic and built
upon modern behavioral psychology. As for the constitutional factors
in criminal behavior, Wilson and Herrnstein identify criminals as
more likely than noncriminals to be young adult males with meso-

morphic (muscular) body types; who have an extra Y chromosome, which correlates with low intelligence; exhibit narcissist, sadistic, defiant, hostile, impulsive, extroverted . . . personality traits; and score higher in measures of psychopathology on psychological tests, such as the Minnesota Multiphasic Personality Inventory (MMPI). Wilson and Herrnstein believe that these constitutional factors are genetically predisposed and cite numerous twin and adoptive studies that support genetic rather than environmental factors in determining physical, personality, and cognitive development, and social behavior. It is not until the end of the book, in the chapter "Race and Culture," that Wilson and Herrnstein argue that Blacks are significantly more likely than Whites to have constitutional characteristics that genetically predispose them to violent criminal behavior.

By locating the cause of criminality within the human body, Herrnstein and Murray can now legitimately rationalize the repression of black people, particularly the youth. This can be inferred given the authors' behavioral psychology orientation in their formulation of social policy to address crime. Critical psychologists believe that followers of such an orientation seek to manipulate "the environment to effect individual adjustment to the status quo." The emphasis is not on the degree to which the environment or a specific set of controls are oppressive, "but that it can and should be made more effective." The result of this is "more effective power for the powerful and more effective control over the powerless" (Bulhan, 1985, p. 56-57). Accepting Wilson and Herrnstein's premise that Blacks are overwhelmingly more likely than Whites to be genetically predisposed toward psychopathology, *The Bell Curve* supports the notion that Blacks generally lack an internal locus of control (conscience) and are therefore in need of external stimulus to control their extroverted and impulsive behavior. According to this perspective, the actual threat of incarceration along with punitive treatment while incarcerated—the basis for moral education—are the only deterrent to black criminality.

This is also implied in Herrnstein and Murray's view that individuals with "low intelligence" are not able to make complex moral decisions; therefore, "the rules about crime must be made simpler and the consequences equally simple" (p. 544). They state that "[p]eople of limited intelligence can lead moral lives in a society that is run on the basis of 'Thou shalt not steal.' They find it much harder to lead moral lives in a society that is run on the basis of 'Thou shalt not steal unless there is a really good reason to'" (p. 545). In making this point, Herrnstein and Murray enthusiastically draw on James Q. Wilson's *The Moral Sense,* in which he states "that people have a natural moral sense, a sense that is formed out of their innate disposition," but that there are "different degrees of [this moral sense] among different people" (p. 2). Wilson infers from this that the "moral sense" of those predisposed to be either criminals and noncriminals is not related to societal rules and conventions but to self-control, which he roots in human biology: "Society's belief that it is important to endow rules about self-control with moral signifi-cance is challenged by evidence that some people are biologically more disposed to lack such control than others. . . . There exists a heritable predisposition to certain kinds of criminality, especially high rates of theft" (p. 95).

What is curious about Herrnstein and Murray, as well as the sources they rely upon (see Wilson and Herrnstein, 1988; Wilson, 1993) to make their arguments regarding criminality and intelli-gence, is how their obsession with control is intimately related to their effort to construct black people as pure body, as mere objects or things, with no consciousness of self except as a physiological self. Herrnstein and Murray's obsession with control must be understood in the context of their more political obsession of wanting to make excuses for racial hierarchies by naturalizing racial inequality and by conjuring up biological explanations for their fear and suspicion of potential transgressors. Eric Fromm, in his study of the psychology of fascism, described this preoccupation with control as being sadistic, that is, "namely to have complete mastery of another person, to make of him a helpless object of our will" (p. 32). The very essence of the sadistic drive, according to Fromm, is the pleasure of complete domination over another person. Fromm says that "the aim of sadism is to transform man into a thing, something animate into something inanimate, since by complete and absolute control the living loses one essential quality of life—freedom" (p. 32). Fromm also has described this sadistic character of fascism as being necrophilic because it relates to persons as objects, as things, only to oppress them, therefore loving death, not life.

Herrnstein and Murray's arguments and social policy recommendations regarding crime are pure and simple about rationalizing the near-genocidal oppression of black people, the final solution. Their erroneous idea that Blacks have a biological predisposition toward crime undergirds the implicit assumptions of the get-tough-on-criminals rhetoric and policy recommendations of the mainstream right-wing Republican *Contract with America* and the *Contract with the American Family*. The crime policy recommendations of the mainstream Right support the reversal of civil and human rights legislation aimed at protecting the accused and incarcerated; increased funding for the construction of new prison facilities to accommodate the higher rate of incarceration expected from new sentencing laws; anti - prison reform and the repeal of court-oversight legislation; and stricter death penalty provisions. Informing much of the right-wing crime policy is a retributive understanding of punishment, but retributive justice is based on vengeance; it is about making another person suffer to show who really is in control. Fromm reminds us that part of the sadistic psychology of fascism "is to make him suffer, since there is no greater power over another person than that of forcing him to undergo suffering without his being able to defend himself" (p. 32). This takes on significant meaning in a society premised on racial hierarchies and prisons that are overwhelmingly black.

Human Rights Watch's investigation of American prisons and jails and of prison litigation over the past ten years showed widespread abuses of the United Nations' minimum standards for the treatment of prisoners (Burkhalter, 1995, p.18). Patricia Williams is fearful of the country's turn toward this culture of vengeance in which crude forms of punishment inflicted upon criminals are gleefully deemed as payback. Criminal suffering as "payback," Williams adds, "has the extra benefit of removing responsibility from fellow citizens because after all criminals bring it all on themselves" (p. 62). I want to close with a quote from which Williams points to the antiblack racism that informs the sadistic culture of vengeance overwhelming the soul of the country, which I believe books like *The Bell Curve* help to create:

> One of racism's many manifestations is the collective death wish that Blacks were not alive—one can hear this expressed over and over again on talk-radio programs around the country any day of the week. This wish that Blacks would just go away and shut up and stop taking up so much time and food and air and then the world would return to its Norman Rockwell loveliness and America could be employed and happy once more. Sometimes it's expressed as an actual death wish, but more often it comes out as a disappearance wish. But the sentiment is no less frightening to those of us on the receiving end of such categoric euphemisms. Moreover, the killing wish takes on such public, even joyous legitimacy when blackness is paired with actual outlaw behavior. (p. 63)

References

Abu-Jamal, M. (1995). *Live from death row*. Boston: Addison-Wesley.

Burkhalter, H. (1995). Barbarism behind bars: Torture in U.S. prisons. *The Nation, 261* (1).

Bulhan, H. (1985). *Frantz Fanon and the psychology of oppression*. New York: Plenum Press.

Bonn, R. (1988, Winter/Spring). The case against using biological indicators in judicial decision-making. *Criminal Justice Ethics, 7*.

Brecht, B. (1990). *Der aufhaltsame aufsteig des Arturo Ui*. Frankfurt: M. Diesterweg.

Frankenberg, R. (1993). *The social construction of whiteness.* Minneapolis: University of Minnesota Press.

Fromm, E. (1968). *The heart of man.* New York: Harper & Row.

Gingrich, N. (1995). *Contract with America.* Washington: Republican National Committee.

Gordon, L. (1995). *Bad faith and antiblack racism.* NJ: Humanities Press.

Hacker, A. (1995). Malign neglect: The crackdown on African-Americans. *The Nation, 26* (1), 2.

Herrnstein R. and Murray, C. (1994). *The bell curve: Intelligence and class structure.* New York: The Free Press.

Horne, G. (1992-93, Winter). Race backwards: Genes, violence, race, and genocide. *Covert Action.*

Morrison, T. (1995). The marketing of power: Racism and facism. *The Nation, 260,* 21.

Murray, C. (1984). *Losing ground: American social policy 1950-1980.* New York: Basic Books.

Observer. (1992). Chief Resigns, Becomes Director of NIMH. *5,* 2.

Omi, M. and Winant, H. (1994). *Racial formation in the United States.* 2d ed. New York: Routledge.

Proctor, R. (1993). Nazi medicine and the politics of knowledge. In Harding, S. *The radical economy of science: Towards a democratic future.* Bloomington, IN: Indiana University Press.

Reed, R. (1995). *Contract with the family.* New York: Time Books.

Williams, P. (1995). Abu-Jamal: Live from death row. *The Nation, 26* (1), 2.

Wiegman, R. (1995). *American anatomies: Theorizing race and gender.* Durham, NC and London: Duke University Press.

Wilson, J. (1993). *The moral sense.* New York: The Free Press

Wilson, J. and Herrnstein, R. (1985). *Crime and human nature: The definitive study of the causes of crime.* New York: Simon and Schuster.

16 THE LAST RATIONAL MEN: CITIZENSHIP, MORALITY, AND THE PURSUIT OF HUMAN PERFECTION

CAMERON MCCARTHY, ED BUENDIA, CAROL MILLS, SHUAIB MEACHAM, HERIBERTO GODINA, CARRIE WILSON-BROWN, MARIA SEFERIAN, AND THERESA SOUCHET

First Citizen—We are accounted poor citizens, the patricians good. What authority surfeits on would relieve us. If they would yield us but the superfluity while it were wholesome, we might guess they relieved us humanely; but they think we are too dear; the leanness that afflict us, the object of our misery, is as an inventory to particularize their abundance; our sufferance is a gain to them. Let us revenge this with our pikes ere we become rakes. For the gods know I speak this in hunger for bread, not in thirst for revenge.

> —*Coriolanus*, Act I,
> Scene I, lines 15-25

The opening speeches in Shakespeare's play Coriolanus launch its characters and their audience into a debate among Roman plebeians about the status and quality of societal membership offered to the lower classes in Rome. This discussion was not simply about the conditions of the people in ancient Rome; Shakespeare was addressing the issue of citizenship in seventeenth-century England. This discussion of citizenship echoes forward into contemporary debates over identity and nation in the United States, in which Richard Herrnstein and Charles Murray's *The Bell Curve* (1994) is just one strand of a larger network of discourses that aim to legitimize and naturalize "white popular wisdom" (Murray, 1984), particularly regarding the inhabitants of the depressed urban centers. Taken as a whole, Herrnstein and Murray's volume is an especially disturbing register of contemporary anxiety over the boundaries of national affiliation and citizenship.

Herrnstein and Murray's book is a project of social normalization par excellence. Their objective is to call attention to the variable distribution of human mental capacity and moral virtue in American society and the implications that these "variables" have for the overall productivity and economic efficiency of the nation. As in Shakespeare's *Coriolanus,* there is a powerful deployment of biological tropes linked to morality and citizenship in *The Bell Curve.* In short, for these two neoconservative social scientists, high-IQ social actors are likely to be good citizens, low-IQ types are likely to be bad. A clear policy implication flows from this formulation: Society must find a way to limit and contain the reproduction of its flawed members. In what follows, we discuss *The Bell Curve* as an example of the popular medical panic prose genre (see for example, the film *Outbreak* [1995], Richard Preston's *The Hot Zone* [1994], or Laurie Garrett's *The Coming Plague* [1994], all of which deal with the threat of invasion of exotic viruses and microbes into pristine American metropolitan suburbs) and its biological treatment of the topic of citizenship. Our primary focus is to discuss chapter 12 and other related chapters of Herrnstein and Murray's book that address the topic of citizenship.

In *Coriolanus,* the plebeians speak for the alienated working classes for all times and all places. They denounce the arrogance and ill-gotten gains of society's patrician elites. But most important, they call attention to the obligations of society's rich to its poor and downtrodden and the obligations of state elites to the lower classes whose surplus value these elites expropriate:

Menenius—I tell you, friends, most charitable care
Have the patricians of you . . .
First Citizen—Care for us! True, indeed! They
ne'er cared for us yet. Suffer us to famish, and their
storehouses crammed with grain; make edicts for
usury, to support usurers; repeal daily any wholesome
act established against the rich, and provide more
piercing statutes daily to chain up and restrain the poor.
                    (Act I, Scene I, lines 66-67, 80-87)

Shakespeare gives the plebeian working classes a voice in *Coriolanus*. In *The Bell Curve*, Herrnstein and Murray take the voice of the poor away. Instead, society's downtrodden are the objects of an imperial biological gaze. In the minds of these authors, the poor exist to be defined, categorized, and regulated. Whereas the plebeians in *Coriolanus* maintain that the issue of inequality is central to any discussion of citizenship, Herrnstein and Murray radically shove the issue of social inequity aside. For these authors, modern American society already offers equality of opportunity to all its citizens. The fact that some individuals and groups do not fare well in this open and freely competitive system has to do with their genes, not their socioeconomic circumstances: According to Herrnstein and Murray, "Low IQ continues to be a much stronger precursor of poverty than the socioeconomic circumstances in which people grew up" (p. 127). *And no policy intervention will change that fact.*

The Bell Curve, then, is an example of theorizing from the top of the food chain. Herrnstein and Murray take advantage of the panic already constructed by neonationalist movements: the cultural literacy movement (Bloom, 1987; Hirsch, 1987), the anti-immigration movement, and jingoistic isolationist groups such as the patriot militias. They elaborate a proto-fascist defense of the existing system of unequal membership status offered to different groups of America's citizenry. The authors pursue this objective of political inoculation of the hegemonic social order by using the discourse of biology to throw up a blanket of ideological protection around America's professional middle class and corporate elites. Herrnstein and Murray then point an accusatory finger at the country's minority and white working-class poor who, for the most part, they contemptuously dismiss as mentally degenerate. They are economically poor, the authors charge, because they are poor in cognitive capital. Instead of addressing the issue of the rights of society's most disadvantaged citizens and the obligations of the state, their focus is the issue of moral responsibility and civic duty and the needs of society for the most efficient deployment of the mental capacities of its citizenry. The view from Herrnstein and Murray's window on the world is decidedly corporatist. Given this emphasis, the authors write off the lower classes as the tragic ballast weighing down the ship of the state.

Interestingly, in Shakespeare's *Coriolanus,* it is Menenius, the apologist for Rome's patrician elite, who, like Herrnstein and Murray, uses poignant biological tropes in his ideological rationalization of the inequality in Rome's social order:

> Menenius—There was a time when all the body's members
> Rebelled against the belly; thus accused it;
> That only like a gulf it did remain
> I' th' midst o' th' body, idle and unactive,
> Still cupboarding the viand, never bearing
> Like labor with the rest; where th' other instruments
> Did see and hear, devise, instruct, walk, feel,
> And, mutually participate, did minister
> Unto the appetite and affection common
> Of the whole body. The belly answered—
> First Citizen—Well, sir, what answer made
> the belly? . . .
> Menenius—Note me this good friend
> Your most grave belly was deliberate,
> Not rash like his accusers, and thus answered:
> "True it is my incorporate friends," quoth he,
> "That I receive the general food at first,

Which you do live upon; and fit it is,
Because I am the storehouse and the shop
Of the whole body. But, if you do remember,
I send it through the rivers of your blood,
Even to the court, the heart, to th' seat o' th' brain;
And, through the cranks and offices of man,
The strongest nerves and small inferior veins
From me receive that natural competency
Whereby they live; and though that all at once"—
You, my good friends, this says the belly, mark me . . .
First Citizen—It was an answer. How apply you this?
Menenius—The senators of Rome are this good belly.
And you, the mutinous members.
      (Act I, Scene I, lines 97-107, 129-142, 149-151)

Of course, Herrnstein and Murray's use of biological metaphors draws on a long tradition in the educational and social sciences. The use of medical or biological imagery to interpolate society runs deep in the sociological and educational literatures, from the writing of Herbert Spencer to Talcott Parson and contemporary structural functionalist curriculum theorists such as Allan Ornstein and Francis Hunkins. This mainstream social science research tradition generally compares society to an organism. Much attention is paid to social norms and social normalization and the role of social institutions in the reproduction and maintenance of a functional equilibrium within the body politic. Similarly, behavioral scientists in the field of psychology have concentrated relentless attention on the measurement of human traits as already given in nature. This, for example, allows for the discursive production of glib taxonomies and systems of classification of individuals and groups into hierarchical categories of competence and efficiency. Early behavioral psychologists such as Henry Goddard, Lewis Terman, and Edmund Thorndike promised a world of human perfection through the unyielding practices of diagnosing and eliminating human decrepitude. In *The Bell*

Curve, Herrnstein and Murray think they have found a pathway to this promised land. And access to the promised land lies in the harnessing and efficient deployment of human intelligence.

In their approach to the assessment of human intelligence and its function in organizing society, Herrnstein and Murray place their work within the most conservative behavioral science tradition of psychology—the tradition that runs through the genealogical line of Charles Spearman, Lewis Terman, Arthur Jensen, and William Shockley to contemporary thinkers such as Phillipe Rushton. This conservative or "classical" approach to cognition maintains that intelligence is massively heritable and that the underlying causal explanation of virtually every social ill—unemployment, poverty, crime, illegitimacy, divorce, and so forth—is a matter of genetic endowment.

In *The Bell Curve* Herrnstein and Murray deploy a tautological net of biological discourses in their analysis of the relationship of intelligence to citizenship. These discourses are used in three interrelated ways: Biological tropes underscore the authors' claims of scientific neutrality; they also help to draw out the lines of demarcation that separate the mentally degenerate working class from the mentally whole in the suburbs; and last, the language of biology is used to displace and suppress more radical discourses of social inequality. Let us take a closer look at the deployment of biological discourses in Herrnstein and Murray's book.

THE CLOAK OF SCIENTIFIC NEUTRALITY

First, these authors use the discourses of biology and nature to wrap their highly motivated and socially prejudicial claims in the cloak of scientific neutrality. The language of genes and heredity suggests a world in which "the social" literally evaporates and the contents of "men's minds" are all that matter. Herrnstein and Murray try on their lab coats and wear them into the murkiest waters in their assault on the poor: "Going on welfare really is a dumb idea, and that is why women who are low in cognitive ability end up there, but also such women have little to take to the job market, and welfare is one of their few appropriate recourses when they have a baby to care for and no husband to help" (p. 201).

Here the discourse of measured intelligence provides a cloak for a highly loaded moral didacticism and a deep suspicion of the autonomy and civic judgment of the nation's female poor. Poor, low-IQ women do not make good citizens because they do not pull their weight. In addition, they endanger the economic (and the military) security of the nation by their hyperfertility. This is just a fact of biology, not politics or ideology, Herrnstein and Murray argue. By emphasizing the scientificity of their work, the authors portray themselves as expert citizens—professionals who are direct and honest with the rest of society; even if, by so doing, it means that they anger liberals and radicals and damn the lives of generations of various racial groups and the poor. This use of the discourse of biology invokes "science" abstractly and generally. Ultimately, the discourse of biology and nature constitutes a language of innocence—a discourse of the future linked to the past. In this recourse to nostalgia, the scientist and the citizen are one: dwellers of suburbia where the pursuit of the good life is the social reward for the best and brightest.

METAPHORS OF HUMAN PERFECTION

The second use of the discourses of biology foregrounds metaphors of perfection and their opposite, metaphors of human degeneracy. This deployment of biology represents the professional middle class (PMC) persona as the human ideal, high in the mystical g—a complete and separate human specimen, distinct and distinguishable from the low cognitive dweller of the inner city. The professional middle-class subject is therefore the natural recipient of the genetic bounty of high cognitive capacity. And from this great bountiful storehouse, this PMC citizen dispenses "civility" and magnanimity to all his neighbors. He is the grand role model, the embodiment of the best in civil society: "Much of what could go under the heading of civility is not readily quantified. Mowing the lawn in the summer or keeping the sidewalks shoveled in the winter, maintaining a tolerable level of personal hygiene and grooming, returning a lost wallet, or visiting a sick friend. . . . [This is] what we are calling civility" (p. 254). As a corollary to this, suburban life is represented as the epitome of wholesomeness and completeness. The suburb is the incubator of civility—an organic environment in which the high-IQ citizen helps his neighbor out, has open-ended, urbane conversations around the picnic table about politics, and enters the voting booth, society's "civic hearth" (p. 255), to do his civic duty. This application of the discourse of biology is linked to a discourse of the natural habitat where the PMC citizen resides. Here also the discourse of nature blends with the discourse of nostalgia: "We do not need statistics to remind Americans alive in the 1990s of times when they felt secure walking late at night, alone, even in poor neighborhoods and even in the largest cities" (p. 236).

What Herrnstein and Murray designate as "citizenship," the middle-class suburban resident already possesses as symbolic capital. This is summarized in the metaphors of self-regulation and self-control:

> To what extent is high intelligence associated with the behaviors associated with "middle-class values"? The answer is that the brighter young people . . . are also the ones whose lives most resemble a sometimes disdained stereotype. They stick with school, are plugging away in the workforce, and are loyal to their spouse. In so far as intelligence helps lead people to behave in these ways, it is also a force for maintaining a civil society. (p. 236)

In subtle and not so subtle ways, Herrnstein and Murray center the polity in the suburb. Outside the acropolis dwells society's problem species: "the dull" and "the very dull," mostly urban inhabitants—Frantz Fanon's "wretched of the earth" (1965). The body politic of the suburban high-IQ citizen is healthy and wholesome. By contrast, the imagery associated with the low-IQ poor is that of disease and degradation. If the problems of the urban centers are intractable or "chronic," as Herrnstein and Murray maintain, it has to do with the people who live there—the low IQ types who wallow in a culture of poverty: "The analyses provide some support for those who argue that a culture of poverty tends to transmit chronic welfare dependency from one generation to the next. But if a culture of poverty is at work, it seems to have influence primarily among women who are of low intelligence" (p. 191).

This culture of poverty is definitively linked to mental frailty. In a striking way, too, such poverty is decidedly gendered. The low-IQ woman of America's working classes makes for a poor citizen because she lacks those values of self-regulation and self-control associated with the middle class. Here again the sense of disease and degeneracy is in the air: "The disquieting finding is that the worst environments for raising children, of the kind that not even the most resilient children can easily overcome, are concentrated in the homes in which the mothers are at the low end of the intelligence distribution" (pp. 203-204).

Herrnstein and Murray draw down the lines between desired citizen traits and behaviors and undesirable ones by pointing to the almost indelible behavioral differences that exist between the woman of "middle-class values" and the "other" woman—the female urban resident who is bereft of these desirable middle-class traits and qualities:

> A woman in the NLSY [National Longitudinal Study of Youth] got a "Yes" if she had obtained a high school degree, had never given birth to a baby out of wedlock, had not been interviewed in jail, and was still married to her first husband. People who failed any one of the conditions were scored "No." Never-married people who met all other conditions except the marital one were excluded from analysis. (p. 263)

In foregrounding issues of biology, reproduction, and sexuality (that is, issues of control over the body), the authors of *The Bell*

Curve separate out the inner-city dweller as an anticitizen, a threat to the future security of the nation as a whole. The authors hint at these dangers throughout chapter 12. They spell out the nature of this threat more definitively, however, in chapter 15, which deals with present and future population and demographic trends. The matter can be summarized as follows. While the patriotic high-IQ suburban resident is a model of restraint, the low-IQ population of the country is aggressively fertile. Thus the overall intelligence in the nation is declining because the very dull are producing too many babies and the very bright too few. Worst yet, immigration policies are too generous to low-IQ immigrants from the Third World. The result is the powerful negative phenomenon of overall decline in intelligence, or "dysgenesis":

> Mounting evidence indicates that demographic trends are exerting downward pressure on the distribution of cognitive ability in the United States and that the pressures are strong enough to have social consequences. . . . The professional consensus is that the United States has experienced dysgenic pressures throughout the century. . . . Women of all races and ethnic groups follow this pattern in similar fashion. There is some evidence that Blacks and Latinos are experiencing even more severe dysgenic pressures than whites, which could lead to further divergence between whites and other groups in future generations. (p. 341)

BIOLOGY AND THE REPRESSION OF THE POLITICAL

The third type of deployment of biological metaphors in *The Bell Curve* involves a strategy of suppression of the discourse of the social and the political and their replacement by the discourse of nature. Here the issue of inequality is displaced from the arena of the economy onto the terrain of mental and moral capacity and adequacy. The social world is naturalized as a world of the survival of the fittest. The best and the brightest of society's citizenry will prevail over the feebleminded. This is nature's law: social Darwinism writ large. Most significantly, Herrnstein and Murray suggest that the socioeconomic class map of America is obsolete, since Americans generally now all coexist on a level playing field for contest mobility. They replace the class map of America with a cognitive map based on the distribution of mental capital. This map corresponds with a gradation of national membership or citizenship in society based on competence. Herrnstein and Murray introduce a five-tiered hierarchy: "the Very Bright," "the Bright," "the Normal," "the Dull," and "the Very Dull":

> The twentieth century dawned on a world segregated into social classes defined in terms of money, power and status. The ancient lines of separation based on hereditary rank were being erased, replaced by a more complicated set of overlapping lines. Social standing still played a major role. . . . Our thesis is that the twentieth century has continued the transformation, so that the twenty-first will open on a world in which cognitive ability is the dividing force. The shift is more subtle than the previous one but more momentous. Social class remains the vehicle of social life, but the intelligence pulls the train. (p. 25)

Following this claim the authors go on to maintain: "Low intelligence is a stronger precursor of poverty than low socioeconomic background. Whites with IQs in the bottom 5 percent of the distribution of cognitive ability are fifteen times more likely to be poor than those with IQs in the top 5 percent" (p. 127).

The cognitive map charts nature's differential order of endowments to different groups of human beings. It is nobody's fault that there is inequality in the land. And indeed, our best political efforts to wipe out such inequality only compound the bad hand that nature has dealt to "the dull" and "the very dull." This is what liberal politicians did in the 1960s. They gave handouts to the poor, the low-IQ types, the congenital criminals, and the welfare sororities. The consequences everywhere were bad, but particularly bad for the poor: "The irony is that as America equalizes the circumstances of people's lives, the remaining differences in intelligence are increasingly determined by differences in genes . . ." (p. 91).

Ultimately, for Herrnstein and Murray, liberal policies elaborated in the 1960s aimed at helping poor Americans overly politicized the function of government in people's lives. The best thing that the government can do now is to step aside and let the law of nature and the invisible hand of the market reestablish a necessary equilibrium in social life. For these authors, the removal of impediments to the efficient sorting of cognitive capacity is the key to national renewal and national well-being.

CONCLUSION

On the whole, *The Bell Curve* must be seen against the backdrop of a deeply conservative phase in the evolution of the American polity. This new phase in American life is reflected in ever more conservative inroads into the academy itself. A significant correlate of these developments has been the deep incorporation of academic scholarship into the culture industry. This is reflected particularly in the ever-expanding commerce of fast-break quasi-academic books aimed at mass consumption that blur the lines among academic scholarship, policy, and entertainment. To put the matter bluntly, right-wing academics have learned that panic prose that manipulates authoritarian popular anxieties and desires sells well. Herrnstein and Murray's *The Bell Curve* joins a steady stream of doomsday books— such as *The Closing of the American Mind, The Disuniting of America, Illiberal Education, Cultural Literacy, Alien Nation,* and Murray's own *Losing Ground*— that focus attention on the internal threats to national identity and national security. Herrnstein and Murray's discussion of citizenship marks the aggressive return of biological arguments in the discussion of the social policy regarding some of the most intractable political and social problems in contemporary American society.

The lived reality in the United States is that though formally citizens, some groups of Americans, particularly working-class Blacks and Latinos, occupy the place of modern-day plebeians; that is to say, they are treated as second-class citizens. There is solid social, economic, and cultural evidence that this is so. In *The Bell Curve*, Herrnstein and Murray, with great fanfare, wipe this evidence away, pointing instead to the relative imperfection of the mental structures of America's lower classes. In their hands, biology becomes a powerful tool for the legitimation of unequal status. The very bright and the very dull are two different types of citizens. One type of citizen lives at the top of the food chain in the hallowed suburb, while the other lives at the bottom in the inner city. Herrnstein and Murray contend that there is not much that government should do about this. Indeed, current policies of government handouts and uncontrolled immigration are leading us down the slippery slope of dysgenesis—the precipitous fall in IQ—as the least endowed multiply and procreate without restraint. This perhaps will be the end of America as we know it. And then what? Maybe, the plebeians will inherit the earth.

References

Barnett, S. (1972). *The complete Signet classic Shakespeare*. New York: Harcourt Brace Jovanovich.

Bloom, A. (1987). *The closing of the American mind*. New York: Simon & Schuster.

Fanon, F. (1965). *The wretched of the Earth*. New York: Grove Press.

Garrett, L. (1994). *The coming plague*. New York: Farrar, Strauss and Giroux.

Herrnstein, R. and Murray, C. (1994). *The Bell Curve: Intelligence and class structure*. New York: The Free Press.

Hirsch, E. D. (1987). *Cultural literacy*. Boston: Houghton Mifflin.

Murray, C. (1984). *Losing ground: American social policy, 1950-1980.* New York: Basic Books.

Preston, R. (1994). *The hot zone.* New York: Random House.

17 THE BELL CURVE, INTELLIGENCE, AND VIRTUOUS JEWS

SANDER L. GILMAN

The recent appearance of Richard J. Herrnstein and Charles Murray's book *The Bell Curve: Intelligence and Class Structure in American Life* has again drawn attention to the debate about the relationship between inheritance and intelligence, a debate that in the American context is read as a comment on "race" (read: blackness) and lower intelligence. (In my discussion of the idea of the "bell curve," specifically looking at chapter 13, it is important to understand that the very existence of such a curve can be drawn into question once the definition of what is being plotted on it is examined.) There is no question that *The Bell Curve* was (and is) read as a book on race and intelligence. When the book appeared, Charles M. Madigan of the *Chicago Tribune* noted that "its adds a layer of scientific glaze to a collection of racial attitudes that seems to have escaped from the 19th century. In that sense, this huge tome is the perfect *Thinking Bigots Beach Book*. If you're looking for data to back up your prejudices, it's all here; David Duke will find much to borrow" (Madigan, 1994, Sec. 4, p. 1). Madigan clearly read the book as one about race, and race in the American context is defined by blackness. In *The Bell Curve,* intelligence becomes a discussion of character and virtue. And this red thread throughout the debates about race and intelligence has been little acknowledged over the past decades. While this debate about the relationship between "race" and "IQ" has been carried out sporadically over the past three decades around the work of Arthur Robert Jensen, William Shockley, and J. Philippe Rushton, little attention has been paid to the ethical and moral questions that adumbrate these studies. As Richard Lacayo (1994) noted in a *Time* essay on the book:

> *The Bell Curve*'s explosive contentions detonate under a cushion of careful shadings and academic formulations. Even so, they explode with a bang. To give credence to such ideas— even when doing so with loud sighs of alas—is to resume some of the most poisonous battles of the late 1960s and '70s, when the sometimes cranky outer limits of the IQ debate were personified by Arthur Jensen, the Berkeley psychologist who stressed the link between race, genes and IQ, and William Shockley, who proposed paying people with low IQs to be sterilized. Murray says the reaction against them shut off a necessary discussion. "The country has for a long time been in almost hysterical denial that genes can play any role whatsoever." (Lacayo, 1994)

All of these writers of the 1960s implicitly or explicitly raised the question of the relationship between "intelligence" and "race" as defined by skin color. They also have implied (explicitly or implicitly) that race and intelligence are related in very specific ways to questions of morality and virtue. Herrnstein and Murray's presentation in this regard is neither the most extensive nor the most hotly contested. Even though it deals with "cognitive class" and not explicitly with race as defined by skin color, it repeats the collateral question addressed by much of the earlier literature. Virtue and morality are the real objects of *The Bell Curve*—and these qualities are posited positively or negatively at both ends of the curve.

In a real sense Herrnstein and Murray are addressing the multiculturalism debate that continues to rage in the United States in the mid-1990s. Central to their argument is the valorization of the idea of multicultural difference. They take the left-liberal advocates of "difference" and "pluralism" at their word, but take it to a biological extreme. You want difference, they argue, we'll show you that difference is real and inescapable; in fact, it's in our genes. In so doing they transform the notion of "difference" from a concept meant to ensure that all "voices" receive equitable attention—that calls hierarchy into question—into a rigid and quantifiable hierarchical notion reminiscent of nineteenth- and early twentieth-century biological determinists. Their rhetoric, which seems to escape the older, 1960s rhetoric of race, with its emphasis on "class," mirrors the rhetoric of the Left but inverts it. Herrnstein and Murray's concern is not solely the lower end of the "bell curve."

There are two ends to Herrnstein and Murray's "bell curve," each of them thin and rare. As rare as is the lowest end of the curve—composed of those of lowest intelligence, according to the "classic" argument—equally rare is the upper end of the curve. It is fascinating that in the analysis within such studies as *The Bell Curve*, little or no attention is given to the "normal" center. The thin ends define the problem—the "normal" center is understood as the model of intelligence and therefore also the model of virtue. This chapter examines the "high" end of the "bell curve," the image of Jewish superior intelligence and the primary source for Herrnstein and Murray's argument. This source, as I shall discuss, reveals a number of the presuppositions about Jewish superior intelligence that haunt *The Bell Curve*. The book and others like it erroneously assume that following the model of the pathological in medicine, only the deviant can provide insight into the normal. And thus the center—the two standard deviations from the norm in this erroneous model—is invisible. The center remains the implicit site of virtue through (or because of) its "average" intelligence.

Given the American political climate of the mid-1990s, it is understandable why the Herrnstein and Murray book has attracted much attention in its evocation of the myth of permanent underclass (read: of African Americans) whose high rate of reproduction, low intelligence, and degenerate sociopathic genes have led to an America where it is dangerous to walk the streets of the big cities. This is not the first time in recent years that there has been an attempt to pin contemporary anxiety about urban crime on inheritance. Or as Herrnstein and Murray note high intelligence does provide protection against lapsing into criminal behavior for people who otherwise are at risk. According to this model, criminals are dumb and dumb people are criminals. This ahistorical reconstruction ignores all of the complex reading of the relationship between "intelligence" (however that is defined) and "crime" (however that is defined) (Pope, 1979). According to contemporaries, New York's "Hell's Kitchen" in the 1860s was full of atavistic Irishmen who made the streets unsafe. They too were seen literally as a race apart and were accused of reproducing at an uncomfortably high rate. The racial sign of their lower intelligence could be seen in their simian brow and saddle nose! Such myths about the relationship of "low intelligence" and "race" are basic to Western science at least since the mid-eighteenth century in its attempts to dispel the established society's anxiety about a source of social instability. Identify your potential enemy and you can control your anxiety! Thus the focus on the lower end of the "bell curve" has been an attempt to locate the origins of the anxiety about individual risk in a stereotyped category.

But what about those who are too smart? Little attention has been paid to the other end of the spectrum, to the thin line at the other end of the so-called bell curve. It is this end that serves as a prophylaxis against crime. Herrnstein and Murray devote only one page to the highest group in terms of intelligence—Ashkenasic Jews of European origins who tend to test higher than other ethnic groups. Based on this model, which equates intelligence with virtue, we would come to expect that the higher the intelligence, the greater the protection against criminality, the greater the virtue of the group. According to Herrnstein and Murray, Jews in the United States and in England have an overall IQ mean between a half and a full standard deviation above the mean, with the main source of the difference in the verbal portion. Such test scores, however, are not sufficient for the authors to establish the superior intelligence of the Jews; they also rely on an analyses of professional/vocational and

scientific attainment by Jews, constantly showing their disproportionate level of success, by orders of magnitude, in various mediums
of scientific and artistic achievement. Jews are not only smart but
they are creative—and, following Max Weber's reading of American
Protestant culture, this is a sign of their virtue, for worldly success is
a sign of a virtuous life. As we shall see, this combination of the two
instruments employed to measure intelligence—catalogues of accomplishments and multiple-choice testing mirrors the history of
the construction of the image of Jewish superior intelligence from
the mid-nineteenth century to the present. But it is equally important to understand that such studies imply that virtue can be
identified and quantified, and such rather crude types of analogies
are just as likely to draw the Jews' virtue into question as to posit
them as the site of virtue.

 This myth originated during the age of biological racism
and it is part of the discussion of Jews as a racial category. The
discourse of racial science quickly absorbed the myth, which, as I
have shown, continues to hold power even today. Richard Herrnstein
and Charles Murray label the "Jews" as a racial group, Ashkenasic
Jews of European origins. Historically this is a racial category. The
arguments about who is smarter than whom reflect the general
debates in the world of nineteenth-century scientific racism. The
argument of the superiority of Northern Jews (Ashkenasic) over
Southern Jews (Sephardic) dates to the nineteenth-century scientific
racism that argued for the improvement of the race the farther north
or east (to a point!) one goes ("Caucasians" versus "Semites"). By the
late twentieth century, the social situation in Israeli seemed to present
this as a given (Ryan, 1995, p. 23). Jewish scientists of the late
nineteenth century often reversed this argument, seeing the Sephardic Jew as the better "type" (Efron, 1993).

 In the recent literature on the intelligence of the Jews,
written after the post-Shoah (Holocaust) creation of the State of Israel
with its overlaying of "Eastern" and "Western" Jews, the idea of the
superior intelligence of the Ashkenasic Jew has reappeared. In studies
of the perception of intelligence in Israel today, for example, social

status and distance create the illusion of Ashkenasic superior intelligence. A revealing Israeli study looked at the meaning attributed to the perceived superior intelligence of the Jews in present-day Israel. Moshe Zeidner (1990) interviewed 60 Jewish and 60 Arab Israeli college students about their perceptions of the modal intelligence and social distance of five Israeli ethnic groups: European Jews, Eastern Jews, Christian Arabs, Muslim Arabs, and Druze. He also explored the subjects' attributions with respect to the determinants of ethnic group differences in ability. The perceived modal intelligence profiles for the ethnic groups varied as a function of each subject's ethnic group membership. There was consensus among them that Jews of Western extraction (Ashkenasic) are the most intelligent of the subgroups. Arab informants, compared with Jewish informants, were more prone to feel that environmental factors explained group differences in ability. Thus perceived Jewish superior intelligence reflects the informant's position and self-definition.

A careful examination of the literature on Jewish superior intelligence reveals that a unitary category "the Jews" always is imagined. At times, this category is divided by those who wish to or need to identify with one subclass or another, as in Zeidner's case. Thus nineteenth-century Central European Jews, such as Theodor Herzl, wishing to relativize their relationship both to Eastern European Jews (understood as primitive) and Central/Western European Jews (understood as assimilated), postulated the Sephardic Jewish experience as the "real" world of the Jews. Arabs in contemporary Israel see the politically most visible Jews in Israel, the Jews of Western (actually Eastern European) extraction, as the most intelligent. The distinction among subsets of the "Jews" is, however, found more frequently among Jewish savants writing about racial science of the nineteenth and early twentieth centuries. When "Jewish" superior intelligence is assumed to be positive, it is rarely seen as "biological." Rather it is understood as an inherited quality that can be attained by any group if only the "right" rules are followed. When Jewish superior intelligence is seen as a negative quality, as merely cleverness or "the cultivation of a single faculty, that of hair-splitting judgment, at the cost of the rest, narrow[ing] the imagination, . . . [without] a single literary product appear[ing] . . . deserving the name of poetry . . . A love of twisting, distorting, ingenuous quibbling . . ." (so said the late nineteenth-century Jewish German scholar Heinrich Graetz about Polish Jewish intelligence, Graetz, 1891-1980), then it is also often seen by Jews as (culturally) inherited but by non-Jews as inherent. In the post-Enlightenment era, forms of creativity, such as the writing of poetry, have come to be indicators of the virtue of a specific group, as aesthetics have come to mark "high" as opposed to "low" values as well as culture. Thus the pseudointelligence of the Polish Jews, according to Graetz, is a form of instrumental or functional rationality rather than substantive rationality. And substantive rationality is marked by aesthetic creativity, which in turn marks the creator as able both to comprehend and to represent the beautiful and the true, that is, the virtuous.

Virtue (or its absence) is thus a quality ascribed to or implicit in nineteenth-century racial categories. While it is evident that that century's concept of race, with its stress on the perfected prototype, is different from the contemporary biological view of race as a probabilistic aggregate, Murray's own views blur this distinction (Peterson, 1988). In a discussion at the Aspen Institute after the book's appearance, the following exchange took place: "An Israeli cellist asks if Murray draws any conclusions about Africa's shortage of ancient literature. Murray says he does, and as the veal chops sizzle, he offers the Israeli a national compliment: 'In terms of IQ, you guys are off the charts'" (DeParle, 1994, p. 52). The "guys" who are "off the charts" are the "Ashkenasic Jews of European origins" who make up a minority of Jews in Israel today; while Murray said this, his source for the comments in *The Bell Curve* counters itself. Thus the "compliment" is not a national one but a racial one. It is also, as we shall see, a gendered argument—for the "guys" really are men. The relationship of categories of gender to those of morality must be kept in mind as we read through the texts that "verify" Jewish superior intelligence.

The slipperiness and interrelationship of the racial categories that haunt the discourse on Jewish superior intelligence—Jew,

Hebrew, Israeli, Ashkenazi of European heritage, Sephardic—present one aspect of the complexity of the "bell curve" as a model for representing the difference of the Jew. Are "Jew" and "Hebrew" religious designations encompassing the widest range of Jews from all corners of the world (and of every possible "racial" label)? Is "Israeli" a label of national identity or, as it has been among German left-wing anti-Semites for decades, a hidden code referring to "the Jews" as a homogenous racial group? Are "Ashkenasic" and "Sephardic" ethnic or cultural labels, or the designation of racial cohorts? Who exactly belongs to what category and why? And why is it that when all is said and done, we are left with the idea of a homogenous "Jew" who is the embodiment of Jewish superior intelligence?

The image of the Jew in *The Bell Curve* haunts the book's reception. Two volumes of essays on *The Bell Curve,* one edited by Steven Fraser and another by Russell Jacoby and Naomi Glauberman, both published in 1995, contain discussions of the image of Jewish superior intelligence that is presented by Herrnstein and Murray. However, virtually all the essays deal primarily with African Americans and intelligence; one, by sociologist Andrew Hacker, rather pointedly ignores the "Jews" when tabulating "immigrant groups" (Fraser, 1995, p. 105).

A number of the commentators, such as Alan Wolfe, stress that IQ testing had its "original use against Jews and Catholics" (Fraser, 1995, p. 119). These commentators see the testing procedure concerning these groups (and by extension others) as inherently flawed at its American origin, regardless of its present use. John Carey, for example, notes that "social scientists 'proved' that the new Americans, many of them Jewish, would drag down the nation's average intelligence." However, he adds "Jews now score some 10 points higher than the white average" (Jacoby, 1995, p. 53). Among the non-Jewish essayists, the conservative African American intellectual Thomas Sowell sees the belief in Jewish superior intelligence as the result of Jews markedly improved scores from 1914 to the 1930s (Fraser, 1995, p. 75.) Sowell does not accept the idea that Jews were mismeasured in the earlier testing, as Herrnstein and Murray state, or that the measurements of the later period reflect the real, unalterable state of Jewish intelligence. Rather he argues for a theory of adaptation, stating that the measurement of Jewish intelligence that placed the Jew at the lower end of the bell curve was remedied in a relatively short period of time through acculturation rather than intermarriage or the elimination of bias in IQ testing. Sowell's equation of the victim status of American Jews and of African Americans leads him to believe that the increase in Jewish intelligence can be matched by an increase in African American intelligence, which he sees as a potential of the American system of acculturation. Jews become smarter because they become Americans.

Jewish savants see the matter very differently. Nathan Glazer, the conservative Harvard sociologist, postulates the inherent reason for Jewish achievement was the "urban and commercial background of many Jewish immigrants in the late nineteenth century and early twentieth century compared to the predominately peasant background of other immigrant groups of the period" (Fraser, 1995, p. 143). Jews were "smarter" than other immigrant groups because they were already predisposed to deal with urban capitalism in fin-de-siècle America. Here the advantage is a social one, dating from much farther back in history, and resulting from the Jews' oppression and the limits placed on their ability to own and till the land. In Glazer's estimation, Jewish superior intelligence and achievement is not an artifact of American adaptation but rather compensates for prior stigmatization.

For some Jewish commentators intelligence and creativity are interchangeable categories. Martin Peretz, the editor of *The New Republic,* stresses the cultural background of the Jews, commenting that "a population which listens to Midori or Itzak Perlman is likely to produce violinists from among its children, and one that doesn't won't. . . . A similar process helps explain why some American ethnicities (like Jews and subcontinent Asians) disproportionately produce physicians and physicists and why others (like Italians and Greeks) also disproportionately produce restauranteurs" (Fraser, 1995, p. 152). The evident flaw in such a view is the assumption that

Jews and Japanese have always been part of Western high culture. (When and how do Eastern Jews and Japanese move from liturgical music or klezmer or traditional Japanese music to Western high culture?) Peretz's view stresses that contexts that create expectations for an ethnic group to produce specific occupations form a link between creativity and intelligence: cultural expectations dominate. Yet Peretz is tempted by the notion that Jews are biologically somehow different. All Jews "are consistently close in genetic constitution" (Fraser, 1995, p. 153), a "fact" that may (if we only knew enough about the human genome, he cries) eventually make it possible to find the genetic basis for Jewish superior intelligence. Indeed Peretz argues that while Jewish genetic diseases may well be a reason for highly educated (and hypochondriacal?) Jews to collect information, the actual desire to collect data (read: science) "has genetic origins." Glazer states this without hesitation:

> We take these differences in intelligence for granted in the case of families, and it stands to reason that such differences might also characterize larger groups that share some common features in genetic inheritance and culture. Otherwise we would have no explanation for the disproportionate presence of Jews and Asians in selective high schools and selective colleges, or in the disproportionate presence of these groups in such occupations as medicine, law, and college teaching. (Jacoby, 1995, p. 339)

Jews are smarter than the average non-Jew, and they are predisposed to become scientists, says Glazer.

Of the Jewish commentators, it is finally Leon Wieseltier, the literary editor of *The New Republic,* who points the finger directly at the source of the problem as well as at his own anxiety about the question of Jewish superior intelligence. Commenting on Herrnstein and Murray's discussion, Wieseltier is "repelled" because he wishes to believe that he is responsible for his own achievements rather than that they are a reflex of a group of which he happens to be a member.

Earlier IQ studies in which Jews "did not 'test higher'" led to "consequences that were catastrophic." (One assumes that he is referring to the Shoah. As we shall see, the role of the Shoah in framing the question of Jewish superior intelligence is most complex.) And Wieseltier makes the appropriate gesture: "What if the 'generalizations' that Murray takes from the study that he calls 'Storfer 1990' had turned out differently? How would he explain my failure to express the limitations of my group? Or would it be more appropriate, in the event of psychometric embarrassment, that I stop pretending and start tailoring?" (Fraser, 1995, p. 159). These are the questions asked by the Jewish savant about his own role as an intellectual. What is there in "Storfer 1990" that provides Herrnstein and Murray with the certainty of their argument and so generates anxiety in Leon Wieseltier, "the Jew," who could be pretending to be a "smart Jew," but of course knows that he really is one?

No clearer example of the pitfalls of the romanticization of the "Jewish intellect" and its problematic relationship to the concept of virtue can be found than in the cited source for Herrnstein and Murray's one-page digest of the upper end of *The Bell Curve,* Miles D. Storfer's *Intelligence and Giftedness: The Constitutions of Heredity and Early Environment.* Published by a legitimate academic publisher, Jossey-Bass, this volume contains a summary of the positive, century-long search for the source for the improvement of the human condition, using "the Jews" as its model. It is thus different from many of the more questionable sources of the Herrnstein and Murray volume. Much like the nineteenth-century discussions concerning the improvement of the human condition through the adoption of Jewish ritual practices such as circumcision (which accounts for the wide practice of this ritual as a medical prophylaxis in the United States among non-Jews) and ritual slaughter (as a prophylaxis against tuberculosis—an argument not generally accepted but put forth at the same period), the question of the duplicable source of Jewish intelligence lies at the heart of Storfer's long chapter on "the nurturing of verbal/conceptual reasoning abilities in Jewish families." It must be noted that Storfer self-consciously places himself in the tradition of the testing studies from the 1920s, such as those by Lewis Terman (Storfer, 1980). He thus sees his work as a continuation of the "scientific" discourse about Jewish superior intelligence that has its roots in nineteenth-century science.

In his chapter on Jewish superior intelligence, Storfer summarizes the bulk of the post-Shoah statistical studies of Jewish superior intelligence based on various modalities of intelligence testing and notes, as Herrnstein and Murray's summary reflects, the superiority of Ashkenasic over Sephardic Jews. But Storfer's summary of the literature that employs this distinction actually draws it into question. Firstly, he makes sure that his reader knows that his idea of "the Jew" has little or nothing to do with religious belief, faith, or practice. He removes "Jewishness" totally from the realm of religion: "The overall intellectual proficiency of American Jewish children does not appear to depend on whether or not their families adhered to the Orthodox Jewish traditions" (p. 321). (Orthodoxy is for Storfer the only legitimate form of Jewish religious practice as it is evidently the most authentic and the least polluted by "non-Jewish" traditions.) Thus whatever virtue is to be associated with Jewish superior intelligence has nothing (according to this argument) to do with religious practice or belief. For Storfer, Jewish superior intelligence is the result of child-rearing practices, the linguistic matrix of the child, and the specific arenas of Jewish accomplishment. None of these is (at least in his initial discussion) seen as an aspect of religious practice.

Storfer employs, however, a Lamarckian, ethnopsychological model of organic memory that itself constitutes the space that defines "the Jews" (Otis, 1994). Lamarck's "evolutionary" theory suggested that new traits appear as a result of a species' attempts to adapt to environmental conditions—the giraffe reaches for leaves in the trees and stretches its neck; the longer neck is then passed down to the subsequent generations. Lamarck's theory was displaced by Charles Darwin's, which suggested that a giraffe might randomly receive a trait for a longer neck and that because this trait enables it to survive in its environment better than shorter-neck giraffes, the trait is passed on through the species. Thus, Storfer destroys any distinction between the Ashkenazi and the Sephardic Jew. The "verbal precocity of the Jewish people" can dissipate "after several generations of 'intellectual neglect'" (which he defines as living in "backward Arab lands for ten or twenty generations and [being] *assimilated into the Arab child-rearing customs"* [emphasis in original]). But the resilience of Jewish intellectual superiority is such that "exposure to a cognitively enriched (primarily Ashkenazi) kibbutz environment may be able to restore as much as two-thirds of this loss in a single generation" (Storfer, 1980, p. 328). For it is the underlying Jewish psyche that is the "source" of the superiority of the Jew, whether that psyche is found in Ashkenazi or Sephardic form. It is indeed "the Jew" as a unitary, racial category about whom Storfer is speaking.

Storfer's own sources for the practices to which he ascribes the origin and/or perpetuation of Jewish superior intelligence are as romanticized as is his own discussion. He evolves an image of "Jewish infant caretaking practices" as his model of shaping the ethnopsychology of the Jew and being, of course, shaped by the resulting superior intelligence of the Jews who developed it—such tautologies are not missing in studies of Jewish superior intelligence. His view of "Jewish infant caretaking practices" is rooted in a post-Shoah textual tradition. His primary source is Mark Zborowski and Elizabeth Herzog's *Life Is with People* (1952), a work that reflects immediately post-Shoah, passionate memories about the sole authenticity of the Eastern Jewish experience in the form of narratives about that world of European Jewry lost in the destruction of the Shoah. Thus Storfer's "Jews" are both universal (all Jews everywhere) but also the most "authentic of the Ashkenazi Jews"—Yiddish-speaking *Ostjuden.* Rooted in fieldwork among survivors of the Shoah, Zborowski and Herzog's text collected post-Shoah legends, myths, and memories of the pre-Shoah world of Eastern Jewry, and presented them as fieldwork about the actual, daily reality of the *shtetl.* But the image of the *shtetl* that Zborowski and Herzog retrospectively constructed was already an invention of late nineteenth- and early twentieth-century Yiddish high culture writers such as Sholem Aleichem. Sitting in the south of France or New York City at the turn of the century, such authors evoked a world at the moment after its dissolution and wrote about a lost world of an integrated, authentic Jewish experience located in Eastern Europe. Such a construction was shared by German Jews during World War I, who also "found" in the East the authenticity that they seemed to lack in their own culture.

The world of the Eastern Jews imagined during World War I and after the Shoah was a constructed image of the East fulfilling very specific ideological needs. The *shtetl* was a product of the Pale of Settlement and land/settlement practices in the Austro-Hungarian Empire—it was certainly *not* paradise. As soon as Jews could move into urban areas in Russia and Central Europe or leave for North America, England, France, South Africa, Australia—anywhere but to remain in that "perfect world"—they fled in overwhelming numbers. The image captured in the narratives in Zborowski and Herzog were early twentieth-century myths about the idyllic nature of the *shtetl* that evolved retrospectively following its dissolution through urbanization and immigration. Certainly such an idealized image also tended to stress the virtuousness of such communities. Zborowski and Herzog's discussion of the verbal environment of the child, of swaddling practices, and of a favorable caretaker ratio based on an extended family (Storfer's terms) is part of their image of coherent, extended families with specific child-rearing rituals. The existence of analogous practices among Russian, Ukrainian, and Polish "peasants" is never invoked to argue the basis of rural Russian, Ukrainian or Polish superior intelligence. Rather such practices seem to be proof of the peasants' (who were merely three generations out of serfdom) "primitive" status. Such stereotypes can be used both in "negative" and "positive" manners. Zborowski and Herzog's image of the Jewish family, which Storfer borrows, certainly does not overlap with the inchoate, complex, difficult world of the widely divergent Jewish Diaspora experiences in the nineteenth and twentieth centuries. It certainly does not at all reflect the four generations of the American experience of Jewish life, which according to the contemporary anxieties expressed within the

Jewish community is moving toward precisely the opposite pole in becoming too American.

The romanticizing that results from Storfer's appropriation of Zborowski and Herzog's world is evident when we focus on Storfer's idea of language, one of the core concepts in his model for the origin of Jewish superior intelligence. The question of the nature of the Jewish language and discourses is an extended trope in Western thought: Graetz commented on the stultifying mental set reflected in "Talmudic" discourse, and, internalizing the anti-Semitic Enlightenment view of a universal Jewish linguistic particularity, identified comments about the intrinsic nature of "Jewish language" and therefore "Jewish thought" with the *Ostjude* and the world of Polish Jewry. However, he saw this discourse as irrational and limiting. The origin of this perspective lies, of course, with Kant's distinction between the rational and the crafty man. His example of craftiness, cunning, and slyness are the Jews, a "nation of deceivers," who use their special command of language for their economic advantage (Kant, 1978, pp. 101-102). Kant associates little or no virtue with the image of the Eastern (Polish) Jew. Indeed, the Eastern Jew becomes the model for the rapaciousness and destructiveness of the Jew. The language of the Jews in this context becomes the measure of their craftiness but not of their intelligence.

Storfer reverses such a negative image of the "natural" language of the Jews and sees "the highly repetitive use of specific words and phases" as capturing specific "expressions of emotions" (Storfer, 1980, p. 327). For him, the "linking of words, melody and strong emotions . . . in the liturgy of the Jewish rituals" represents the Jews' ethnopsychological sensitivity to the nuances of language. But again such a view is tautological in its basic argument: Is it the liturgy (religious practice) that makes the Jew so (positively) sensitive to language, or is it the Jewish predisposition to language manipulation that generated the liturgy? There is no end to such a circle.

According to Storfer, there is no specific link between religious belief and Jewish superior intelligence. There is, however, an ancient tradition that has imprinted itself on the Jewish psyche so that it is believed that the liturgical practices (of the Temple) account for the contemporary Jew's facility with language. (Such an argument is analogous to the arguments of both the nineteenth and twentieth centuries that Jewish males have a much higher incidence of congenital circumcision than non-Jewish males because Jews have practiced circumcision over such an extensive period of time.) Thus, Storfer links two arenas in the nineteenth-century discussion of Jewish superior intelligence: "creativity" (music) and "intelligence" (verbal ability). But, as we have seen, he is not original in this linkage.

Storfer cites P. M. Sheldon's 1954 study of 28 children in New York City who had Stanford-Binet tests of 170 or higher: *"twenty-four . . . were Jewish"* (emphasis in original, Sheldon, 1954, p. 59-61). Similar studies (and Storfer cites dozens of them) show that Jews are much smarter, at least in terms of verbal and numerical ability, than non-Jews. *But is smarter better?* Given his heavy reliance on such studies, Storfer still does not feel that they are sufficient to make his point. For Storfer, the discussion of Jewish superior intelligence ("cleverness") must answer the more traditional European view of Jewish superior intelligence as a negative sign, a view found even in the psychological literature of the early twentieth century that Storfer evokes. Storfer needs to equate Jewish superior intelligence with virtue—just as Herrnstein and Murray argue that the transmission of low intelligence must be linked to vice. He equates Jewish superior intelligence with virtue in unusual ways.

Storfer turns to a model of Jewish superior intelligence from the age prior to psychological testing (which has its own deep history). This model catalogs Jewish achievements in order to correlate Jewish intellectual ability with "the contribution of the Jewish people to human progress." Jews are not only smarter, Storfer notes, but they are also better. For Jews' "verbal and/or numerical (conceptually based) mechanism for analyzing and integrating knowledge" enables them to "attain proficiency in conducting and playing classical music, acting, selling, and practicing psychotherapy" (Storfer, 1980, p. 314-319). These are, well, most of these are, good occupations. They are a sign of the "educated man," the *Bildungsbürger*, whom Western Jews ever since the Enlightenment took as the model for the "good" (and one might add "smart") Jew. High culture is the mark of accomplishment in this model.

Storfer turns to cataloging lists of "Jewish genius" (to use the nineteenth-century term). He begins with the paradigmatic smart who are also good "Jews": Albert Einstein and Sigmund Freud (Storfer, 1980, p. 322). But, as we have seen, such attributions are themselves fraught with problems, as the question of what such Jewish superior intelligence means to the individual so characterized is complex. American conservatives dealing with intelligence and race at the close of the Cold War need to abridge the normal catalog of smart Jews (as either positive and negative examples). Marx suddenly vanishes from the triumvirate of Marx, Einstein, and Freud. Storfer then turns to the tabulation of Nobel Prizes in science (including economics) and follows the Jewish scholar Raphael Patai's tabulation listing the "Jews" who have been awarded prizes. Patai, who is the author of the major study *The Jewish Mind* (1977), argues for and attempts to document Jewish superior intelligence. Had he turned to Armin Hermann's 1978 study of Noble Prize winners, however, he would have found a number of the "Jewish" winners labeled as "German" winners.

The difficulty in such catalogs is, of course, in how "the Jew" is defined. For Storfer it must be defined racially, for only then can such a list of "Jews" cutting across the national designation of winners be compiled. Having shown Jewish intellectual preeminence in science, he turns to "classical" music and lists performers from Vladimir Ashkenazy to Bruno Walter. With a bow to American popular culture, he throws in Irving Berlin and Benny Goodman for good measure. (By 1990, the age of rock and rap, both Berlin and Goodman are no longer seen as belonging to the realm of popular culture.) Here again it is the standard of the "educated man," the *Bildungsbürger*, that defines Jewish superior intelligence. The confusion between "talent" and "genius" standard in nineteenth-century analyses of catalogs of accomplishments is repeated here with all of the high culture bias of the nineteenth-century savant. The Beastie Boys, Jewish rap performers, or even more innovative klezmer artists such as The Klezmatics, need not apply for admission into the pantheon of talented Jews! Chess champions, another standard model for Jewish intellectual superiority in the nineteenth century, is the next category of Storfer's listing; and he extends the model of the "brilliant chess master" into the world of contract bridge players. While the "intelligence" of "Jewish" chess and bridge players is assumed because of their facility at their games, the facility of "Jewish" boxers and baseball players is seen as an absence of Jewish superior intelligence.

Jews, according to Storfer's listing of accomplishments, do not have the equivalent rank as painters, architects, and the "more observational sciences" such as geology, botany, zoology in the catalogs he examines (Storfer, 1980. p. 323). Jewish intelligence is the intelligence of the word, not the eye. But this exclusion is as much a comment on the anxiety associated with the role attributed to the Jews in the creation of the "modern." For conservative thinkers in the late twentieth century, art and architecture mark the bounds of the modern. Without any doubt, the impressionistic and culturally loaded compilation of such source books is subjective. A contemporary study of Jewish achievement, for example, dismisses a standard biographical handbook on American art as a questionable source because none of its editors appear in *Who's Who in America* (Weyl, 1989, pp. 57-58). But, in his reading of Zborowski and Herzog, Storfer takes the print record as a mimetic representation of a "real world." For him, the accomplishments recorded in these "best of . . ." lists all illustrate the results of the inheritance of "left hemisphere" skills. Thus the Jewish brain has certain advantages of training. In 1899 the Jewish savant Joseph Jacobs commented that "in races where progress depends upon brain rather than muscle the brain-box broadens out as a natural consequence" (Jacobs, 1899). One is not very far from nineteenth-century craniometric claims in Storfer's view about left-hemisphere development among Jews. Indeed, the last half of his monograph deals with the question of brain anatomy and intelligence. He thus explains

Jewish superior intelligence as the transmission of acquired physical characteristics of the brain over generations.

Storfer has now provided "statistical" detail about Jewish superior intelligence as well as a catalog of Jewish accomplishments. He has foreshadowed his argument as to how these qualities of mind become qualities of race. Yet this catalog does not completely fulfill his initial promise to explain how Jewish superior intelligence is shown in Jewish ability in conducting and playing classical music, psychotherapy, acting or sales (Storfer, 1980). Classical music (Bruno Walter) and psychotherapy (Sigmund Freud), are accounted for, but "acting" and "selling" seem to be missing. Acting, even that of Woody Allen, is part of the sphere of contemporary American popular culture, but the role of the actor, or at least the "actress," has a much different space in nineteenth-century accounts of Jewish genius. And the "salesmen" of the opening list of accomplishments seem to have vanished here as they vanished in most nineteenth-century accounts. Jewish stock brokers, savings and loan owners, and bankers, given the climate of the late 1980s and early 1990s could not appear. Michael Milken and Albert Einstein in the same list of "smart Jews?"—an impossible task for the tabulator of genius. Indeed, the anxiety about the central stereotype of the Jew in the late twentieth century, the economic stereotype, makes it virtually impossible to evoke the "merchant" in such a context (Krefetz, 1982). The conflation of the seeming economic success of the Jew and the representation of Jewish superior intelligence harkens back to older myths of the relationship between virtue and capital. This view harks back to Mark Twain's comment in 1898 that noted the Jew's "contribution to the world's list of great names in literature, science, art, music, finance, medicine, and abstruse learning" as "way out of proportion to the weakness of his numbers." But Twain also attributed the hatred of the Jews to "the average Christian's inability to compete successfully with the average Jew in business" (Twain, 1985, p. 12). The subject of business and the Jews is virtually taboo in contemporary evaluations of Jewish superior intelligence, as it raises the hoary question of Jews and white collar crime. Andrew Hacker obliquely raises this issue in an essay published in Steven Fraser's anthology of essays on *The Bell Curve*, in which he stresses "the high level of mental ability needed to perpetrate corporate crimes, ranging from verbal versatility to mathematical sophistication" while not relating this to any specific group discussed in *The Bell Curve* (Fraser, 1995, p. 103).

Such a list of accomplishments makes sense only if the ideological presumptions of Storfer's positioning of Jewish superior intelligence and his definition of it are explored. And Storfer makes this very easy for us. Having constructed a unilateral category of the Jew—for even his Sephardic Jews can be brought back into the fold of smart Jews with a minimal exposure to the "outstanding" form of Israeli life, the kibbutz—as much of a myth as the idealized life of the *shtetl* (Storfer, 1980, pp. 222-224), he ends his chapter on Jewish superior intelligence with a call for action. We (the human race) must and can all become smart Jews:

> What an optimistic scenario this Jewish model offers the human race! If the child development principles employed by the Jewish family can generate such a *multifold increase in the rate of productive genius*, then understanding and utilizing this knowledge for the betterment of all mankind could and should be viewed as a golden opportunity—not just an opportunity to develop a future population of highly intelligent people but, most importantly, an opportunity to use these heightened gifts of intellect to promote the kinds of achievements exemplified by the Jewish mission. (p. 330)

Thus Storfer's chapter on "smart Jews" ends. But even in Storfer's eyes, the ending needs clarification. What is the "Jewish mission" (as opposed to "the mission to the Jews," which historically was part of European discourse on the conversion of the Jews)? He provides his truly dedicated readers with a footnote:

> In virtually every one of the so-called helping professions—medicine, psychology, the shaping of legal and ethical

standards, the education of young minds, or the shaping of public opinion, the "people of the book" have made their presence keenly felt. It is almost as though (irrespective of whether the researcher/practitioner was a devout practitioner of the Hebraic faith) his or her efforts have been dedicated to the fulfillment of the "Jewish mission": "To help make the world a better place to live, in the hope that God will finally say 'You have done well my children,' and will cast down his countenance to shine upon the human race and reveal himself anew. (p. 333)

Intelligence is virtue, and both reflect a divine plan. We must indeed pause here and consider. Is economist Miles J. Storfer, former chief economist of the Department of Social Services, Bureau of Program Forecasting and Economic Analysis, whatever his self-definition, himself possessed of Jewish superior intelligence by dint of his professional role in the "helping professions"? With his superior intelligence, can he tell us all how to improve the species? All human beings can become like Jews—just swaddle your children and talk to them for 30 or 40 generations until Jewish superior intelligence is so imprinted on your gene pool and the structure of your racial brain that you will never lose it. You will thus become virtuous (like the good Christian or a good economist) and prepare for the second coming of Christ, when he reveals himself anew. The evocation of the priestly blessing evoked in the final quote is thus double edged. The Christian notion of Christ the (Jewish?) physician curing the sick as part of his mission to redeem mankind haunts this passage. And, in this scenario, the smart economist is the surrogate of Christ or at least of the priest. This is not too far from the claims of eugenics for the eventual perfection of the human species. We do not have to quibble with the notion of whether lawyers are necessarily part of the "helping professions" to realize that the pattern of Jewish professional employment was historically tempered by those professions into which Jews could enter and by a Western tradition of family patterns of employment. Freud's choice of his profession as a physician was overdetermined not by the representation of Jewish superior intelligence but by the options open to Jews even in as "open" a society as late nineteenth-century Vienna. As the son of a truck driver and the grandson of a junkman, my presence in a "Jewish profession" dedicated to "the education of young minds" was motivated primarily by a desire to move into the middle class, as my father's luckier Jewish contemporaries were able to move into white-collar jobs during the Depression by getting jobs in the post office. Storfer's text provides a sense of mission in these discussions of Jewish superior intelligence. But it is a mission not limited to the Jews—it only has value if it can be infinitely replicated.

According to the late Richard J. Herrnstein, a Jew, and his non-Jewish collaborator, Charles Murray, Jews are disproportionately smarter than non-Jews. They play this image off against the assumption that the other end of the "bell curve" is predominately African American. Storfer postulates that "frequent intrauterine problems and less-favorable family configurations" account for the lower end of the bell curve (Storfer, 1980, p. 19). But this deficiency becomes imprinted on the African-American brain as surely as does the Jewish superior intelligence on the brain of the Jew. One unspoken aspect of this contemporary American view is that if the Jew is smarter then he is also physically weaker. Again we can contrast the comment made by Joseph Jacobs at the turn of the century: "If they [the Jews] had been forced by persecution to become mainly blacksmiths, one would not have been surprised to find their biceps larger than those of other folk; and similarly, as they have been forced to live by their exercise of their brains, one should not be surprised to find the cubic capacity of their skulls larger than that of their neighbors" (Jacobs, 1899); linking to the historical assumption of the physical difference of the Jew and to the hidden notion that this intelligence is a form of biological compensation. Franz Kafka's friend Felix Weltsch wrote in the Prague Zionist journal *Self-Defense* that the Jews must "shed our heavy stress on intellectual preeminence . . . and our excessive nervousness, a heritage of the ghetto. . . . We spend all too much of our time debating, and not enough time in play and gymnastics. . . . What makes a man a man is not his mouth, nor his mind, nor yet his morals, but discipline. . . . What we need is manliness" (Pawel, 1988, p. 205). This lack of manliness is compensated for by genius. The Jewish physician Martin Engländer commented in 1902, "the inheritance and the quality of life [in the ghetto] evidenced two grotesque parallel facts: the skull size of the Jews is on average greater than that of the non-Jewish population; on the other hand, their chest circumference absolutely and relatively in relationship to body length is less than for non-Jews" (Engländer, 1902, pp. 11-12). Engländer did not need to interpret these "facts" for his Jewish readership at the fin de siècle, as they could easily do it for themselves: Thin-chested Jews may have "insufficient muscles and badly developed breathing apparatus," may "live with poor nutrition and conditions which harbor infection" and may therefore "have an enormous rate of tuberculosis," but they are smarter than non-Jews. Intelligence is the compensation for the physical weakness signified by small chest circumference and tuberculosis; big psyche rather than big biceps or chest.

Framing *The Bell Curve* in such a manner, Herrnstein and Murray show how alive and real the myth of American Jewish superior intelligence and its anti-thesis, African American muscular development, remain in contemporary discourse and in a wide range of contexts. They raise the problem of the masculinity of the male Jew and his relationship to his intelligence as part of the discourse on Jewish superior intelligence. Are smart Jews tough Jews, in Paul Breines's terms (Breines, 1990)? The right-wing adoption of multiculturalism continues to sort out qualities ascribed to fixed, limited groups. Those qualities ascribed to the "Jew" focus on the image of Jewish superior intelligence to the exclusion of Jewish physicality. Placement on the upper end of the "bell curve" is as much of a disadvantage as placement on the lower end if such placement means a person is reduced to the stereotypical qualities ascribed to his or her "race."

References

Breines, P. (1990). *Tough Jews: Political fantasies and the moral dilemma of American Jewry.* New York: Basic Books.

DeParle, J. (1994). Daring research or "social science pornography". *The New York Times Magazine.* October 9, 48-80.

Efron, J. (1993). Scientific racism and the mystique of Sephardic racial superiority. *Leo Baeck Yearbook, 38,* 75-96.

Engländer, M. (1902). *Die auffallend häufigen krankheitserscheinungen der jüdischen Rasse.* Vienna: J. L. Pollak.

Fraser, S., ed. (1995). *The Bell Curve wars: Race, intelligence, and the future of America.* New York: Basic Books.

Gilman, S. (1991). The indelibility of circumcision. *Koroth* (Jerusalem), *9,* 806-17.

Gilman, S. (1993). Mark Twain and the diseases of the Jews. *American Literature, 65,* 95-116.

Graetz, H. (1891). *History of the Jews.* Philadelphia: Jewish Publication Society of America.

Herman, A. (1978). *Deutsche Nobelpreisträger.* Munich: Moos.

Herrnstein, R. and Murray, C. (1994). *The Bell Curve: Intelligence and class structure in American life.* New York: The Free Press.

Jacobs, J. (1899). Are Jews Jews? *Popular Science Monthly, 55,* 507.

Jacoby, R. and Glauberman, N., eds. (1995). *The Bell Curve debate: History, documents, opinions.* New York: Times Books.

Kant, I. (1978). *Anthropology from a pragmatic point of view,* trans. V. L. Dowdell. Carbondale: Southern Illinois University Press.

Krefetz, G. (1987). *Jews and money: The myths and the reality.* New Haven, CT: Ticknor and Fields.

Lacayo, R. (1994). Essay. *Time Magazine.* October 24.

Madigan, C. (1994). Column. *Chicago Tribune, Section 4,* 1.

Otis, L. (1994). *Organic memory: History and the body in the late nineteenth and early twentieth centuries.* Lincoln: University of Nebraska Press.

Pawel, E. (1988). *The Nightmare of reason: A life of Franz Kafka.* London: Collins Harvill.

Peterson, W. (1988, February). Jews as a race. *Midstream,* 35-37.

Pope, C. (1979). Race and crime revisited. *Crime and Delinquency, 25,* 317-357.

Ryan, A. (1995). Apocalypse now? In Jacoby, R. and Glauberman, N., eds., *The Bell Curve debate: History, documents, opinions.* New York: Times Books.

Sheldon, P. M. (1954). The families of highly gifted children. *Marriage and Family Living, 16,* 59-60.

Storfer, M. (1980). New York City. New York: City of New York, Human Resources Administration.

Twain, M. (1985). *Concerning the Jews.* Philadelphia: Running Press.

Weyl, N. (1989). *The geography of human achievement.* Washington: Scott-Townsend.

Zborowski, M. and Herzog, E. (1952). *Life is with people: The culture of the shtetl.* New York: International Universities Press.

Zeidner, M. (1990). Perceptions of ethnic group modal intelligence: Reflections of cultural stereotypes or intelligence test scores? *Journal of Cross-Cultural Psychology, 21,* 214-231.

18 CHAOS AND COMPLEXITY: A QUANTUM ANALYSIS OF *THE BELL CURVE*

PATRICK SLATTERY

Ian Malcolm, the scientist and chaos theorist in Michael Crichton's novel *Jurassic Park,* challenges the modern notion of strict linearity and refutes the assumption that sudden, radical, irrational change is impossible. Despite protestations from researchers committed to Enlightenment notions of positivistic science, postmodern scholars and researchers recognize that chaos and complexity are built into the very fabric of existence. Crichton (1990) writes:

> Chaos theory teaches us that straight linearity, which we have come to take for granted in everything from physics to fiction, simply does not exist. Linearity is an artificial way of viewing the world. Real life isn't a series of interconnected events occurring one after another like beads strung on a necklace. Life is actually a series of encounters in which one event may change those that follow in a wholly unpredictable, even devastating way. That's a deep truth about the structure of our universe. But, for some reason, we insist on behaving as if it were not true. (p. 171)

Writers such as Richard Herrnstein and Charles Murray (1994) in *The Bell Curve* perpetuate the modern myth that the universe is wholly knowable and controllable. This chapter challenges their underlying philosophical argument in chapter 14 that by "controlling for IQ" they can "deduce with accuracy" a social commentary on the issues of ethnic inequalities in occupational status, wages, annual income and poverty, unemployment and labor force participation, marriage, illegitimacy, low-birthweight babies, children living in poverty, home environment, child development, crime, and middle-class values. I contend that "controlling for IQ" is not only impossible but inappropriate in the emerging postmodern global society. For some reason writers such as Herrnstein and Murray continue to believe that straight linearity is the natural state of the universe, despite the devastating impact of this modern philosophy on the human psyche, the environment, and social structures.

The entire argument in chapter 14 that "inequality between Whites, Blacks, and Latinos" is narrowed—and in some cases eliminated—when IQ is factored into the measurement equation fails on two accounts. First, identifying homogeneous ethnic control groups for comparative purposes is impossible; and second, expanding research variables to include IQ measurements increases complexity, uncertainty, and unpredictability in the resulting data rather than insuring more accuracy of interpretation. By "factoring in IQ" Herrnstein and Murray actually increase complexity in their equation and undermine their contention that the statistical data demonstrate ethnic and racial equality in American society.

The basis of this repudiation of Herrnstein and Murray's thesis is not rooted in modern notions of scientific validity and reliability of research models. With the appearance of a postmodern philosophy and the accompanying deconstruction of modern notions of linearity, an emerging science of complexity offers an alternative vision of the universe that makes obscene the reduction of racial, ethnic, and social issues to statistical certainties. The postmodern vision rejects traditional research metanarratives such as those underlying *The Bell Curve.*

Rational and statistical studies of decontextualized survey results, student behaviors, and intelligence tests that have driven educational research and promised inevitable progress in the task of human betterment and social improvement have been deconstructed. The modernist attempt to measure complex systems with an eye toward generalizable conclusions has been undermined.

The construction of "White, Black, and Latino" as categories of study begins the problematic in chapter 14 of *The Bell Curve*. In the postmodern era, the scientific effort to limit human beings with categories of race or ethnicity is being reevaluated. Examples of people discovering diverse biological ancestry later in life abound. Gregory Howard Williams (1995), professor at Ohio University and author of *Life on the Color Line*, is not an isolated example. Interracial marriage, adoptions, sperm donors, multiracial heritage, and social construction of racial and ethnic categories all undermine the simplistic notion of controllable racial variables.

In 1995 several Florida school districts were mandated by court decisions to include the category "multiracial" on student records. How many parents and students will now identify themselves as multiracial? With a genealogical search of just a few generations, possibly the majority of students will be identified as multiracial. William Faulkner's investigation of mixed bloodlines of white, black, and native peoples in the South foreshadows the reemergence of this issue in the 1990s. As another example, a major controversy has emerged in some Native American communities over the question of who should be accepted for tribal membership as applications expand during a time of financial growth and social recognition. Should a person with a single great-grandparent who was Native American in the last century be accepted for membership? Should a multiracial adopted child who has been immersed in the native culture and who has no biological ancestry in this local community, but whose family has lived in the native community for generations, be given precedence for membership over a person with a great-grandparent who had been a member of the community, even though this person has never had social or cultural contact with Native American people? Race is a complex political, social, biological, economic, theological, and autobiographical construction and cannot simply be reduced to biological determinism. Thus, the major premise of chapter 14 is undermined in contemporary postmodern scholarship.

Postmodern studies challenge rational and scientific studies of decontextualized human characteristics, student behaviors, and test results such as those in *The Bell Curve*. Research on linear progress and sequential development is coming under increasing scrutiny as critical scholars deconstruct the grand narratives of progress, arguing that historical outcomes are produced that run counter to the promises of linear progress and emancipation they espouse. Jean François Lyotard (1992), for example, writes:

> In the course of the past fifty years, each grand narrative of emancipation—regardless of the genre it privileges—has, as it were, had its principle invalidated. All that is real is rational, all that is rational is real: "Auschwitz" refutes this speculative doctrine. . . . All that is proletarian is communist, all that is communist is proletarian: "Berlin 1953," "Budapest 1956," . . . refute this doctrine of historical materialism. . . . All that is democratic is by the people and for the people, and vice versa: "May 1968" refutes this doctrine of parliamentary liberalism. . . . Everything that promotes the free flow of supply and demand is good for general prosperity and vice versa: "Crises of 1911 and 1929" refute the doctrine of economic liberalism, and the "Crisis of 1974-1979" refutes the Post-Keynesian modification of that doctrine. (p. 40)

Lyotard provides a critique of the modern project of linear progress, reason, and emancipation in which humanity seeks to master its own destiny and historical condition. The failure of modernity—as exemplified by *The Bell Curve*—to fulfill the promises of all grand narratives is not the result of incomplete data or inaccurate application. Additionally, the failure of modernity is not the result of refusing to pursue modernity to its end, as does *The Bell Curve* when its authors neglect to seek more accurate information.

Rather, its failure is due to the contingency, irony, and complexity of historical and social events that escape the clutches of reason, rationality, segmentation, and linear progress. Advances in the study of ethnic inequalities by "controlling for the IQ" factor add to the historical problems that destroy the modern project while giving the impression of completing it. Thus *The Bell Curve* may appear "reasonable" on first reading. However, Lyotard and other critical postmodern scholars remind us that controlling variables for linear progress is not reasonable and, thus, no longer tenable because it leads to the demise of that progress.

An example of this phenomenon from natural processes highlights this postmodern premise. Consider the Mississippi River. Since the great floods of the 1920s, the Army Corps of Engineers has developed an elaborate flood-control system consisting of levees from St. Louis to New Orleans, concrete blankets along the levees, locks at the Atchafalaya River, diversion canals, spillways, and other flood-control projects. Cities have been built in floodplains, and wetlands have been reclaimed for farming and industry, which have necessitated more expensive control structures to insure protection from annual floods. However, even with massive expenditures of money to build protective levees, the Mississippi River flooded and devastated the midwestern United States in 1993 and threatened to do so again in 1995. Many environmentalists and engineers recognize that the control structures themselves contribute to the flooding and exacerbate property destruction. Complexity and chaos are natural phenomena, and rivers must have wetlands and floodplains to absorb spring runoff and allow for shifts in the currents. Attempting to predict the flow of the river and eliminate the floods has been futile and ecologically disastrous. It is now recognized that some control structures must be removed to provide more wetlands. In the same sense, controlling for IQ in the Herrnstein and Murray research will only lead to further disaster. The complexity and contextual milieu of the human condition defy such linear analysis.

Chaos theory, according to William Doll (1993), gives meaning and substance to the language of disequilibrium, reflective intuition, surprise, puzzlement, confusion, zones of uncertainty, nonrationality, and metaphoric analysis. Doll contends that metaphoric analysis is hardly possible within a model structured around behavioral objectives, competency-based performance, accountability, mastery learning, and effective teaching. It is the very disequilibrium itself that provides opportunities for creative tension and self-reflection. "Chaos theory" was first coined by physicist Jim Yorke. He writes, "We tend to think science has explained how the moon goes around the earth. But this idea of a clock-like universe has nothing to do with the real world" (Briggs, 1992, p. 12). John Briggs (1992) describes chaos as a natural state of the universe, and he uses weather as an example: "With its variability, general dependability, and moment to moment unpredictability, weather infiltrates our schedules, sets or undermines our plans, affects our moods, and unites us with the environment and each other. Weather is also an example of a mysterious order in chaos" (p. 13).

In 1961 at the Massachusetts Institute of Technology (MIT), Edward Lorenz discovered a disturbing fact. He realized that the mere accumulation of more information about variables related to the weather such as wind speed, humidity, temperature, lunar cycles, and even sunspots do not help to increase the accuracy of long-range weather forecasts. Dynamic and complex systems such as weather, he discovered, are composed of many interacting elements, and the slightest perturbation has a significant impact on future patterns. Garmston and Wellman (1995) explain the impact of Lorenz's discoveries:

> At that moment, two fresh understandings of the world were born: First, that minor changes in initial conditions will produce major changes in dynamic systems. Lorenz's minute rounding of a number produced a significantly different pattern for the weather ahead. Second, more data will not permit more accurate predictions in such systems. Since each event affects another, which in turn affects another, more information complicates forecasting to the point of uncertainty. (p. 10)

The Bell Curve ignores this important discovery in the new sciences. Human beings, like weather patterns, are complex systems that defy predictability and linear certitude.

Following Lorenz, researchers have examined all dynamic systems, from the human brain to electrical circuits, for evidence of chaos. Chaos theory and complexity can help us to understand the postmodern vision that challenges the static and controllable universe on which Herrnstein and Murray rely for their philosophical grounding. Here the traditional social science approach to research is challenged; complexity replaces certainty. Prigogine and Stengers (1984) have demonstrated that systems in equilibrium and disequilibrium behave differently and that order can emerge out of chaos. James Gleick (1987) and Paul Davies (1988) contend that there is an emerging science of complexity that is built in part on the fact that hidden in apparent chaos are complex types of order. Postmodern research celebrates chaos, nonrationality, and zones of uncertainty because the complex order existing here is the place where critical thinking, genius (Kincheloe, Steinberg, and Tippins, 1992), reflective intuition (Doll, 1993), and global problem solving will flourish. The standardization of rote memorization, conformity, and controlling for an IQ variable, following from the faculty psychology movement and scientific management, restrict learning and success to a one-dimensional level imposed uniformly.

Cartesian-Newtonian models and mechanistic systems on which modern research paradigms are constructed ignore the developments in the new sciences that indicate that social systems are interactive and open-ended. Einstein set the stage for the emergence of the new physics and new ways of understanding the universe that inform chaos theory and complexity in the postmodern era. Complex systems can improve in the midst of turmoil. No longer must every person conform to predetermined principles, cultural forms, social structures, or, in the most egregious example from Herrnstein and Murray, definitions of "success in prestigious occupations." Rather success is based on a new science: a complex, multidimensional, kaleidoscopic, relational, interdisciplinary, and metaphoric system.

These complex systems challenge the Second Law of Thermodynamics, which sees the universe as running down as entropy increases. Paul Davies (1990) contends that there is no claim that the Second Law of Thermodynamics is invalid, only that it is inadequate because it applies only to closed systems that are isolated from their environments. Davies writes, "When a system is open to its environment and there can be an exchange of matter, energy, and entropy across its boundaries, then it is possible to simultaneously satisfy the insatiable desire of nature to generate more entropy and yet have an increase in complexity and organization at the same time" (p. 10). The universe as a whole can be seen as a closed system while subsystems of the universe remain open to their environments. Thus human beings cannot be "controlled for IQ," as the authors would lead us to believe. Humans are "open systems" associated with diverse subcultures and environments that increase the complexity of the human dynamic. After observing open and closed systems and their environments, the French Jesuit paleontologist Pierre Teilhard de Chardin (1959) wrote, "We are now inclined to admit that at each further degree of combination something which is irreducible to isolated elements emerges in a new order. . . . Something in the cosmos escapes from entropy, and does so more and more" (cited in Davies, 1990, p. 10).

William Doll (1993), David Bohm (1988), and David Ray Griffin (1988) turn to Werner Heisenberg's Uncertainty Principle to provide further support for this claim. In traditional modern physics, scientists believe that if they can improve their measurements and calculate with infinite precision, then absolute understanding of the universe and its physical properties will follow. Heisenberg disagreed, and he demonstrated that it does not matter how accurate the instrument or measurement because the act of measuring influences the outcome of the measurement process itself.

The Heisenberg Uncertainty Principle examines the subatomic world and contends that if we choose to measure one quantity (such as the position of the electron), we inevitably alter the system itself. Therefore, we cannot be certain about other quantities (such as how fast the electron is moving). Since an interaction is involved in every measurement, and since measurements are involved in observations in modern science, some physicists contend that the act of observation changes the system.

In classical physics, everything that can be known can be measured. In quantum physics, uncertainty is built into the metaphysical reality. Position and velocity of an electron cannot be measured simultaneously, not because the observer is not looking carefully but because there is no such thing as an electron with a definite position. In a parallel argument, there is no such thing as a human with a definite and unchanging IQ that can be measured with certainty. Electrons are "known" only in their relationship to other electrons. Electrons do not orbit the neutron like a planet; rather, an electron exists in a cloud like a twin. Neither a particle nor a wave, the electron is described more by its relationship and potentiality rather than its actuality. Each electron, in a sense, enfolds in itself the universe as a whole and hence all its other parts, emphasizing internal relatedness. This implicate order is also true of human beings who cannot be reduced to single measurements. In postmodern research it does not make sense to evaluate persons based on classical physics, for like the elusive electron, relationships and potentialities explain human existence—and not predetermined structure or IQ tests. Fritjof Capra (1975) explains:

> The exploration of the subatomic world in the twentieth century has revealed the intrinsically dynamic nature of matter. It has shown that the constituents of the atom, the sub-atomic particles, are dynamic patterns which do not exist as isolated entities but as integral parts of an inseparable network of interactions. These interactions involve a ceaseless flow of energy manifesting itself as the exchange of particles; a dynamic interplay in which particles are created and destroyed without end in a continual variation of energy patterns. The particle interactions give rise to the stable structures which build up the material world, which again do not remain static, but oscillate in rhythmic movements. The whole uni-

verse is thus engaged in endless motion and activity; in a continual cosmic dance of energy. (p. 211)

Investigations of the subatomic world cause contemporary scholars to reexamine the entire relation of research to cosmic and quantum phenomena. Herrnstein and Murray's attempt to ignore the complexities of the human dynamic as they "control for IQ" in order to dismiss issues of injustice and inequality in American society must be challenged. The new sciences provide an important source of research that allows the modern notions of control and linearity to be deconstructed and the philosophical foundations of *The Bell Curve* to collapse.

References

Bohm, D. (1988). Postmodern science and a postmodern world. In Griffin, D., ed., *The reenchantment of science*, 57-68. Albany: State University of New York Press.

Briggs, J. (1992). *Fractals, the pattern of chaos: Discovering a new aesthetic of art, science, nature.* New York: Simon and Schuster.

Capra, F. (1975). *The Tao of physics.* Berkeley, CA: Shambhala.

Crichton, M. (1990). *Jurassic park.* New York: Knopf.

Davies, P. (1988). *The cosmic blueprint: New discoveries in nature's creative ability to order the universe.* New York: Simon and Schuster.

Davies, P. (1990). Cosmogenesis. *Creation Spirituality, 6* (3), 10-13.

Doll, W. E., Jr. (1993). *A post-modern perspective on curriculum.* New York: Teachers College Press.

Herrnstein, R. and Murray, C. (1994). *The Bell Curve: Intelligence and class structure in American life.* New York: The Free Press.

Garmston, R. and Wellman, B. (1995). Adaptive schools in a quantum universe. *Educational Leadership, 52* (7), 6-13.

Gleick, J. (1987). *Chaos: Making a new science.* New York: Viking Press.

Griffin, D. R. (1988). *The reenchantment of science: Postmodern proposals.* Albany: State University of New York Press.

Kincheloe, J. L., Steinberg, S. R., and Tippins, D. J. (1992). *The stigma of genius: Einstein and beyond modern education.* Durango, CO: Hollowbrook Publishing.

Lyotard, J. F. (1992). *The postmodern explained to children: Correspondence 1982-1984.* London: Turnaround.

Prigogine, I. and Stengers, I. (1984). *Order out of chaos: Man's new dialogue with nature.* New York: Bantam.

Williams, G. H. (1995). *Life on the color line.* New York: Penguin Books.

19 DYSGENESIS AND WHITE CULTURE

GREG TANAKA

The neatly dressed young woman laughed out loud. Her "dirty" blond hair was cut short, just above the collar. She wore a conservative black dress and new black pumps. A simple gold pendant hung from her neck. She had been singing a few lines of a song to herself: "Come ye from the hills, come ye from the fields. . . . Hear ye everywhere, don'tcha care, there's a fair, down on MacConnachy Square!" Hearing her own "made-up" words, she smiled.

Melanie Healy remembered her first class assignment in International Arts: Give an oral report about the moment you realized you had a cultural or ethnic identity different from others. She reported she was six when she came home skipping and smiling after watching a musical with her mother. She was so proud to finally learn who she was—to see a visual image of the people who were her ancestors. The musical was about a magical place called Brigadoon. It was only recently that her mom corrected her, saying "Brigadoon's Scottish, and you know, you're Irish and there's a difference between (laugh) this and Scottish. Here's the place on the map."

Melanie told the class her mother did not want to correct her when she was six because she had seemed so "into bagpipes." Her International Arts Program—IAP—classmates laughed along with her and she knew immediately she had come to the right major. She wanted to learn about herself and others—in a place where it was safe to do so.

But as she looked up now at the exposed wood beam ceiling of the university placement center, Melanie wondered about the road she had taken. The four years had zipped by. Observing the naked simplicity of this Frank Gehry–designed building—its bold red and yellow air ducts hanging from the ceiling—Melanie realized she was just the opposite. She had become more complex. Just as America itself was undergoing dramatic social and demographic change, her own location in society was in real flux.

WHY BRING UP DYSGENESIS NOW?

In responding to chapter 15 of The *Bell Curve,* I choose to write not in the style of Herrnstein and Murray—which I feel would add unnecessary credibility to their claims—but in my style, which is novelistic and emphasizes multiple perspectives. To accommodate the increased significance of race and ethnic heterogeneity in the United States, I will apply a postcolonial framework that recontextualizes, historicizes, and problematizes their claims.

Herrnstein and Murray assert that immigrants of color pose a threat to U.S. intelligence, a phenomenon they label "dysgenesis." But the idea that different races have different IQ levels was dealt a crippling blow some years ago when Stephen Gould showed that IQ tests were statistically designed to measure the variation between *individuals* and not between *groups.* In *The Mismeasure of Man,* Gould (1981) concludes, that the average difference between the scores of Whites and Blacks might still only reflect the environmental disadvantages of Blacks. Since then, there have been *no new advances* in the argument that race determines intelligence. In the face of this, Herrnstein and Murray only offer vague disclaimers: "Foreign-born blacks score about five IQ points higher than native-born blacks, *for reasons we do not know.*"

Perhaps the problem lies in the use of standardized tests. Suppose, for example, that IQ tests were rewritten, this time by the five top-ranked African American scholars. Theoretically, whatever these professors come up with will be worthy of use in the IQ tests because these are the premier scholars in their fields. Would it make any difference *who* prepared these tests to the white parents whose children will be taking them? Of course it will matter—and that's precisely the point. There is something inherently biased about IQ tests written by people from only one cultural background.

Suppose instead someone sues the University of California at Berkeley law school under a claim that all black applicants with Law School Admissions Test (LSAT) scores in a certain range were admitted—while none of the white applicants in the same range were admitted. (In fact there is such a case.) What this lawsuit overlooks is the fact that black graduates of Berkeley typically outperform white graduates as a group on state bar exams, three years later, suggesting bias in the LSAT as well.

Recontextualizing Herrnstein and Murray's claims in a heterogeneous society, it is apparent that what has changed is not the research findings about intelligence but rather the social environment. Herrnstein and Murray argue that evidence indicates that African Americans and Latinos are reproducing at a faster rate than middle-class Whites, forcing the national IQ to decline. Such a reality creates a new social context with serious social consequences for Americans. But if the authors raise nothing new and persuasive about the race and intelligence debate, the larger question is: "Why bring up dysgenesis now?"

Melanie Healy remembered the early promise of the university's International Arts Program. Only the best students were admitted. Frannie Chu, the program chair, had wowed the entering class that year with a rousing orientation speech: It would be up to us to shape not only how we see the world, she said, but also how to know ourselves. There would not be one historical view here of what constituted good art. Instead, students would spend time accessing their own feelings and histories, learning about other people's histories, and then creating art based on those journeys.

Melanie wanted to learn about American musicals and about theater from other cultures—such as Noh and Kabuki. She recalled talking to the student sitting to her left on orientation day. He was a Chinese American from the Bay Area and he believed IAP could help him learn about his identity. Eyes shining and chin held forward, he was already a full convert to the cause. He said he would pursue a dual major in math and IAP music.

The student sitting to her right was a Chicano. An artist and musician before coming to the university, he had entered IAP in order to learn how to make "world art" as opposed to "personal art." He thought that art of the future would be "intercultural" and resonate human experience rather than theory. Melanie's head was spinning from the excitement and richness of the experience that was barely beginning.

IS DYSGENESIS A SMOKESCREEN FOR SOMETHING ELSE?

The willingness of Herrnstein and Murray to use the veil of science to make race and intelligence claims suggests a desire to whip the American public into a frenzy about future immigration. They tell us that since the ethnic groups differ in their average IQ, a shift in America's ethnic makeup would imply a change in the overall average IQ.

But does another reason exist for this fear of immigrants? One psychiatrist, Francis Cress Welsing (1991), concludes from years of practice that Whites harbor a fear of losing their identity to interracial marriage because whiteness derives from a recessive gene: A baby coming from white and black parents will invariably be "not white."

Others have suggested that the self-image of Whites in the United States has not been based on their own positive ethnic histories, which many sought to discard when leaving Europe for the Americas, but on artificial comparisons with black slaves who were not free and therefore were inferior to them (hooks, 1992; Morrison,

1992; West, 1994). On what, then, is the identity of the European American to be based? What will constitute the shared set of norms, beliefs, and behaviors for European Americans? It has gone largely unnoticed that many Latinos, Asians, and Africans who now come to the United States voluntarily bring with them intact ethnic identities—and their arrival may trigger a realization among some Whites that they don't possess a clear identity.

According to Morrison (1992) and West (1994), the white identity always has been parasitic on blackness, upholding a race superiority. But if this is still a democratic society and equality is still a cherished value, then there remains a fundamental tension in America: Whites *as Americans* can no longer look themselves in the democratic mirror and continue to bask in an identity of race superiority.

Does the presence of so many who seem to know and value their ethnic histories remind many European Americans that they have *no* ethnic identity? If so, what would happen to the psyches of European Americans? While I can only guess, some researchers are starting to come forward to speak on this. Herbert Stein, former chair of the President's Council of Economic Advisors, writes in the *Wall Street Journal* (1995), "Why is the white American male so angry? Because he is white, American and male. The security and pride he had in all three characteristics is threatened, which makes him fearful and angry." What are white males to do? "The white American male will learn. He will learn that he doesn't have to be king of the hill to value himself and to be valued by others."

Apparently, one product of losing an identity based on race and gender superiority is rage. If so, then the "dysgenesis" claim—a direct attack on immigrants of color—almost sounds like a projection of the authors' own rage about a perceived threat to their identity. Stein hopes that "98% of the world's population that is not white American male will understand that he is going through a period of stress and will try to be sympathetic and tolerant."

By locating the dysgenesis claim in a wider continuum of time spanning Western colonialism—by *historicizing* it—we see how some writers may feel tempted to bring it up now, prior to an election year, to assuage the emotions of white voters. The alternative—stripping an identity of race superiority from a people who already lack an ethnic identity—would leave white America conceivably with *no* identity.

HAD DANCE LOST ITS MEANING?

Melanie watched a woman with fair skin, short light brown hair, and a long sinewy body running around the stage in wide circles. Dressed in a diaphanous outfit, the dancer seemed to be winding herself up to perform a traditional modern dance. Melanie recalled how this dance had turned vaguely unsettling. Although the performance began with form, music, and lighting that was clearly Western, it quickly turned "fragmented." The dancer was becoming imbalanced, decentered, without compass. It was as if this woman seemed bent on seeing something—even though that something did not exist. The final segment was decidedly multicultural with many dancers joining in—men and women of color plus other Whites. Yet instead of implying harmony or integration, the overall effect of this piece was jarring, and Melanie didn't quite know why.

On another night a dark woman with bells on her feet moved diagonally across the stage. Ten times she moved—each time calling forth one of the mythic transformations, each time crashing Father Time (linear time), each time elevating Mother Time (cyclical time). Indian music, lateral darting eyes, a pretty dark head shifting left, shifting right—the South Asian woman moved in contrasting motions, first Western, then ancient Indian. At the front of the stage she interacted with a white man who held a camera and was dressed in tourist garb. Apparently, this white man's gaze could record only linear time, time captured by his Polaroid—as if time could actually stand still! In contrast, the beauty of cyclical time was its freshness—its harmony, its rejuvenating quality.

But Melanie wondered what would become of Western linear time, her time. Was this dance too binary—in the sense that it forced humans into two camps, one Western, the other Eastern? If it was, then didn't it operate, ironically, just as the Western aesthetic had—this time by exoticizing and essentializing the white male "Other?"

Melanie thought about her decision to rush a sorority. She had been accepted on Sorority Row—but then immediately ostracized by her nonsorority classmates at IAP. Simply by joining a sorority, had her membership at IAP become *less* valued?

DYSGENESIS AND WHITE IDENTITY

Many Americans may in fact be so cut off from Europe that they are deracinated—rootless. Is there any basis to white identity other than its own whiteness? *Perhaps the debate about intelligence and race is and always has been about whiteness.*

The problem with dysgenesis is that it hinders the development of cultural identity for European Americans by directing attention away from their own need and focusing instead on those who trigger this defense mechanism, immigrants of color. By posing dysgenesis in the context of a white identity problem—*problematizing* it—we see it operates as a subversive symbol: By concentrating and then reasserting the misdirection inherent in the genetic intelligence debate, it removes from European Americans any responsibility for examining and developing their own positive identities.

At a time when the need for self-awareness is arguably the most keen—when a homogeneous racial grouping is forced to confront its own history of colonialism and a future of dark democratic faces—the authors would have us dwell only on fear. Sadly, the panic cry of "Dysgenesis!" induces a *withdrawal* from one of the most significant sociological events in U.S. history: the turn-of-the-century inquiry into what it means to be an American.

Balloons rose up in bunches from a dozen folding tables displaying food choices: Nikkei Student Union, Jewish Student Union, Iranian Students Association, Ethiopians, Thai Smakom, MECHA, World

Hunger Project, and others. Hundreds of people were milling about. The crowd at north campus was 90 percent of color. Under one tree folkloric strummers stood dressed in red and black, and practiced with their guitars. Not far away, Melanie heard someone chanting—a Native American. His resonant voice floated across the warm air as he punched his rattle again and again.

On the other side of the wide, grassy garden, a small troupe of musicians was preparing to make Western folk music. Their attire made them look like an old group from the 1960s called The Band. At another corner of this Western art garden, a Korean woman was concluding her dance near a Brancusi-like brass sculpture, her ghostlike white-robe costume sweeping left then right. A loud shallow drum punctuated the air and the audience around her seemed as if in a trance.

The IAP annual music and dance festival always was widely attended by students and employees of the university. It was a grand time. As the South Asian dancer tried to show, perhaps time was not always linear! Hey, wasn't this also like the L.A. Arts Festival several years earlier—where the director announced he would move the appreciation of culture away from the dualistic and in the direction of "a multiplicity"? Melanie remembered him asking: "How do you construct a cultural institution that has a permanent sense of movement?" He said the answer was "to create a space in America where you can have discussion and sustain it" so that there would always be many views of art in the same conversation.

But Melanie was wondering if festivals like these didn't leave something out. Did they have room, for example, for *her* identity? She knew she had come from a well-to-do Republican family and that it had been a long journey for her just to be open to other cultures. But did the path at IAP just lead to a new kind of elitism—where other ethnicities were celebrated and European American identities were left out? Even in class, she was starting to notice how the "in" students wore ethnic clothing from Africa or South America or Asia. Meanwhile, there she was looking like "Little

Miss Nice" dressed in her gold crew-neck sweater and light blue jeans. Was *this* why she often felt ignored by her classmates? Was her culture now going to be *de*-valued?

DYSGENESIS AND "MISSED OPPORTUNITY"

By using science as a smokescreen—in effect celebrating as fixed truth their own racial perspective—Herrnstein and Murray create a convenient disguise for their own polemic. But rather than hide their polemic about issues of race, what writers should be doing is examining such questions *as polemic.*

I feel the long-term answer to all this gnashing of teeth lies in some form of interculturalism (Hwang, 1994: Marranca and Dasgupta, 1991). The focus on interaction *between* cultures offers more potential than either the separate enclaves of early multi-culturalism—or the self-defeating ethnocentrism of Herrnstein and Murray. Was it in elementary school we learned that in order to interact successfully with others, we have to have a secure sense of who we are? But if interculturalism will ultimately include the stories of all Americans, we face this new question: *Who is responsible for European American participation?*

Perhaps the greatest harm from *The Bell Curve* is that it cuts off possibility by preventing European Americans from directing their attention to the creation of new cultural identities not based on race superiority. Having said this, should anybody care about their absence?

The last few weeks had been draining. Right and left, professors she knew from dance were quitting or retiring. It was a wholesale riot. Decades of national leadership in dance were being swept out the window in one swift turn of history. Was this the collapse of something cherished—or merely the inevitable?

What bothered Melanie most was a document proposing that IAP be merged into the Dance Department. The new department would cast off the dance descriptive and be renamed the

Department of International Arts. Was this new department going to *eliminate* Western dance? What would happen to Western culture then? To ballet? Would Broadway musicals fall too? The document was worded in a way that almost *excluded* European cultures. For the first time, Melanie realized her whole experience at IAP had been exclusively *ethnic.*

Melanie knew about the numbers. Everyone had been talking about them. The Dance Department had the money and the teaching positions—but it was admitting 150 students into each freshmen class and graduating only three or four seniors four years later! In contrast, IAP had grown from 10 to 12 graduates per year in the early 1980s to almost 40 in the coming year. The numbers favored IAP. Why not give the successful program the money?

As she continued to wait for her interview at the Placement Center—which was now running late—Melanie wondered what would become of the program she loved. She had taken a risk by staying in IAP: While many of her sorority friends were landing jobs at IBM, AT&T, and other corporations, here she was interviewing with the L.A. Arts Festival—the only entity all year that was interested in interviewing her. Well, at least the IAP major was good for one kind of job! Melanie tried not to worry as she fingered the gold pendant that hung from her neck.

WHO CARES?

When this decade's public furor dies over race and IQs, affirmative action, and illegal immigration, what will the European Americans have gained? Brown, black, red and yellow people will still be here. Will Whites still lack symbols of shared meaning that derive from intrinsic worth?

Herrnstein and Murray tell us that their purpose has been to point out that the stakes are extremely large—but once we unpack their concept of "dysgenesis," we see that what is at stake is far larger than even they imagine: feelings of worth, the irrepressibility of human spirit, and perhaps most important of all, the ability to connect with others.

Melanie heard the clicking of heels and looked up tentatively. An Asian woman was smiling at her. It was the assistant director of the center. Melanie watched the assistant director's mouth moving but did not hear the words. She did not need to. The employer had canceled the interviews. It seemed the L.A. Arts Festival had lost its funding and would not be hiring this year. Melanie nodded politely, got up and moved like a ghost through space. Her eyes were tearing as she exited the building, and she reached down deep for something to hold on to. She began to sing: "Brigadoon, Brigadoon, you'll be under sable skies. Brigadoon, Brigadoon, there my heart forever lies. . . ."

References

This narrative was constructed from interviews and observations made during a six-month period at a large public university in California. Only the final scene in the placement center waiting room was fabricated; all others were as depicted. The L.A. Arts Festival did lose its funding permanently—when wealthy white donors became disenchanted with the multicultural tone of the 1993 event. Melanie is a fictitious name for one acutely perceptive interviewee. The only job interview she had in her senior year was in fact with the L.A. Arts Festival, just before it lost its funding.

Gould, S. (1995). Curveball. In Fraser, S., ed., *The Bell Curve wars: Race, intelligence, and the future of America.* New York: Basic Books.

Gould, S. (1981). *The mismeasure of man.* New York: W. W. Norton & Company.

Herrnstein, R. and Murray, C. (1994). *The Bell Curve: Intelligence and class structure in American life.* New York: The Free Press.

hooks, b. (1992). Representing whiteness in the black imagination. In Grossberg, L., Nelson, C. and Treichler, P. eds., *Cultural studies*. New York: Routledge.

Hwang, D. (1994). Facing the mirror. Foreword to Aguilar-San Juan, K., ed., *The state of Asian America: Activism and resistance in the 1990's*. Boston: South End Press.

Marranca, B. and Dasgupta, G., eds. (1991). *Interculturalism & performance*. New York: PAJ Publications.

Morrison, T. (1992). *Playing in the dark: Whiteness and the literary imagination*. Cambridge, MA: Harvard University Press.

Solorzano, D. (1992). Education in a cross-cultural perspective. Title of a graduate course taught at UCLA.

State Notes. (1995, June 16). *Chronicle of Higher Education*, A30.

Stein, H. (1995, February 9). White male rage sweeps America. *Wall Street Journal*.

Welsing, F. (1991). *The Isis papers: The key to the colors*. Chicago: Third World Press.

West, C. (1994 fall). Speech given at Claremont McKenna College. Pomona, California.

20 A SUBURBAN TALE: REPRESENTATION AND SEGREGATION IN SPECIAL NEEDS EDUCATION

GLENN M. HUDAK

As a parent of a child having "special needs," I was greatly concerned with the data presented by Richard J. Herrnstein and Charles Murray in chapter 16, "Social Behavior and the Prevalence of Low Cognitive Ability," of their book *The Bell Curve* (1994). In particular, I was troubled by their mountain of data intending to show the correlations between individuals labeled with "low cognitive ability" and major societal problems such as poverty, high school dropouts, unemployment, being in jail, receiving welfare, and so on. The chapter concludes with a short commentary referring to the virtues of middle-class values (the Middle Class Values Index). I found this equally troubling. As I pondered the numerous graphs and figures that comprise the bulk of the chapter, I became increasingly concerned about my son, Ben.

I am worried about my son's present circumstance and his future possibilities. My son has been tracked into "special needs" classrooms since preschool. The issue of "cognitive ability" is present in all our discussions with his teachers, especially with regard to his proper placement in school. Last year my wife, Kathy, and I requested and then insisted that Ben be included in a "regular" second-grade classroom (with the necessary support services), reasoning that the segregation of special needs children from other children was hurtful. We worried that Ben's growing sense of not fitting in would cause him to withdraw from schooling in general. We worried about his being marginalized from mainstream activities. We worried about self-fulfilling prophecies and a myriad of other tensions that eat away at the soul of parent's where their child is concerned.

Throughout his second-grade year, Kathy and I attended several meetings at Ben's school to discuss his progress and his Individual Education Program (IEP). During these meetings we were told how Ben scored on a battery of tests. At these meetings, school personnel described Ben's performance in the classroom in detail, usually settling on a sober discussion of his social behavior (quiet and withdrawn) and his cognitive ability. We were told that Ben's return to a segregated special needs classroom would be "for his own good."

I found a certain convergence in thinking between the thesis put forward by Herrnstein and Murray, that is, there is a place for everyone, and Ben's teachers, who argue that he is best served by being segregated, "placed" into a special needs classroom. From Herrnstein and Murray's perspective, the question of place—where one is to be located in school and society—is very much related to the issue of intelligence. It is easy to identify the legacies of the Platonic tradition and the social efficiency movement as shaping their concluding chapter, "A Place for Everyone."

Indeed, during the early decades of the twentieth century, the creation of an orderly and stable society where each individual had a place, a location, was espoused by the proponents of the social efficiency model of education—a model that sought to discover the individual needs and capacities of the child as a way of locating his or her future role in society. To accomplish this task of educating the child according to his or her needs, new theories and techniques were developed to measure the child's intelligence quotient (IQ). As Herbert Kliebard (1986) notes, I.Q. became a powerful tool by which society could be regulated. In an effort to eliminate waste and make school more efficient in training students for the growing demands of industrialization, differentiated curriculums were created. In 1928 the sociologist Ross Finney argued that the point of schools was to fit the individual into a slot in society, thereby separating the leaders from the followers. As Kliebard notes, what angered Finney was the persistence of the "rise-out-of-your-class" philosophy of society that continued to dominate educational policy in the face of conclusive evidence that "the great majority are predestined never to rise at all. . . ." Finney's solution was to teach that half of the population without the power to "secrete cogitations," to follow dutifully what those who have the power tell them to do. In fact, in curriculum terms, he envisioned one curriculum for leadership and another for "fellowship" designed for that purpose (pp. 110-111).

The social efficiency model conceived of individuals as being "essentially" different, where differences between individuals, particularly with regard to intelligence, were viewed as "natural," a part of nature itself. Consequently, a few people are very smart while most are average and a few are far less than average. This idea is illustrated by drawing a bell curve.

But it is fair to ask: What are the moral/ethical criteria for such sifting and sorting of our children? In chapter 16, Herrnstein and Murray evoke the Middle Class Values Index as their standard, their criteria. They initially developed this index from their work with the National Longitudinal Survey of Youth (NLSY). The Middle Class Values Index is scored only in terms of a yes or a no response. To score a yes, one had to give a yes answer to each of four questions: one had to be married to his or her first spouse, be in the labor force (if a male), bearing children within wedlock (if a female), and never have been interviewed in jail (p. 385). Those who answered yes to each of these four concerns received a composite score of yes on this survey and subsequently were identified as fitting "the middle-class stereotype." According to Herrnstein and Murray (p. 264), there is a correlation between cognitive class and middle-class values. Of those identified as "very bright" (Class I), 74 percent scored yes on the Middle Class Values Index (hence fitting the middle-class stereotype), while on the other extreme, those labeled "very dull" (Class V), only 16 percent scored a yes.

Herrnstein and Murray tell readers how much they enjoyed preparing the Middle Class Values Index:

> [I]ts modest goals are to provide a vantage point on the correlates of civility in the population of young adults and then to serve as a reminder that the old-fashioned virtues represented through the index are associated with intelligence . . . high intelligence also seems associated . . . , perhaps surprising to some, with the behaviors that we identify with middle-class values. (pp. 265-266)

Here we have civility, high intelligence, and middle-class values united together as the ethical base from which to judge others. Left out of this triad of virtue are the voices of marginalized individuals or groups. Left out are those unable to speak on their own behalf precisely because of these middle-class values: Those segregated and labeled as demonstrating "low cognitive ability." Here, as Cameron McCarthy and Warren Crichlow (1993) argue, "issues of identity and representation directly raise questions about who has the power to define whom, and when, and how" (p. xvi). At issue is the painful struggle over the "proper" placement, location, and identification of children like Ben, who are labeled as "special." Ben's narrative provides testimony to the stigma, segregation, and growing feeling of inadequacy often attached to children labeled this way. Left out of Herrnstein and Murray's discussion of place and the "civility" of middle-class values is the realization that the term "place" is itself a contested, political terrain struggled over by parents, teachers, administrators, and the like. The force of this contested terrain is revealed by the difficulties we had in trying to include Ben in a "regular" second-grade class (with appropriate support services) located in our largely professional, middle-class community.

Ben is now eight years old. We also have an older daughter, Nicole. Kathy and I began to have concerns about Ben's speech and language development when he was two years old. When he was two and a half, we had him evaluated by a speech/language pathologist.

She told us that Ben's speech was "unlike anything she had ever heard" and advised that we watch him and have him reevaluated if there was no improvement. At three, Ben and his sister began attending a local family day care home. Not long after their arrival, the day care provider alerted Kathy and me that Ben was "different" from other children. We were told that "he seemed to be in a world of his own"—that he was having a great deal of difficulty doing simple tasks, most important, "potty training." Kathy and I had Ben evaluated by a child psychologist. After the session, and after much deliberation over the proper label, he was pronounced as having a pragmatic language disorder. To this day I'm not sure what this label designates. Admittedly Ben has certain handicapping conditions, including fine- and gross-motor difficulties (such as holding a pencil, zipping his pants, or tying his shoes). Speech and language have been a struggle for him, but he has made immense progress and can now ask and answer questions and hold a conversation. Ben is "shy" around other children; he usually chooses to play by himself. He enjoys the company of adults. He enjoys reading books, is fascinated by science topics, and likes using the computer. He is an inquisitive child. All of his teachers point out that he is mild-mannered and not a behavior problem. On standardized tests he reads close to grade level; he struggles with math. Ben's test scores are not consistent; they fluctuate, excelling in some areas and dipping low on others.

Ben began attending a special pre-K program when he was three and a half. Since then, he has been assigned to various special needs classrooms. He had made a great deal of progress upon entering second grade, and we requested that he be "included" with appropriate supports into the "regular" classroom. Kathy and I told teachers and administrators that our concerns were not simply over the curriculum. Rather, our concern was that Ben should not feel excluded and that, regardless of certain handicapping conditions, we wanted him to be part of a diverse, heterogeneous classroom.

Second grade has not been easy. Upon learning, at the last minute, of Ben's teacher assignment, Kathy took Ben to visit his new school. The teacher was in the classroom, setting up for the new school year. She said that she had "no time to talk now." Kathy encouraged her to call us with any questions or concerns she might have. Kathy also told the teacher she would buy a special notebook to be used for home-school communications. We never have heard from the teacher.

About 15 children ride the bus from Ben and Nichole's stop. Nicole talks with friends and does not seem aware of Ben's presence. Ben stands holding onto his mom's hand and is quiet. He has never been on a school bus without an adult aide. Kathy and I are apprehensive. We have argued with the Committee on Special Education (CSE) for Ben's inclusion into a regular class with appropriate support. Apparently "appropriate support" does not include an aide on the bus.

Two weeks into the school year, a Saturday, Kathy and Nicole were out shopping. Ben sat on my lap, put his arm around my shoulder, and asked, "Dad, will you be my friend? No one wants to sit next to me in school."

There were meetings between ourselves and various school personnel in the early fall over promised support services for Ben. From the beginning his schedule was very, very chaotic. His regular classroom teacher and other school staff members were confused. The teacher complained that she had not been prepared for Ben's arrival in her room and stated that she (and Ben) were not getting the support they need. On his IEP, an aide was to be in her classroom at .3 (33 percent of full time) time to work with Ben. However, the teacher feels the aide is never in class at the needed times.

The CSE board called a meeting for us and the staff who worked with Ben (the regular classroom teacher, resource room teacher, speech specialist, occupational therapist, and adaptive PE teacher). Also in attendance were the school psychologist, a social worker, the school principal, and the CSE chairperson. We were gathered to discuss the "wisdom" of Ben's second-grade placement. The mood was cautious. The resource room teacher said Ben was making good progress in her classroom. The regular classroom teacher mentioned that she saw a need for more aide time for Ben. Each staff member presented his or her perception of Ben. In turn, we were told that Ben was reportedly reading at grade level; he was still struggling with math but was making progress. He was learning, but we were told he had difficulty keeping up with the mainstream class. The principal and CSE chair wanted us to rethink/reconsider Ben's placement.

One of the committee's concerns, and one of ours as well, was that Ben was being pulled out of the regular classroom too often in order to receive special services. The issue of this pullout time became one of the bases for the CSE recommendation that he be transferred after winter break to a self-contained special needs classroom located at another school building. Our reply was that a midyear transfer to another building with a new set of teachers and support staff would be extremely disruptive for Ben and could be devastating to his self-esteem. Further, we wondered why Ben couldn't stay in his current placement and continue his studies at his own pace. We wondered why more of the support services couldn't occur in the regular classroom. The reply was that scheduling was difficult and that there were not enough resources available. During this meeting, I felt a growing tension that Kathy and I were not following "the program" and were creating extra work with our requests for an inclusion program. In short, we were not following Herrnstein and Murray's dictum; we didn't readily accept our place in the suburban social order.

The meeting concluded when the principal agreed to "maintain" Ben for the remainder of the school year and to look at making some changes in his current schedule and support time. As we left this meeting, one of the staff members who worked with Ben motioned me aside and said, "Your son is a wonderful child. He is strong and very resilient. Given the pressures, he is handling things well and seems in good spirits."

By midwinter it became obvious that we would share no communication with the regular classroom teacher. Kathy wrote periodic notes to her to ask questions and share information. There was no reply. We were later informed that Ben was withdrawing in the regular classroom for unknown reasons. The other children would invite him to join them, yet he chose to be alone. We found out that he was eating lunch by himself. We were informed that Ben had begun to come into the classroom in the morning and "just sit" during the time allotted for students to write in their journals. Since Ben has difficulty writing with a pencil, he was using one of the two computers in the classroom at journal-writing time. However, he was reluctant to use the computer. We wondered as to the reasons for this change, and Kathy asked if anything had occurred at school to explain this. The response was no.

Spring arrived. Ben's sister, Nicole, had just had her birthday party. Ben was sad. I sensed he would like to have friends like his sister does. She was always going off to birthday parties. Except for his sister's, Ben had been invited to none that year. For a long time he had been happy just being the "king of reading." He would sit at home and read for extended periods of time. Obviously he was harboring anxiety about his social position. Now I can only guess that this is related to his growing awareness of his peers, the formation of a social consciousness; he observes the other children and seems to be struggling as to how to join in their play, and he expresses concern about what they think of him.

Ben began making strange gestures with his hands. I asked him what he was doing. He replied, "I was talking in sign language. Children at school think I can't speak. I have no voice. So I'm learning sign language to talk to them." My heart was breaking.

My concerns are constantly rising. What is going on in his school? What kind of identity is being constituted for Ben within this school context? And as parents, what are Kathy and I to do? The CSE committee is set in their ways; they want to send Ben back to a special needs classroom.

Being segregated from other children and "learning one's place" is a painful, dehumanizing process. Herrnstein and Murray conclude chapter 16 with a "lesson": that large proportions of people who exhibit behaviors and problems that dominate the nation's social agenda are people with limited cognitive ability—that future social policies must focus on those who have the most difficulty in society: "the least intelligent people" (p. 386). But Ben is already the focus of many intense debates over his proper placement. We need not to pay more attention to Ben's propensities, but rather to situate Ben's predicament within the context of larger social practices and policies. Ben is not the problem. The issue of segregation is the problem.

My concerns over this and the gatekeeping of special needs children led me to investigate my own community. Were there other practices of segregation going on in what appeared to be a pleasant suburban community, or is there something endemic about special needs education that warrants the separation of children? In my investigations I was fortunate to interview Dr. Barbara Williams, a high school principal in a neighboring school district. Talking with her helped situate me into the history of my own community as well as suburban life and educational practices. She explained that many suburban counties, like our own, are communities "by design" where small enclaves exist within the larger affluent neighborhood. These enclaves are composed of families who live on incomes far below that of the surrounding community. These enclaves are created out of scarcity, hope, and greed. Many city families are attempting to move into affluent suburban communities in the hope that their children will attend better, safer schools. As such, the competition for housing is quite intense. In our county, for example, African American, Latino, East Indian, Pakistani, Middle Eastern, and recent immigrants from Eastern Europe, along with working- and middle-class Whites, all compete for affordable housing.

Given the scarcity of housing, realtors have acted as the gatekeepers—in a way determining who can or can't move into the neighborhood. Practices of segregation are evident as realtors and banks have engaged in illegal tactics commonly known as "blockbusting" and "redlining." In blockbusting, realtors play off of racist fears that immigrants or persons of color moving into the neighborhood will lower property values. This creates a panic in local residents, who sell at a lower price. In redlining, certain areas of a community are boxed off by an imaginary "red line." Persons with lower incomes are lumped together with the incentive of lower mortgage rates. In both instances, the renter's/buyer's are unaware that they are being segregated into a specific enclave due to race, class, and/or economic resources. According to Williams, real estate practices keep in check who comes into the community and hence who attends the local school.

I realized that the representation (the created image) of our community as an affluent, respectable, safe place to live and the perceived high status (the reputation) of the school district would ensure high real estate values. These real estate values are maintained, in part, through segregation practices both in and out of school. The school provides the link between current material wealth for the affluent middle class and the future (the reproduction) of that class. However, as Barbara Ehrenreich (1990) notes, the professional middle class is an anxious class. It is afraid of misfortunes that might lead to a downward slide. In the middle class there is also another anxiety: a fear of inner weakness, of growing soft, of failing to strive, of losing discipline and will. Even the affluence that is so often the goal of all this striving becomes a threat, for it holds out the possibility of hedonism and self-indulgence. Whether the middle class looks down toward the realm of the less, or up toward the realm of more, there is the fear, always, of falling.

Indeed, I suspect that the segregation of special needs children is grounded in this notion of a fear of falling. Fear grounded in the possible loss of material wealth for themselves and for their children. Parents at PTA and other school meetings seem often to indicate that if special needs children, like Ben, were included in regular classrooms, the quality of education would fall for everyone. "This is not a place for 'them.'" Further, they fear that their children might somehow "catch" the handicapping condition and hence weaken their wills, their drive to succeed in a tough competitive world. I get the sense from these parents that the inclusion of a child like Ben into the regular classroom was tantamount to a kind of pedagogical "blockbusting." One's cultural capital might be diminished by association with a special needs child. Where is the middle-class "civility" that Herrnstein and Murray hold in such high esteem?

Many members of my community are really not interested in helping or aiding anyone who is "disadvantaged." The issue of low intelligence is more of a smokescreen for the more pressing concern of "putting" people in their place. There is a cold callousness to their remarks about children such as Ben—children who are perceived as just "slowing up everything."

John D. Anderson reflects on the suburbs and the relations between power, privilege and public education by focusing on Jonathan Kozol's book *Savage inequalities* (1993). Anderson has used Kozol's book for two semesters in a graduate education course. He was surprised that many of his students ("the vast majority are both white and from suburban backgrounds") were convinced that Kozol exaggerated the plight of inner-city children. That Kozol was sensationalizing in order to sell the book. When Anderson pressed his students for reasons as to why they felt the way they did, it was clear that they had no experience or proof on which to base their belief that Kozol had focused on the most extreme conditions of inner-city education. What interested Anderson was the response by well-to-do youth both in his class and in Kozol's book. If anything, Anderson suggests, *Savage inequalities* tells us as much about the affluent suburbs as it does about the inner city.

Anderson found that in present public education, a class and racial war is being acted out whereby suburbanites siphon off a disproportionate share of taxes for public education. The rub, so to speak, is that logic which claims that increased spending in education does not matter, particularly for inner-city poor. For Anderson, while these arguments are varied, illogical, contradictory, and complex, they are characteristic of the "pathological detachment" of the rich. Anderson highlights several of Kozol's interviews with high school students and laments how parents of well-to-do children do an excellent job of transmitting their opinions of inequality to their offspring. Kozol's interviews with students are revealing: "The point," said one high school student, "is that you cannot give an equal chance to every single person. If you did it you'd be changing the whole economic system. Let's be honest. If you equalize the money, someone's got to be shortchanged. I don't doubt that children in the Bronx are getting a bad deal. But do we want everyone to get a mediocre education?" (p. 9). Another student: "Well, it's easy for me to be sitting here and say I'd spend my parent's money. I'm not working. I don't earn the money. I don't need to be conservative until I do. I can be as open-minded and unrealistic as I want to be. You can be a liberal until you have a mortgage" (p. 9).

These comments reveal the relations among privilege, segregated practices, and the dollar. While we may talk about differences and diversity at the cultural level, the bottom line for middle America is the fear and anxiety of falling, losing one's place in a society where economic advantage literally buys privileges in a scarce market. Anderson reports that as of 1990, 1 percent of the population owns 37 percent of the wealth of this country and that the gap between the rich and the poor continues to widen. His point is that the pathology, as well as the political smokescreen, is to deny that money matters, particularly to those who don't have it. Anderson points out that middle-class values, ideology, and interests about schooling are intimately interwoven into existing economic conditions.

Herrnstein and Murray go to great lengths to argue that human intelligence differs for reasons "that are not any one's fault" (p. 535). Intelligence is a "natural" occurrence, something we are born with, an essential quality of who we are. The role of education then, becomes, in part, discovering the child's natural intelligence and then locating the child's proper place in school (and society). They claim the individual will then live a more satisfying, complete life when placed within the parameters of his or her needs and capacities. Left out of their discussion are the issues pertaining to representation and segregation of those labeled as having low cognitive ability. At issue is not simply the individual who may or may not have a handicapping condition, but the societal values within which the individual is situated. That is, we must ask here: *Who determines this placement for our children? Why do they place our children there? And whose interests are served by such a placement?*

To address these concerns, I have taken up bell hooks's (1990) suggestion that struggle also includes a struggle of memory against omitting. Ben's second-grade school experience was a tough year for him and Kathy and me. In my efforts to investigate Ben's being segregated, I found parallel practices of segregation in community real estate practices. I discovered that the bottom line which drives many upper-middle-class suburbanites is not some abstract notion of middle-class virtue but rather the angst, that "fear of falling" in losing one's property and place in a brutally competitive society. Some of my neighbors are afraid of upsetting the school system, a system that they perceive as working for them. In short, the middle-class civility that Herrnstein and Murray link with intelligence and virtue (pp. 265-266) remained opaque in my investigations. Instead what was revealed most clearly to me was the attitude taken by parents and officials in their efforts to maintain order and control over school policies through questionable practices of segregation.

There are no easy solutions. At the end of Ben's second-grade year, Kathy and I met one more time with the CSE board to determine his third-grade placement. It was not a friendly meeting. We were told that there were only two options for Ben: a large regular class or a small special needs class. Kathy and I argued for a smaller, multi-ability, self-contained classroom. We cited concrete examples of these classrooms found in neighboring states: classrooms where children of varying abilities worked together, learned together. We were told that these options are not available in our school district. Framed narrowly, with no ready alternatives available, we very, very reluctantly agreed to Ben's placement in a special needs classroom. The lesson: We must never forget that behind the seemly benign slogans used by Herrnstein and Murray, such as "A Place for Everyone," lie issues of power and authority—that is, the power and authority invested in historically defined institutional practices and policies to label, frame, and place our children.

For now, Kathy and I have bent to the CSE board, but we have by no means given up our struggle. It is precisely the place of a narrative to provide an organic connectedness between the individual and the community in which he or she lives. No narrative exists in a vacuum. Indeed, it is the friendships that are made, the alliances that are formed, the actions pursued in struggle, that are reasons for telling these stories. At issue are the politics of labeling and the attendant practices of segregation that are hurtful to all and especially to children. As such, our struggle is to break down the walls of segregation everywhere and develop a language of empathy, compassion, and understanding that enables students to grasp the complex diversity of our society. We can begin by demystifying and dispensing with highly problematic categories/criteria used in chapter 16 to classify and ultimately marginalize a sizable proportion of our population: the Middle-Class Values Index that privileges the few at the expense of all our humanity.

CODA

Ben started out of our door to third grade with a positive attitude. We walked him down to the corner bus stop, where he waited with his neighborhood buddies for the school bus. Because he was being sent to a different school, his bus came first. He looked confused, as he realized that no one else was getting on this bus with him. One boy said, "Hey, where is Ben going?" Another asked, "Why isn't he coming with us?" Ben sat down in his seat and gazed out the window with a confused look on his face. He looked as if he were about to cry as his bus pulled away.

References

Anderson, J. D. (1993, winter). Power, privilege, and public education: Reflections on *Savage inequalities. Educational Theory,* 43, (1), 1-10.

Ehrenreich, B. (1990). *Fear of falling.* New York: Harper Perennial Inc.

Herrnstein, R. J., and Murray, C. (1994). *The Bell Curve: Intelligence and class structure in America.* New York: The Free Press.

hooks, b. (1990). *Yearning: Race, gender, and cultural politics*. Boston: South End Press.

Kliebard, H. (1986). *The struggle for the American curriculum: 1893-1958*. New York: Routledge Press.

Kozol, J. (1993). *Savage inequalities*. New York: Crown Publishers.

McCarthy, C., and Crichlow, W. (1993). *Race, identity, and representation in education*. New York: Routledge Press.

21 THE BELL CURVE AND TRANSRACIAL ADOPTION STUDIES

WILLIAM E. CROSS, JR.

In the final section of The Bell Curve, chapters 17-22, Richard Herrnstein and Charles Murray argue that all forms of social engineering, which might benefit the poor in general and African Americans and Hispanic Americans in particular, should be terminated. They display unbridled enmity toward Head Start, affirmative action programs, and public welfare for the poor. They advocate what amounts to a return to the southern strategy of yesteryear, in which white supremacy is affirmed, black and Hispanic obsequiousness is encouraged, and limited developmental resources are directed toward changing the socioeconomic status of the poor. Their perspective combines notions of white supremacy with a sense of hopelessness toward Blacks and Hispanics. It is derived, in large measure, from Herrnstein and Murray's interpretation that the most radical form of social intervention, the adoption of black children by middle-class white families, has failed to result in any appreciable change in the IQ scores of the adopted black children.

Based on their readings of Sandra Scarr and Richard Weinberg's study, Herrnstein and Murray suggest that had the "pure" black children been "left" in their homes of origin (that is, had they remained in the "ghetto"), their IQs would have reached a level, on average, of 85. Placing them in white homes, through transracial adoption, resulted only in a negligible IQ change of four points. Consequently, Herrnstein and Murray conclude, less radical interventions, such as Head Start, which seek to "change" selected parts of the child's environment, can be expected to increase IQ scores only by a fraction of that which is possible through the more comprehensive change strategy of transracial adoption. But since adoption results in a change of only four IQ points, it logically follows that participation in Head Start can be expected to change IQ by less than four points. In short, Herrnstein and Murray believe that, whether raised in the ghetto or in white homes, and whether they attend Head Start or not, variations in the environment of black children has little or no effect on their IQ development, which, on average, tends to level off at 85, or 15 IQ points below the average for Whites. With "scientific evidence" showing black IQs are almost impervious to manipulation, whether through transracial adoption or Head Start, they conclude that Head Start, in particular, is a wasteful venture.

Most of the evidence Herrnstein and Murray present about IQ and race is indirect; consequently, many of their arguments, for the text as a whole, "turn" on their interpretation of the Scarr and Weinberg transracial adoption IQ data, which provides a more direct test of the relationship among race, socioeconomic status (SES), and IQ development. In a project known as the Minnesota Transracial Adoption Study, Scarr and Weinberg have studied the cognitive development of members of a unique set of middle- to upper-middle-class white families, who, starting in the 1970s, became involved in transracial adoptions. IQ scores have been collected on the fathers, mothers, their biological daughters and sons, as well as the children they have adopted. The adopted children are white, black (adopted black children whose birth parents were both black), mixed racial black and white (adopted children born of a black and white relationship) and mixed racial Asian/Indian. IQ scores were first collected when the children were around seven years of age (Scarr and Weinberg, 1976) and then ten years later, when they were in late adolescence or early adulthood (Weinberg, Scarr, and Waldman, 1992).

Herrnstein and Murray's interpretation of the Scarr and Weinberg transracial adoption study allowed them to make two points:

1. IQ rankings and race: Factoring out the effects of environment, Herrnstein and Murray believe the Scarr and Weinberg study shows that Whites achieve the highest rank, racial hybrids, such as the offspring of black and white partners, fall below the scores attained by pure-white progeny but above the IQ for pure-black children, with pure-black children bringing up the rear.

2. Null effects of SES: Since the average IQ of pure-black children raised in middle-class white homes is not that much higher (IQ = 89) than cohorts raised in an all-black, low-income environment (IQ = 85), Herrnstein and Murray conclude that socioeconomic status has little or no effect on IQ development. According to the authors, pure-black children are handicapped less by SES factors and more by the biogenetics of their racial ancestry.

Before any meaningful interpretation of the Scarr and Weinberg results can be attempted, two corrections must be introduced: (1) There must be a correction for the type of experiences a child had before placement in a home (preplacement history); (2) There must be a correction for the effects of attrition (that is, the researchers must make certain that the characteristics of the persons who stay in the study are the same as those who, for whatever reason, are lost to the study). When these two corrections are introduced, the interpretation by Herrnstein and Murray is shown to be in error.

RACIAL IQ RANKINGS WHEN THE CHILDREN WERE YOUNG

In their interpretation of the Minnesota Transracial Adoption Study, Herrnstein and Murray state that the biological children of the white parents recorded an average IQ of 117, while the figures for the white-adopted, mixed racial (black and white), and pure-black children were 112, 109 and 97, respectively. Herrnstein and Murray suggest that this early testing shows the emergence of a rank order for race and IQ that will become more demonstrative when the children grow older. However, the rank order stressed by Herrnstein and Murray does not take into account the preplacement history of the children. Few, if any, of the white adopted children, a handful of the mixed racial (black and white) children, but a large number of the pure-black and Asian/Indian children had problematic preplacement histories. *Both the research and applied literature on adoption have demonstrated well that problematic preplacement histories are associated with less optimal development across a wide range of sociopersonality variables.* The Minnesota Transracial Adoption Study has produced evidence that the same holds true for IQ development. For example, Weinberg, Scarr and Waldman (1992) report that the difference between early-placed (IQ = 110.2) and late-placed (98.5) black children was 11.7 IQ points. Thus, when interpreting the Minnesota data for racial trends, valid comparisons should only involve black children who were early placed (that is, children with optimal preplacement histories). For the first testing, the 86 black and biracial children who were early placed registered an average IQ of 110.2, and the white adopted children had an average IQ of 111.5, which is to say, there was no difference between the two groups.

    It cannot be determined whether the early-placed biracial children had an IQ that was different from the early-placed pure-black children, because Scarr and Weinberg have never reported the IQ means, standard deviations, and IQ ranges for these important categories. This may be related to the fact that to actually publish these figures would reveal a major shortcoming of the study. Scarr and Weinberg had hoped to make a major contribution to the discourse on IQ and race, especially as it applies to "pure" black children. However, in their study, which originally incorporated 29 pure-black adopted subjects and now includes only 21, perhaps as many as half were late placed. In effect, only a fraction of the pure-black adoptees who remain in the Minnesota Study had optimal preplacement histories. Such small numbers greatly limit the generalizability of findings that pertain to the IQ development of pure-black persons.

RACIAL IQ RANKINGS AT ADOLESCENCE

Herrnstein and Murray state that at the second testing, conducted ten years later, when the Minnesota subjects were adolescents or were approaching early adulthood, a rank ordering of the races by their IQ scores was transparent. The biological offspring had an average IQ of 109.4; the white adopted siblings achieved an average IQ of 105.6, the biracial Blacks, an average IQ of 98.5; and the pure-black children, an IQ score of 89.4. As before, the authors did not correct for preplacement histories. With such a correction, however, there remains the hint of a racial ranking, because the early-placed black/biracial IQ was 99.2, or 6.4 points less than that achieved by the white adoptees and 10.2 points less than the IQ score associated with the biologic offspring of the adopting families. (Comparisons with the biologic children are not really at issue, as previous research suggests that adopted children do not achieve the same IQ as the biologic progeny; the question is whether the black and white adopted children have similar IQs.) *However, Herrnstein and Murray made a glaring error by not checking the data to see if the effects of attrition in any way skewed the results.*

Not everyone who participated in the study at time-1 stayed on to participate at time-2. As in any longitudinal study, there was attrition. Generally speaking, attrition was low for almost all of the participant categories (fathers, mothers, biologic offspring, and the various adoptee clusters). Furthermore, the baseline IQ for any particular group did not change significantly when attrition was taken into account. For example, 99 fathers were tested at time-1, and they achieved an average IQ of 120.8. However, not every father who was tested at time-1 agreed to be tested at time-2. Only 74 of the original 99 fathers were tested at both periods, which works out to an attrition rate of 25 percent. It must be determined whether the average IQ for the smaller group of 74 fathers matches the average IQ for the larger group of fathers. The IQ for the smaller sample of 74 fathers was 121.7, which suggests that, despite attrition, the smaller sample of fathers is representative of the larger group. In repeating this analysis across all participant categories, it is clear that low attrition, as well as a good match between the IQs for the original and smaller samples, is characteristic of the study as a whole, with two exceptions. The Asian/Indian group registered an attrition rate of 42 percent, as there were 21 Asian/Indian children in the original sample, but only 12 at the time of the second testing. But more important is the white adoptee attrition rate. Originally numbering 25, after attrition the white adoptee group was reduced to 16 (attrition = 37 percent). Furthermore, the baseline IQ for this smaller subsample (N = 16 and IQ = 117.6) was significantly higher than the baseline IQ for the larger sample (N = 25 and IQ = 111.5). Another indication of the dramatic effect attrition had on this category is the change in the range of IQ scores that resulted from attrition. The range of IQ scores for the original sample of 25 white adopted children was 62 to 143, while the range after attrition was only 92 to 138. *Practically all the below-average IQ scores were eliminated through attrition. No other category of participants experienced a significant upward or downward change in IQ due to attrition.*

Recall that, at the time of the second testing, the IQ for the white adopted children was 6.4 points higher than the IQ for the early-placed black and biracial children. When attrition is added to the equation, the actual difference between the early placed black/biracial and white adoptee groups is more like 0.3 IQ points. In other words, as was the case at time-1, there really is *no difference* in IQ level between early placed black/biracial adoptees at time-2. For either time-point, one group cannot be ranked above or below the other.

In summary, when preplacement patterns and attrition are taken into account, the (early-placed) black/biracial and white adoptees evidence the same level of IQ development at time-1 and time-2.

In addition, each group displayed the same degree of IQ perturbation over the ten-year period, with the early-placed black/biracials showing an IQ swing of 11.6 points and the white adoptees a 12.0-point swing. Weinberg, Scarr, and Waldman (1992) also have reported on the academic performance of the adoptees. However, because they did not adjust their analyses for the effects of attrition and preplacement histories, every single one of their additional findings, such as on high school class rank and high school grade point average, has limited scientific validity.

SES, RACE, AND IQ RANKINGS

Observing that the average IQ of pure-black children raised in the middle-class white homes of the Minnesota Study is not that much higher (IQ = 89) than cohorts raised in all-black, low-income environments (IQ = 85), Herrnstein and Murray concluded that socioeconomic status has little or no effect on black IQ development. They believe the pure-black children are handicapped less by SES factors and more by the biogenetics of their racial ancestry. I have already shown that this component of the Minnesota Study is highly contaminated by late-placement factors. Of the 21 pure-black subjects who remain in the study, perhaps as many as ten or more may fall in the late-placement category, and 11 or so may fall in the more favored early-placed cluster. Based on how Weinberg, Scarr, and Waldman (1992) have reported their data, it appears that at both testing points, early-placed pure-black children had IQs in the 100 range. Regardless of how these data on the early- and late-placed pure-black adoptees eventually turn out; Hernnstein and Murray point out that the "racial IQ gap" has been recorded in comparisons between Blacks and Whites who share the same middle-class status. In most instances, advocates of the white superiority model scoff at the notion that environmental factors, such as racism, could play any significant role in blunting middle-class black IQ development. *However, another important transracial adoption study (Moore, 1986),*

which Herrnstein and Murray reference but do not analyze, found that
environment does account for differential IQ development among mid-
dle-class Blacks.

Elsie Moore (1986) studied the IQ development of 46 black and biracial adoptees, all of whom were placed in middle-class homes. Half of the children (N = 23) were placed in intact middle-class black homes (traditional placement) and an equal number (N = 23) were placed in two-parent middle-class white homes (transracial adoption). All of the children had positive preplacement histories and were adopted at around two years of age; the IQ testing was conducted when the children were between the ages of 7 to 10.

While it was not Moore's primary objective, her results underscore something that has long been noted by scholars of the black American experience. Mainly, Blacks and Whites who share the same SES, in this case, middle-class, do not "experience" the same quality of life often associated with that status. This suggests, among other things, that the adopted and biologic children of black middle-class families will develop higher IQs than cohorts raised in poor black homes, but the constraints on the quality of their middle-class existence may "cap" their IQ development. If such is the case, black children adopted by black and white middle-class families should evidence differential IQ patterns. The Moore study makes possible a test of this proposition.

Let us begin the analysis by looking at what happened to the black children who were placed in the black middle-class homes. One would expect that being exposed to black middle-class life, black children would achieve an above-average IQ, and they did. The average IQ for black children nationally is 85, but the black children from the Moore study who were adopted by black families achieved an average IQ that was 19 points higher than the black "norm."

For reasons that need not concern us here, Moore anticipated that the achieved IQ of the children would differ by type of adopting household, to the favor of white homes. However, in all likelihood, she must have been startled by the magnitude of the difference she found. Black (IQ = 118) and biracial (IQ = 117) children raised in white middle-class homes developed IQs that were almost one standard deviation higher than the black (IQ = 103) and biracial (IQ = 105) children raised in black middle-class homes.

How can we account for this finding? Some of the difference may be traced to the fact that the two types of adopting homes were not "perfectly" matched for SES characteristics, although all homes were decidedly middle-class, by anyone's definition. Also, Moore explored family dynamics that might explain some of the difference. There is no evidence that the children placed in the white homes were of a different "genetic stock" than the children placed in the black homes, as all the placements were handled by the same adoption agency and all the children had excellent preplacement histories. Because Moore's sample included both "pure" black and biracial children, there is the possibility that the "mulatto" thesis may account for the difference. However, Moore's data provides absolutely no support to the notion that high IQs among black people are only to be found among biracials or "mulattos." The average IQ for the 20 biracial or "mulatto" children was 110.72, the figure for the 26 "pure" black children was 110.65, and the pattern of IQ development was the same across the two types of adopting households.

We must turn to other explanations. As scholars of the black experience point out, Blacks equated with Whites on middle-class status are not able to translate this equal status into the same quality of life (Cross, 1995; Massey and Denton, 1993). Jeanne Brooks-Gunn (1993) has cited census data showing that one in five black children, but only one in fifty white children, live in neighborhoods where 30 percent or more of the individual neighbors are poor. In contrast, three in five white children, as opposed to only one in ten black children, reside in neighborhoods where less than 10 percent of the individuals are poor.

Complementing these findings, Massey and Denton (1993) report that rising economic status for Blacks has little or no effect on the level of housing and neighborhood segregation African Americans experience. As a case in point, they cite data from Los Angeles, California, which show that the poorest Hispanics are less segregated than the most affluent Blacks. Massey and Denton report also that Hispanics, Asians, and, of course, Whites, are able to translate their improved SES status into high-quality and less-minority-dominated neighborhoods. Blacks, on the other hand, find it much more difficult to "buy" their way into a community that makes possible the quality of life normally associated with their middle-class status. This means that black middle-class families may be able to purchase a "good" home on a "good" block, but, in all likelihood, the more immediate neighborhood may present a striking contrast to their lifestyles and aspirations. Finally, the public schools their children attend may cater not only to the middle-class but to a large segment of the desperately poor. Despite the mismatch between themselves and their communities, black middle-class parents are still able to help their children achieve above average intelligence, but their children's developmental outcomes may not reach the heights of those to be found among (white) middle-class families living in homes, neighborhoods, and communities that are consistently middle-class in demographics, character, and dynamics (Cross, 1995).

CONCLUSIONS

Herrnstein and Murray used data from the Minnesota Transracial Adoption Study to construct a racial rank ordering of IQs that favored notions of white superiority; however, they did not control for preplacement histories and attrition. Early-placed black and biracial children recorded the same IQ level as the white adopted children. This pattern was repeated when they were adolescents. The comparison at adolescence required control for the effects of attrition, as well as preplacement histories, because attrition made the mean IQ of the white adopted children seem much higher than it would have been, except for the effects of attrition

Herrnstein and Murray also avoided considering the significance of another important transracial adoption study conducted by Elsie Moore (1986). The Moore study revealed that (1) the "mulatto" thesis has no validity, as biracial and "pure" black children show the same pattern of IQ development, whether adopted by black or white middle-class families, and (2) adopted black children placed in black and white homes, which have been matched for middle-class characteristics, develop higher IQs in white than in black homes, primarily because black middle-class parents are not able to translate their middle-class status into the same quality of life as are Whites. These *environmental* rather than genetic factors help explain why a "racial IQ gap" may persist between Blacks and Whites, even after Blacks have achieved middle-class status.

Whether an adopted black child has a positive or negative preplacement history appears to have a profound effect on IQ development. Most of the "pure" black children in the Scarr and Weinberg study were *late placed*, and their average IQ was far below that recorded by the early-placed black children. This fact was further confirmed by the adopted black children found in the Moore study, all of whom had excellent preplacement histories and high IQs.

The transracial adoption studies to date have the following to say about IQ development: (1) When black children are confined to slums and limited opportunities, their developed IQ is typically 85; (2) when black children are adopted by black middle-class families, their developed IQ is typically 104; (3) for black children who are early placed into white middle-class homes, they achieve IQ scores that are from 14 to 32 points higher than the norm for black children who are poor and live in hyper-segregated communities.

Overall, a more objective interpretation of the transracial adoption literature than can be found in *The Bell Curve* indicates that social policymakers should continue to search for efficacious ways to assist the poor. Early-placed and healthy black children respond to their improved environments with IQs that are from 14 to 32 points higher than the IQs of cohorts raised in segregated, inner-city circumstances. There is every reason to believe that effectively designed interventions, such as Head Start, if well funded and spread across grades one through twelve, can positively affect IQ development.

References

Brooks-Gunn, J. (1992, September 8). Growing up poor: Context, risk, and continuity in the Bronfenbrenner tradition. Lecture and paper presented at a conference honoring Urie Bronfenbrenner, Cornell University.

Cross, W. E., Jr. (1995). Oppositional identity and African American youth. In Hawley, W. D. and Jackson, A. W., eds., *Toward a common destiny*, 185-204. San Francisco: Jossey-Bass.

Dorfman, D. (1995). Soft science with a Neoconservative agenda. *Contemporary Psychology, 40* (5), 418-421.

Herrnstein, R. and Murray, C. (1994). *The Bell Curve: Intelligence and class structure in American life*. New York: The Free Press.

Massey, G., and Denton, N. (1993). *American apartheid: Segregation and the making of the underclass*. Cambridge, MA: Harvard University Press.

Moore, E. (1986). Family socialization and the IQ test performance of traditionally and transracially adopted black children. *Developmental Psychology, 22,* 317-326.

Murray, C. (1995). *The Bell Curve* and its critics. *Commentary, 99* (5), 23-30.

Scarr, S. and Weinberg, R. A. (1976). IQ test performance of black children adopted by white families. *American Psychologist, 31,* 726-739.

Weinberg, R. A., Scarr, S., and Waldman, I. D. (1992). The Minnesota transracial adoption study: A follow-up of IQ test performance at adolescence. *Intelligence, 16,* 117-135.

22 WHITE SUPREMACY AND THE POLITICS OF FEAR AND LOATHING

PETER MCLAREN

It has never been so obvious that the forces of egalitarianism in this country are in tatters. The stench of racism permeates the air, as the winds churned up by the backlash against affirmative action sweep the nation. Last week some of the mean-spirited pawns of Governor Peter Wilson—some members of the Regents of the University of California—voted to abolish affirmative action, bringing their dream of a Jeffersonian "natural aristocracy" a step closer to reality. Virulent exchanges between Chicano/a and white students continue to occur in several of my summer classes at The University of California at Los Angeles (UCLA). There are no African American students enrolled in the teacher education program. The classes are heating up, even as the quarter is winding down. Bolstered by the Regent's history-making vote and with their sense of natural superiority supported by books such as *The Bell Curve,* some white students smugly dismiss challenges to white privilege initiated by classmates of color. I am especially troubled when a number of Asian students join in support of the angry white students who now proclaim that the white male is the most oppressed person in today's society. As I watch a group of the "cognitive elite" prepare to join the ranks of the teaching profession, I feel a stab in my heart. The liberal integrationist attitude pervading their education has sustained their white privilege rather than challenged it. Why, they ask, are they suffering through all of this protest by Chicano/a students here at UCLA, when a degree from the university will bestow upon them the gift of honorary whiteness?

All through 1995, my anger and disgust at Governor and former presidential wanna-be Pete Wilson escalated, it reached one of its many peaks when Proposition 187 passed. I continue to marvel at the smoothly orchestrated efforts of the nation's political right to suture the ideological coordinates of xenophobia, Euro-American superiority, and neoliberal politics into a victory for a national discourse motivated by racism. Such a discourse is stitched together by a specious biodeterminism that is driven by and based on natural selection and a scientifically bankrupt epistemology. It rests on a platform of social Darwinist principles of necessary class stratification, a shameful ethics supported by a white supremacist ideological foundation, and a hate-fueled aversion to the low-IQ poor whose intelligence is supposedly genetically disabled. Its intended victims are those groups such as African Americans and Latinos, who are disproportionately represented among the poor.

In chapter 18 of *The Bell Curve*, our faith in Western science is continually exploited through a study of population genetics that is more conservative ideological propaganda than sound scientific research. First of all, the scientific basis of *The Bell Curve* has already been discredited. Genetic patterns of heritability are multifarious and complex since genes interact with their environment in ways that reflect a variable expressivity (Andrade, 1995). As Noam Chomsky points out, *The Bell Curve*'s central argument—that 60 percent of the IQ in any given person is heritable—is a meaningless argument. The book lacks any evidence about unknown genetic factors and how they might interact with environmental conditions to produce deficiencies in IQ. Contrary to the position charted out in *The Bell Curve*, the evidence that Herrnstein and Murray present is entirely compatible with the conclusion that IQs of Blacks are 15 points higher than those of Whites (Chomsky, 1995). The issue is really one of ideological choice. If genetic science fails to link genes to destiny, then Herrnstein and Murray are walking on scientific eggshells; they are either dishonest or unscrupulous racial elitists—or both. Herrnstein and Murray's project brings to mind those painful historical moments that have figured most shamefully in our collective human consciousness, moments stretching from Hitler's Germany to the ethnic cleansing in Bosnia.

The authors lead their readers astray on a number of accounts: First, there is no theoretical evidence offered for the "general factor" of intelligence; it is based on a form of factor analysis that has been challenged elsewhere; the question of cultural bias in testing is not seriously explored; the statistics are woefully suspect. For instance, the regression curves of their variables against IQ and parental socioeconomic status do not reveal the strength of the relationships or the amount of variation in social factors explained by IQ and socioeconomic factors. That is, the relationships between genetic inheritance and IQ and between IQ and social class are not nearly strong enough to draw the inference that genes are mainly responsible for a person's social status; in fact, about 90 percent of the factors related to socioeconomic status do not bear any relationship to measured IQ. The fact that Herrnstein and Murray's own data reveal that IQ is not a major factor in determining variation in nearly all the social behaviors they study causes all their conclusions to collapse (Gould, 1994).

Herrnstein and Murray treat capitalist society as synonymous with nature. According to them, it's only natural for some people to be born with a higher IQ, and these "natural leaders" need to be given privileges the lesser humans neither deserve nor require. The exploitative structures of global capitalism are never challenged, never seriously interrogated, only accepted as a natural given.

What, exactly, do Herrnstein and Murray want the crumbling educational establishment to do? They work from the following premises. Some students possess more genetically determined capacity to absorb education than others; individuals with the most capacity should become the most educated; those who occupy the top layers of cognitive ability are generally the children of the socioeconomic elite; the diluted, dumbed-down curriculum created by misguided liberal reforms has been a boon to the mediocre students from the low-IQ, high-breeding populations and a veritable plague for the more genetically talented sons and daughters of the ruling classes; funds for the cognitively deficient are disgustingly wasteful and should be eliminated or, better still, be channeled immediately to school programs serving the cognitive aristocracy; schools are a waste of time for the 98 percent of the academic low-lifes; academic protectionism is justifiable if it serves the interests of the cognitive elite; a 12-minute intelligence test is a better measure for judging a job applicant than a high school diploma; and parents are to blame because they don't push teachers to increase their academic work-loads or to create higher national educational standards.

Herrnstein and Murray lament the fact that the U.S. education system cannot get away with the authoritarian elitism practiced by countries such as France and Germany. Unfortunately, democracy just isn't working for U.S. students because it doesn't unapologetically favor the children of the upper classes. In other words, too many concessions have been made by bleeding-heart liberal educational reformers—such as attempts in some schools at detracking—and this puts our national brain trust at risk. Herrnstein and Murray believe that it is mostly the parents of the best and the brightest who desire an ambitious education for their children. Guided by this pathetically misinformed and condescending logic, they believe scholarships should be more competitive and that some portion of existing elementary and secondary federal aid should be taken from programs for the disadvantaged and reallocated to programs for the gifted students (who overwhelmingly come from families of the economic elite). In a repugnantly smug assertion, the authors maintain that the gifted are not more deserving of funds but rather that the welfare of the United States depends on the accumulated wealth of the nation's genetic cognoscenti. It is futile, they argue, to imagine that everyone is up to the challenge of becoming educated. Only a few students can profit from the best that the world's Western intellectual heritage has to offer. Predictably, the authors hate public school education, support school vouchers, and urge that parental choice be extended to private and religious private schools.

In the 1920s, the developer of the Scholastic Aptitude Test (SAT) test, Carl Brigham, hoped that Eastern Europeans would be weeded out of institutions of higher learning by college entrance exams; in those days he never could have dreamed that Latinos and Blacks would become the educational "problem" of the twenty-first century. Were he alive today, Brigham surely would admire Herrnstein and Murray's efforts to keep the struggle alive to demonize the undeserving poor—especially people of color. Smacking of eugenics, and betraying the grim determination of the fascist's steel-toed march to ethnic purity, Herrnstein and Murray argue that most of the dregs of society—those who possess measured IQ scores considerably lower than their own—are to be taken in custody and warehoused (so to speak) in a space that prevents them from intermingling with the cognitive elite. They describe this custodial state as a more lavish, high-tech form of the Indian reservation. While Whites no longer display non-Whites in cages as they did in the nineteenth- and early twentieth-centuries—consider the case of Maximo and Cartola, the microcephalics (pinheads) from Central America who toured the United States in P. T. Barnum's circus as Aztecs shortly after the annexation of Mexico; the Hottentot Venus, whose genitalia were preserved after her death in order to confirm the hypersexuality of black people; or Ota Benga, the Pygmy boy exhibited in the Monkey Cage in the Bronx Zoo—they continue to support the ideologies necessary for the reproduction of the cultural logics that support such racism.

CONCLUSION

Herrnstein and Murray are dishonest in their discussion of genetic determination; they refuse to deal with the fact that there is no scientific factor in IQ differences. Intelligence determines social futures not through biological determinism but rather in the sense that the tacit racist assumptions upon which current IQ tests are based, such as those developed by Herrnstein and Murray, become socially reproduced. The authors' indebtedness to scientists supported by the Pioneer Fund (which is committed to the reproduction of the genetic stock of white descendants from the original 13 colonies and which subsidizes the Federation for American Immigration Reform, which fought on behalf of Proposition 187 and the English-only group, U.S. English) assists the emotional attack on affirmative action by U.S. conservatives by lending scientific credibility to the nation's ideologically motivated xenophobia, stimulating the social reproduction of hierarchies based on race, class, and gender, and sustaining white privilege. *The Bell Curve* gives a new vitality to the colonial unconscious of the United States. That Murray received $1 million to research the book from the ultra-conservative Bradley Foundation should come as no surprise.

Herrnstein and Murray want to believe that the high-breeding immigrants of color and the undeserving poor in general lack character as well as intelligence since they believe character depends somewhat on IQ. Children from intellectually inferior families will never have the intelligence to understand the ethics books imported from Western Europe and naturally will be given over to lawlessness. The understaffed elite—who could provide the nation with the moral direction it needs—is preventing us from increasing the public good. That these eugenicist sentiments masquerading as the language of benevolent civic-mindedness drive the book (it is certainly not driven by scientifically credible psychological assumptions) is scandalous. Equally as scandalous is the fact that the pseudo-science of *The Bell Curve* has turned some poorly argued science into a manifesto for justifying a special status for the meritocracy of the self-proclaimed, hereditary elite. The truth is that biology does provide human beings with certain competencies; we do inherit mental abilities. Physically healthy human beings all have the same biological equipment that creates distinctive intelligences. We cannot say some of these intelligences are superior to others due to race, class, or gender (Mensch and Mensch, 1991), since the issue is not intelligence but the assessment of intelligence, which is a political issue (McSwan, 1995).

Chomsky provides a hypothetical solution to the dilemma charted out by the authors of *The Bell Curve* and by other conservative thinkers, such as Malcolm Browne:

> Suppose we grant the most ominous facts he [Malcolm Browne] conjures up about decline of IQ and achievement, and its causes. There's an easy solution to the problem: simply bring here millions of peasants driven from the countryside in China under the "reforms," and radically reduce Browne's income and that of his friends and associates, making sure to deprive their daughters of opportunities and education, while Black mothers are placed in Manhattan high rises and granted every advantage. Then the Asian influx will raise the IQ level; and as serious inquiry demonstrates, the fertility rates of Blacks is very likely to drop while that of the journalistic elite, Harvard psychology professors, and associates of the American Enterprise Institute will rapidly rise. The problem is solved; there is nothing to fear. (1995, p. 12)

Social, cultural, and political institutions secured over the last several decades to enforce racial hierarchies have received some powerful reinforcement from Herrnstein and Murray, members of the "bought priesthood" of the New Right ideologues. It is up to concerned parents, teachers, administrators, and citizens to challenge these institutions and the ideologies that give life to their racist assumptions. A failure to do so is a capitulation to irrationality, fear, and the demonization of difference.

References

Andrade, K. (1995, December-January 5). Head trips: Debunking *The Bell Curve* and the new wave of biodeterminists. *LA Village View*, 30-32.

350   Peter McLaren

Chomsky, N. (1995, February). Rollback II: Civilization marches on *ZNet*,
1-12.
Gould, S. (1995, November 28). Curveball. *The New Yorker*, 39-43.
McSwan, J. (1995). Mental aspects of biology and the meritocratic elite:
What psychological theories really say about status. Unpublished.
Mensch, E. and Mensch, H. (1991). *The IQ mythology: Class, race, gender,
and inequality.* Carbondale: Southern Illinois University Press.

23 THE BELL CURVE, AFFIRMATIVE ACTION, AND THE QUEST FOR EQUITY

ROBERT M. HENDRICKSON

INTRODUCTION

Affirmative action as a national policy is not only the primary issue of the last half of this century but one whose importance will dominate public opinion well into the next century. The social, economic, political, and psychological implications for the body politic of affirmative action policy continue to have far-reaching effects on the achievement of our national and constitutional goal of equity. In chapter 19 of *The Bell Curve,* authors Richard Herrnstein and Charles Murray use performance on intelligence tests to explain why class structure is based on race in American society. They argue that measures of intelligence are accurate measures of the individual's intellectual capacity or, as they call it, "cognitive ability." They hold that "cognitive ability," as measured by IQ tests is relatively stable over time, not subject to racial or ethnic bias, and clearly an inherited trait over which environment has little influence. This fact has resulted in the emergence of a cognitive elite in this century and a strong positive correlation between higher "cognitive ability" and education level, occupation, economic independence, and civility and citizenship. Low "cognitive ability" they maintain, is correlated directly with involvement in crime, dependence on welfare, unemployment, divorce, out-of-wedlock and teenage pregnancy, and family dysfunction (Graham, 1990). They eliminate race or gender bias as explaining the differences in "cognitive ability" they found between Whites and other racial or ethnic groups. Further, they leap to a presumption that standardized tests such as the SAT, LSAT, GRE and MCAT are also acceptable measures of "cognitive ability" not affected by gender or race bias. Finally, they argue that a social policy such as affirmative action, which was based on the assumption that there are no differences in "cognitive ability" across racial and ethnic groups, should be scrapped, and that scores on standardized tests should be used as appropriate measures of merit in admission to higher education institutions.

This chapter specifically addresses the fallacies of the authors' premises about federal affirmative action policy and the use of standardized tests to establish merit-based admissions policies. I review the historical origins of federal policy on affirmative action. Supreme Court decisions addressing the constitutionality of race as a criteria in public sector decisions and the Court's extensive review of college and university admissions policies provide the legal perspective to this policy question. Affirmative action literature, including Critical Race Theory, is used to focus on the pivotal issues surrounding affirmative action. These analytical perspectives will be used to refute the crux of *The Bell Curve* argument that standardized tests constitute absolute merit. I conclude the discussion by suggesting that we need to rethink the criteria we use to select and admit students to higher education and the precision with which we use these criteria in making admissions decisions. The goal is to have decisions that are free of racial bias and truly level the playing field so that all will have equal opportunities. To achieve this goal, it may be appropriate to act affirmatively to promote gender and ethnic diversity in the makeup of various constituencies in institutions of higher education where a compelling interest to act affirmatively exists.

AFFIRMATIVE ACTION POLICY

The civil rights era spawned the notions of equal opportunity and affirmative action. Title VI and Title VII, among other titles of the Civil Rights Act of 1964 serve as the basis for the conceptualization of affirmative action. Both the Justice Department (later the Office of Civil Rights [OCR]), which enforced Title VI nondiscrimination policies in the award of federal funds, and the Equal Employment Opportunities Commission (EEOC), which administered the employment nondiscrimination provisions of Title VII, helped to illuminate the notions of affirmative action. However, technically the actual origins for affirmative action came from President Johnson's Executive Order #11246, issued in 1965, which authorized government agencies to develop regulations promoting equal opportunities for all races (Graham, 1990). The words "affirmative action" were used in the part of the executive order dealing with the award of federal contracts. The sections of the executive order on federal employment spoke about "additional affirmative steps" and "positive measures" to eliminate discrimination in federal employment.

In 1970, the Nixon administration adopted the concepts of what was then called the Philadelphia Plan, designed to set racial goals for employment by contractors holding federal contracts. This plan saw the full maturation of the affirmative action policies as we know them today. It required that due to the history of past inequities, employers should plan to achieve a proportional representation of the races to mirror that found in the larger community (Graham, 1990). These plans or goals immediately raised the question of the use of quotas based on race. However, the Supreme Court rejected the use of quotas saying they violated the equal protection clause. Yet, the government still expected that the regulations would require employers and institutions to act in an affirmative way and to employ a diverse workforce or admit a diverse student body.

Proponents of affirmative action requirements reached agreement on the policy from two conflicting viewpoints. One view was that this policy of giving preference based on race and gender was defensible only as a temporary bridge to the goal of a color-blind society as mandated by the Constitution's provisions protecting individual rights. The other maintained that this new proportional representation model was required as a permanent fixture to protect group rights and equal results within the society's social and political structure. Thus some proponents speak of the temporary nature of these policies while others look at affirmative action as an entitlement. In the current debate, if one listens carefully, both of these voices emerge and serve to weaken and divide affirmative action proponents. However, the most significant challenges to affirmative action have come through litigation in the courts, including the most recent Supreme Court decision in June 1995.

THE SUPREME COURT SPEAKS ON AFFIRMATIVE ACTION

Over the last three decades, the United States Supreme Court has spoken on the issue of affirmative action from a constitutional perspective. Its decisions emanate from the language of the Fourteenth Amendment, establishing state obligations to provide equal protection under the law, and the Fifth Amendment requiring federal equal protection. While there may have been one or two sidetracks, the majority opinions of the Court have interpreted the amendments as protecting individual as opposed to group rights. Further, when governmental entities use suspect categories, defined as race, creed and national origin, the Court has applied the doctrine of strict scrutiny—it requires the public entity to show that there is a compelling interest to use the suspect category. A compelling interest can be reached through an administrative, judicial or legislative finding of discrimination necessitating the remedy. The remedy also must be narrowly tailored to eliminate the specific wrong without causing undue harm to other individuals. This does not mean that the public entity must be color-blind; rather, while race may be one of a number of factors, it cannot be the only factor upon which the governmental benefit was granted. The following review of cases substantiates this position.

The first affirmative action case involved a claim of reverse discrimination in the denial of admission of a white applicant to the University of Washington Law School. In *Defunis v. Odegard* (1974), the law school had set aside spaces for minority applicants and used a separate process to determine who would fill those positions. While Whites were not allowed to compete in the special process, minority applicants successfully competed in the regular admissions process. Defunis brought suit claiming he was discriminated against because of his race. Since the lower court opinion was vacated, Defunis was in the final year of study in the law school and the Court dodged the question by declaring the case moot. However, the dissenting opinion of Justice Douglas points out how the Court would later rule.

The Court would face the same decision four years later in the *Regents of the University of California v. Bakke* (1978). While this case involved a medical school, the issues were very similar. The medical school had a dual admissions process with a set number of spaces reserved for minorities and a separate admissions process for those spaces. Like the University of Washington, minorities successfully competed for positions in the general admissions process but Whites could not compete in the minority process. Allen Bakke sued claiming discrimination in admission based on race in violation of the equal protection clause. In one of the more complicated decisions ever to emanate from the Court with four justices joining in a dissenting/concurring opinion and four other justices developing concurring/dissenting opinions, Justice Powell wrote the opinion of the Court. In this five to four decision, the Court ruled that the Fourteenth Amendment protects individual or personal rights not those of groups defined as "discrete and insular minorities." It applied the concept of strict scrutiny, requiring a compelling state interest to allow a suspect category (race) to be used to award admission. The Court also challenged the notion that setting proportional goals or quotas was permitted. This case is cited in subsequent cases as striking down the use of quotas. The state failed to support its argument of a compelling state interest to justify the existence of the special race-based admissions program. However, joined by the four dissenting/concurring justices, Powell established that race could be one of a number of criterion used in the admissions decision as long as it was not the sole criteria. The Court in Bakke rejected the notion of a color-blind admissions process and allowed race to be one of a number of criteria. In subsequent decisions to the present day, the Court seems to have upheld and reinforced this decision.

The Court continued to grapple with the notion that when government uses suspect categories, strict scrutiny should apply. For example, in *Fullilove v. Klutznick* (1980), a case involving 10 percent set-aside in the Public Works Employment Act of 1977 for minority-owned business, while not applying the strict scrutiny test, the Court found that congressional power allowed Congress to pass such legislation and the limited use of race to achieve affirmative action goals was within the scope of Congress. The majority argued that their opinion was consistent with the several tests advocated in the several opinions in Bakke.

In 1986, the Court struggled with whether to apply strict scrutiny in a case involving use of race to determine which teachers to lay off. In *Wygant v. Jackson Board of Education* (1986), the majority opinion applied strict scrutiny, which required that the school's decisions must be based on a compelling governmental interest and be narrowly tailored to inflict the least harm. The Court found that the school's efforts to provide teachers who are minority role models was not compelling when it was based on a showing of past societal discrimination.

The Court clearly applied the doctrine of strict scrutiny to situations involving race based preferences given by state and local governments in *Richmond v. J. A. Croson Co.* (1989). In a case involving the city setting aside 30 percent of its contracts for minority owned businesses, the Court applied strict scrutiny, finding that the city's evidence supporting the race based preference would not sustain remedial action. However, in the 1990 case,

Metro Broadcasting, Inc. v. FCC (1990), involving the federal government and the fifth Amendment, the Court applied a less strict review of race preference policies. It found that "benign federal racial classifications" require only intermediate scrutiny, and went on to elaborate that benign racial classifications could be identified by analyzing the legislative scheme and its history. With this case separate standards were applied at the federal and state/local levels. The 1994-1995 term of the Supreme Court would see the end to these differing standards.

In June 1995 the Court issued its long-awaited decision in *Adarand Contractors, Inc. v. Pena* (1995), which involved federal agency contract rules giving contractors a financial incentive to award subcontracts to minority-controlled business. A white-owned sub-contractor who was the low bidder sued when the general contractor for a federal highway project in Colorado awarded the subcontract to a minority-owned business. The six to three opinion, written by Justice O'Connor, rejected the *Metro Broadcasting, Inc.* (1990), case as an error and applied the concept of strict scrutiny to federal race preference cases. Since strict scrutiny would require that the federal government establish a compelling governmental interest for the race-based preferential policy and that the remedy be narrowly tailored so as to expose others to the least harm, the Court remanded the case for the application of these standards by the lower court. While the popular press has labeled this case as the final blow to affirmative action programs, the opposite may in fact be the case. It could be argued that the discussions of *Bakke* within this case seem to support the conclusions that race may be a factor as long as it is not the *sole* factor in granting of governmental benefits. Further, it would appear that there are some cases in which government can show a compelling interest to justify the racial preference as long as the remedy is narrowly designed to reach only the justified governmental interest. Given the votes of the current justices, it does not appear that the Court will adopt the color-blind standards advocated by some. While these standards set by the Court are stricter than those under which the legislation and executive orders were originally written, governmental entities should still be able to show a compelling governmental interest and tailor a narrow enough remedy to meet constitutional requirements.

AFFIRMATIVE ACTION AND CRITICAL RACE THEORY

While the Courts have been setting the constitutional parameters under which affirmative action policy must be established, politicians and scholars continue to debate the merits of affirmative action policy. For example, some people advocate the end of affirmative action and, basing their arguments on the premise that the Constitution mandates that government be color-blind, maintain that race should not be considered in the award of any governmental benefit or privilege. Another group that favors affirmative action bases much of its argument on the fact that the basis for discrimination is the categorization by society of racial groups and that one group, the white race, dominates the others. Since discrimination is based on groupings, than governmental remedies should be based on group rights and preferences. Some scholars maintain that we are mired in this debate and no new creative solutions seem to be emerging that help to reach the goal of equity. However, an emerging group of writings on what is called Critical Race Theory appears to have some promise for moving us out of this stalemate.

Critical Race Theory (CRT) is an outgrowth of frustration with the Civil Rights movement of the 1960s. It has its origins in the 1970s but officially came into its own at a workshop in Madison, Wisconsin, in 1989 (Nan, 1994). CRT is primarily composed of scholars of color who espouse eight basic premises according to Richard Delgato (Farber, 1994). Delgato outlines these eight premises as (1) an insistence on "naming our own reality"; (2) the belief that knowledge and ideas are powerful; (3) a readiness to question basic premises of moderate/incremental civil rights law; (4) the borrowing of insights from social science on race and racism; (5) critical examination of the myths and stories powerful groups use to justify racial subordination; (6) a more contextualized treatment doctrine; (7) criticism of liberal legalisms; and (8) an interest in structural determinism—the ways in which legal tools and thought structures impede law reform.

CRT demands that a new perspective, the perspective of color, be used to translate affirmative action policy into results that level the playing field and leads to roughly proportional representation in the schools, colleges, and employment ranks within society. While some CRT scholars promote the continuation of affirmative action, others argue that it actually demeans people of color because their attainment is compromised by such policies. This debate mirrors the larger debate and lead to a similar stalemate. However, one theme cuts across CRT: The field is unanimous in its challenge of the current standards used to determine merit. This challenge to the merit standards, I believe, is just the approach to break the stalemate and move to the next level in our quest for equity. CRT scholars would argue that the standards of merit, that is, standardized tests, used in *The Bell Curve*, are a "white" perspective on the notions of what constitutes merit for admission to a college or university and are not valid measures from the perspective of a person of color. In the next section I use the approach of challenging and analyzing the criteria used to determine merit for admissions purposes, to analyze the fallacies of notions of affirmative action put forth in *The Bell Curve*.

FLAWED PREMISES LEAD TO ABSOLUTE MERIT

In *The Bell Curve*, the authors attempt to refute the basic premises of affirmative action admissions policy by demonstrating that racial groups are not the same on measures of "cognitive ability." For purposes of higher education admission, they use standardized tests as measures of "cognitive ability." Like the other measures of "cognitive ability" discussed in the book, these tests are found, according to Herrnstein and Murray, to be free of cultural bias. They argue that these tests are adequate measures of merit and because Blacks and Hispanics have average scores substantially lower than Whites, these minority groups are given unfair advantage over Whites in admission decisions. Given these premises, I first cannot help but wonder why our institutions are not being taken over by minority populations. All sarcasm aside, there are several glaring problems with the logic of the authors' arguments.

First, the notion that the standardized tests used in admission decisions measure "cognitive ability" was a given for the authors and was never substantiated in the text. While these tests may have some bearing on "cognitive ability," their most significant connection is with the quality of the learning environment and the individual's utilization of that opportunity at the high school or undergraduate level. I doubt whether even the manufacturers of these tests would argue that they measure "cognitive ability" as defined in *The Bell Curve*. This also raises questions about the validity of maintaining that these tests are free of cultural bias. While the research may substantiate that the test questions are free of cultural or race bias, that does not remove the cultural bias emanating from the quality of the high schools many minority students have been educated in. We know there are differences in the educational environment of predominantly white suburban schools and predominantly minority inner-city schools. If these standardized tests are measuring the learning environment and individual utilization of that environment, then the differences found between students from these differing environments are not surprising.

The second problem with The *Bell Curve* argument lies with the correlations Herrnstein and Murray are willing to accept as "big." A correlation coefficient, when squared (R2), will provide the percentage of the variance within the sample that is explained by the measure. The authors maintain that correlations between .2 and .4 are good and a correlation of .2 in the social sciences is "big." It is hard to believe that a measure that explains 4 percent (.2) to 16 percent (.4) of the variance within groups in a population should be given such importance. The problem with these standardized tests is that they have very low correlations to academic success after admission (grade point average [GPA]). For example the correlation of the SAT to college GPA is .31, and the correlations of the other standardized test to academic performance in graduate or professional schools is less than .5 (Willingham, 1995). Further, the correlation of academic performance with high school or undergraduate GPA is also less than .5 If the test measures less than 25 percent of the variance, why should we give it such absolute importance as a determinant for admissions? Coupled with the cultural bias just discussed inherent in what these tests measure, serious reservations should arise about how much importance should be ascribed to these tests in the admissions decision and how they serve to perpetuate a societal structure based on race.

Third, these standardized tests tell us some things about the tails of the bell curve but they cannot tell us very much about the vast majority who lay in the middle of this normal distribution. In the *Defunis* (1974) case, Justice Douglas made this point in his dissenting opinion. Douglas noted that the law school can make distinctions between those with 750 on the LSAT, who should be admitted, and those with lower than 500, who should be rejected. "The problem is that in many cases the choice will be between 643 and 602 or 574 and 538" (*Defunis v. Odegard*). David Weber, in an article on the *Defunis* case, illustrated the point more fully. Weber reviewed the admissions formula for the University Washington Law Schools, which looked at the "predicted first year average" (PFYA). The PFYA included the undergraduate GPA + the LSAT + writing sample. He then looked at two examples that were close to the cutoff point at Washington, which is 74.5. (Scores below this are automatically rejected). In the first case, the person has a GPA of 3.5, a writing sample of 60, and LSAT of 550, which equals a PFYA of 74.7. In the second case, the person has the same GPA of 3.5 and writing sample of 60, but his LSAT is 520, yielding a PFYA of 74.3 and rejection. Some would say, well some have to be rejected, but the LSAT has a standard error of measure of ± 30, which means that on any given day, a person's score on the test could vary ± 30 points. Thus the test is being used with more precision than it was ever designed to be used. Many admissions processes use the standardized tests in exactly this way. Even when we know the limitations of these tests, they are being used for administrative expediency.

I have been overseeing a very competitive admissions process for a doctoral program for the past 11 years. During that time we have used the GRE as one of a number of measures used to make admissions decisions. What we have found is that when someone gets a composite score (verbal and analytic portions of the test) below about 700, we are relatively sure that person will have difficulties in their graduate program, particularly with the conceptual and writing tasks faced in developing a doctoral dissertation. We like to see at least a 1,000 composite score; however, if other factors indicate that the student has the ability to complete the work, we accept the person, even though the GRE may be lower than 1,000. Because we know the limitations of the GRE and that it correlates so poorly with later performance, we include a number of other variables in our admissions decision. Unlike the authors in *The Bell Curve*, we are unwilling to ascribe absolute merit to a test that has so little predictability. While it is true that minority applicants in some cases have lower standardized test scores, other variables indicate an individual who will successfully complete a doctoral degree, and those students are admitted to our program. As Justice Douglas pointed out, it is the student who has had to struggle for academic success who will, over the long haul of a professional career, have made a better contribution than the applicant who had high test scores, a high undergraduate GPA, and for whom academics were always easy.

ADMISSIONS DECISIONS AS A SUBJECTIVE PROCESS

In *The Bell Curve*, the authors, like admissions officers across the country, have ascribed too much importance to scores on standardized tests. The authors of *The Bell Curve* believe that these scores are absolute measures of merit and point to the unfairness of affirmative action programs. The Critical Race Theorists on the other hand have recognized that this issue of what constitutes merit is where the affirmative action battle needs to be fought. If the criteria used to make admissions decisions are fair, then we will no longer need to give consideration to "suspect categories" as identified by the Court. One of those criteria, according to the Court, can be the racial or ethnic origins of the applicant as long as it is one of several criteria used to make the decision. As long as there is disparity between the quality of education available to students in inner-city and suburban schools, race will continue to be one of the criteria we need to evaluate in making admissions decisions. The differences in "cognitive ability" across ethnic groups are another reflection of the long history of discrimination and all of its manifestations. For some 30 years we have acted affirmatively to mitigate the past and pursue a future grounded in equity. While some progress has been made, there is much more to do. We need to focus the debate not on whether we need affirmative action but rather on the admissions process itself and the criteria we use to measure merit.

References

Baida, A. (1994). Not all minority scholarships are created equal: How to develop a record that passes Constitutional scrutiny. *Journal of College and University Law, 21,* 307-352.

Carnegie Council on Policy Studies in Higher Education. (1975). *Making Affirmative Action work.* San Francisco: Jossey Bass.

Delgoto, R. (1990). When a story is just a story: Does voice really matter? *Virginia Law Review, 76,* 95.

Duster, T. (1995). What's new in the IQ debate. *The Black Scholar, 25,* 25-31.

Early, G. (1995). *The Bell Curve:* As the meaning of the academic will. *The Black Scholar, 25,* 32-38.

Farber, D. (1994). The outmoded debate over affirmative action. *California Law Review, 82,* 893-934.

Ford, C. (1994). Administering identity: The determination of "race." *Race Conscious Law, 82,* 1231-1285.

Graham, H. (1990). *The Civil Rights era: Origins and development of national policy.* New York: Oxford University Press.

Hawkins, B. (1995, February 9). A multiple-choice mushroom: Schools, colleges rely more than ever on standardized tests. *Black Issues in Higher Education, 8.*

Herrnstein, R. and Murray, C. (1994). *The Bell Curve: Intelligence and class structure in American life.* New York: The Free Press.

Hudson, B. (1995). Scientific racism: The politics of tests, race and gender. *The Black Scholar, 25,* 3-10.

Jackson-Johnson, J. (1995). *The Bell Curve:* What's all the fuss about? *The Black Scholar, 25,* 11-20.

Joseph, D. (1994). Constitutional law—Statistical evidence of discrimination and affirmative action: The numbers game. *Maryland Troopers Assn. Inc. v. Evans,* 993 F.2d 1072 (4th Cir. 1993). *Temple Law Review, 67,* 451-472.

Lewis, E. (1995). The fallacy of positivist reasoning. *The Black Scholar, 25,* 21-24.

Malveaux, J. (1994, November 17). Snatching back the welcome mat. *Black Issues in Higher Education, 41.*

Morrison, J. (1994). Colorblindness, individuality, and merit: An analysis of the rhetoric against affirmative action. *Iowa Law Review, 79,* 313-366.

Nan, C. (1994). Adding salt to the wound: Affirmative action and Critical Race Theory. *Law and Inequality, 12,* 553-572.

Quaye, R. (1995). The assault on the human spirit: *The Bell Curve. The Black Scholar, 25,* 41-43.

Sindler, A. (1978). *Bakke, Defunis, and minority admissions: The quest for equal opportunity.* New York: Longman.

Wanza, K. (1995). Plus ca change, Plus ca reste la meme chose. *The Black Scholar, 25,* 39-40.

Whatley, W. (1995). Wanted: Some black long distance runners—The message of *The Bell Curve. The Black Scholar, 25,* 44-46.

Willingham, W. (1995). *Success in college.* New York: College Entrance Examination Board.

Table of Cases

Adarand Constructors, Inc. v. Pena, 115 S. Ct. 2095 (1995).
Defunis v. Odegard, 416 U.S. 312 (1974).
Fullilove v. Klutznick, 448 U.S. 448 (1980).
Metro Broadcasting, Inc. v. FCC, 497 U.S. 547 (1990).
Regents of the Univ. Cal. v. Bakke, 438 U.S. 265, (1978).
Richmond v. J. A. Croson Co., 488 U. S. 469 (1989).
Wygant v. Jackson Board of Ed., 476 U.S. 267 (1986).

24 ATTACKING AFFIRMATIVE ACTION: SOCIAL DARWINISM AS PUBLIC PROLICY

CATHERINE A. LUGG

In chapter 20 of The Bell Curve, Richard Herrnstein and Charles Murray lay out their rationale for demolishing affirmative action programs in the American workplace. In the rest of the book, much of their argument rests on the heroic assumptions that both IQ scores and various standardized measures of aptitude are bias-free and synonymous with competency, ignoring the substantial historical evidence to the contrary. Additionally, the authors are obsessed with the menacing specter of the supposed genetic intellectual inadequacies of African Americans and the implications for U.S. society writ large. They present a dizzying array of statistical data to reinforce their contention that Whites comprise the American meritocratic elite. Herrnstein and Murray argue that governmental efforts to insure equity in employment impede this "natural superiority." Accordingly, the United States courts social disaster by promoting the intellectually unworthy (African Americans) over the worthy (Whites) in employment.

However, much of the statistical analysis upon which their argument is built uses smoke and mirrors. They unintentionally revived the joke "You can get what you want out of statistics if you torture them enough," for as educational researchers Ernest House and Carolyn Haug acidly note, "if there were such a thing as social science malpractice, these authors would be at risk" (1995, p. 263). Rather than wading through the varied statistical murkiness, I will instead focus on the historical foundation for Herrnstein and Murray's overriding political agenda. It is important to realize that although *The Bell Curve* has the appearance of social science research, it is more propaganda than science, more recapitulation than innovation. The authors' proposals have the potential to inflict great economic harm on the *majority* of U.S. citizens, once we recall that the majority of the citizenry is not comprised of white males

The Bell Curve is significant because the authors have effectively marketed their policy proposals for eliminating affirmative action, cloaking their rhetoric in notions of merit and white supremacy. As legal scholar Donald Judges has observed, "what busing was to school desegregation, affirmative action has become to workplace desegregation" (1992, p. 629). Like many earlier antibusing advocates, Herrnstein and Murray have directly appealed to a powerful electoral constituency, conservative Whites, in building popular support for their proposals. Since Richard Nixon's 1968 campaign based on the "Southern Strategy" (see Phillips, 1969, p. 468), no presidential candidate who has angered this constituency has subsequently been elected (Cramer, 1992; Hacker, 1992; Haldeman, 1994; Cramer, 1992; Lugg, 1996; Phillips, 1969). White conservatives comprise the voting majority in key electoral states, and they wield disproportionate influence in policy debates and the shaping of federal affirmative action policies. American politicians ignore white conservatives at their peril. This is Herrnstein's and Murray's target audience.

Since the inception of federal affirmative action programs in 1970, conservatives of various ideological stripes have been hostile, claiming that it interferes with the natural order of things and/or the "divine" workings of the market. President Nixon was very aware of this dynamic when he helped formulate the original employment policies, hoping the bland initiatives would not antagonize white conservatives while concurrently giving him some political breathing space over his failed appointment of segregationist Harold Carswell to the U.S. Supreme Court (Haldeman, 1994). Nevertheless, throughout this century, politically conservative white Americans have opposed not only various affirmative action programs but also the enforcing of basic civil rights protection. As one unsigned editor at *The National Review* mused in 1957:

> The central question that emerges—and it is not a parliamentary question or a question that I answered by merely consulting a catalogue of the rights of American citizens, born Equal—is whether the White community . . . is entitled to take such measures as are necessary to prevail, politically and culturally, in areas where it does not predominate numerically? The sobering answer is *Yes*—the White community is so entitled because, for the time being, it is the advanced race. (1957, p. 149)

By employing dubious data to appeal to appeal to politically historic notions of "the advanced race," Herrnstein and Murray have waged an updated form of American cultural warfare or symbolic crusade (Gusfield, 1963) that is better known as social Darwinism.

SOCIAL DARWINISM

Charles Darwin's 1859 *Origin of the Species* revolutionized how individuals viewed their world. Prior to its publication, Western Christianity and, increasingly in the eighteenth and early nineteenth centuries, Christianity with a smattering of science or at least what sounded scientific provided the rubrics regarding the nature of "things." With the arrival of Darwin, and more important his various American disciples, Western Christianity was displaced as the provider of all truth. Thanks to its newly found prominence, science quickly stepped in to fill the void. As the historian Richard Hofstadter observed, "Many scientific discoveries affect ways of living more profoundly than evolution did; but none have had a greater impact on ways of thinking and believing" (1955, p. 3).

In the fledgling social science field of sociology, a combination of Darwinian biology and the teachings of English sociologist Herbert Spencer held enormous implications. If biology "evolved," and societies were comprised of living beings who also evolved, it only seemed reasonable that various ethnic and racial groups were more or less "evolved," more or less "civilized." It was only a quick intellectual leap to employ the new "science" to rationalize prejudice into an elaborate hierarchy of greater to lesser races, ethnicities, and genders, with Anglo Americans at the top and African Americans and women at the bottom of the social order (Bannister, 1979; Ehrenreich and English, 1978).

It was Spencer, not Darwin, who coined the phrase "survival of the fittest" and who had perhaps the larger influence upon American social thought. According to Hofstadter, "In the three decades after the Civil War it was impossible to be active in any field of intellectual work without mastering Spencer" (1955, p. 33). This vogue coincided with a spectacular era of "heyday capitalism," or the *Gilded Age* (Phillips, 1990), where corporate giants such as Standard Oil grew powerful enough to buy members of congress; vast personal fortunes were made; financial speculation and political corruption were rampant; immigration exploded; and corporations were provided with civil rights protection while African Americans lost many of their Reconstruction gains (Coontz, 1992; Woodward, 1974).

With the emergence of the United States as a major global industrial power, it was realized that not everyone was capable of "cashing in." The enormous economic disparities that existed among differing ethnic and racial groups were rationalized through the rubrics of social Darwinism. Dismal, dreary, and dangerous, urban sweatshops were plentiful, with most of the labor force composed of immigrants who were barred from more lucrative areas of employment due to both their ethnicity and/or religious beliefs. African Americans were relegated to a new separate and despised economic caste, typically shut out of all but the most menial of jobs. Many of the restrictions limiting the economic, political, religious and social rights of non-Anglos reflected the Darwinism of the era. The new science also counseled that there was little anyone could do to change the current conditions. Social change, if it happened at all, was evolutionary and would take many generations to occur (Hofstadter, 1955).

Gender was also a powerful determinant with social and economic roles tightly circumscribed (for example, see Sangster, 1901). In the view of social Darwinists, women were valued for their reproductive capacity and little else. With economic expansion and growing educational opportunities for women, especially middle-class white women, the birth rate for middle-class Whites began to decline. Various academics and politicians thundered about the impending "race suicide" for Whites if white women continued to shirk their biological duties. More than a few blamed the decline on the popularity of "female" education, claiming it had "sterilized" women. (See Clarke, 1873.)

During the Gilded Age, the American notion of the self-made man became the stuff of instant legends. It has remained a vital part of American popular culture (Coontz, 1992; Vidal, 1993). For example, Horatio Alger penned popular tales of plucky young lads from very humble beginnings who succeeded through their hard work and moral rectitude. Subsequently, the poor were poor due to their sloth, moral, and otherwise. Yet thanks to the influence of social Darwinism upon American social thought, the real game of "survival of the fittest" was fixed. During a time when many decent work opportunities were limited to white Protestants, the meritocratic mythology was as powerful as it was pernicious.

This notion of economic success, if not outright salvation, through hard work also drove much of the belief systems of white Protestants. The tenor of the times was such that "other" European immigrants were expected to assimilate (that is, become Anglo) as quickly as possible, and non-Whites and women were to accept their lower status. Many Anglo Americans of the late nineteenth and early twentieth centuries devoutly believed that the social hierarchy reflected the natural order of things. Anglo Americans were in positions of power by dint of their hereditary superiority and hard work. Not only were non-Anglos and women mentally inferior, they also tended to be morally unfit if removed from their "proper" roles. The "new" immigrants were especially suspect.

> These Southern and Eastern Europeans were of a very different type from the North and West Europeans who preceded them. Largely illiterate, docile, lacking in initiative, and almost wholly without the Anglo-Saxon conceptions of righteousness, liberty, law, order, public decency, and government, their coming has served to dilute tremendously our national stock and to weaken and corrupt our political life.
>
> The new peoples, and especially those from the South and East of Europe, have come so fast that we have been unable to absorb and assimilate them, and our national life, for the past quarter of a century, has been afflicted with a serious case of racial indigestion. (Cubberley, 1919, p. 338)

One antacid for such indigestion was the public school. Modeled after factories, the early twentieth-century schools "efficiently" selected and sorted students for their future roles as adults and workers, largely along lines of class, race, ethnicity and gender. It was seen as *the* institution that would "Americanize" (that is, Anglicize) the hordes of students flooding into the public schools. Schools developed differentiated curricula (or tracks) as a means of training students to better meet the needs of business. This process was greatly aided by the creation of the World War I–era standardized tests. The most notable were the alpha and beta tests developed during World War I, originally to classify U.S. recruits, not measure intelligence (Cremin, 1961; Tyack, 1974). After the war, the government held a "fire sale" and school districts eagerly snapped up millions of unused test booklets to aid in their selecting and sorting process (Spring, 1994; Tyack, 1974).

The new field of educational psychology tapped into the growing demand for standardized measures of aptitude and intelligence, with various academics scrambling to design and then market their own instruments. By 1917 there were well over 100 different tests (Cremin, 1961, p. 187). These early tests were promoted as a scientific means of predicting future individual academic and social performance. They were touted as *the* method to divine "merit." One such promoter, Carl Bringham, examined the results of various tests and found that "Nordic groups were intellectually superior to Alpine and Mediterranean groups, Alpines were superior to Mediterraneans, and Mediterraneans were superior to Negroes" (Spring, 1994, p. 264). Bringham subsequently created the Scholastic Aptitude Test (SAT) for college admissions, with those results mirroring his earlier findings. The SAT became an effective tool for restricting the college admission of Roman Catholic and Jewish students (who were typically non-Anglo) as well as African American and female students.

However, by ascribing merit (or lack thereof) to class, racial, religious, gender, and ethnic characteristics, the principal value of standardized tests was to strengthen the established social hierarchy during a time of ongoing social and economic flux. Additionally, intelligence was hazily defined in most tests, with many of the pioneers in educational psychology equating intelligence with moral virtue. Since non-Anglos tended to do poorly on the standardized measures, there was a successful movement during the 1920s to restrict immigration and to sterilize "undesirables" (specifically African American and Native American women; see Davis, 1981) to limit the "criminal element" within the United States. Standardized tests also became an inexpensive tool for weeding out "undesirables" in the workplace, touted as a means of ameliorating "perceived labor problems such as turnover, accidents, and strikes" (Baker and Stites, 1991, p. 141).

By the 1920s standardized testing with its Darwinian base was a cost-efficient (cheap!) and popular means of selecting both students and potential employees. Since testing took on airs of science and merit while conveniently reinforcing prejudice, it has become a part of the American culture. Debates have raged since the 1920s regarding the level of bias within standardized tests, with their popularity rising and falling in conjunction with shifts in the larger political environment. Since the 1960s various legal challenges, based on solid research, successfully questioned standardized tests' predictive validity and the more blatant misuse of standardized tests has been restricted (Persell, 1977). However, standardized testing remains problematic, for it still tends to rewards a narrow social, gender, racial, and ethnic status more than it asses any real notions of "merit." (See Sadker and Sadker, 1994.)

THE BELL CURVE AS PUBLIC PROLICY

Herrnstein and Murray address this history in only the most superficial of terms, indicative of their overriding political agenda. At the beginning of this chapter, I claimed that Herrnstein and Murray were targeting a specific audience (white conservatives) in "selling" their agenda for repealing affirmative action. According to the authors, only African Americans, and occasionally other ethnic minorities, do poorly on standardized tests and are therefore (the authors imply) covered under affirmative action employment policies. What is missing from their equation is any mention of gender. This is a critical mistake on a number of levels. First, women as a whole do not fair well in standardized testing (Sadker and Sadker, 1994). Second, the group that has benefitted the most from affirmative action policies in the workplace is white women (Hacker, 1992). Following Herrnstein and Murray's logic, white women should be the most socially "pampered" and inept group, and their economic advancement would present the biggest threat to the stability of American society. Yet the authors remain silent regarding gender. Why?

    To begin with, much of *The Bell Curve* could be defined as public PRolicy or public relations public policy. (See Lugg, 1996.) It has far more to due with the marketing of an idea than framing actual policy. Tied to the rise of American "think tanks," PRolicy has become a large part of the civic discourse. The goal of all think tanks is to both shape the debate surrounding policy formation and to lobby for the enactment of specific policies through the skillful use and manipulation of policy tools (Lugg, 1996). While ostensively nonprofit and nonpartisan, most think tanks have a none-too-subtle political agenda that is woven into their policy analysis and proposals. For example, one will probably never see a feminist or an Afrocentrist critique of welfare policy issued from either American Enterprise Institute or the Heritage Foundation. This is not to boldly claim that all research done by think tanks or "think-tankers" is glorified ad copy for either the Democratic or Republican parties. However, such endeavors should be viewed through jaundiced colored glasses.

One of the authors, Charles Murray, has had a highly visible career working for various conservative think tanks. Yet he is not particularly respected as an academic (Coontz, 1992; House and Haug, 1995). Nevertheless, Murray has been very effective during the last decade in grabbing spectacular headlines with his neo-Darwinian approach to welfare policy (Coontz, 1992; Murray, 1984), and has become the darling of white conservatives. Thanks to his intellectual "bad-boy" image, he is a frequent guest on numerous "talking head" television news shows, gaining a certain instant credibility that any policy entrepreneur needs. Murray knows how to "sell" policy. It is no accident that he and Herrnstein, a longtime devotee to the heritability of intelligence, coauthored *The Bell Curve.*

The Bell Curve has also brilliantly exploited the ongoing American economic upheaval that is savaging working-class and poor Whites. But their anxiety has far more to do with a profound and irreparable rift in the old-world economic order since the 1973 OPEC oil embargo (see Neuberger and Tyson, 1980) than with the specter of "reverse discrimination." While various politicians, (especially Senator Jesse Helms), have successfully placed the blame for this economic angst squarely upon the shoulders of ethnic and racial minorities, the standard of living for most Americans has declined since 1973 (Phillips, 1990), with working-class women and minorities disproportionately affected (Coontz, 1992; Phillips, 1990). By appealing to historic (and Darwinian) notions of white entitlement to society's "goodies" and attributing merit to heredity while ignoring issues of gender bias in testing and employment, *The Bell Curve* plays to conservative Whites without splitting this powerful, and increasingly angry, electoral constituency over gender. In other words, the authors get to have their political cake and eat it too, by telling too many white Americans the lies they halfheartedly believe (Hacker, 1992).

Finally, if affirmative action has greatly reshaped or warped the workplace, as Herrnstein and Murray claim, there should be some empirical evidence to reveal these drastic changes, especially at the upper levels of management were merit supposedly reigns. However, the current reality is that women and minorities "hold just 5 percent" of senior-level executive jobs and tend to quit up to two and one-half times as frequently as white males (Galen and Palmer, 1995, p. 60). White managers, in particular, are perceived as being willing to mentor white employees, while concurrently holding lower expectations for minority employees (Galen and Palmer, 1995).

If the authors seem unperturbed by such messy realities, American businesses are not. As the authors of a recent article in *Business Week* stated, "The attrition of minorities and women from the ranks of Corporate America is nothing new. What is surprising is that after years of trying to improve, companies are still so often seen as inhospitable places" (Galen and Palmer, 1995, p. 60). Herrnstein and Murray are correct in calling for a new and vigorous debate over affirmative action. In many respects, it has been a program that has been designed to fail through half measures and inconsistent enforcement. Unfortunately, Herrnstein and Murray seem far more interested in reinventing social Darwinism by conjuring up notions of the "advanced race" for political gain than in addressing the inequities in employment faced by most Americans. In the final analysis, *The Bell Curve* rings false.

References

Baker, E. L., Stites, R. (1991). Trends in testing in the USA. In Furhman, S. and Malen, B., eds., *The politics of curriculum and testing: The 1990 yearbook of the Politics of Education Association,* 139-157. New York: The Falmer Press.

Bannister, R. C. (1979). *Social Darwinism: Science and myth in Anglo-American social thought.* Philadelphia: Temple University Press.

Clarke, E. H., M.D. (1873). *Sex in education or a fair chance for the girls.* Boston: James R. Osgood.

Coontz, S. (1992). *The way we never were: American families and the nostalgia trap.* New York: Basic Books.

Cramer, R. B. (1992). *What it takes.* New York: Random House.

Cremin, L. E. (1961). *The transformation of the school: Progressivism in American education, 1876-1957.* New York: Vintage Books.

Cubberley, E. P. (1919). *Education in the United States: A study and interpretation of American educational history.* Boston: Houghton Mifflin Company.

Davis, A. Y. (1981). *Women, race and class.* New York: Vintage Books.

Ehrenreich, B. and English, D. (1978). *For her own good: 150 years of the experts' advice to women.* New York: Anchor Books.

Galen, M. and Palmer, A. T. (1995, August 14). Diversity: Beyond the numbers game. *Business Week,* 60-61.

Gusfield, J. R. (1963). *Symbolic crusade: Status politics and the American temperance movement.* Urbana: University of Illinois Press.

Hacker, A. (1992). *Two nations: Black and white, separate, hostile, unequal.* New York: Charles Scribners' Sons.

Haldeman, H. R. (1994). *The Haldeman diaries: Inside the Nixon White House.* New York: G.P. Putman's Sons.

Herrnstein, R. J. and Murray, C. (1994). *The Bell Curve: Intelligence and class structure in American life.* New York: The Free Press.

Hofstadter, R. (1955). *Social Darwinism in American thought,* rev. ed. Boston: Beacon Press.

House, E. R. and Haug, C. (1995, Summer). Riding *The Bell Curve:* A review. *Educational Evaluation and Policy Analysis, 17,* (2), 263-272.

Judges, D. P. (1992, Spring). Bayonets for the wounded: Constitutional paradigms and disadvantaged neighborhoods. *Hastings Law Review, 19,* 599-714.

Lugg, C. A. (1996). *For God and country: Conservatism and American school policy.* New York: Peter Lang.

Murray, C. (1984). *Losing ground: American social policy, 1950-1980.* New York: Basic Books.

National Review. (1957, August 24). Why the South must prevail. *The National Review,* 4, 148-149.

Neuberger, E. and Tyson, L. D., eds. (1980). *The impact of international economic disturbances on the Soviet Union and Eastern Europe: Transmission and response.* New York: Pergamon Press.

Persell, C. H. (1977). *Education and inequality: The roots and results of stratification in American's schools.* New York: The Free Press.

Phillips, K. P. (1969). *The emerging Republican majority.* New Rochelle: Arlington House.

Phillips, K. P. (1990). *The politics of rich and poor: Wealth and the American electorate in the Reagan aftermath.* New York: Random House.

Sadker, M. and Sadker, D. (1994). *Failing at fairness: How our schools cheat girls.* New York: Touchstone.

Sangster, M. E. (1901). *Winsome womanhood.* New York: Fleming H. Revell.

Spring, J. (1994). *The American school, 1642-1993,* 3rd ed. New York: McGraw-Hill.

Tyack, D. B. (1974). *The one best system: A history of American urban education.* Cambridge: Harvard University Press.

Vidal, G. (1993). *United States: Essays 1952-1993.* New York: Random House.

Woodward, C. V. (1974). *The strange career of Jim Crow,* 3rd rev. ed. New York: Oxford University Press.

25 QUESTIONING "THE WAY WE ARE HEADED"

KYLE L. PECK

In chapter 21, "The Way We Are Headed," Richard Herrnstein and Charles Murray "speculate about the impact of cognitive stratification on American life and government" (1994, p. 509). Their speculation is quite depressing, as they predict increased cognitive stratification, an isolated cognitive elite walled off in protected havens similar to those currently found in Third World nations, and a continued deterioration of the quality of life experienced by the cognitively disadvantaged. They predict that the political power of the cognitive elite (a group they identify as approximately 5 percent of American families and between 10 and 15 percent of the voters) will continue to increase, while increasing numbers of people at the low end of the cognitive ability distribution become "increasingly expendable in economic terms" and "unable to perform that function so basic to human dignity: putting more into the world than they take out" (p. 520).

The result, as Herrnstein and Murray see it, is a nation in which many communities do not have the cognitive resources necessary to sustain themselves and in which "a coalition of the cognitive elite and the affluent continues to accept the main tenets of the welfare state but are increasingly frightened of and hostile toward the recipients of help" (p. 523). They believe that child care will become a government responsibility in urban areas, that more shelters will be constructed to eliminate homelessness and to "reassert control over public places," and that stricter responses to crime will be instituted, including the use of technology to enforce "house arrest." They believe that the underclass will grow and will be increasingly geographically concentrated and that racism will increase, resulting in a "custodial state" they describe as a "high tech and more lavish version of the Indian reservation for some substantial minority of the nation's population, while the rest of America tries to go about its business" (p. 526).

It seems clear that the primary purpose of chapter 21 is to frighten the reader into changing current policy. Throughout the book the authors contend that the current system of welfare and remedial programs is ineffective, and they suggest a host of policy changes (in what seems to me as perhaps the ultimate demonstration of their contention that members of the cognitive elite will exert increasingly inappropriate levels of influence on policy [see top of page 518]).

WHERE ELSE MIGHT WE BE HEADED?

Herrnstein and Murray use this image of "the way we are headed" to call for major shifts in social policy. Are there other likely alternatives, or is the future predicted in *The Bell Curve* inevitable unless we abandon our programs to improve the lives of the disadvantaged? In the remainder of this chapter I argue that: (1) While there is a neurological foundation upon which intelligence rests, intelligence can be developed to a sufficient extent that an amplification of strategies designed to help the disadvantaged would be more productive than the reversal of current policies called for in *The Bell Curve*; (2) investigations of environmental influence on the development of intelligence should focus on the presence of cognitive challenge, cognitive mentoring, and modeling rather than factors such as income and education level of parents, which are only indirectly related to cognitive development; and (3) differences in challenge and mentoring are likely causes of much of what appears to be the heritability of IQ and the differences in intelligence among races. After expanding on these three ideas, I propose that our current course may not be leading to high-tech reservations for the cognitively disadvantaged but rather toward a society in which acceptable levels of cognitive functioning can be developed in all individuals with normally functioning nervous systems.

THE MODIFIABILITY OF COGNITIVE ABILITY

The Bell Curve presents many correlations between cognitive ability and other variables, and demonstrates that in almost all cases, cognitive ability is a better predictor than socioeconomic status or level of education. As other authors in this book have pointed out, correlation does not imply causation. Relationships between IQ and social problems do not mean that IQ caused the social problems. Some other factor or combination of factors may be influencing both IQ and the variables reported as correlated with it. But let's assume for the moment (as Herrnstein and Murray warned us not to and then did) that there is a causal link between IQ and other variables. A response more obvious than "So, let's create social programs that work for recipients with low cognitive ability" or "So, let's abandon attempts to lift people from poverty" might be "So, let's expand our efforts to find ways to improve cognitive ability." Herrnstein and Murray predicted and tried to fend off this reaction by presenting in chapter 17 what they considered to be evidence that attempts to improve cognitive ability have been ineffective. Despite a rather bleak history of attempts to raise IQ (Spitz, 1986), I feel compelled to propose that IQ can be improved, and that other factors (such as ethics and decision making) more directly related to the detrimental effects Herrnstein and Murray attribute to low IQ are much more easily modifiable. I challenge the assumption that cognitive ability is not modifiable and the recommendations that flow from this assumption.

IS IMPROVING COGNITIVE ABILITY DESIRABLE?

Suppose we could improve cognitive ability. Would that be important? Herrnstein and Murray report that a drop of three points in IQ has serious implications (p. 365). Conversely, an increase of three points must also have important implications. They report that programs successful in increasing IQ tend to achieve these increases by elevating scores at the low end of the distribution, as if that is disappointing news (p. 390), but isn't that precisely where we would choose the gains to occur? Changes at the low end of the spectrum would, according to Herrnstein and Murray's argument, have the greatest influence on reducing unwed pregnancy, crime, unemployment, and other problems.

To further discourage attempts to raise cognitive ability, Herrnstein and Murray argue that it's really where you are in the distribution of cognitive ability that makes a difference, and that if we lift the low end they will still be at the bottom (p. 309). But let's think about that. While where you are in the distribution may influence how well you can compete with others in the distribution, does it influence whether you will have a baby out of wedlock or commit violent crimes? These social problems are associated with levels of cognitive ability (or perhaps to levels of a specific aspect of cognitive ability) rather than how your ability compares to the rest of the distribution. There are benefits to be realized by raising the cognitive ability of a population, especially if the gains are concentrated in individuals at the lower end of the spectrum, and, according to Herrnstein and Murray, even if these gains reflect only a few points in IQ.

IS IMPROVING COGNITIVE ABILITY POSSIBLE?

Let's begin this discussion by reviewing what intelligence, or "cognitive ability," is. In *The Bell Curve* it is described as "a measure of a person's capacity for complex mental work" (p. 4). Contemporary scholars in educational psychology and learning systems design believe that complex mental work involves the functioning of the nervous system, the learner's base of knowledge and experience, affective factors, and cognitive strategies. In other words, people consistently demonstrating higher cognitive ability may have well-developed nervous systems, richer pools of experience, broader knowledge, better attitudes toward learning and other forms of mental work, and more and better-refined processes with which to acquire information and make judgments. Researchers in this area also tend to agree that a compounding occurs: Those advanced in these ways will continue to advance more rapidly, drawing on the strength these factors offer in learning situations. The strong get stronger, faster.

David Perkins, a colleague of Herrnstein and Murray's at Harvard, a prolific author on the development of thinking skills and a collaborator with Herrnstein in the early 1980s on a project that raised IQ scores of Venezuelan children, recently published a Theory of Learnable Intelligence (1995). (Project Intelligence, a project involving both Perkins and Herrnstein, is discussed later and is mentioned briefly in *The Bell Curve,* but none of Perkins's work, beliefs, or theory can be found in *The Bell Curve*'s 800 pages.)

Perkins's Theory of Learnable Intelligence proposes that intelligence has neural, experiential, and reflective "dimensions," that these dimensions interact to determine cognitive capability, and that experiential and reflective intelligence can, in fact, be learned (Perkins, 1995).

Perkins contends that the neural dimension of intelligence is influenced by genetics and maturation and that it forms the infrastructure for cognitive ability. Neural factors influence general intelligence as measured by intelligence tests, but Perkins contends that people should not "think of themselves as imprisoned by their native neurology" (p. 105), since the experiential and reflective dimensions play such pivotal roles. The "experiential dimension" of intelligence reflects a large and constantly growing pool of context-specific knowledge. It is the "accumulated knowledge and know-how"—the "specialized knowledge thoroughly internalized through extended experience" (p. 107)—that contributes to thinking in a particular situation or domain. The reflective dimension of intelligence contributes "strategies for various intellectually challenging tasks, attitudes conducive to persistence, systematicity, and imagination in the use of one's mind, and habits of self-monitoring and management" (p. 103). It is seen as the control system governing the resources offered by neural and experiential dimensions.

The neural, experiential, and reflective dimensions of intelligence work together, "amplifying the impact of one another" (p. 109), making distinctive contributions, and only partially compensating for each other's limitations. The neural dimension supports the development of the experiential and reflective dimensions and supports the development of general human talents. The experiential dimension supports day-to-day expert thinking and allows the formation of complex routines that simplify life and allow concentration on more challenging tasks and the reflective dimension allows us to respond to novel situations for which our experiential intelligence is not prepared and allows us to think in creative ways. Perkins contends that intelligence is "learnable" because, although neural intelligence appears relatively fixed, the experiential and reflective dimensions of intelligence develop.

Important insights into this theory of learnable intelligence become clearer following Perkins's analogy with the development of a hypothetical construct "AQ," or "general athletic ability," during which he reminds us that an athlete's development is determined to an extent by inherited capabilities, but that these inherited capabilities interact with diet, coaching, practice, and other experiences. He points out that attempts to raise general athletic ability, after a certain point in the athlete's development, will be difficult, although it will be quite possible to improve tennis-playing ability by coaching in tennis, soccer ability by work in soccer, and so on. This is a crucial point in interpreting *The Bell Curve* and in setting social policy.

Perkins acknowledges the rather dismal history of attempts to raise intelligence, but cites four important examples of efforts that have been successful. He also reminds readers that while attempts to raise general intelligence (IQ) might produce less-than-exciting results, attempts to improve experiential and reflective aspects of intelligence—the aspects that control the undesirable consequences relayed in *The Bell Curve*—can be very productive. In numerous studies, attempts to improve IQ through training in decision making, reasoning, and ethics have produced modest, if any, improvements in IQ, but have demonstrated that growth in the targeted areas does occur. That's good news that should not be swept under the carpet when setting social policy, because these aspects of intelligent behavior more directly control behavior than general IQ. (Does a woman become pregnant because of inadequate general intelligence or because of shortcomings in the practical skills of decision making?)

Despite a chapter devoted to dispelling the thought that cognitive ability can be raised, Herrnstein and Murray do, in several places, display their belief that environmental influences play an important role and that significant progress in this area may be possible in the near future. Perhaps due to Herrnstein's involvement in Project Intelligence (with Perkins), which raised the IQ of Venezuelan children by .4 standard deviation (about 6.5 points) more than gains experienced by a control group, *The Bell Curve* includes the following concessions, among others:

1. Intelligence as measured by IQ tests possibly can be increased by interventions after children enter school.
2. Since cognitive ability is not completely inherited, it will be possible someday to raise the intelligence of children.
3. Maybe new teaching technologies will improve education for people with the lowest IQs.
4. In a timeframe as short as two decades, environmental changes may narrow the racial gap in IQ scores.
5. Schools of the 1990s are better than in the 1950s. If we assume that education affects cognitive ability, then increased investment especially benefits students at the lower segment of the socioeconomic continuum.

Herrnstein and Murray contend that since social pathologies are found more frequently among individuals with low IQ, these
problems are reduced as IQ increases. Indeed, the study of IQ
indicates that such cognitive improvements occur most quickly at the
lowest end of the distribution. Why then should we not formulate a
national strategy to increase IQ? If IQ is 20 percent to 30 percent
inheritable (or, as some argue, 50 percent to 60 percent), why not?
Whatever the percentage, the authors contend, "eliminating the
disadvantages that afflict people in poor surroundings should increase
their relative cognitive functioning" (p. 390).

Pay close attention to the last sentence. Like many others,
they assume that improving environments to build IQ involves the
removal of disadvantages rather than the addition of crucial influences that may be missing. Consider, for example, a single variable,
"cognitive challenge."

COGNITIVE CHALLENGE

"Environment," as a variable in a scientific study of cognitive ability,
is silly. It is a compilation of many factors, some of which may be very
important, while others clearly are not. Socioeconomic status (SES)
is not much better. Herrnstein and Murray described the ineffective-
ness of "environment" as a variable in the struggle to raise intelligence
and began to look inside environment for characteristics of its critical
aspects. Much to their surprise, the authors contend, evidence is
mounting that whatever variation remains for the environment to
explain (40 percent of the variation, if heritability is assumed to be
.6), little can be attributed to shared environments produced by
families. Environmental influences that individuals experience, they
conclude, are unknown at present.

Which aspects of environment might we realistically expect
to influence cognitive ability? Affluence? Only indirectly. Education
of the parent or parents? Perhaps, but only to the extent that
education results in the development of cognitive strategies in the

parent that are made visible to and are transferred to the child through social interactions. By looking at intelligence with a new lens, such as that offered by Perkins's Theory of Learnable Intelligence, we can make different predictions about the most important sources of variation in the development of intelligence.

Let us begin with the assumption that neural intelligence, experiential intelligence, and reflective intelligence all play important and complementary roles. What factors might influence each, and which of these factors can we manipulate? Neural intelligence, for the most part, is genetically determined. While the effects for nutritional interventions may indicate some neural influence, they may also influence attention or motivation. It seems that working in the neural domain offers little promise of increasing cognitive ability. Experiential intelligence is built through the constant stream of interactions that make up work and daily life. While this might suggest something as nebulous as environment as a factor in intelligence, certain aspects of the environment would obviously have more impact than others. For example, "activity" might be a more appropriate variable, probing the extent to which the child engages in active rather than passive experiences—for example, building a fort or learning to play an instrument rather than watching television. Remember, however, that reflective intelligence influences the contents of experiential intelligence.

It is when we consider reflective intelligence that significant opportunities for developing intelligence emerge. Remember that reflective intelligence is the set of strategies used when faced with various intellectually challenging tasks and when interpreting and making sense of unusual events, and that it encompasses attitudes conducive to persistence, self-monitoring, self-management, systematicity, and imagination. How might reflective intelligence be acquired? Perhaps it might be developed by repeatedly facing cognitive challenges, by repeatedly receiving expert mentoring while engaged with these challenges, by repeatedly witnessing experts model reflective strategies while engaged in cognitive challenge, and by engaging in activities designed and delivered by educators to develop thinking skills, problem solving, logic, ethics, and creativity.

Could differences in these variables (challenge, mentoring, modeling, and instruction in reflective skills) be sufficient to cause what Herrnstein and Murray appear willing to attribute to genetic differences among races? They propose that environments would need to be vastly different to cause differences of the magnitude displayed by different races, and that differences of such magnitude are difficult to imagine. Consider, however, the compounding that takes place. If children are engaged in cognitively challenging experiences, if they see experts modeling successful strategies, if experts are available to help them think through their strategies in novel and challenging situations, and if they are trained to use promising strategies, growth can occur. But perhaps more important, this growth will facilitate further growth, which will, in turn, facilitate even more growth. A compounding effect that causes the strong to get stronger means that the environments need not be that different to cause ultimate differences to be sizable. Perhaps this is why it is difficult to predict adult IQ from measures taken before children reach age six. It may be that during this time their reflective strategies and what educator Ted Sizer might call the "habits of mind" undergo rapid development and compounding.

Might the environments of Blacks, Whites, and Asians be different enough in the variables that might influence reflective intelligence to cause a difference in it that might compound to the extent documented in *The Bell Curve?* Yes. While Herrnstein and Murray point out that public education has surely improved since the 1950s (especially for Blacks), great disparities remain between predominately Black and predominately White schools in America. While there are certainly a number of fine teachers in virtually all schools, and while the gap may have closed to an extent, great disparities in virtually all aspects of schooling still exist. As Jonathan Kozol (1991) describes in *Savage Inequalities,* "urban schools were, by and large, extraordinarily unhappy places. With few exceptions, they reminded me of 'garrisons' or 'outposts' in a foreign nation" (p. 5).

Factors in the home are at work as well. A higher percentage of Black and a lower percentage of Asian parents are single parents, and many urban Blacks with reflective skills to pass on have multiple jobs. Both factors reduce the time available for parent/child interaction, time that is necessary to pass on the skills and to allow the high-level interactions that produce reflective intelligence. In addition, there exists a great disparity in terms of the availability of many of new technologies that engage students in meaningful cognitive challenge and the people who know how to put children in touch with them. While children in some communities use on-line encyclopedias and "surf the Internet" for ideas to include in their multimedia reports, children in other communities watch TV.

While the suppositions I offer are far from conclusive evidence, I'll end by urging readers to consider another view of "The Way We Are Headed." Remember, people were very ready to give up on air flight after centuries of attempts made it look futile. But shortly after the Wright Brothers made a few very short "hops" across a sandy field, major breakthroughs were achieved and the dream of flight was realized. It's time for us to realize, not abort, a far more important dream—the development of new levels of cognitive ability. Please consider the following alternative to the predictions of Herrnstein and Murray.

THE WAY WE ARE HEADED: A SECOND OPINION

Based initially on the objective evidence presented in *The Bell Curve,* funding for research on the development of cognitive ability will increase dramatically. Researchers will accept evidence in *The Bell Curve* that highlights the importance of cognitive ability in everyday life but will reject faulty interpretations and recommendations for social policy based on these faulty interpretations. Instead, researchers who suspect that general intelligence (if a worthwhile notion at all) is a composite of multiple factors, many of which can be developed, will redouble their efforts to determine which aspects of intelligent behavior are most closely tied to individual social problems. They will conduct research needed to identify ways to develop levels of these

390   Kyle L. Peck

dimensions of intelligence that dramatically reduce the incidence of crime, unwed pregnancy, and unemployment. Inequitable funding practices across the nation's school districts will be seen as unconscionable, revenues to support schools will be allocated equitably, and the schools and services provided to all students will be "reinvented" to reflect the needs of different communities. Modern technologies will be harnessed not to provide "house arrest" but to provide engaging, cognitively challenging activities to be used at school and at home and to provide expert coaching in skills seen as components of reflective intelligence. Numerous combinations of promising strategies and technological tools will emerge, tailored to fit the needs of different communities and individuals, and students from across the cognitive ability spectrum will experience unparalleled growth.

Sure, that picture may be too optimistic. But is my scenario as optimistic as Herrnstein and Murray's was pessimistic? As usual, reality probably lies somewhere between these extreme views. The way we are headed will be determined by the actions of a relatively small number of people. Reject the notion that little can be done to improve cognitive ability, especially in the areas that most directly influence real-world decisions. Accept, instead, the premise that important aspects of cognitive ability *can* be developed, and mount, or at least support, efforts to prove it.

References

Herrnstein, R. and Murray, C. (1994). *The Bell Curve: Intelligence and class structure in American life.* New York: The Free Press.
Kozol, J. (1991). *Savage inequalities: Children in America's schools.* New York: Crown Publishers.
Perkins, D. N. (1995). *Learnable intelligence.: Breaking the IQ barrier.* New York: The Free Press.
Spitz, H. H. (1986). *The raising of intelligence: A selected history of attempts to raise retarded intelligence.* Hillsdale, NJ: Lawrence Erlbaum Associates.

26 ON REFUSING ONE'S PLACE: THE DITCHDIGGER'S DREAM

DEBORAH P. BRITZMAN · ALICE J. PITT

Terrifying visions of sex and violence, of bodily destruction and monstrous procreation, are served up for children's delight and, according to some critics, their instruction.
—Mandy Merck, 1993, p. 207

A standard horror [movie's] format calls for a variety of positions and character sympathies in the early phases of the story, but, as the plot goes on, a consolidation at both levels (story and cinematography), and in the final phase a fairly tight organization around the functions of victim and hero (which may be collapsed into one figure, or alternately, split into many).
—Carol Clover, 1992, p. 8

[I]t is justified to pay the high IQ businessman and engineer more than the low IQ ditch digger, producing some inequality, because that's the only way to make the economy grow and produce more wealth in which the ditch digger can share.
—Richard Herrnstein and Charles Murray, 1994, p. 527

The horror story, as J. A. Cuddon (1991, p. 416) points out in his dictionary of literary terms, is a genre meant to shock the reader "and/or perhaps induces a feeling of repulsion or loathing." Ghosts, demonic pacts, diabolical possession, and vampires (among other horrible creatures) are its major players; their locale covers various kinds of hell. The economy of affects structured by horror include "intense grief, an overwhelming feeling of irredeemable loss, acute fear, irrational foreboding or physical pain" (p. 417). Typically, then, horror stories recount tales of violence, crime, and irredeemable chaos: Things are out of place or things revolt in their place. Simply put, something is horribly wrong in the horror story.

For the horror story to take hold, the reader must be willing to suspend disbelief and derive pleasure from being scared and from scaring others. It requires that the pleasures of the reader coincide and therefore identify with the moralism of the teller. The narrator of the tale may have a didactic or moralistic purpose but is hardly capable of admitting the enjoyment that derives from ridding the self of anxiety through the projection of her or his own fears, repressed desires, and neuroses onto the story's characters or into the places of other folks' bedrooms. This structure of pleasure is dependent on the order of the self ordering others and producing those others as otherness. Those who have lost their place and those with little room to maneuver—that is, the narrated—become the objects to be berated.

The notion of losing our place, of being displaced or replaced, or of finding our place haunted may well be the underside of Herrnstein and Murray's last chapter, "A Place for Everyone [And Everyone in His Place]." Noticing this, we begin our chapter with a note on the uses of horror. Ostensibly, chapter 22 is haunted by the ghosts of intelligence and perhaps the desire for a social policy where even the ghosts stay put in their place. Between the dream and the waking thought, before the ditchdigger referred to in the last epigraph jumps into the ditch, covered over by his acceptance of place, and within the social policy that has as its desire the termination of the question, there still remains the anxiety of things not staying put. So, while Herrnstein and Murray's chapter title could also be read ironically, for of course there is a place for everyone on the bell curve—even if one's place is a place of failure—we read this chapter through another lens, one also interested in uncanny places: psychoanalysis. Having a place or being put into one's place should conjure a certain wariness and recall, perhaps, a thought of the one who compulsively puts things in place.

We bring a few psychoanalytic insights to bear on our reading of chapter 22 because behind its seemingly reasonable tone is a view that discontentment and misery stem from refusing the demands for social convention rather than the idea that social convention may well induce misery. We demonstrate how the work of putting things in their place functions much like the work of repression. In the first part of our chapter, we bring Freud's observations to bear on those of Herrnstein and Murray because of their mutual interest in the problem of happiness and how it is possible to be happy in society. To raise such a question means that *un*happiness and its causes must also be considered. But as we shall see, our defenders of the bell curve and our Freud are diametrically opposed in their views of the causes of unhappiness and on the possibility of happiness itself. It may be instructive to think through the antagonistic answers offered from both sides. Briefly, Herrnstein and Murray advocate sexual repression whereas Freud, as a way to come to terms with an Eros beyond its repression, argues for less restriction on the libido. In the last part of this chapter, we argue that what social policy puts at stake is a vision of happiness and liberty. Rather than putting happiness and liberty in its place, what is actually required is a thought that can exceed the limits of place, a thought that can tolerate what de Certeau (cited in Bensmaia, 1986, p. xi) calls "the impossibility of one's own place." Anyone has a right to an everyday not organized by eugenics, family values, or compulsory heterosexuality. The problem of liberty and happiness requires an inessential ethic that can begin, in the words of Derrida (1994, p. 22), to "think the possibility of a step beyond repression."

In *Civilization and its discontents*, Sigmund Freud (1975) calls the compulsion of putting things into place a compulsion for order; he links it to Western civilization's obsession for cleanliness and the compulsion to repeat the cleaning and therefore the finding of dirt. That first place of dirt is, of course, the body. But in linking the body to its social regulation, Freud understands that the compulsion for order is not just for the order of one's own body. Rather, the compulsion is satisfied and provoked through the repetition of ordering others. In Freud's words: "Order is a kind of compulsion to repeat which, when a regulation has been laid down once and for all, decides when, where and how a thing shall be done, so that in every similar circumstance one is spared hesitation and indecision" (p. 30). One is spared a thought; thought itself has been displaced.

At the same time, regulations can never be set down once and for all; hence their repetition. Moreover, the very regulation installed produces not just the limit but the transgression, or at the very least a decision to be made. And with the possibility of a decision comes the possibility of liberty. Wryly, Freud notes the conflict: "The liberty of the individual is no gift of civilization" (p. 32). This is so because liberty demands something other than social compliance and something other than the renunciation of bodily instinct or, in Freud's terms, sexuality. But there is more than this, for behind the renunciation of the instinct resides a hatred for the body, for the body's capacity for a certain pleasure in excess of what the social deems as proper. The compulsion for cleanliness, order, and mastery (of the body) can then be considered a demand for repression. One might say that the insistence that objects stay in their proper place once and for all is a demand that depends upon a hatred for uncertainty, for being out of control, and for the (improper) body.

Certainly a theory of involuntary returns signaled Freud's interest in how individual pathology had its complement in the dynamics of social practices and in the structure of institutions. Within the wish for cleanliness is an obsession for purity, order, and certainty, for the making of boundaries and rules, for putting things into place. Julia Kristeva (1982, p. 41) in her study *The power of horror: an essay on abjection,* terms such a compulsion "a phobia [that] functions under the aegis of censorship and repression." Abjection, Kristeva suggests, "disturbs identity, system, and order" (p. 4). She argues that the one who is haunted by disorder and the intolerable asks the wrong question: "Instead of sounding himself as to his 'being,' he does so concerning his place: 'Where am I?' instead of 'Who am I?'" (p. 8). We will return to this formulation and what it supposes for agency, that is, the capacity to act, near the end of our chapter.

Early on, Herrnstein and Murray ask a deceptively simple question: "how people might live together harmoniously despite fundamental individual differences" (p. 528). The primary difference they engage is intellectual difference; they insist that the measuring of intellect need not inflict misery given the proper social order. They fantasize a nostalgic version of history as a past where "it used to be easier for people who are low in ability to find a valued place than it is now" (p. 536). For these authors, what made life easier were the "valued places" of marriage, parenthood, and neighborhood. They do admit that lots of misery existed back then (and we need only consider how the past lives in the present in legal segregation, economic disfranchisement, antichoice legislation, sodomy laws, and so on). Still, their imperatives of nostalgia demand that all grieve the idea that something was lost between then and now. Whatever its commonsensical appeal—and here it can only appeal to those who situate themselves as outside of such misery— the unsaid in this sort of fantasy, according to de Certeau (1988, p. 85), is that the writing of history is always ambivalent and "the figure of the past keeps its primary value [by] representing *what is lacking*." For Herrnstein and Murray, the lost object—the everpresent lack—is the sort of rewards and punishments doled out for social compliance, for staying in one's place.

In their section called "Making It Easier to Live a Virtuous Life," they lament the complicity of the U.S. criminal system where punishment is no longer meaningful and where the state has gone soft on punishing criminal acts. That the United States has one of the largest populations of people in prison in the world, that chain gangs are being reinstituted, and that prisoner rights are becoming an oxymoron do not seem to matter here. For remember, we are speaking of haunted places where suffering from reminiscences imposes its own kind of order. These authors jump from lamentations of criminality unpunished to what they imagine as the demise of state-sanctioned heterosexual marriage. In both instances, they seem to argue that those with low ability are given plenty of excuses to commit crimes and hardly any reason to get married. Their concern is with aimless men, even as they seem to address only men already in place.

For Herrnstein and Murray, what seems to tie the criminal to the one who refuses to marry is a moral aimlessness, ostensibly induced by the loss of moral codes and severe forms of punishment. In the case of marriage, Herrnstein and Murray argue there is no longer any reason (for men) to get married because sex outside of marriage and children outside of marriage are no longer stigmatized as they were from the time of Nathanial Hawthorne's *Scarlet Letter* up to the 1970s, when pregnant unmarried girls were expelled from school and, if white and middle class, sent away to homes for unwed mothers. They write, "The sexual revolution is the most obvious culprit" (p. 544) and thus introduce another kind of ghost, the so-called spirit of an age. And while the spirits of feminism, gay and lesbian civil rights, the civil rights movement, the antiwar movement, children's rights movements, alternative education, and other social movements for a less authoritarian social systems seem to haunt the margins of this chapter, for these authors, any movement away from phobic state authority, fundamentalist family values, the law of the father, and moral certitude is a descent into hell. In this horror story, the "culprit" is the body in revolt. These sorts of accusations are reminiscent of Kristeva's definition of phobia, what she refers to as a barricaded discourse, one which functions under the "aegis" of repression and censorship.

Herrnstein and Murray recommend sexual repression through marriage and the policy of "return[ing] marriage to its formerly unique legal status" (p. 545), as if such a status were not already operative and inflected through every attempt at antigay and lesbian legislation. Without acknowledging any social contestation against the definition of the family, their policy would further consolidate present efforts to foreclose legal redress for single parents, gays and lesbians, children, and those who would live without state sanction. Punitive measures of thoroughly coupling heterosexuality with the state apparatus are suggested, banishing to the margins of illegality and unintelligibility the question of how individuals and groups choose to organize their own economy of affection and sociality. The justification for such measures stems from Herrnstein and Murray's philosophy of value already bonded by marriage and the production of children within marriage: "You occupy a valued place if other people would miss you if you were gone. . . . If a single person would miss you and no one else, you have a fragile hold on your place in society, no matter how much that one person cares for you" (p. 535). As if to assure the anxious reader, it is not the "average" or "normal" American who is fragile, unless it is the fragility that comes from the feeling that the "normal" are becoming a minority. The social policies suggested in *The Bell Curve* are meant to rein in "the discontented," those who refuse to differentiate between, say, a marriage and anonymous sex.

Indeed, while these authors insist they are concerned with human dignity, the rules and regulations they offer depend on a society that narrows the range of identifications to those of "family values" and their attendant disavowals. The very possibility that human dignity requires no justification, that there is, in Levinas's terms, "a dignity of intelligibility" (1993, p. 1)—whether understood or not by the larger social—a dignity that knows no rules, boundaries, or constriction, is unthinkable in *The Bell Curve* authors' formula. What must be foreclosed is a value of singularity and the value of the question. If value depended on social regulation and social regulation is organized through exclusionary practices, then all that can be valued is the social regulation of conformity. Who shall miss the stranger?

For Freud, the problem of happiness is the problem of the libido, or the pleasure principle. In *Civilization and its discontents,* Freud suggests there are three sources of human suffering: ". . . the superior power of nature, the feebleness of our own bodies and the inadequacy of the regulations which adjust the mutual relationships of human beings in the family, the state and society" (1975, p. 23). It is the last form of suffering that is the most painful, the one requiring, as a prerequisite for joining with others, the renunciation of instinct (a renunciation that is grounded in the inadequacy of its own demand). What must be renounced and then sublimated through the structures of compulsory heterosexuality, monogamy, and child legitimacy is sexuality. Freud claims that "civilization" can barely tolerate the idea of sexual pleasure without utility, without reason or justification. Indeed, he argues that civilization "is only prepared to tolerate [sex] because there is so far no substitute for it as a means of propagating the human race" (p. 42). The very strictures of sexual regulation and their command that individuals view sexuality as rational utility rather than pleasure that wants no justification induces unhappiness.

But Freud also acknowledges something more. It has to do with the fact that while the grounds for the social are in conflict with the individual, even as they set in motion conflicts between the individual and the group, the sorts of solutions that are offered— namely, the sublimation of love and the disavowal of conflict itself—foreclose the possibility of engaging conflict in ways that do not produce the very discontentment that civilization attempts to restrict. Essentially, where there is civilization there will be discontentment. In acknowledging the conflict between instinct and the forces of social repression, Freud can offer "no consolation." He understands that strengthening the strictures of the super ego through the severity of punishment, censorship, and repression can only lead to individuals who identify with the aggressor. And in the process of identifying with the aggressor, the individual introjects bodily hatred and projects this hatred onto another object.

The struggle between Eros and Death is what preoccupied Freud's concluding thoughts in *Civilization and its discontents*. The text was written between the world wars and Freud was convinced that civilization itself, however defined, produces the very social suffering it must disavow through its strictures and laws. It disavows suffering through its insistence on the impossible commandment of "Love thy neighbor as thyself" and thus promises something that is impossible to deliver: a social without conflict. Can unhappiness be avoided? Or, more specifically, what becomes of a social that cannot tolerate what is beyond repression? Freud was also clear on this point: "It almost seems as if the creation of a great human community would be most successful if no attention had to be paid to the happiness of the individual" (1975, p. 77). But what of the pursuit of autonomy if no attention is paid to happiness?

The social harmony imagined by the authors of *The Bell Curve*, a harmony fashioned from a nostalgic view of a past that never was, distinguishes less between happiness and unhappiness than it does between true and false happiness. One succeeds in finding true happiness when one accepts one's "place" in the social matrix of IQ and within socially sanctioned heterosexual coupling. What this vision of happiness cannot tolerate is anyone's enjoyment of what it seeks to repress. Contra Freud, *The Bell Curve*'s vision of happiness relies on the conflation of individual desire and the laws of the social. It also relies on the conflation of intelligence with moral righteousness.

Yet, as we have seen, Freud offers no way out of the dilemma of the impasse between the instinctual demands of sexuality and the social demands of repression. Indeed, his famous pronouncement that healing, education, and government are the three impossible professions seems to invite—at least for those who demand closure—the conclusions reached by Herrnstein and Murray. A radically different perspective is developed by Cornelius Castoriadis (1994), who reconfigures the impossibility of these professions, renaming them psychoanalysis, pedagogy, and politics. What makes these professions impossible becomes for Castoriadis the very grounds of possibility for any ongoing project of democracy. He rejects the notion of a natural social order and argues instead that societies institute themselves and create their own means of reproduction through the institutions and imaginary significations that give meaning to their members. These twin

dynamics of conflict—individual and institutional—are the necessary conditions for a democratic state that practices a politics of
autonomy. For Castoriadis, conflict within individuals and within
societies holds the potential for something beyond the acceptance of
one's place, namely the capacity to question injustice.

What Castoriadis has in mind when he refers to a politics
of autonomy is not the unleashing of individual libido (as if that
were possible), nor is it chaos at the level of the social. Rather, the
contention Castoriadis holds is that, while institutions push for
social stasis or conformity, the individual capacity to exceed the
institution is an ever-present and creative potential. What is at
stake is the possibility of autonomy, that is, the "collective,
self-reflexive and deliberate activity" (1994, p. 7) of its members to
call into question and to alter its institutions. He contrasts the
nongiveness of autonomy with a notion of the state as heteronomous. There, the society's role in self-institution and reproduction
is hidden from view, disguised as the predetermined order of the
natural. A heteronomous society, in Castoriadis's view, relies
heavily on the production of conformable individuals, that is,
individuals who have internalized without question the existing
social institutions and their place within them. Such a society is
what Kristeva terms "phobic."

Repetition takes form in a heteronomous society, both at
the level of the individual and the collective, as an obsessive
preoccupation with "real or symbolic representations of a perennial
meaning and an imaginary immortality in which everyone is supposed to participate. . . ." (Castoriadas, 1994, p. 11). What
repetition wards off is death, whether figured as the specter of
mortality that we all face or "the meaninglessness of meaning"
(p. 11). This should recall de Certeau's earlier claim of "the
impossibility of place," where everyone is precarious precisely because we are human. And yet social policy in a heteronomous society
must disavow its own tenuous grounds. To do so it represents
community as already given, as a place-holder waiting for occupants.
A politics of autonomy, however, begins with a view of community

as nongiven and as something to do. The work of community is much like the work of the individual engaged in analysis.

An investigation and working through of structures of repetition may free the radical imaginary of the individual and permit the development of the capacity to engage in self-reflexive deliberation. The central question for such a working through is not, as it must be for the compulsive phobic described by Kristeva, "Where am I?" Nor is the process of working through exhausted by articulating a response to the question "Who am I?" for this question ultimately runs aground in the confrontation with the Other. Rather, what characterizes analytical work is the ongoing alteration of the self as a project of becoming. The question "What is the place of the agent?" becomes refused since it forecloses the potential for liberty in favor of authority, order, and certitude.

An inessential ethic centers *becoming*, as a question of practice, instead of *being*, as a state of existence. It is *not* place that conditions autonomy but the actions of making relations. What becomes valued and, indeed, necessary is the interest in putting to question the justice and appropriateness of any law, relation, or practice. But the making of ethics now raises a significant problem that returns us to Freud and his insistence that there are three impossible professions: healing, education, and government.

Castoriadis's project of linking together psychoanalysis, pedagogy, and politics suggests that these social practices are impossible—and not merely difficult—for two reasons. First, he argues that the project of developing self-reflective subjectivity relies on the use of "an autonomy which does not yet exist" (1994, p. 6) and cannot be given. Second, he points to the difficulties inherent in trying to help individuals develop into autonomous human beings in a society that teaches us "to absorb and internalize existing institutions" (p. 7). Given these two dynamics, the value of an individual cannot reside in where he or she is but must begin with what he or she can become. The potential and singularity of becoming is dependent on the free play of critique and the capacity to become worried when critique becomes foreclosed, repetitious, and phobic.

Herrnstein and Murray, however, desire institutional absorption and hence must emphasize place. But as we have argued, putting things into place shuts out the very problem of a nongiven autonomy that can tolerate democracy and community as something to make. If there can be a social policy that refuses the structure and pleasure of horror, it will have to begin with an idea that can bear the nongiveness of autonomy and the uncertainty of being in no particular place. This, perhaps, is the ditchdigger's dream.

References

Bensmaia, R. (1986). Forward: The Kafka Effect. In Deleuze, G. and Guattari, F. *Kafka: Toward a minor literature*, trans. Dana Polan, ix-xxi. Minneapolis, MN: University of Minnesota Press.

Castoriadas, C. (1994). Psychoanalysis and Politics. In Shamdasani, S. and Muchow, M., eds., *Speculations After Freud: Psychoanalysis, philosophy and culture*, 1-12. New York and London: Routledge.

Clover, C. (1992). *Men, women and chain saws: Gender in the modern horror film*. Princeton, NJ: Princeton University Press.

Cuddon, J. A. (1991) *A dictionary of literary terms and literary theory*, 3rd ed. Oxford: Blackwell.

de Certeau, M. (1988). *The writing of history*, trans. Tom Conley. New York: Columbia University Press.

Derrida, J. (1994). *Specters of Marx: The state of the debt, the work of mourning, and the new international*, trans. Peggy Kamuf. New York and London: Routledge.

Freud, S. (1975). *Civilization and its discontents*, trans. Joan Riviere. London: Hogarth Press.

Kristeva, J. (1982). *Powers of horror: An essay on abjection*, trans. Leon Roudiez. New York: Columbia University

Levinas, E. (1993). *Outside the Subject*, trans. M. Smith. Stanford: Stanford University Press.

Merck, M. 1993. *Perversions: Deviant readings*. London: Vergo.

PART IV

TALKING ABOUT
THE BELL CURVE

27 INTERVIEWING AND FINDING SOUND BITES

RONALD E. CHENNAULT · SHIRLEY R. STEINBERG

When we began this project, we decided to interview prominent speakers, teachers, and political scientists. People such as Cornel West, Angela Davis, bell hooks, Stanley Aronowitz, Paulo Freire, Donaldo Macedo, Michael E. Dyson, Douglas Kellner, Noam Chomsky, Harvey Kaye, Ivor Goodson, and Molefe Asante. Most of our contacts were receptive, so we set up times to interview them. In the middle of our interviewing, the O.J. Simpson verdict came down. Consequently our interviews halted—many of the people we wanted to speak with were "on the circuit," answering questions from across the United States on the issue of this one black man who was acquitted of murdering his white wife and her friend. The irony of our inability to contact some of our interviewees in time for our publication deadline lies in the fact that they were summoned to address the same racist sentiments that ground *The Bell Curve.* Many of our contacts were needed by the media to assuage the temperaments of the enraged (white) masses. Blacks were the recipients of white anger, once again blamed for the ills that have befallen our society. This recovery of racism, as labeled by Aaron Gresson, is exemplified by the response to the verdict and validates Herrnstein and Murray's cry of white victimization.

   While Afrocentrist Molefe Asante denied our interview request due to his refusal to participate in any promotion of *The Bell Curve,* feminist writer bell hooks was not ready to comment, nor did she plan to in the near future. Noam Chomsky told us that he wrote about Herrnstein's first effort along these lines in the early 1970s *(For Reasons of State);* obviously, he was more future-sighted than many of us.

Cultural studies scholar and philosopher Douglas Kellner told us:

> *The Bell Curve* is throwing us a curve ball to get us to duck and not see the problems of American education and society. The problem is not that certain races are inherently inferior, but certain subcultural groups—of every color and ethnicity—are disadvantaged, not given adequate education and opportunity. Resources and action must be directed toward these groups to level the playing field, to provide equal opportunities and in particular to provide better education—through new and innovative programs, providing resources like computers and attendant training and to make an effort to lift up the disadvantaged, to provide hope and not despair.

Marxist historian Harvey Kaye admitted not having read the book but had a visceral reaction to the text. He felt "it signified the attempt by the Right to completely refashion public policy and public opinion on this public policy." Not wanting to specifically address the racial aspect of the book, he acknowledged that many others would focus their remarks on race and went in another direction.

In the past five, ten, twenty years in society, Kaye noted, we've seen three things:

1. The publication of Fukiyama's book *The end of history,* which promotes the argument that history has indeed ended.
2. The rhetoric of free-market education and school choice, and the breakdown of the separation between church and state.
3. [Charles] Murray's argument for ending welfare.

Furthermore, Kaye suggested that there were two dimensions to Herrnstein and Murray's position: "that we all have unequal [intellectual] capacities; and that the cognitive elite should feel legitimate in their accumulation of capital." Kaye concluded with the feeling that the book and its position is crudely ideological in its attempt to justify the existence of the elite.

Ivor Goodson, a prominent scholar with joint academic appointments in the United Kingdom, the United States, and Canada mused about his own history as Phillipe Rushton's colleague at the University of Western Ontario. He spoke of the controversy surrounding Rushton's work, "Evolutionary Biology and Heritable Traits," referred to by Herrnstein and Murray in *The Bell Curve*. Goodson was torn between the concepts of academic freedom and the blatant hatred that Rushton displayed within his "scholarship." Following is Ivor Goodson's account of reviewing the Rushton work in 1989.

SCIENCE AND SOCIAL RESPONSIBILITY BY IVOR S. GOODSON

In responding to *The Bell Curve,* I want to review the controversy surrounding Dr. Rushton of the University of Western Ontario (used as a scholarly resource by Herrnstein and Murray) and his work entitled "Evolutionary Biology and Heritable Traits" and of academic freedom towards a more broadly-based conception of social responsibility. For me the main issue is that of the relationship between science and *social responsibility:* these two matters cannot be divided, they are both crucial and integral.

At the time, there were two presentations in London, Ontario which allowed us to get a closer grasp of what is at issue. First, there had been the play *Einstein* at the Talbot Theater. In this play we saw a world-renowned scientist spending the last years of his life pondering the question of social responsibility and science. As we know, Einstein was partially responsible for the scientific breakthroughs which led to the development of the atomic bomb. However, in the play, we view him speculating on the fact that although all this was "good science," impeccably executed, it was not socially responsible science. Einstein ultimately felt that this called the value of his life's work into question. A second presentation was the film, *Mississippi Burning*. The film showed in graphic detail what may happen when one racial group believes itself to be superior to another racial group. The result was a series of murders, lynchings, house burnings and church bombings. Pushed to an extreme, it can be seen how such a belief in racial superiority can lead to historical episodes like the Nazi treatment of the Jews. It is salutary to remember that much of the Nazi action was underpinned by a well-worked-out theory of racial superiority provided by psychologists and other scientists. We would do well to recall the role of science in such historical episodes.

Moving back to the work of Dr. Rushton, it becomes clear that the issue is not a narrowly defined one of "is this technically good science?"; rather the question should be "is this socially responsible science?" Here widespread testimony from many of the ethnic groups in London and the surrounding communities provides a fairly conclusive response. Without doubt, many, many people feel a sense of anger and despair about this work. It is now up to the university community to listen to those testimonies and make a judgment about Rushton's work. A judgment will be informed not by some narrow definition of whether this is technically competent science (about which I believe in the long run there may be some very serious and substantial questions), but whether it is a socially beneficial science. Here I think the balance of the evidence is fairly overwhelming. Above all, a university's mission should be a humane one of seeking to further equal treatment of women and men of all kinds. If work is conducted which moves us in the other direction, it should be plainly seen as against a university's mission. The issue then, before the academic community as it faces these questions is not, I repeat *is this good science?* Or even, *is this correct science?* But, clearly, *is this socially responsible science?*

I believe the answer for once is fairly clear. For my own part, I would feel deeply ashamed if my university were to defend and/or sponsor a socially irresponsible science. My commitment to university scholarship has always been allied to the ideal that such scholarship would promote the treatment of all men and women as equal. The university may take the view that if scholars want to undertake socially damaging science and if funding agencies are willing to pay for such work, then that is their individual right. Individuals have the right to negotiate with their own consciences. Well—maybe. But what of the issue of *teaching* this socially irresponsible science? Rushton declared to and continues to *teach* his theories. (As does Charles Murray). If we judge his theories to be socially irresponsible, surely this matter should be adjudicated within scholarly circles and the arena of media/public opinion.

Where does this leave us? I can only say it leaves me to defend Rushton's right to continue his studies, even if they are judged as socially irresponsibile. I would not recommend his (or Murray's) suspension from undertaking scholarly work. I would however, question to what extent the academy in general, a university in particular as a bastion of humane and civilized values, or any public media would want its own name associated with his work and with the implicit legitimation of that work. Further, I would be deeply concerned if socially irresponsible science were taught to students. If the academy fails to monitor social responsibility successfully than other groups may come in to do the job instead. In the end, academic freedom will be lost by another route—not just for Rushton, Herrnstein, or Murray, but for all of us.

28 INTERVIEWS

Shirley: Let's talk about your reactions to *The Bell Curve.*

Stanley: The first thing that has to be said about *The Bell Curve* is that it is déjà vu all over again—it repeats a debate that has been going on for decades. The last time was about 20 years ago, when Richard Herrnstein, the coauthor of *The Bell Curve,* and William Shockley, with many others, raised the issue of black inferiority. At that time, a bevy of liberal and radical responses successfully beat back what promised to be a new assault on equality. In fact, a book was published with Noam Chomsky, myself, and others called *The new assault on equality.* But, more significantly perhaps, was Stephen J. Gould's *The mismeasurement of man,* which came out in 1981. At the level of biological scientific analysis, it showed distinctively and irrefutably that all of this psychometric talk was largely fabrication and had nothing beneath it. Herrnstein and Shockley's work was just another attempt to subordinate black people at a time when the United States was going through a very difficult period of history. The Vietnam War was winding to a halt. There was tremendous fear concerning the future of a country which might have to severely cut back its arms budget, its commitment to military spending.

Second, there developed during this period an increase in unemployment, a recession at the middle of the Vietnam War. There was a lot of feeling that this was a very bad time. In that period, recall the gains of the Black Freedom Movement, which had really developed from about 1954 with the Supreme Court decision and 1955 with Rosa Parks refusing to go to the back of the bus. Of course, the Montgomery Bus Boycott followed. There had been 15 years of unbroken progress in the development of a discourse of equality. And the backlash, the attack against this was inevitable. It took place in part with the election of Richard Nixon in 1968. And it became in many ways a conjuncture between the end of the war, the beginning of the recession, and Nixon's election. People feared that the period of tremendous economic expansion and the liberal push for equality were over. This perception pretty much paralleled what went on in the late 1980s and early 1990s. We had a stock market crash in 1987, and, following the crash, significant restructuring of large international corporations. This corporate restructuring initiated a series of layoffs of technical professional as well as industrial workers. We had a new foundation, if you will, for "scapegoatism." Combined with that was the conservative mood against the maintenance of the welfare state and the growth of the social welfare budget in the broader sense.

What we see now is a historical parallel to the attack on Blacks in the early 1970s. The attack on Blacks is not simply gratuitous or demeaning but is designed to establish the intellectual and political basis for the devictimization of Black people—that is to say, the refusal of the historical judgment made by progressive Americans that Blacks suffered systemic discrimination. If one could establish that they were essentially "not worthy" of the compensatory programs that had been put in place for them since the 1960s, then society wouldn't have to spend all this money on education, job training, and welfare. The argument went something like this: "These people are lazy, these people are inferior, these people are not worthy of the kind of support that is represented by the broad programs of the welfare state." Because of the large commitment of this country to equality and to educational opportunity, Blacks must be responsible for their own oppression. Having been granted "equal opportunity," Blacks are now held to the same standard that anyone else would be held to in this country: "You are an individual, if you can't cut it, you deserve to sink."

The Bell Curve provides the intellectual basis for saying "Why throw good money at bad people?" Why support all these programs, when, in fact, these people are less than human? They can be citizens, because we believe in citizenship. They can vote, they can walk the streets—but what we can't do is treat them as if the society is responsible for their poverty and the discrimination that they suffer. That discrimination is really not the issue; the actual issue is what Moynihan and Glaser argued back in 1966: that there was a cultural deterioration of the black family. According to Herrnstein and Murray, this familial deterioration may or may not have a genetic basis. The cause really doesn't matter: Whether you believe it is natural talent or culture, black people simply do not deserve the rights and privileges provided by our society.

The fundamental point to be made about *The Bell Curve* and its predecessors is that none of this can be refuted by facts. Even though Steve Gould, Noam Chomsky, and many others buried the intellectual basis of the Herrnstein/Murray/Shockley thesis, it recurs because it is essentially historically, politically, economically, and culturally based. It is not based on some scientific standard. Thus it cannot be refuted on scientific grounds except at the most abstract intellectual level. In this context, it is a mistake for opponents to engage Herrnstein and Murray at this level. It is a trap, actually, to say "I will debate you fact for fact—we will show that none of the research supports your contentions." I suppose that is okay, but it is really beside the point. What people have to understand is what is entailed by this debate. There is a requirement, at least among conservative forces and a number of erstwhile liberal forces, that ways be found to release the federal government, powerful corporations, and large sections of the upper crust of any responsibility for racial discrimination.

Shirley: So the ideological level is the only honest level in which to engage this discussion?

Stanley: The point we have to face is that America's political commitment to equality in this country has always been dependent on the unique position that the United States holds the global economy and the global polity—namely, that this country has had, at least in its own mind, the resources to broadly distribute its goods among all sections of the population. The point has been not that there would be equality, but that there would be provision for mobility. The educational system has been a major institutional instrument for the achievement of this. Now, what is happening (which I would argue is the most important point) is that we are facing a generalized transformation of our economy. We no longer have a national economy—we have a global economy. The United States stands in relation to that global economy as just another place. Its industrial base, which was at one point awesome, has now been, to a significant degree, dismantled. The people who were most adversely affected by this dismantlement were black people. At the same time, however, white workers, engineers, and people in the professions were economically hurt. Now we are facing what my coauthor William Di Fazio and I call *The jobless future*.

Economic equality does not come easy—and now it is not just Blacks that are being discriminated against, but also the general working class. In the 1990s the lower-middle-class population, both black and white, is being victimized by the internationalization of capital. Under those conditions the attack against Blacks provides a convenient way for Whites to displace their own anger, frustration, and sense of defeat. This displacement is politically unfortunate and inaccurate: white anger should be directed toward the cruel policies of the transnational corporations. *The Bell Curve* provides the basis for this white displacement and also redefines the function of the educational system from providing a broad basis for equality to the establishment of a new and more rigid kind of hierarchy. In this new context, certain people can make it and other people can't—the reason why they can't is that they weren't meant to make it in the first place. According to Herrnstein and Murray, God said "you're just not ready to cut the mustard."

Shirley: Absolutely. So we're back to a viewpoint that god makes choices as to who is worthy to "make it."

Stanley: That's right. And at this point, Social Darwinism comes into the picture in the evolutionary scale; certain people (or the cream) rise to the top.

Shirley: Which means certain people are destined to fail.

Stanley: Right.

Shirley: So we have a recovery of white supremacy.

Stanley: Yes. Also, Francis Galton, Darwin's cousin, co-invented the IQ test to basically act as a sorting machine.

Shirley: Of course, the tests were invented for and based on white males.

Stanley: Right. Basically for Irish, Scottish, and Welsh workers— saying how do we prevent the schools from being flooded by people who don't deserve to be there? We establish a standard, and against that standard, they will not measure up. And the Herrnstein/Murray position reinvents that earlier Social Darwinism to argue on the basis of standard testing: Who can qualify and who cannot? And those who cannot (although Murray vehemently denies it) belong in the scrap heap. They simply do not belong in the precincts of higher education—we have to recognize that those people are just not simply fitted for the intellectual rigor that is required by institutions of higher learning. This goes for academic secondary education as well.

Shirley: So white supremacy becomes civic duty in a sense. A duty to keep the cream at the top.

Stanley: That's right. Because if you don't do that, the country will go down the drain.

Shirley: Herrnstein and Murray can be viewed as saviors in a sense.

Stanley: Yes, they are preventing the country, in the name of democratization and equalization, from sinking into mediocrity. And I think you have to confront that argument. What is it that will make this country or prevent this country from not sinking into this mediocrity? The answer has nothing to do with IQ tests, nothing to do with racial distinctions with respect to the meritocracy in general.

Shirley: And Herrnstein and Murray are saving America from dysgenesis.

Stanley: Right.

Shirley: Let's talk about O.J. Simpson.

Stanley: Bluntly, I think he was guilty—but I think the sense that Blacks have of being deracinated, de-legitimated, put in a position of exclusion except for the affirmative action types who came in due to Richard Milhous Nixon, the affirmative action president. The reason, of course, that he pushed affirmative action was because it would have been much more expensive to have a genuinely egalitarian educational system. So what he did was to establish affirmative action, so the O.J.'s of this world would rise to the top. There are relatively few of them, but because of the increasing exclusion of Blacks in the polity and civic culture from any sense of being part of the American promise, the black jurors had no way to say "Look, he is an individual who may or may not be guilty of a crime against a woman and a man. We have to vote, we have to act on the basis of our general sense of outrage at the discrimination against us.

Shirley: After Rodney King, Mike Tyson, Michael Jackson, it almost becomes the expected outcome—it was about time, in a sense.

Stanley: Right. The problem is that what happened with O.J. due to the incredible shadow of race is that he was a wife-beater—he attacked and killed this woman. That 50 percent of all murders in the United States concern men killing women.

Shirley: Incredible. Have you heard D'Sousa speaking on his new book, *The end of racism?*

Stanley: Yes, I have.

Shirley: Do you have anything to say to that? Did you notice that Andrew Hacker nonendorsed, endorsed the book. Isn't that interesting?

Stanley: Yes. And in a way there is a certain return to Moynihan and Glazer—the liberals who jumped ship, who let the cat out of the bag by arguing that the real reason for black oppression is the disintegration of the black family. Blacks suffer from a cultural poverty, they maintained. Oscar Lewis, the anthropologist, agreed with them. Sure, let's assume there is a cultural poverty, and let's assume equally that there are factors in the history of slavery that produced a black family which is something less than solid. But to turn around and infer that black family pathology is the cause of black poverty is ludicrous and monstrous. Such arguments set the stage for policies that will make black living conditions worse than they are now.

Shirley: It chills me, hurts, and chills me. I understand your thoughts on O.J. Simpson—I feel pretty much the same way you do.

Stanley: Yes. You understand what happened, but it doesn't quell my sense of outrage that people can be blinded to the point that they can't see that this man, or any individual like him, can be responsible for a crime.

Shirley: It wasn't the victory I wanted to see against racism.

Stanley: A victory against racism would have been to convict him.

Shirley: It is amazing what we see and hear about the Simpson trial, outrage based on a phrase like "Once again, race wins out over justice." An incredible rewriting of history.

Stanley: In the context of the trial, nobody takes into account Herrnstein and Murray—they don't take into account D'Sousa, they don't take into account the enormous neoconservative attack (neoconservative because many of them are liberals—not Dinesh, but Herrnstein certainly thought of himself as a liberal), they don't take into account this backlash, this attack. This bears on the Simpson trial and its conclusion.

Shirley: Obviously it is a mistake to not take Herrnstein, Murray, and D'Sousa into account.

Stanley: Absolutely.

INTERVIEW WITH ELLEN WILLIS BY JOE L. KINCHELOE

Joe: What prompted you to write an article on *The Bell Curve* for *The Village Voice?*

Ellen: I was a media columnist, and this was the debate everyone was obsessing about—including me. I like to write about issues that become huge public debates and what they say about our cultural unconscious—the underlying impulses and attitudes that both reflect and influence the way the culture is going. I certainly felt *The Bell Curve* was a good subject from that point of view. Also, there were many things about the book that nobody was talking about.

Joe: Such as class?

Ellen: Class *and* culture—the significance of the class argument and the implicit culture argument and how they might relate to race. This was not simply a book about race, although everybody immediately pounced on race. Herrnstein and Murray invited that kind of pouncing by the way they presented the book and by their *New Republic* essay. Also, people really wanted to talk about race—Americans are totally obsessed about the subject. That obsession tends to take the place of actually dealing with race relations.

Joe: You wrote in your article that the issue of class was virtually ignored by the press. Was addressing class one of the main things you were trying to do in your piece? Of course, not to simply dismiss race, but to look at the class dynamics that were involved?

Ellen: Yes. I wanted to draw attention to the paradox that, on the one hand, Herrnstein and Murray were trying to use IQ to make judgments about people; they wanted to set up a hierarchy of intelligence. But, paradoxically at the same time, they also took a dim view of a society organized by intelligence. They were nostalgic for the old feudal kind of society organized by rank fixed at birth.

Joe: So how can this book be, or is this book being, used politically?

Ellen: Now that we have Dinesh D'Souza's new book, the two are perfect compliments to delegitimizing the demands of black people. Murray and Herrnstein suggest that Blacks are biologically inferior; D'Souza says no, it's black culture that is the culprit.

Joe: Do you plan to write about D'Souza's new book?

Ellen: Probably not. Unless I have something to say that no one else has said. It's hard to figure out how to write about a book with an argument that's so totally crude.

Joe: Naturally none of us wants to buy the book. There seems something so ludicrous about *The end of racism* that it almost doesn't demand a response on some level. It was similar to writing this response to *The Bell Curve*. Do you ignore it or do you reveal what it is saying and its implications?

Ellen: More important than the book itself is the whole argument about IQ. This is not a new argument—it was made in the 1960s, now once again in the 1990s. The other part of the book, the class argument, isn't really new either. But it's interesting to see it in conjunction with the other argument. What was most compelling about *The Bell Curve* wasn't the book itself but the debate it touched off, the concerns that were expressed. If D'Souza's book turns out to be a runaway bestseller that everyone talks about, then there will be something to say about it. As a book, I don't have much to say about it.

Joe: In a sense, it is not as much about the books per se, it is about the public reaction that they have elicited. The legitimation that say,

Herrnstein and Murray found within mainstream television talk shows.

Ellen: Yes. What's important is the larger cultural conversation.

Joe: Your article mentioned that the attack on intelligence reeked of anti-Semitism. Could you expand on that?

Ellen: The basic argument Herrnstein and Murray are making is that the Enlightenment destroyed the organic culture—the great chain of being. That it destroyed the medieval wholeness of the culture, where everybody had a place and knew their place. With the idea that reason is abstract and something anybody can latch on to, culture can be organized around reason. Reason becomes the most important human value, which leads to universalism and cosmopolitanism. The culture of the village and its settled hierarchy and tradition cannot withstand the onslaught of reason. The village is suddenly opened up to the possibilities of this universal, global interchange. And, of course, Jews have always been criticized for exactly this. For their universalist, "rootless cosmopolitan" subversion of culture, for their outsiderness. Whenever there's a critique of intellectuals, often Jewish is the unspoken adjective, the unspoken modifier. It's not that Herrnstein and Murray are making any kind of argument about Jews; the only time they mention Jews is to say that Ashkenazi Jews had higher IQs on average. But you can see an anti-Semite reading this book and appropriating the argument.

Joe: Once the argument about rationality begins and these types of assumptions are being made it can turn in a variety of directions, some very ugly. Often Jewish intelligence can be distorted to read as crafty—as in the Jews are a *race* of schemers, maybe even subversives. The notion of Jewish intelligence can be transformed into the *innate* ability of Jews to use their cunning for financial gain at *our* expense. You mentioned in your article white anger: What is the relationship between this book and white anger?

Ellen: White anger at their own declining economic position? I think white people in general (working-class to upper middle-class whites, including journalists, people in my circle) are probably the first to deny that their jobs too are eroding, as is their precarious standard of living. But I think there's an enormous insecurity and/or outright anger, and a lot of it is displaced onto race.

Joe: What has been the reaction to your piece?

Ellen: I've gotten a lot of noises of approval. I don't think I got a single angry letter. It is hard to say these days, there is not enough of a community, at least on the left, of people reading and responding to each other's writing. It is often hard to figure out what people think of my writing.

Joe: You didn't get that many responses?

Ellen: No. I didn't feel as if I got particularly many responses.

Joe: I wouldn't have guessed that.

Ellen: Some told me they liked the piece, and Jacoby reprinted it in *The Bell Curve Debate.*

Joe: I did enjoy the piece; it was beautifully written.

29 SCIENTISM AS A FORM OF RACISM: A DIALOGUE

PAULO FREIRE · DONALDO MACEDO

Donaldo: If it were not for the amnesia prevalent within U.S. Society, it would be very easy to understand that the present cruel and frontal attack on affirmative action, immigrants, and unwed mothers is a mere continuation of a historical context where Blacks were "scientifically" relegated to a subhuman existence which, in turn, justified the irrationality of their alienating reality as slaves. After the abolition of slavery and with the eradication of laws that protected the existence of slavery the dominant white ideology resorted to "science" as a means not only to demonize but to also dehumanized Blacks in the United States. These race-based ideological mechanisms were very much prominent during the Reconstruction as succinctly described by black historian, W. E. B. Dubois:

> The South proved by appropriate propaganda the Negro government was the worst every seen and that it threatened civilization. They suited their propaganda to their audience. They had tried the accusation of laziness but that was refuted by a restoration of agriculture to the pre-war level and beyond it. They tried the accusation of ignorance, but this was answered by the Negro schools. It happened that the accusation of incompetence impressed the North. . . . Because the North

had never been thoroughly converted to the idea of Negro equality. . . .

Did the nation want Blacks with power sitting in the Senate and the House of Representatives, accumulating wealth and entering the learned professions? Would this not eventually and inevitably lead to social equality . . . ? Was it possible to contemplate such eventualities?

Under such circumstances, it was much easier to believe the accusations of the South and to listen to the proof which biology and social science hastened to adduce the inferiority of the Negro. The North seized upon the new Darwinism, the "survival of the fittest," to prove that what they had attempted in the South was an impossibility; and they did this in the face of the facts before them, the examples of Negro efficiency, of Negro brains, of phenomenal possibilities of advancement. (Jackson, 1995, p. 15)

Sadly, after over one century, the United States continues to be embroiled in the debated centered on the false notion of the genetic inferiority of Blacks. The publication of the book, *The Bell Curve*, authored by Richard Herrnstein and Charles Murray, once more presents "evidence" in support of genetic inferiority. This book has not only activated what had appeared to be a dormancy of racism in the United States after the enactment of the Civil Rights laws, but it also has resurrected an old form of intellectual lynching that, unfortunately, has been embraced by ever-more powerful representatives of the far Right and, with some exception, by Liberals through a form of silence.

Paulo, can you comment on the reemergence of the legitimization of racism through pseudoscientific methods?

Paulo: When I am confronted with the problem of racial discrimination, independently of the insidious explanations that a racist pretends to give in order to maintain his or her attitude that negates the existence and equal rights of the other, my first reaction is one of anger mixed with pity. By pity I am not referring to the victims of discrimination. I pity those who discriminate. I pity their lack of human sensibility. I pity their exaggerated arrogance with respect to the world and their lack of humility.

These expressions of both anger and pity are obviously understood by those who discriminate, particularly those who use pseudoscience to legitimatize their racism, as empty platitudes, empty and incompetent discourses. But, for me, the use of science to prove the inferiority of Blacks is also an incompetent discourse. Between these two incompetent discourses, I prefer the humanism and humility that exist in my position.

I remember very well when I was at Harvard and a professor there published an infamous and highly controversial article in the *Harvard Education Review*. In this article, the author, Arthur Jensen, argued that he would be more than happy to say that there is no racial inferiority between races, but science would not permit him to do since, according to his calculations, Blacks are inferior, even though they excel in their ability as runners. When I think about the reaction I had when I read his argument, I feel the same way today when the authors of *The Bell Curve* strive to resurrect the mechanism of dehumanization parading, once again, under the veil of science.

Another thing that I want to point out is that when I oppose these pseudoscientists and their scientism for their cruel and racist approach to scholarship, I remain unafraid of being criticized for not having a scientific basis upon which to make such a claim. I would like to say here, to proclaim, if you will, that there is no other basis upon which to judge one another than upon the basis of membership in the human race. I am not interested in going to a laboratory in an effort to attempt to prove that Blacks are inferior to Whites or vice versa. I find this pseudoscientific endeavor absurd. It is absurd to claim the inferiority of human beings because of their historical accident of birth along the lines of race, gender, and ethnicity. If there is on e thing that distinguishes humans from animals, as Francois Jacoby notes, it is our innate ability to learn. This is, in my view, scientific affirmation. It is not a mere dream to say that we are beings who are programmed to know and to learn.

Jensen, Murray, Herrnstein, and others would have to demonstrate that Blacks are programmed to know and learn less than Whites. I would argue otherwise. Even if their claim were to be scientifically true, there would have to be no exceptions to the rule. In other words, we could not have a Dubois, a Martin Luther King, a Toni Morrison, a Nelson Mandela among a constellation of great black leaders and intellectuals in the world. If the claim of inferiority were to be true, all Blacks in the world would have to be inferior in all domains and respects, in both time and space. They would have to be inferior ethically, aesthetically, physically, and so forth. In fact, this never is the case. If, in fact, Blacks were genetically inferior, Amilcar Cabral, the leader of the movement for the independence of Guinea-Bissau and Cape Verde, would not have created so many problems for the Portuguese government and, indirectly, its supporter, the United States. Amilcar Cabral and his black army defeated completely the Portuguese white army. When I say Amilcar Cabral, I also have in mind other African leaders and their people who also defeated the European colonizers. It was the African intelligence and its ethical conscience that enabled the indigenous population to reacquire not only its land but also its human dignity by removing the yoke of a vicious colonialism. It is this intelligence that triumphed over the human exploitation, the dehumanization, the cowardice and deceitful attitudes of the European colonizers. The Africans won the war and the Europeans had to flee.

Donaldo: Let me interrupt you for a moment. I think it is important not only to point out the Africans' intelligence in devising battlefield strategies that led to the defeat of European colonialism, but it is also crucial that the ethical and moral issues involved in the struggle for independence be analyzed. In other words, how can the Europeans who, according to these pseudoscientists, are holders of superior intelligence, this civilization, justify the dehumanizing effects of colonialism and the barbaric and cruel atrocities committed by them in their pursuit of ways to satiate their greed? As supposedly superior and more civilized beings, how can Europeans justify the quasi-genocide inherent in the process of colonialization designed to secure and help them consolidate European cultural hegemony? If the white race is intellectually superior, and, in turn, supposedly represents the bastion of civilization, how can these pseudoscientists justify the worldwide human exploitation engineered by Whites, the mass killings of the elderly, women, and children by our Western-developed smart bombs; the mass killings and raping of women, including children as young as five years old in Bosnia, as Western civilization watches from the sidelines? The supposed white European superiority is directly compromised in the following historical observation:

> If you were a colonist, you knew that your technology was superior to the Indians: You knew that you were civilized, and they were savages. . . . But your superior technology proved insufficient to extract anything. The Indians, keeping to themselves, laughed at your superior methods and lived from the land more abundantly and with less labor than you did. . . . And when your own people started deserting in order to live with them, it was too much. . . . So you killed the Indians, tortured them, burned their villages, burned their cornfields. It proved your superiority, in spite of your failure. And you gave similar treatment to any of your own people who succumbed to their savage ways of life. But you still did not grow much corn. (Zinn, 1980, p. 184)

How can Herrnstein and Murray and their cultural legionnaires justify the superiority of the white race, when technology and military intelligence fashioned by Whites leads American GIs to commit horrendous crimes against humanity as described by Vietnam veterans themselves?

> The girls were unconscious at that point [after repeated rapes]. When they finished raping them, three of the GIs took hand flares and shoved them in the girls' vaginas. . . . No one needed

to hold them down any longer. The girls were bleeding from
their mouths, noses, faces and vaginas. Then they struck the
exterior portion of the flares and they exploded inside the girls.
Their stomachs started bloating up and they exploded. The
stomachs exploded and their intestines were just hanging out
of their bodies. (Gibson, 1988, pp. 202-203)

If Herrnstein, Murray, and Jensen, among others, were to be true to
the claim of the objectivity of their science, they would factor in why
the higher white IQ predisposed the white civilization to commit
grotesque, barbaric, and horrendous crimes against humanity, as has
been the case throughout history. It is precisely because of these
pseudoscientists' selective selection of historical facts in their determination of IQ that we need to keep dangerous historical memories
alive as reminders of the consequences of all forms of dehumanization, particularly the type of dehumanization sanctioned by science.
It is for this reason that for each museum of fine arts we build in a
given city, we should also build a museum of slavery with graphic
accounts of the dehumanization of African Americans, when entire
families were split and sold on the block to the highest bidder and
where pictures of lynching would remind us of our racist fabric. For
each museum of science built in a given city, we should also build a
museum of the quasi-genocide of American Indians, their enslavement, the raping and killing of their women, and the appropriation
of their land. Although there has privately been built a Holocaust
Museum in Washington, D.C. 50 years after the Nazis' horrendous
crimes against Jews, Gypsies, Communists and homosexuals, we also
need to build a governmentally supported Vietnam War Museum
along with the Vietnam Memorial, where graphic accounts of rape
and killing of Vietnamese women, children, and innocent by Western heritage trained Gis would be described thus keeping the
dangerous memories of My Lai alive.

    Although the existence of these museums would represent
historical truths, I doubt it very much that our society is willing to
confront its demons as exemplified in the watering down and

rewriting of history in the case of the proposed exhibition of the *Enola Gay* at the Smithsonian. After ferocious protests by veteran's groups, the exhibition not only presented no historical analysis, it also suppressed historical truths, rendering the exhibition a mere presentation of artifacts without any connection with historical analysis.

For me, more important than proving white IQ superiority is the design of scientific studies that engage students in the archaeology of a white generic map that may be responsible for the barbaric crimes against humanity through colonialism, slavery, the Holocaust, among other historical atrocities. It is only through our willingness to confront the demon in us that we become willing to stop demonizing and dehumanizing the other.

Paulo: I agree, Donaldo. You see, for me it is far more important to study the interrelationship between white supremacy and dehumanization than to spend time and energy to maintain white supremacy through the enactment of a pseudoscience that attempts to prove black inferiority dislodged from the sociocultural conditions that may, in fact, hinder normal intellectual development. For instance, the ignorance laws that made it a crime for slaves to learn how to read and write certainly represent a socially constructed context for lack of reading ability. You cannot isolate in a scientific study the genes that seemingly are responsible for black inferior intellectual capacity while ignoring the material conditions that adversely affect cognitive and intellectual development. What is needed is not yet another study like *The Bell Curve,* designed to rationalize the further abandonment of Blacks. What is needed is the courage to transcend the deficit orientation supported by a suspect and racist scholarship hidden under the guise of scienticism, so we can move beyond the pipe dream of a democratic education and create the reality. However, in order to make education democratic, we must simultaneously make the society within which it exists democratic as well. We cannot speak of democracy while promoting racist policies.

Donaldo: Well put. Democracy in a racist society is an oxymoron.

Paulo: Exactly. Thus the humanization and the democratization of society must imply the necessary transformation of an oppressive and unjust apparatus that guides and shapes society. Since racism is a form of oppression, you can never achieve any substantive humanization by accommodating to racist structures. For me, there can never be any humanistic dimension in oppression, nor is there dehumanization in true liberation. The fact that Blacks in the United States continue to be dehumanized, their liberation from slavery is compromised, as indicated in W. E. B. Dubois's pronouncements. In order to maintain new forms of slavery, the dominant white class must attempt to eliminate Blacks' capacity to think. An attempt such as this can be characterized as nothing less than an aggression against nature and against humanity. It is for this reason that authors such as Herrnstein and Murray have so attempted, with technology and "science" at their disposal, to generate dubious studies like those published in *The Bell Curve*.

Donaldo, when I am confronted with the arguments in *The Bell Curve,* I say strongly and loudly that we should not respect these arguments scientifically or humanistically.

Donaldo: The near-euphoric embracing of the debate generated by *The Bell Curve* puts your reaction against its racist propositions in the minority. In fact, *The Bell Curve* has been embraced not only by right wing ideologues who had been impatiently waiting for science to legitimize their racism, it also has been embraced willfully by the media, which gave many authors space to shape and define the agenda on race issues in the United States. Even when the media would contest the racist propositions presented in *The Bell Curve,* it nonetheless facilitated wide dissemination of these propositions, which, in turn, reinforced the racist fabric of our society that is presently launching frontal attacks on affirmative action and immigrants. As David Duke, a presidential candidate in 1992, put it, "America is being invaded by hordes of dusty third world peoples, and with each passing hour our economic well-being, cultural heritage, freedom and racial roots are being battered into oblivion" (Duke, 1991, p.1). One could argue that David Duke represents the fringe, but I find little substantive difference between the unveiled racism of David Duke and the scientifically veiled racism of Richard Herrnstein and Charles Murray. In fact, one could easily consider Charles Murray as a David Duke in academic regalia. That a major portion of the data used to provide the basis for the main arguments in *The Bell Curve* was funded by the Pioneer Fund, an organization with a long history of association with Nazi groups should have been a wake-up call for those who profess to combat racism. Instead, Charles Murray has appeared in all major media outlets, from conservative to the so-called liberal media such as *Nightline, MacNeil/Lehrer, All Things Considered,* the *New York Times Book Review,* to mention only a few. The question remains as to whether or not the media would give an antiracist book that indicts our racist society equal time. Given our society's preponderance to oppose an open debate concerning our ethical posture concerning the *Enola Gay* exhibition and given the marginalization of major dissident scholars like Noam Chomsky, even though he is considered the most influential intellectual alive in the world today, we can easily understand the celebration of questionable scholars such as Charles Murray and society's complicity with his racist tirades. Although, on the surface, it may be hard to comprehend that our so-called democratic society is obviously in complicity with racism, upon further analysis it becomes less difficult to unveil the racist structures that continually debilitate our ever-more fragile democracy, as demonstrated by John Sedgwick who writes: "[They] shouldn't be hard to find, in a country where Blacks are far more likely than Whites to grow up poor, fatherless, malnourished, badly educated, and victimized by crime and drugs. Then there is the matter of racism in America, which, like bloodstains on the hands of Lady Macbeth, cannot be washed away" (p. 158). Richard Herrnstein's and Charles Murray's book *The Bell Curve* represents the bloodstain of American racism. It cannot be washed away without the total transformation of the present oppressive racist structures that characterize our democracy in crisis.

References

Duke, D. (1991). *Boston Globe,* October 24.

Gibson, J. W. (1988). *The perfect war.* New York: Vintage Books.

Jackson, D. (1995). Reconstruction part two. *Boston Globe,* July 5.

Sedgwick, J. (1995). Inside the Pioneer Fund. In Jacoby, R. and Glauber-man, N., eds., *The Bell Curve debate.* New York: Random House.

Zinn, H. (1990) *A people's history of the United States.* New York: Harper Perennial.

CODA: "COGNITIVE ELITISM" VERSUS MORAL COURAGE

AARON D. GRESSON III

In the preceding chapters, scholars from several different fields and perspectives have critiqued *The Bell Curve.* Arguing from within the canons of sound scholarship, they have provided a point by point refutation of the major scholarly claims of this book. They have, on the whole, been more than persuasive in this pursuit. Yet, there remains a dimension of response which may serve both as a recapitulation of their efforts and an extension of them as well. In the Introduction, Joe Kincheloe and Shirley Steinberg observe the unfortunate necessity of responding to Herrnstein and Murray. Fully appreciating the likely political suicide of silence, they cogently argue for response in terms similar to those most empha-sized by Herrnstein and Murray: reason, logic, evidence. And yet within each of the responses to *The Bell Curve,* there has been an essential and imminent tension, for underpinning this work is a passion suffused with power. Various authors in the preceding chapters have named this passion in terms of its various incanta-tions: racism, classism, sexism, capitalism, elitism.

In this concluding chapter, I want to access the issues and themes under contestation by a brief bit of biographical reflection. I do this as a way of placing flesh on the single critical matter implicit in the Herrnstein and Murray volume: What shall we do with the "wretched other" when so many of those called to "whiteness" will themselves become canonfodder in the years to come?

I AM A "COGNITIVE ELITIST" NOT!

My students call me "Dr. Gresson." To them, this seems "natural" and correct: I am a university professor in good standing and my institution, unlike some of the more elitist colleges, does not assume that everyone has a doctorate and hence ought to be called "Mr.," "Mrs.," or "Ms." Perhaps this is so because my institution serves a largely working, middle-class white student body, and they have yet to attain the precise level of "cognitive elitism" attributed to more prestigious educational institutions. And so, they call me "Dr. Gresson."

I, of course, am anxious that they see me as I know myself to be—and as I want them to see me in relation to themselves and the minorities I represent for them. So I frequently begin each class with a brief biographical reflection. For example, I often share that I have a jail record for shining shoes: at fourteen, I used to shine shoes for the white sailors on the streets outside the segregated USO; routinely the police would raid the streets surrounding the USO, picking up all the little black boys who were shining shoes there. This was done at the behest of the local vendors who ran the civvies shops (civilian clothes) and whose business competitors we were.

Students are usually mesmerized by this story of that ancient period called the "old days." It is hard for them to reconcile their image of a small black youth shining shoes for white sailors with this short, fat, middle-aged academic standing before them. To them, I am the "Cognitive Elite." But I remember all of those really smart black kids I grew up with in the segregated South; many of them are dead now from the Vietnam War, drugs and AIDS, premature cancers, strokes and heart attacks, and plain street violence. If they had lived, they might have become successful in ways that Herrnstein and Murray view as consonant with cognitive superiority. But then maybe they would have not fared much better than they did, for ultimately, a great part of my own ultimate success was due to the confluence of the so-called radical 1960s and my good fortune in being adopted by several "white fathers."

My education might be broken up into roughly two periods: the segregated black education I received in Norfolk, Virginia and Baltimore, Maryland; and the white education I received after I became a Catholic and aspirant to the priesthood in the mid-1960s. In the early 1960s, my parents divorced and we moved from Norfolk to Baltimore; during the week my mother and younger sister lived in the home of the wealthy white family my mother worked for; they said they could not have me living in the same house with their two young daughters and I stayed with a black family my mother attended church with. Through a series of fortuitous events I ended up converting from Southern Baptist/Pentecostal to Roman Catholic and found myself beginning preparations for the priesthood. At this time the Archdiocese of Baltimore was suffering a deep embarrass-ment: traditionally, no white bishop would permit a black to be ordained as a priest for the archdiocese—yet Baltimore was the oldest diocese in the country. Given my interest in the ministry, I was encouraged to pursue the priesthood in order to help Baltimore enter the new era.

To assist me along the way, I became the "spiritual son" of some half dozen or more Roman Catholic priests; each was a holy man as well as learned cleric and respected community leader. This was an incredible group of men for anytime, but they were perhaps typical for the radical Catholic Church of the 1960s. (I recall many occasions on which I shared conversation and antiwar strategies with the Berrigan Brothers, Dan and Phil; and several of the so-called Harrisburg Seven were seminarian friends.) Yet and still, my "fathers" were certainly unusual to me. First, there was Monsignor Healy, patrician pastor of St. Martin's, a working-class parish in the heart of southwest Baltimore's poor white community; he got me summer employment when even white boys my age were finding summer work scarce. Also at St. Martin's were Frs. Jordan and Hiltz; the former, an effeminate, upper-class scholar, the latter, a poor working-class boy whose crew cut belied his tremendous racial courage and compassion and deep spirituality. Each gave me something special: Fr. Jordan introduced me to Salvatore Dali's works (he had several prints hanging in his suite of rooms at the parish rectory), guided my entry into the world of classical music, served me coke in wine glasses and cookies on gold paten plates, and taught me Latin for the day I would enter seminary. Fr. Hiltz took me to the New York World's Fair, taught me to budget my money, and to courageously enter the streets and homes of working-class whites as an ambassador of good will. He also chose me to be one of the first blacks given scholarships to the elitist and envied Calvert Hall College High School in Towson, Maryland. There, under the guidance and encouragement of the brothers I would learn first that my "brain power" was not less than whites; that not all whites were brilliant; and that I could compete with the best white minds on cognitive, affective, and moral planes.

But before Calvert Hall, which came my last year of high school, I met three other "fathers" who would further insure that I succeed despite the destiny earlier prepared for me in a race-conscious society that held me as intellectually, socially, and morally inferior to whites. These were Frs. Reed, Connolly and Lee. Frs. Reed and Connolly were, respectively, pastor and curate at St. Gregory the Great. Fr. Reed, a retiring, gentle, and conservative person, was nonetheless extraordinary in his sincerity and compassion; his deep religious conviction made him a standout in this predominately black parish set in the middle of West Baltimore's most depressed black neighborhood. Father Connolly was his exact opposite: A former Marine, this working-class Irishman stood five feet six but seemed a giant to the blacks who loved his persona: a hard-drinking, chain-smoking, profane man consumed by a relentless courage and finesse in promoting the interests of Baltimore's Black Catholics. Each alone and both together, they nurtured and encouraged my emotional and cognitive growth; gently chiding, always expanding my horizons and opportunities. No one father could have given so much love and good counsel. And when they had done all that they could, they gave me over to my final and more memorable "white father," Fr. William "Lugger" Lee.

A member of the Order of St. Sulpice, Fr. Lee was my first academic mentor: a doctorate in Sociology, he taught at St. Mary's, the minor seminary in Baltimore (later he would serve as President of the world famous St Mary's University and Seminary in Roland Park, Md). Each week I would make my way through the inner city streets of my youth—the streets "cognitive inferiority" had destined to be the home of my old age—to the seminary that set just on the edge of the ghetto. There, gently yet firmly, patiently and prophetically, Fr. Lee, a middle-class product of suburban Ohio, served as a "holding environment"—a safe yet dynamic space—for my unfolding black manhood. I now often think how very critical he was to my finding enough inner calm during precisely that time most working-class males, especially minority males, "fall by the wayside."

I am sure that there are others who might tell similar stories of this surrogate parentage and its role in their academic success. Were it only to rehearse this somewhat familiar trajectory, I would not have shared this bit of biography. But it is clear that this over-all process had a tremendous impact on my cognitive growth and on my recorded performance. I entered the "cognitive elite" through my "fathers." When I first came to Baltimore from Norfolk, I tested at the low normal range of intelligence on the WISC; when I began Calvert Hall some two years later, I scored at roughly 105. I recall how Bro. Jim, a Ph.D. in Counseling Psychology, was relieved at my "normal performance" when I entered Calvert Hall, but even more pleased when I retested at 119 by the end of 12th grade. (As a certified School Psychologist and Ph.D. in Counseling/Clinical Psychology, I now understand some of the problematic dynamics Bro. Jim engaged in on my behalf.)

What my "white fathers" and schooling at the Christian Brothers of Ireland elite private high school (Calvert Hall College High School) gave me was not a shift in IQ through improved testing skills or gerrymandering of standard testing procedure. Rather, they gave me those opportunities that buttress the operationalization of the intelligence construct. When I left Calvert Hall, I graduated with white men—there were only two blacks in the entire graduating class of 1965—who belonged already to a "cognitive elite" and expected to achieve even greater things than their forefathers. They would go off to Princeton, Yale, Harvard, Dartmouth, Villanova, Annapolis, and West Point. I too was going away, to Waterloo and Toronto universities, to prepare for a leadership role among black people. And it was because of this tremendously important role that I was to assume—if not as priest, at least, as one priest put it, as "a fine black Catholic family man"—that so many resources had been made available to me.

MORAL COWARDICE AND CONTEMPORARY RACE RHETORIC

This, of course, is the message I want to convey from my narrative: I received so very much more than a minority person in America was suppose to have; and it is clear to me that my academic achievements—which include two Ph.D.s—were due less to my "cognitive superiority" than to the "preferential treatment" I (and a few like me) received. What I am insisting from my own story is the fact that most human beings, given the optimal environment, are capable of achieving at levels Herrnstein and Murray mystify with notions such as "cognitive elitism." Moreover, I have been at pains to acknowledge and accolade my "white fathers" not because they did so much more than the many dozens of "black mothers and fathers" I had in the years before I entered the "white world," but rather because their courage, compassion and commitment belie the cowardice of those "cognitive elitists" who would return to the racist differentiations dominating the American landscape before 1954. Shame!

Shame to the memory of those who recognized and heeded the call to democratize American Education and to equalize the opportunities for enriched qualities of life. And if I seem to have abandoned the way of dispassionate, academic discourse, it is true. This is not the time for trading academic-talk; for while this book has been painfully careful to walk the ways of reason and logic, clearly what is driving the contemporary political, social, and cultural agenda of the so-called Right is anything but reason and logic. *We cannot go back to where we have been as a Nation.*

In a peculiar yet pertinent article, Clarence Thomas, the Supreme Court Justice, is reported to have said that "God's Law" required that he vote against Affirmative Action. He added:

> [A] tremendous burden has been placed upon the righteous Black man of today to rise above the wrongs done to him and help right America. . . . Black people have a critical role in bringing to fruition the promise of 1776. The signatories of the Constitution had the ideas, but never the courage to carry them forward for all mankind. We must have more strength than they had to do what is right. We can't give in to our passions and expediency and compromise the way they did. We must get it right this time, at all costs. (*National Report,* 1995, p. 8)

Clarence Thomas's identification of Christian teaching as the basis for his reactionary assault on affirmative action is indeed ironic given the reflections I have made above. It is perhaps all the more ironic because Thomas, like myself, grew to maturity as a member of a progressive, forward looking Catholic Church, one intensely self-conscious of the need to make affirmative changes on the behalf of all historically disenfranchised Americans. I recall vividly my first summer job after entering seminary: Monsignor Healy had found me a job working as a psychiatric medical aide in a Catholic run psychiatric hospital; Sister Mary Gregory, upon hiring me, noted that I was receiving this rare opportunity—no black male attendants were employed in this facility before me—because the diocese was looking forward to the day I would assume my role as Baltimore's first black priest.

For Sr. Mary Gregory, in 1965, affirmative action was "God's Plan." For her generation, racist scholarship aimed at keeping blacks and other groups "in their place" had been rejected, and so had the notion—implicit in Clarence Thomas's comment—that blacks could or ought to assume a self-hating, sacrificial posture toward affirmative action. Because she and my "white fathers" were prepared to assume responsibility for the white construction of race, intelligence and bell-shaped curves, I was "freed" to grow intellectually, to make problematic the constructed meanings of the bell shaped curve. Indeed, because of their actions—and numerous others like them—I can now use my status as a member of Herrnstein's and Murray's "Cognitive Elite" to challenge the very underpinnings of this construction.

Thus, the challenge of affirmative action, introduced in the 1960s, remains intact despite efforts to destroy it by a renewed assault on the meaning of intelligence and its imminent significance in the everyday lives of Americans. That challenge is the courageous acceptance of the multicultural mandate—the inclusion of all Americans as full participants in the pursuit of a compassionate and communal enjoyment of the American way of life.

Reference

Thomas, C. (1995). *National Report.*, p.8.

BIOGRAPHIES

Editors:

JOE L. KINCHELOE teaches Cultural Studies and Pedagogy at Penn State University. He is the author of numerous books, including *Teachers as Researchers: Qualitative Paths to Empowerment, Toil and Trouble: Good Work, Smart Workers and the Integration of Academic and Vocational Education,* and (with Shirley Steinberg) the editor of *Thirteen Questions: Reframing Education's Conversation* and *Kinderculture: The Corporate Construction of Childhood.* Along with his scholarship, he is actively involved in a newly formed Indigenous Knowledge Group and many university service organizations, including a sponsor of the Gay and Lesbian student organization. He is a well-known lecturer and travels frequently with Shirley Steinberg presenting workshops and keynote addresses on popular culture, pedagogy, and issues of race, class, and gender.

SHIRLEY R. STEINBERG teaches part-time at Adelphi University. She is an educational consultant and drama director. Along with the books written with Joe Kincheloe, she is also the co-author of *The Stigma of Genius: Einstein and Beyond Modern Education.* She is the senior editor of *Taboo: The Journal of Culture and Education,* and with Joe Kincheloe, she edits four book series dealing with issues of critical pedagogy, popular culture, and children. Her recent research deals with the corporate curriculum and the construction of childhood consciousness. Her latest book is *Ain't We Misbehavin'? A Pedagogy of Misbehavior* (in press). Steinberg and Kincheloe are the parents of Ian, Meghann, Chaim, and Bronwyn and three cosmic dogs. They live in State College, Pennsylvania.

AARON D. GRESSON, III is Associate Professor of Education in the Department of Educational Policy Studies at Penn State University. Formerly Director of the Center for the Study of Educational Equity, also at Penn State, he currently teaches courses in multicultural education, education and equity policy, social foundations of education, and cultural studies. A former community clinical psychologist and special educator, his research interests include such diverse areas as aging policy, alcoholism and special populations, the psychology of political symbols, and intergroup communications and conflict management. His most recent book is *The Recovery of Race in America.*

Contributors:

MICHAEL W. APPLE is the John Bascom Professor of Education at the University of Wisconsin, Madison. He has written extensively about the relationship between education and inequality. Among his most recent books are *Official Knowledge, Education and Power,* and *Cultural Politics and Education.*

STANLEY ARONOWITZ is Professor of Sociology at the Graduate Center of the City University of New York. He is the author of eleven books, including *The Jobless Future* (with William Di Fazio), *False Promises, Working-Class Hero,* and *Science as Power.* He has also coauthored several books with Henry Giroux.

ALAN BLOCK is an Associate Professor in the Department of Education at the University of Wisconsin-Stout. He is the author of two books, *Anonymous Toil* and *Occupied Reading,* and has published many articles on curriculum, education, and critical reading.

DEBORAH P. BRITZMAN is an Associate Professor in the Faculty of Education, York University (Toronto) with cross appointments in the programs of Social and Political Thought and Women's Studies. Research interests include: psychoanalysis and education and questions of social difference. She is the author of *Practice Makes Practice.*

ED BUENDIA is a doctoral student in the Department of Curriculum and Instruction at the University of Illinois at Urbana-Champaign.

PHIL FRANCIS CARSPECKEN is Associate Professor of Cultural Studies at the University of Houston. He conducts research in sociological social psychology, educational sociology and pursues scholarly work in social theory and research methodology. He is the author of two books: *Community Schooling and the Nature of Power* and *Critical Ethnography in Educational Research.*

RICHARD CARY is Professor of Art and Chair of the Art Department at Mars Hill College. His academic background includes advanced studies in studio art and aesthetics and in social and educational research methodology with a special interest in meta-analysis and quantitative research synthesis. He serves as art editor of the journal *Taboo* and is completing work on a book tentatively titled *Critical Art Pedagogy: Theorizing Foundations for Art Education in the Postmodern Era.*

RONALD E. CHENNAULT is a doctoral candidate in Education and Cultural Studies at Penn State University. His research interests surround issues of critical cultural studies, race, class, and gender.

WILLIAM E. CROSS, JR. is Professor of Psychology and African American Studies at The Pennsylvania State University. A major figure in the field of Black Psychology, Professor Cross's early work on black psychological identity was the impetus for a generation of research in this area. His most recent book is the highly acclaimed *Shades of Black: Diversity in African-American Identity.*

PAULO FREIRE is the author of *Pedagogy of the Oppressed, Education for Critical Consciousness, Pedagogy in Process (the Letters to Guinea-Bissau), Learning to Question,* and *Pedagogy of Hope: Reliving "Pedagogy of the Oppressed."* Admired and cherished around the globe, the former education minister of Brazil, Freire is a liberation theologist, critical theorist, and strong proponent of *radical love.*

SANDER L. GILMAN is the Henry R. Luce Professor of the Liberal Arts in Human Biology in Chicago. The author of more than 28 books on diverse topics in medical history, race and ethnic politics, and Jewish Studies, Professor Gilman's recent works include *Picturing Health and Illness* and *Reading Freud's Reading*. He is also currently at work on a volume that critiques the assumptive underpinnings of *The Bell Curve;* his chapter in this volume is drawn from this larger work.

HENRY A. GIROUX is the Waterbury Chair Professor at Penn State University. His latest books include: *Border Crossings, Living Dangerously* (which recently was named an "Outstanding Book on the subject of human rights in North America" by the Gustavus Myers Center for the Study of Human Rights), *Disturbing Pleasures*, and *Fugitive Cultures: Race, Violence and Youth*. He is internationally known in the areas of critical pedagogy and cultural studies.

HERBERTO GODINA is a doctoral student in the Department of Curriculum and Instruction at the University of Illinois at Urbana-Champaign.

IVOR S. GOODSON teaches at the University of Rochester Graduate School and at the University of Western Ontario with a visiting appointment at King's College, University of London. The author of many books and articles on education and social change, he is well-known throughout North America and the United Kingdom.

STEPHEN N. HAYMES is an Assistant Professor in the social and historical foundations program at DePaul University-Chicago. He is the author of *Race, Culture and the City: A Pedagogy for Black Urban Struggle*. Some of his research interests include: black existentialism and critical studies in black pedagogy and culture. He is currently working on a new book titled *Pedagogy of Our Ancestors: Educating for Black Critical Consciousness*.

ROBERT M. HENDRICKSON is currently Head of the Department of Educational Policy Studies and Professor of Education at Penn State University. His areas of expertise in teaching and research include legal aspects of higher education and organizational and administration theory in higher education.

GLENN HUDAK is an Assistant Professor of Foundations at Teachers College at Columbia University. A frequent author of scholarly articles, his interests include critical pedagogy, the pedagogy of jazz, and special needs children. His latest article is published in *Taboo: The Journal of Culture and Education* and his new book is *The Technologies of Marginality and Other Essays on Suburban Schooling: 1986-1996* (in press).

JOYCE KING is Associate Vice Chancellor for Academic Affairs and Diversity Programs at the University of New Orleans. She is a sociologist of education whose publications address sociocultural foundations of education, African-centered thought, pedagogy and curriculum transformation. She is coauthor of *Black Mothers to Sons* (with Carolyn Mitchell), and coeditor of *Teaching Diverse Populations* (with Etta Hollins and Warren Hayman)

YVONNA S. LINCOLN is Professor of Higher Education and Head of the Educational Administration Department at Texas A&M University. Her research interests include new-paradigm inquiry and research ethics. She is the coeditor of *The Handbook of Qualitative Research* and the new journal, *Qualitative Inquiry*, and the coauthor of *Naturalistic Inquiry and Fourth Generation Evaluation*. She is also at least liberal, and therefore, deeply despairing of the racist rhetoric embedded in the Herrnstein-Murray book.

CATHERINE A. LUGG is Assistant Professor of Education in the Department of Educational Policies Studies at Penn State University. She teaches courses in Social Foundations of Education and is the author of *For God and Country: Conservatism and American School Policy* and a new book on the pedagogy of kitsch. Obsessed with Ronald Reagan, she identifies both Ron and Nancy as the two most influential people in the twentieth century.

DONALDO MACEDO is Professor of English and Graduate Program Director of Bilingual and ESL Studies at the University of Massachusetts-Boston. He is a leading authority in language education and has published widely in the area of critical literacy. His latest book is *Literacies of Power: What Americans are not Allowed to Know.* He has also coauthored many articles and books with Paulo Freire.

CAMERON McCARTHY teaches courses in Cultural Studies, Media and Curriculum at the University of Illinois at Urbana-Champaign. He is the author of *Race and Curriculum: Social Inequality and the Theories and Politics of Difference in Contemporary Research on Schooling,* and the editor (with Warren Crichlow) of *Race, Identity and Representation in Education.* He is the book review editor of *Educational Researcher.*

PETER McLAREN teaches at the Graduate School of Education and Information Studies, University of California, Los Angeles. He is the author of *Critical Pedagogy and Predatory Culture, Schooling as a Ritual Performance,* and the award-winning *Life in Schools* as well as numerous other books and articles. McLaren lectures throughout the world on liberation politics and social justice.

SHUAIB MEACHAM is a doctoral student in the Department of Curriculum and Instruction at the University of Illinois at Urbana-Champaign.

CAROL MILLS is a doctoral student in the Department of Educational Psychology at the University of Illinois at Urbana-Champaign.

JO ANNE PAGANO is Associate Professor of Education and Chair of the Department at Colgate University. She is the author of *Exiles and Communities: Teaching in the Patriarchal Wilderness* and, with Landon Beyer, Walter Feinberg and James Whitson, *Preparing Teachers as Professionals: The Role of Education and Other Liberal Studies.* She is the author of numerous articles in curriculum theory and philosophy of education from a feminist theoretical perspective.

KYLE PECK is an Associate Professor of Education at Penn State University. He is the director of a major collaborative project on restructuring public education, funded by the Hershey Foundation of Pennsylvania. He also teaches courses in instructional systems and design and is coauthor of *The Design, Development, and Evaluation of Instructional Software.*

WILLIAM F. PINAR teaches curriculum theory at Louisiana State University, where he serves as the St. Bernard Parish Alumni Endowed Professor. He has also served as the Frank Talbott Professor at the University of Virginia and the A. Lindsay O'Connor Professor of American Institutions at Colgate University. He is the author of *Autobiography, Politics, and Sexuality,* and the senior author of *Understanding Curriculum.* His newest book is *Curriculum: Toward New Identities in/for the Field.*

ALICE J. PITT is an Assistant Professor in the Faculty of Education at York University in Toronto. Research interests include: psychoanalytic study of learning and Feminist theory, pedagogy, and questions of subjectivity.

TOWNSAND PRICE-SPRATLEN is Assistant Professor of Sociology at The Ohio State University. His current research focuses on the effects of social ties and community development on residential mobility and neighborhood change, and the influence of neighborhood context on well-being and other individual outcomes. He is also interested in the relationship between criminal sanctioning and individual and community marginalization.

SUSAN SEARLS is finishing her doctorate in the English Department at Penn State University. Published previously in *The Review of Education and Cultural Critique,* her research interests focus around the prevailing importance of race and the shaping of American literature in the discipline of English literature and the concept of professionalism.

MARIA SEFERIAN and THERESA SOUCHET are doctoral students in the Department of Educational Policy Studies at the University of Illinois at Urbana-Champaign.

LADISLAUS SEMALI is Assistant Professor of Education at Pennsylvania State University. Originally from Tanzania, his major areas of research are Language, Communication, and Literacy Education. Interests also include the study of intergroup relations from sociocultural perspectives and the creation of a new consortium on indigenous knowledge. His work has been published in *The International Review of Education* and *Comparative Education Review.* He is a coeditor of a new book series on indigenous ways of knowing.

ALLEN SHELTON is visiting professor of sociology at SUNY-Geneseo. With Joe Kincheloe, he is the author of *The Sign of the Burger: Double Takes on McDonald's.* He has publications in *The Journal of Symbolic Interaction* and a chapter in *Social Perspectives on Emotion.* Recent publications are "The man at the end of the machine" and "Anal Geometry," which will appear in *Taboo: The Journal of Culture and Education, Volume 2, Number 4.*

PATRICK SLATTERY is Associate Professor in the Department of Education at Ashland University in Ohio where he teaches curriculum theory and educational foundations. His books include *Curriculum Development in the Postmodern Era* and the coauthored *Understanding Curriculum.* He has recently published articles on curriculum theory in *The Harvard Educational Review, Curriculum Inquiry,* and *The Journal of Curriculum Theory.* With Joe Kincheloe and Shirley Steinberg, he is the author of *Contextualizing Teaching,* a critical foundations text.

DON STEPHENSON is Professor and Chairperson at University of Wisconsin-Stout, Department of Education, Counselling and School Psychology. He has spent over thirty years in education during which time he has published several articles and made numerous presentations to state and national organizations.

GREG TANAKA writes about education and culture. A James Irvine Dissertation Fellow and lecturer at Loyola Marymount University, he has completed a book on the breakdown of common culture in America. An eclectic scholar and writer, he is also a former lawyer.

MARIA VIDAL is an Assistant Professor of Social Work at Loyola University-Chicago. Her research and publications focus on gender, poverty, and Latino family formation; economic incorporation of Latino immigrants; child welfare; and social welfare policy. Her research is informed by her active involvement with several Chicago area Latino community organizations and state policy advisory boards.

ELLEN WILLIS teaches journalism at New York University. She is a free-lance writer and writes for *The Village Voice;* she is the author of *Beginning to see the light, pieces of a decade* and *No more nice girls, countercultural essays.*

CARRIE WILSON-BROWN is a doctoral student in the Institute of Communication Research at the University of Illinois at Urbana-Champaign.

INDEX

Adler, Mortimer 199
affirmative action 23, 312, 352, 352, 353, 354, 355, 358, 367, 369, 374, 376, 381, 423, 439, 440, 439
Africa 163, 167, 168, 172, 186, 190
Afrocentricity 231
Agnew, Spiro 4
Aid to Families with Dependent Children (AFDC) 219, 220, 221, 222, 225
Ailes, Roger 26
Aleichem, Sholem 277
Alger, Horatio 371
Alien Nation 262
American College Testing (ACT) 32, 100
American Enterprise Institute 4, 80, 375
Anna Karenina 211, 212
anti-citizen, 260
anti-intellectualism 232
anti-Semitism 76, 232, 420
Armed Forces Qualification Test (AFQT) 154, 220
Armed Services Vocational Aptitude Battery (ASVAB) 154
Arnot, M. 60
Asante, Molefe 405
Ashkenasic Jews 268, 269, 270, 271, 272, 276, 277, 420
Asians 80, 162, 343

Bacon, Francis 31
Baker, Josephine 97, 98
Bane, Mary Jo 222
behavioral psychology 244, 255
The Bell Curve Wars 104
Bellow, Adam 3
Benjamin, Walter 100, 102, 103, 105
Bennett, William 199
Binet, Alfred 33,
Bradley Foundation 4
Brecht, Bertold 237
Bringham, Carl 347, 373
Brown, Rap 241
Buchanan, Patrick 84
Burt, Cyril 79,162
Bush, George ix, 27, 225

California Aptitude Test (CAT) 101
Capps, Donald 233

Carmichael, Stokely 241
Cartesian-Newtonian paradigm 28, 297
Castoriadis, Cornelius 399, 400, 401
Caucasoids 80
Chaos theory 291, 295, 296, 297
Chomsky, Noam 349, 406, 413, 411, 431
Christian morality, values, 54, 61
citizenry 254
citizens 112, 257, 263
citizenship 67, 79, 251, 252, 253, 258, 261
civic leadership 79
civil rights laws 353, 396, 424
Civil Rights Movement 42, 241, 353
Cleaver, Eldridge 232
Clinton, Bill 26, 74, 82, 83
The Closing of the American Mind 262
cognitive ability 37, 94, 183, 185, 195, 204, 205, 224, 321, 346, 351, 352, 360, 381, 382, 386, 390
cognitive elite 110, 111, 116, 127, 128, 343, 379, 380, 407, 434, 435, 437, 438, 440
cognitive psychology 22, 32
colonialism 309, 426, 429
color-blindness 240, 241, 354, 356, 357, 358
conservatives 53, 59, 72, 83, 86, 368, 374, 375
Contract with America 72, 82, 247
Contract with the American Family 247
Coontz, Stephanie 189
corporations 10, 138, 412
correlation coefficients 157
Cose, Ellis 186
Critical Race Theory 352, 358, 363
Crossfire 84
cultural capital 52
cultural diversity 37
cultural literacy 253
Cultural Literacy 262
custodial state 85, 113, 114, 380

Darwin, Charles 276, 369, 370, 415
Darwinism 9, 78, 370, 424, 370, 371
Davidson, Basil 169
Deaver, Mike 26
Decartes, Rene 31
Delgato, Richard 358
democracy 113

Denton, Nancy A. 207
Derrida, Jacques 393
deskilling 19
Dewey, John 199
discourse 31, 35, 66, 79, 227, 258
  biological 256
  community 36
  cultural 38
  discursive context 33
  European 284
  psychological 38
  racial 244
  Talmudic 279
discrimination 177
The Disuniting of America 262
Dole, Robert 74
D'Sousa Dinesh 24, 37, 416, 417, 418, 419
Dubois, W. E. B. 190, 423, 426, 430
Duke, David 27, 265, 430, 431
dysgenesis 22, 25, 37, 303, 304, 307, 309, 416
Dyson, Michael E. 405

economic dependency 65
educational policy 120
educational psychologists 43
Einstein, Albert 33, 34, 94, 281, 283
Ellison, Ralph 186
Ellwood, David 222
The End of Racism 24, 416
Enola Gay 429, 431
entropy 298
Equal Opportunities Commission (EEOC) 353

family 59, 60, 61, 62, 189, 211, 212, 213, 229, 230, 231, 232, 234, 275, 278, 286, 319, 335, 338, 340, 379, 397
Fanon, Frantz 258
Fascist future 43
Faulkner, William 293
Federation for American Immigration Reform (FAIR) 39, 348
feminists 53
Fordism 16, 17, 18
Forrest Gump 212, 215
Foucault, Michel 92, 97
The Frankfurt School 103
Fraser, Nancy 64, 65
Fraser, Steven 272
Frasier, Mary 165
Freud, Sigmond 283, 393, 394, 397, 398, 399

Fromm, Eric 246
Fuhrman, Mark 42
fundamentalists 54

Galton, Francis 415
Gardner, Howard 7, 37, 121, 195, 165, 214
gay talk show 81
Gayre, Robert 39
gays and lesbians 53, 396, 397
General Aptitude Test Battery (GATB) 145, 151, 152
General Education Diploma (GED) 194, 201, 202
Giddens, Anthony 180
giftedness 161, 165, 166
Gingrich, Newt 21, 26, 72, 73, 82, 87
Glauberman, Naomi 272
Glazer, Nathan 77, 273
Goals 2000 83
Goldberg, David Theo 85
Goodlad, John 37, 200
Gordon, Linda 64, 65
Gould, Stephen J. 92, 96, 99, 165, 181, 225, 304, 411, 413
Graduate Record Examination (GRE) 100, 352, 361
Graetz, Heinrich 271
Grant, Bob 81
Gulf War ix
Gunther, Hans 41

Hacker, Andrew 186, 242, 272, 283
Havel, Václav 88
Head Start 83, 84, 341, 381, 382
Hedges, Larry 149
hegemony 52, 62, 103, 178, 182, 253, 427
The Heisenberg Uncertainty Principle 298
Helms, Jesse 27, 199, 375
Heritage Foundation 375
Hofstadter, Richard 369
Holmes, Oliver Wendell, Jr. 93
Holocaust (Shoah) 24, 76, 102, 269, 275, 276, 277, 278, 428, 429
homophobia 232
homosexuals 428
hoo doo social science 7, 178, 179, 180, 182
hooks, bell 405
Horton, Willie 27
Human Rights Watch 247
Hunter, Ian 54
Hunter, John 149

Illiberal Education 262

immigration 260, 273, 312, 423
Individual Education Program (IEP) 316, 320
"inFORMation" 96
interculturalism 311

Jackson, Michael 416
Jacoby, Russell 272
Jamal, Abu 242
Jefferson, Thomas 95, 113
Jensen, Arther 8, 79, 162, 256, 266, 425
Jim Crow 65
Jurassic Park 291

Kafka, Franz 91, 92, 96, 98, 99, 100, 101, 102, 104, 286
Katz, Michael 66
Kaus, Mickey 77
Kaye, Harvey 406
Kellner, Douglas 406
Kessler, Harry 97, 98
King, Martin Luthur, Jr. 71, 72, 88, 241, 426
King, Rodney 416
Kozol, Jonathan 24, 325, 388
Kristeva, Julia 394, 401
Kristol, William 225
Ku Klux Klan 8, 27, 83

labor 55, 61, 78, 129, 130, 132, 145, 154, 203, 207, 208, 292
Labor, U.S. Department of 24, 145, 154
Law School Admissions Test (LSAT) 352, 361, 305
liberals 86, 424
Limbaugh, Rush 21, 77, 81
Losing Ground 221, 240, 241, 262
Lynn, Richard 79
Lyotard, Jean 294

Mandela, Nelson 426
Marcuse, Herbert 100
Marx, Karl 101, 131, 212, 281
Massey, Douglas S. 207
measured intelligence 257
Meta-analysis in Social Research 147, 148
Michels, Robert 131
Middle Class Values Index 315, 317, 318, 328
Milken, Michael 283
mimesis 95
Minnesota Multiphasic Personality Inventory (MMPI) 245

Minnesota Transracial Adoption Study 332, 333, 334, 337, 340
The Mismeasure of Man 92, 165, 181, 304, 411
misogyny 232
modernism 3l, 32, 294, 295, 300
Mongoloids 80
moral aimlessness 396
moral commitment 199
moral education 245
The Moral Sense 246
Morrison, Toni 41, 184, 237, 238, 426
multicultural mandate 440
multiculturalism x, 162, 174, 287
multiple intelligences 7

National Institute of Mental Health (NIMH) 240
National Longitudinal Survey of Youth (NLSY) 163, 188, 220, 259, 317
National Research Council 139
Nazis 27, 38, 39, 41, 76, 238, 239, 408, 431
neo-Darwinism 375
neo-Nazi 75, 79
neoconservatism 52, 56, 60, 61, 72
neoliberalism 52, 56, 57
The New Republic 104, 273, 274
The New Republican Majority 26
New Right 54, 57, 233, 234, 240, 349
Newton, Issac 3l
Nietzsche, F. 103
Nixon, Richard Milhous 26, 27, 353, 368, 412, 416
non-gifted students 161
Northern League 41

objectivity 5, 6, 7, 13

Parks, Rosa 412
The Pearson Product-Moment Corelation Coefficient 142, 148
Pearson, Roger 41
Pell Grants 83
penis size 40, 80
Peretz, Martin 273
Perkins, David 165
Pioneer Fund 38, 40, 79, 348, 431
positivistic science 291
post-Fordism 9, 18, 19
post-formal thinking 7
postmodernism 29l, 292, 293 294
poverty 13, 14, 18, 59, 60, 65, 66, 182, 188, 221, 259

power relations 15
practical intelligence 7
productivity differences 139, 141
Project Intelligence 383, 385
Project for a Republican Future 225
Proposition 187 39, 82, 344, 348
psychoanalysis 393
psychology 177
psychology of fascism 246, 247
psychometrics 7, 8, 10, 13, 21, 30, 32, 34, 37
Pulp Fiction 84

race wars 13
Reagan, Ronald 25, 26, 27, 217, 240
Reaganomics 26,
recovery of racism 405
reductionism 31
Reed, Adolph 165
Reich, Robert 130
retribalization ix
rhetoric of race 267
Right 53, 60, 66, 67, 68
right-wing movement 240, 247
right-wing talk radio 81
rightist policies 52, 62
Rockwell, Norman 248
Rushton, Phillippe 40, 80, 256, 266, 407, 408, 409

Sartre, Jean Paul 186
Savage Inequalities 24, 325, 388
Scalia, Antonin 82
Schmidt, Frank 149
Scholastic Aptitude Test (SAT) 32, 100,109, 118, 199, 347, 352, 361, 373
scientism 423
Sedgwick, John 431
segregation 71, 207, 208
Sephardic Jews 269, 270, 272, 276, 277, 284
Shoah, *see* Holocaust
Shockley, William 8, 162, 266, 411, 413
O. J. Simpson 405, 416, 417
slavery 62, 63, 71, 79, 171, 172, 177, 306, 417, 423, 428, 429, 430
social behavior 164
social Darwinism 12, 52, 67, 261, 344, 367, 369, 370, 371, 373, 376, 415
social justice 199
social policy 392
social theory 114, 115, 119

societal discrimination 82
Sowell, Thomas 272, 273
Spearman, Charles 7
Spencer, Herbert 255, 370
Springsteen, Bruce 130
Stanford-Binet tests 280
statistical misconduct 134
statistical significance 156
Sternberg, Robert 7, 165
Storfer, Miles D. 275, 277, 279, 280, 284, 285, 286
suburbs 62, 63
Supreme Court 82, 93, 353, 354, 356, 357, 363, 369, 412
talk shows 81, 82, 84
Taussig, Michael 97
Taylor, Fredrick 92, 93
Terman, Lewis 255, 256, 276
Thatcher, Margaret 55
Thomas, Clarence 439, 440
To renew America 73
Tolstoy, Leo 211, 212
Tumin, Melvin 131
Tyson, Mike 416

United States Labor Department 74
Upward Bound 83

values 218
values, Christian 26, 61
virtue and morality 266
virus 170, 252
von Linné, Carl 173
voodoo 179

Wallerstein, Immanuel 174
Weber, Max 269
West, Cornel 405
Weyner, Harry 38, 39
white anger 25, 420
white supremacy 23, 25, 38, 166, 170, 171, 178, 179, 180, 181, 183 184, 185, 344, 347, 381, 415, 427, 429
Wieseltier, Leon 274
Williams, Gregory Howard 293
Wilson, James Q. 246
Wilson, Pete 39, 343, 344
Wolfe, Alan 272
women 59, 60, 61, 218, 259, 371, 372, 376, 427
world systems theory 174